MW01089924

PHILOSOPHY, REASONED BELIEF, AND FAITH

AN INTRODUCTION

PAUL HERRICK

University of Notre Dame Press

Notre Dame, Indiana

Copyright © 2022 by the University of Notre Dame
Notre Dame, Indiana 46556
undpress.nd.edu

All Rights Reserved

Published in the United States of America

Library of Congress Control Number: 2021949121

ISBN: 978-0-268-20268-2 (Hardback)
ISBN: 978-0-268-20269-9 (Paperback)
ISBN: 978-0-268-20270-5 (WebPDF)
ISBN: 978-0-268-20267-5 (Epub)

Philosophy, Reasoned Belief, and Faith

To Art DiQuattro and Steve Duncan.

I've learned so much from our conversations over
forty plus years that words alone cannot express my gratitude.
Our back-and-forth debates, weekly discussions, trips to
conferences and symposia, the books we've read together —
you have helped me sort things out and clarify my thinking
on just about every issue discussed in this book.
Although neither of you agrees with every position
I defend here, you have influenced every chapter.

CONTENTS

Acknowledgments   ix

To the Instructor   xi

To the Student   xiii

UNIT I.   Three Things to Know before You Dive into Philosophy

ONE. How Philosophy Began   3

TWO. The Socratic Method   23

THREE. And a Few Principles of Logic   39

UNIT II.   Philosophy of Religion

FOUR. The Design Argument   57

FIVE. Design and Evolution   83

SIX. The Cosmological Argument   107

Interlude One. A Survey of Modern Cosmology   140

SEVEN. The Problem of Evil   157

UNIT III. Epistemology

EIGHT. What Can We Know?   185

NINE. C. S. Lewis and the Argument from Reason   211

UNIT IV. Philosophy of the Human Person

TEN. The Mind-Body Problem   229

ELEVEN. Do We Have Free Will?   267

UNIT V. Philosophical Ethics

TWELVE. Can We Reason about Morality?   303

Interlude Two. Or Should We All Become Moral Relativists?   344

THIRTEEN. Moral Reasoning Applied to the State   359

FOURTEEN. God and Morality   393

Notes   407

Index   447

ACKNOWLEDGMENTS

Socrates was right. We learn best when we learn with others, giving and receiving helpful feedback. Many colleagues have given me wise counsel and valuable feedback as I wrote this book. Steve Duncan and Jim Slagle read an early draft and the entire penultimate draft and made many helpful suggestions. Art DiQuattro, Andrew Jeffery, Mark Storey, and Larry Fike read earlier drafts of the manuscript and also made helpful comments.

I thank Stephen Little, former acquisition editor at the University of Notre Dame Press, for his encouragement and good advice as the manuscript was reviewed. I also thank two anonymous reviewers for UNDP for their constructive suggestions.

This book in various places benefited from memorable conversations I've had with my Shoreline Community College colleagues: Larry Clarke, Terry Taylor, Robert Francis, Tim Payne, Tim Wright, Steve Goetz, William Lindenmuth, Larry Fuel, Lou Tarrant, and Robert Thompson. This text has also benefited in many places from discussions I've had with two former students who became philosophy professors, Brian Glenney and Robert Bolger. Long walks with my former teacher Bob Richman and many talks with colleagues Mark Storey, Russ Payne, Tom Kerns, Catharine and Greg Roth, Larry Stern, Steve Layman, Daniel Howard-Snyder, Bill Talbott, Jim Slagle, Michael Matriotti, Andrew Tadie, Richard McClelland, Michael Adeney, Claire Bright, Andrew Jeffery, David Sanders, and Paul Pardi led to insights that I included in this book.

I thank most sincerely my fellow members of Philosophers on Holiday. Our weekly meetings since 1981 have helped me clarify many of the issues that I treat in this book. The members of this informal group, formed by graduate students in philosophy at the University of Washington, have collectively been the Socrates in my life: Steve Duncan, Richard Kopczynski, Art DiQuattro, Liz Ungar, Shawn Mintek, George Goodall, Brad Rind, Mitch Erickson, Nancy Jecker, Bob Kirk, John Burke, Carol Weibel, Terry Mazurak, Todd Currier, Rich Kang, Mike Schmitt, Richard Curtis, Jeff Clausen, and Kristian Kofoed.

I thank the Department of Philosophy at Gonzaga University in Spokane, Washington, for inviting me to address the Gonzaga University Socratic Club. The discussion after my talk helped me clarify my thinking on C. S. Lewis's argument from reason (chapter 9). I thank Howard Segermark for inviting me to present my treatment of the cosmological argument (chapter 6) to the colloquium on big ideas that he hosts and for the wonderful discussion that followed. I also thank the Bellevue College Department of Philosophy for inviting me to give two public lectures on political philosophy. Chapter 13 benefited from those valuable discussions.

Numerous parts of this book were improved thanks to papers I read and feedback I received at annual meetings of the Society of Christian Philosophers and the Northwest Philosophy Conference.

I thank the students who have taken my classes. Every quarter they amaze me with brilliant responses to the class readings, often causing me to think to myself, "I wasn't that sharp when I was in college." I have learned from students as they have learned from me.

I thank Karen Olson and Scott Barker for their superb copyediting skills.

Finally, I thank my wife, Joan, for her love and support during the years I spent writing this book. And I thank our sweet little grandson, Lucca. The time spent taking him to the park and doing other little-kid things with him was not time away from writing, it was inspiration.

TO THE INSTRUCTOR

Philosophers are as affected by fashion as anyone else. It seems to be the fashion today, at least among many who write introductory textbooks in our subject, to present short, easy-to-refute synopses of the traditional arguments for God's existence, the soul, free will, objective truth, and objective moral value rooted in God's nature. These arguments are usually followed by strong objections stated as if they are the last word. This formula may make philosophy easier to digest, but it gives many students the impression that there are no longer any good reasons to accept the traditional beliefs just mentioned.

I wrote this book for philosophy instructors who want their students to take a deeper and more respectful look at the traditional arguments and who believe, as I do, that many traditional views can be rigorously defended against the strongest objections. Many textbooks cover scores and scores of arguments, each presented in a couple of paragraphs or so; this book focuses on fewer arguments so that each can be examined with greater logical rigor and care. My experience in the classroom is that students can handle the rigor and will think more deeply as a result.

I call this book a "Socratic introduction" for several reasons. First, Socrates argued for the existence of God, the soul, objective truth, and objective moral truth. Furthermore, his method of self-examination and individual reform presupposed the existence of free will and moral responsibility. These Socratic issues form the core of this text.

Second, Socrates asked people questions designed to cause them to look inward and examine their fundamental beliefs and values on the basis

of their best reasoning. As students examine the classic philosophical arguments and the main objections to those arguments, I ask Socratic questions
without giving answers.

Third, Socrates challenged some of the popular outlooks of his day,
including the relativism and skepticism taught by the Sophists, such as
Protagoras and Gorgias. This text challenges the dominant outlook in the
academic world today. I am speaking of *naturalism*, which Alvin Plantinga
defines as the "belief that there aren't any supernatural beings—no such
person as God, for example—but also no other supernatural entities, and
nothing at all like God."[1]

I make no apology for the theistic orientation of this textbook. Theism has been the mainstream in philosophy from the beginning. It is true
that two of the most famous philosophers of the nineteenth century were
atheists—Karl Marx and Friedrich Nietzsche—but neither gave a philosophical argument for atheism and neither critiqued a philosophical argument for God's existence. It is also true that during the first half of the
twentieth century many philosophers rejected the traditional arguments
for God's existence on the grounds of either scientism or verificationism,
but both research programs proved to be failures in the end. Since the birth
of analytic theism during the 1960s, many of the leading philosophers in
such fields as modal logic, metaphysics, epistemology, ethics, and philosophy of religion have been theists. I am speaking of Kurt Gödel, Alvin
Plantinga, Saul Kripke, Peter van Inwagen, Peter Geach, Elizabeth Anscombe, Robert Audi, Eleanor Stump, Linda Zagzebski, Richard Swinburne, Robert Adams, Marilyn McCord Adams, William Alston, Alasdair
MacIntyre, Bas van Fraassen, and Nicholas Rescher, to name only a few. To
paraphrase Mark Twain, reports of the death of theism in philosophy have
been greatly exaggerated.

Like most textbooks, this one contains more than can be covered in a
single term. Although a Socratic theme runs from the first through the last
chapter, each chapter is an independent discussion. I plan to assign eleven
or twelve chapters each term, with one reserved for extra credit. Every
major section of each chapter ends with class-tested "Questions for Reflection and Discussion," exercises that stimulate good discussions online and
in the classroom.

I welcome feedback. My email address is available on the website of
Shoreline Community College.

TO THE STUDENT

You are about to study a subject that has been considered a core part of a higher education since the beginning of the Western educational system. The study of philosophy can help you think more deeply about the most fundamental questions of all. The answers you give to these questions form the basis of your worldview or general outlook on life. Those answers matter, for your worldview affects just about everything you do in life. A philosophy class will also help you develop valuable intellectual skills, including precise thinking, the power of abstraction, and the ability to follow a complex train of reasoning to its conclusion.

Some people believe that philosophy is a waste of time. They draw a distinction between "theoretical" and "practical" disciplines and then argue that only the practical subjects matter. By *theoretical* they mean "concerned only with thinking," and by *practical* they mean "concerned with getting things done." On the basis of some such distinction, they claim that philosophy doesn't matter because it is all theory and no action. Philosophy, in other words, is a waste of time because it has no practical application.

However, we must think before we act, or we will be acting blindly. Imagine, for example, campaigning for a candidate without having given any thought beforehand to the candidate's own positions and to the meanings of *justice*, *equality*, and *democracy*. Would that be wise? The more complex our activity, the more thought we need to put into it before we act. Life requires both theoretical and practical thinking.

One of the biggest lessons of life is that action without forethought can have negative consequences. This is why medical schools, for example, include theory as well as practice. (Would you want to be treated by a doctor who knows no medical theory?) The point is that our thinking cannot all be merely practical.

The ancient Greek philosopher Socrates (470–399 BC), whom you will meet in this book, argued that philosophy is actually the most practical of all disciplines, for it is aimed at attaining the most realistic worldview possible. Certainly, we are more likely to accomplish our life goals if our choices proceed from a realistic foundation rather than from fantasies.

One of the themes of this book is the following: if none of our ancestors had thought philosophically about the most fundamental questions of all and debated the answers, our vocabulary today wouldn't include words and concepts such as *critical thinking, debate, theory, evidence, science, human rights, freedom, democracy, rule of law, separation of powers*, and *"government of the people, by the people, for the people."*

Thinking deeply about fundamental worldview issues can be hard work. But if we have not reasoned carefully about the most basic questions of life, how can we be sure our answers to the less basic questions are as good as they can be? For the answers we give to the less basic questions logically depend on the answers we have already given to the more fundamental ones.

The history of ideas is full of cases in which the philosophical examination of fundamental issues enlarged our understanding of the world and led to major advances in the human condition. This is why almost no one today believes that slavery is morally acceptable, that the sun orbits the earth, or that government should control every aspect of society. In the course of this book, we'll be examining ideas that have real-world consequences.

Three Things to Know before You Dive into Philosophy

ONE

How Philosophy Began

FROM MYTH TO REASON

As far back as historical records go, human beings have asked fundamental questions about life, the universe, and the human situation. Why does the universe exist? Does God or a supreme being exist? Why are we here? What is truth? How do we distinguish knowledge from opinion, right from wrong, justice from injustice? Questions like these are fundamental in the sense that the answers we give to many *other* questions depend on the answers we have already given to these. The "big questions," as they are sometimes called, are important because the way we answer them forms the foundation of our worldview, that is, our general understanding of the universe and our outlook on life. Each of us has a worldview. And whether we realize it or not, the choices we make in life all reflect, to one degree or another, the worldview we hold.

The ancient myths record humanity's first attempts to answer the big questions. Usually presented in the form of colorful stories passed down orally from generation to generation, myths can be found in the earliest documents of every ancient civilization. Here are four, from ancient Egypt, China, Africa, and Greece, respectively.

- A god named Khnemu, depicted as a man with a ram's head, built an egg. When the egg hatched, the sun popped out. Khnemu then "sculpted the first man on a potter's wheel." This is the origin of man.[1]
- The world started as . . . a giant cosmic egg. Within the egg, a huge giant named Pangu grew and slept for 18,000 years. Upon awakening, he broke free from the egg and pushed upward. As he pushed, he separated the top and bottom halves of the egg, each to become heaven and earth respectively.[2]
- In the beginning, Mbombo was alone, darkness and primordial water covered the earth. . . . Mbombo came to feel an intense pain in his stomach, and then Mbombo vomited the sun, the moon, and stars. The heat and light from the sun evaporated the water covering the earth, creating clouds, and after time, the dry hills emerged.[3]
- In the beginning Chaos, the nothingness out of which the first objects of existence appeared, arose spontaneously. The children of Chaos were Gaia (the Earth), Eros (desire or sexual love), Tartarus (the Underworld), Erebus (Darkness) and Nyx (Night).[4]

A new way to answer the fundamental questions of life made its first appearance in history in the land of the Greeks during the sixth century BC when a group of thinkers there rejected the customary myths of their society and began seeking answers to the big questions on the basis of independent reasoning and observation alone. We know a great deal about these individuals because they put their hypotheses and supporting reasons into written form and circulated their thoughts for the sake of rational debate and discussion.

Their motivation sounds surprisingly modern. Myths, they argued, suffer from a fatal defect. Although they offer answers to the most fundamental questions of all, those answers are not backed by reasoning and observation. But if there is no reason at all to believe the stories they tell, then why believe them?

This insistence on reason and observation may sound commonplace today, but it was a radical innovation in the early sixth century BC. Historians call the shift from mythical to reason-based explanations of the world a "revolution in human thought."

The ancient Greeks named these independent thinkers "philosophers" (from the Greek roots *philo* for "love" and *sophia* for "wisdom"), and a new subject was born: *philosophy* — "the love of wisdom." As the Greeks originally understood the word, philosophy is the search for answers to the most fundamental questions of all using unaided reason and careful observation alone.

INTRODUCING THALES

We have little factual information about the lives of most individuals around the world in the sixth century BC. However, we know quite a bit about the life and thought of the very first person in recorded history to reject the myths of his society and pursue reason-based answers to the big questions because the ancient Greeks preserved the biographical information and thoughts of their leading thinkers to an extent unparalleled in ancient times.[5] For the details, we turn to Aristotle (384–322 BC), one of the greatest of the ancient Greek philosophers and the first to write a history of philosophy. (We'll meet Aristotle in chapter 3.)

Aristotle traced philosophy back in time through a succession of writers to the prosperous Greek seaport of Miletus and to an individual there named Thales, whom he called "the first philosopher." His historical research has since been confirmed: Thales of Miletus (ca. 625–ca. 546 BC) deserves the title Aristotle conferred on him, for no documented record has been found of any individual anywhere before Thales rejecting the customary myths of his or her society and proposing hypotheses supported by independent reasoning and observation alone.[6] Evidence also exists that Thales published his hypotheses and supporting arguments in written form, hoping to stimulate rational discussion and debate.[7]

One of his students — for Thales was a teacher — raised logical objections to his teacher's hypotheses and proposed alternative answers. That student, Anaximander (ca. 610–546 BC), the second philosopher in recorded history, supported his hypotheses with reasoned arguments that he circulated in a manuscript titled *On Nature*. There is no record of any student anywhere in the world before this time writing a treatise criticizing on reasoned grounds the philosophical arguments of his teacher while offering new arguments of his own.

Anaximander's student Anaximenes (585–528 BC), the third philosopher on record, criticized *his* teacher's reasoning on logical grounds and proposed new ideas that he too circulated in a book containing his reasoning and evidence. The philosophical tradition of argument and counterargument had begun.

In standard histories of the ancient world, the Greeks are presented as the founders of philosophy as an academic discipline. This distinction is deserved, for in no other society of the sixth century BC or before is there a verified historical record of independent thinkers proposing nonmythological, reason-based answers to fundamental questions while their students, in turn, write books challenging the hypotheses of their teachers using arguments of their own.

THE FIRST PHILOSOPHICAL QUESTION: THE PROBLEM OF THE ONE AND THE MANY

Thales began with one of the most fruitful questions ever asked. Here is one way to put the first documented philosophical issue:

> The universe contains many diverse things: plants, animals, consciousness, mountains, stars, ideas, love, hopes, and people. Yet everything is interconnected in some way, for the universe has an overall order that allows us to make accurate predictions and live from day to day. Why doesn't it all fly apart? What unites the many into one to make this a *uni*verse? Is there something—a One over the Many—that joins everything into one interconnected system?

Historians call this a "gateway question" because of the many lines of research it opened and the advances in thought it sparked. Thales's question, known as "the problem of the one and the many," has been raised by nearly every major philosopher, East and West, since his day. It has also been addressed by many of the greatest scientists, including theoretical physicists working on the cutting edge of big bang astrophysics today searching for something they call a "grand unified theory" of the physical universe.

Thales's opening question has also been applied within every academic subject, with fruitful results. Applied to economics, for example, his question becomes, What holds a modern economy together? What are the fundamental principles that explain the way an economic system works? Applied to a nation, the question is, What unites the many different people into one nation? The problem of the one and the many remains a cutting-edge idea today.

The hydrological (water) cycle especially interested Thales. He observed that water comes up from underground (wells, springs), ascends to the sky (evaporation), and comes back down in the form of rain. He also noted that water is necessary for all forms of life. The cycle from earth to sky to earth thus makes life possible. There is evidence that he also argued that the water cycle wouldn't exist if water did not have a unique property. It appeared to be the only substance capable of existing in three phases (liquid, solid, gas). That's a lot of interconnectedness.

Among the ancient Greeks, the term *arche* (pronounced ar-KAY) meant "a foundational principle explaining and unifying everything within a specified domain" (as in "architecture"). For a modern example, the U.S. Constitution is the *arche* of U.S. law. According to Aristotle, Thales was searching for the *arche* of the entire universe — one ultimate principle or source that would explain the interconnectedness of everything and make rational or reason-based sense of the whole system.

> Without some kind of unity within diversity, we could have no thought or language, and thus nothing would be intelligible. Even the simplest concept — for example the concept "dog" — unites many individual things under a single idea.
>
> —James Fieser and Norman Lillegard[8]

AN INTELLIGIBLE UNIVERSE?

Thales's quest for the *arche* of the universe led him to raise a second gateway question, one that also ranks as one of the most fruitful questions of all time. If there *is* an *arche* of the universe — a One over the Many — can its existence and nature be known by the human mind through unaided reason and careful observation? In other words, is the *arche* rationally intelligible? Thales had a hunch that the answer is yes, and on that assumption, he set out to see how far his own cognitive abilities might take him.

We can easily miss the significance of Thales's second gateway question. His working assumption—that we live in a rationally intelligible universe—was a revolutionary step. The historian of philosophy David Stewart calls Thales's rational intelligibility thesis a "brilliant leap forward in the history of thought . . . an advance absolutely essential to the development of modern physical science."[9] L. P. Gerson, another scholar of ancient thought, writes that it is "a remarkable advance on common sense to intuit that there are reasons for the regularity [of the universe] and that different sorts of regularity or patterns in nature are linked by common underlying principles [that can be grasped by the human mind]." The hypothesis of the intelligibility of the universe, Gerson claims, is one "without which any scientific enterprise cannot hope to begin."[10] The philosopher Thomas Nagel writes that "science is driven by the assumption that the world is intelligible . . . that [its basis] can not only be described but understood. . . . Without the assumption of an intelligible underlying order, which long antedates the scientific revolution, [its major] discoveries could not have been made."[11]

Albert Einstein placed himself in the tradition of Thales when he wrote more than twenty-five centuries after Thales, "Certain it is that a conviction, akin to a religious feeling, of the rationality or intelligibility of the world lies behind all scientific work of a higher order."[12]

Indeed, the idea that the universe is rationally intelligible is a presupposition not just of science but of every academic subject. In chapter 4, we'll explore some logical implications of this gateway idea, the working assumption that we live in an intelligible rather than a random universe.

Philosophy and Belief in God

Thales's first hypothesis concerned the water cycle. His hypothesis was naturalistic, that is, it referred only to physical or material elements within the observable or natural universe. However, according to the doxographers—ancient Greek historians who commented on the great texts of their culture's past—Thales did not believe his naturalistic hypothesis went deep enough. They tell us he also argued for the existence of a supernatural *arche* of the universe, characterized as a "divinity, an immortal being, something living that, precisely because it is living, is capable of self-initiated movement and change."[13] Thus, in *Lives and Opinions of Eminent Philosophers*,

Diogenes Laertius (third century AD), one of the greatest doxographers, attributes this statement to Thales: "God is the most ancient of all things, for he had no birth: the world is the most beautiful of things, for it is the work of God."[14]

If Thales conceived of the One over the Many in divine terms, which he likely did, he was the first philosophical monotheist (Greek *mono*, "singular" and *theos*, "God," literally, "someone who believes that God or a supreme being exists"). Of course, in his day the word *theos* did not carry all its modern connotations. As philosophy developed and as philosophers reasoned further about the problem of the one and the many, *theos* acquired deeper meanings. Today an entire field of learning is concerned with this subject: theology.

The historical evidence indicates that both Anaximander and Anaximenes also argued for the existence of a superintending *arche* of the material universe that they characterized in terms of divinity, personhood, and intelligence.

Thus, the first three philosophers argued that our natural power to reason points beyond the material universe to a mind. Arguments for the existence of God or a supreme being can be found throughout the ancient Greek philosophical tradition. This helps explain the fact that by the fifth century BC, most educated Greeks were monotheists.[15] We'll examine some of the first theistic arguments — and modern successors to those arguments — in the course of this book. As we'll see, philosophical reasoning for God's existence brings to light deep logical connections between the intelligibility of the universe and the validity of science, math, ethics, and reason itself.

THALES IN RETROSPECT

Thales is most famous for his hypothesis that all the diverse substances in the material world are composed of one underlying element, water. He supported his conjecture with at least six lines of empirical (observable) evidence, circulated his idea, and sought critical, reasoned feedback. The specific details of his hypothesis are of historical rather than philosophical interest today. His proposal was primitive by modern standards, just as one would expect of a theory twenty-six hundred years old. It has been superseded, obviously. However, all of this should not detract from the importance of what Thales did. The important fact is that he supported his hypothesis with rational arguments presented apart from myth, magic, superstition, and unquestioned priestly authority.

The historian of philosophy Wallace Matson calls the emergence of the first nonmythological, reason-based theories of the universe in Greece during the sixth century BC "the most stupendous intellectual revolution in recorded history."[16] J. V. Luce, also a historian of philosophy, calls Thales "the first thinker to propound a comprehensive account of the *physis* [nature] of the world, based largely on his own observations and inferences. He seems to have outlined a daring and unified scheme . . . thought out along rational lines, which justly marks its author as a major innovator in the history of thought."[17]

The ancient Greeks maintained a special roster honoring their wisest thinkers, or sages. The greatest were known as the "Seven Sages of Greece." Although archeologists have discovered differing lists, the name Thales of Miletus appears in first place on each one.

A DEFINITION OF OUR SUBJECT

This abbreviated account of the birth of philosophy has covered a lot of ground. Can the basic idea be encapsulated in a concise definition? Wilfrid Sellars (1912–89) characterizes philosophy as the rational effort "to see how things in the broadest possible sense of the term hang together in the broadest possible sense of the term."[18] Referring to the method rather than the goal of our subject, Laurence BonJour (b. 1943) writes that philosophy is "essentially dialectical in nature, consisting of arguments, and responses, and further arguments and further responses back and forth among the different positions on a given issue."[19] These statements by major philosophers describe academic philosophy as it is practiced today, yet they are equally true of the way philosophy was practiced in the beginning. The independent use of our own cognitive abilities, combined with the goal of understanding the whole of reality in a rational way, is the common thread linking Thales's thoughts to ours today.

Pulling all the foregoing threads together, I believe the following definition captures the core meaning that hasn't changed since the beginning:

Philosophy is the search for answers to the most fundamental questions of human existence using our cognitive abilities alone, including reason and observation.

Defined in this way, philosophy may sound too abstract to be of any significance. However, several considerations already stated suggest otherwise. The answers we give to the fundamental questions of life form the basis of our worldviews. But our worldviews influence the choices we make in life and therefore the way we live. In addition, philosophy gives expression to one of the most universal of all human needs, namely, the need to make sense of life as a whole.

Questions for Reflection and Discussion 1.1

1. What do philosophy and myth have in common? How do they differ?
2. Take an inventory of your worldview by listing some of your core beliefs and values.
3. Does your worldview affect your life?
4. What would it be like to live with no worldview at all?
5. Do you recall being perplexed by a philosophical question? If so, did you discuss it with others? What was the question, and what conclusion did you reach? Do you recall your reasoning?

THE CHALLENGE OF SCIENTISM

Since ancient times, philosophy has been considered a place to go for carefully reasoned discussions regarding the most fundamental questions of all. In recent years, however, an increasing number of people have been turning to other sources. Many today believe that we should reject philosophy (and religion) and rely solely on science when deciding what to believe, including what to believe regarding the most fundamental matters. The only real knowledge, they say, is scientific knowledge. Nothing counts as known unless it has first been validated by science. According to this view, known as "scientism," science is our only path to truth, our only legitimate form of knowing. Anything not proved by science is merely unfounded (and expendable) opinion.

If scientism is true, philosophy is as outmoded as the horse and buggy. But is it true? As we proceed, keep in mind the distinction between science and scient*ism*. Science is *not* the same thing as scientism. Science refers to those subjects (physics, chemistry, biology, geology, etc.) that restrict themselves to research based on the scientific method of hypothesis testing. The sciences have certainly enlarged our knowledge. All philosophers today agree on this. The scientific method is surely *one* guide to truth. However, it doesn't follow, from the fact that science is one guide to truth, that science is the *only* guide to truth. Scientism claims, not that science is one guide to truth but that science is our only guide to truth.

However, as many philosophers have pointed out, scientism is false according to its own method of validation. Consider the following sentence, which we shall name S:

S: Science is our only path to truth—nothing is known unless it has been proved by science.

Exactly which scientific experiment or series of experiments has ever proved that S is true? Which verified scientific theory appearing in the standard textbooks shows that science is the one and only path to truth? No scientist has ever carried out an experiment or established a theory showing scientifically that S is true. Which is why scientism is neither presented nor defended in any reputable physics, chemistry, or biology textbook.

The sentence S has neither been tested nor proved by science because it is not a scientifically testable thesis. But if scientism cannot be established using the only method it claims is valid—the scientific method—then why believe it? Considered critically, scientism is self-defeating, in the sense that if you accept it, then you have sufficient logical grounds to reject it.

I know of no scientists who explicitly endorse scientism. But I regularly see the view expressed in student papers. Certainly, none of the founders of modern science in the seventeenth century held the view—most gave philosophical arguments for God's existence. Numerous prominent scientists today have given philosophical arguments on fundamental issues—including arguments for the existence of God—indicating that they reject scientism. Francis Collins, for example, the director of the National Institutes of Health, who served as the head of the Human Genome Project, wrote a book in which he argues philosophically for the existence of God based on the apparent design in the genetic code.[20] The founder of big bang cosmology was the mathematician and astrophysicist Georges Lemaître (1894–1966), a Catholic priest of the Jesuit Order.

In the course of this book, we'll see that many beliefs about matters of fundamental importance are reasonable — and are supported by good reasoning — even though they do not fall within the boundaries of the physical sciences. Scientific knowledge is a fraction of the sum total of all knowledge and needs to be interpreted within that sum total.

Going deeper. As we have seen, scientism is the claim that science is our only path to truth. Some advocates of scientism go further and argue that the only things that are real are those objects recognized by science. The philosopher Ed Feser presents the usual argument given for this view:

1. The predictive power and technological applications of science are unparalleled by those of any other purported source of knowledge.

2. Therefore, what science reveals to us is probably all that is real.

Feser comments:

This, I maintain, is a bad argument. How bad is it? About as bad as this one: 1. Metal detectors have had far greater success in finding coins and other metallic objects in more places than any other method has. 2. Therefore, what metal detectors reveal to us (coins and other metallic objects) is probably all that is real. [The problem with this argument is that] metal detectors are keyed to those aspects of the natural world susceptible of detection via electromagnetic means (or whatever). But however well [metal detectors] perform this task . . . that simply wouldn't make it even probable that there are no aspects of the natural world other than the ones they are sensitive to. Similarly, what physics does (and there is no doubt that it does it brilliantly) is to capture those aspects of the natural world susceptible of the mathematical modeling that makes precise prediction and technological application possible. But here too, it simply doesn't follow that there are no other aspects of the natural world.[21]

THE FIRST FREE MARKETPLACE OF IDEAS

At the start of a new subject, it is the questions that matter most, not the first answers given. Thales asked questions that stimulated reasoned discussion and opened new fields of rational investigation. The discussion he started grew into a *dialectic* (Greek *dia*, "between," and *legein*, "to speak," or a "dialogue"). In a dialectic, (1) one person puts forward a hypothesis backed by careful reasoning in an intellectual environment in which people are free to think for themselves, speak their minds, and reason together; (2) others offer critical feedback in response, also based on reasoning; (3) the first speaker either defends his hypothesis, revises it, or rejects it; and (4) the process repeats itself. Economists call this "information spill-over" because freely traded ideas tend to give birth to new ideas that give birth to still more ideas spilling from mind to mind.

The dialectic started by Thales and his students must have spread quickly, for we know that by the fifth century BC, at least *one hundred* philosophers scattered across about two hundred Greek city-states were formulating and debating accounts of the universe based on reasoning that they circulated for debate and critical feedback. This is an amazing number of independent thinkers, given the stage of history at the time and the small size of ancient Greece. Today we are accustomed to large numbers of people publishing, sharing, and debating ideas in a climate of intellectual freedom. This was unheard of anywhere in the world outside Greece during the sixth century BC. The world's first free marketplace of ideas was open for business.

Historians call the earliest Greek philosophers the *pre-Socratics* because they lived before Socrates (470–399 BC), an awesome human being and philosopher whose personality and method of thought revolutionized the nature of the subject, as we'll see in chapter 2.

The pre-Socratics are a remarkable group. Sir Karl Popper, one of the most distinguished philosophers of the twentieth century, argued that it is part of the pre-Socratic philosophical tradition

> to be critical, and to try and improve not only the founder's teaching, but also that of the later teachers. Perhaps for this reason, each generation produced at least one major change, and the name of the innovator is openly transmitted . . . not only were the doctrines, the theories, and the innovations traditionally transmitted, but so was a kind of

second-order methodological advice: "Try to improve upon the theories! Try to make them better for they are not perfect.". . . I suggest that this self-critical methodology must have come from the founder, Thales, and that it was transmitted . . . to [his successors].[22]

The historian of philosophy Wallace Matson writes that the "core achievement" of the pre-Socratics was "the invention of critical or dialectical thought about the world. . . . Myths are not conversations. Their format is that of the speaker addressing the silently listening audience. But Anaximander *criticized* Thales . . . [and] Anaximenes likewise criticized Anaximander."[23]

Commenting on the pre-Socratic tradition, the historian of philosophy J. V. Luce writes:

It is impossible to over-emphasize its pervasive effect on subsequent European thought. The whole fabric of Western culture is still deeply colored by its assumptions, methods, and terminology. Atomic theory and ethics, mathematics and logic, metaphysics and theology, are more than just ancient Greek words. They are key modern ways of ordering experience and comprehending reality, and they remain closely patterned on their original models [in ancient Greece].[24]

Nearly all the great issues that will occupy the rest of this book—and that occupy philosophers today—make their first appearance in the historical record in a strictly philosophical context in the writings of the pre-Socratics.[25]

One of the lessons of history is that reasoning together peacefully can lead to discoveries that advance both knowledge and the human condition. Certainly a partial proof of this is that the philosophical dialectic launched by the pre-Socratics led to many advances in human thought, including the birth of mathematics as a theoretical, proof-based subject.

PHILOSOPHY AND THE BIRTH OF MATHEMATICS AS AN AXIOMATIC SYSTEM

A thousand years before the Greeks reached a stage of civilization advanced enough for mathematics, the Egyptians and Babylonians had discovered many important mathematical principles. However, neither Egyptian nor Babylonian mathematics advanced beyond mensuration: rules for measuring parcels of land and constructing large buildings. The art of measurement was limited because it contained no method of proof and no procedure for systematic theoretical inquiry.[26]

It was Thales, "the founder of the earliest school of Greek mathematics," who advanced mathematics to the theoretical level in the form of an axiom system.[27] As you may remember from your geometry class in high school, an axiom system has three parts: (1) axioms, considered self-evident; (2) exact definitions of all terms; and (3) theorems derived from the axioms using strict definitions and step-by-step, gap-free reasoning. The Greek discovery of the axiomatic method of proof turned math into the abstract, theoretical subject we know today and unleashed a flood of new discoveries. By the third century BC, the Greek mathematician Euclid (ca. 350–ca. 250 BC) was able to record *thirteen* books of proven geometrical theorems and take giant leaps in several other areas of mathematics.

Thus, the noted historian of mathematics Sir Thomas Heath writes, "With Thales . . . geometry first becomes a deductive science depending on general propositions."[28] The historian of mathematics David Burton writes: "The Greeks made mathematics into one discipline, transforming a varied collection of empirical rules of calculation into an orderly and systematic unity [based on a system of proof]. Although they were plainly heirs to an accumulation of Eastern knowledge, the Greeks fashioned through their own efforts a mathematics more profound, more rational, than any that preceded it."[29]

And in math, as in philosophy, what mattered at the start was the nature of the questions asked. Thales and his students went beyond mensuration by asking (and answering) theoretical rather than merely practical questions. Although the Egyptians and Babylonians knew many practical formulas, Thales was the first to look at the known formulas and ask, *Why* are these true? What makes them true? The historian of mathematics Dirk Struik writes:

Modern mathematics was born in this atmosphere [of Greek rationalism] — the mathematics that not only asked the question "How?" but also the modern scientific question "Why?" The traditional father of Greek mathematics is the merchant Thales of

Miletus. . . . [In the figure of Thales we find] the circumstances under which the foundations, not only of modern mathematics, but of modern science and philosophy, were established.[30]

Burton credits the Greeks' preference for abstract thought that

distinguished them from previous thinkers; their concern was not with, say, triangular fields of grain but with "triangles" and the characteristics that must accompany "triangularity." This preference for the abstract concept can be seen in the attitude of the different ancient cultures toward the number $\sqrt{2}$ [square root of 2]; the Babylonians had computed its approximation to a high degree of accuracy, but the Greeks proved it was irrational.[31]

Which raises an interesting question: Is there a math–philosophy connection? Struik suggests a deep one:

The early Greek study of mathematics had one main goal: the understanding of man's place in the universe according to a rational scheme. Mathematics helped find order in chaos, to arrange ideas in logical chains, to find fundamental principles. It was the most rational of all sciences, and although there is little doubt that the Greek merchants became acquainted with [Egyptian and Babylonian] mathematics along their trade routes, they soon discovered that the [Egyptians and Babylonians] had left most of the rationalization undone. Why did the isosceles triangle have two equal angles? Why was the area of a triangle equal to half that of a rectangle of equal base and altitude? These questions came naturally to men who asked similar questions concerning biology, cosmology, and physics.[32]

Are math and philosophy partners in the same quest? The quest to make rational sense of the universe as a whole? Pythagoras (570–495 BC), one of the early Greek mathematicians, thought so, as have many mathematicians, physicists, and philosophers since. Pythagoras founded a religious community in which mathematics and philosophy were considered spiritual pursuits jointly pointing the soul upward toward God, the One over the Many.

The philosophical search for rational principles led to another major advance: the birth of democracy and the first public debates on the nature of freedom, constitutionalism, and the rights of citizenship.

PHILOSOPHY AND THE BIRTH OF DEMOCRACY

The ancient Greeks were the first people in history to set up a working democracy (Greek *demos*, "people," and *kratein*, "to rule," thus, "rule by the people"), complete with voting machines, jury trials with members selected by lot, citizens running for paid public office, government officials (including generals of the armed forces) who could be removed from office by vote of the people or their representatives, public speeches, and written laws passed by elected legislatures and posted in public for all to read. The Greeks were also the first to produce constitutions limiting established governments by written law. These revolutionary advances stemmed from an earlier and equally significant Greek innovation: the Greeks were the first to give philosophical expression to—and to publicly debate—the ideals of civic freedom, individual rights, the rule of law, and citizen participation in government.

The democracy they established was not perfect, that is, they did not fully realize or institute their professed ideals. For instance, as in most societies around the world at the time, slavery was legal. In addition, only male adults of a certain social status were citizens and sometimes one man controlled the assembly. (Should we expect humanity's first steps toward freedom to have been perfect? Have *we* achieved perfection 2,500 years later?) Yet the Greek experiment in democracy was the first documented step in recorded history in the direction of our modern idea of freedom. We saw that there is a logical connection between philosophy and mathematics. Is there a similar connection between philosophy and democracy?

SCIENCE, MEDICINE, AND HISTORY

The philosophical search for rational principles led to three further historic advances that will conclude this brief survey of what historians have called "the Greek miracle." The first is the birth of science, with science under-stood as the rational or reason-based investigation of nature. Natural science began as a branch of philosophy, which the Greeks named "physics" (Greek *physis*, "nature").

The next advance was the birth of scientific medicine. In the ancient world, disease was generally believed to have a supernatural origin, which explains why it was usually treated with spells and magical incantations performed by shamans or priests. The Greek scientist Hippocrates (fl. fifth century BC) is considered the founder of scientific medicine because he was the first person in history to write treatises presenting medicine as a strictly reason-based academic discipline to be practiced apart from magic, myth, and superstition. By placing the study of medicine on a rational rather than a mythical or magical basis, he turned medicine into an empirical, scientific subject. Hippocrates was also the first person in history to argue that the study of medicine should include ethical as well as rational standards, and the first to establish an academic medical school based on the rational investigation of disease.

The third advance is the birth of history as an academic subject. The Greek scholar Herodotus (484–425 BC) is called "the founder of history as an academic subject" because he was the first person on record to write a critical, reason-based analysis of the past that is not merely an uncritical glorification of a ruler or a list of events. He also directed rational criticism wherever he felt it was deserved, including at his *own* society. Writing at the dawn of Western civilization, Herodotus proposed that free people are more creative, inventive, and productive than those who live like slaves under the oppressive hand of unelected authoritarian rulers. Has history borne out his claim?

Many historians have observed that the major subjects that form the basis of the modern college curriculum — science, math, and the humanities — began within Greek philosophy before branching off to become specialized subjects in their own right. The subjects that remained within philosophy were those treating matters too fundamental for the specialized subjects that branched off. In this book we'll examine six fields of philosophy: critical thinking, logic, philosophy of religion, epistemology (the theory of knowledge), philosophy of the human person, and philosophical ethics.

RETROSPECTIVE ON THE PRE-SOCRATICS

In his history of the world, the University of Oxford historian J. M. Roberts writes that the Greeks

> produced quite suddenly a rush of achievements many of which were startlingly novel. Ever since, people have wondered how it happened. Some have called it "the Greek Miracle," so amazing do they find it. . . . In about four hundred years, Greeks invented politics, philosophy, much of arithmetic and geometry (those are all in origin Greek words). . . . This huge step shows how different was Greek civilization from its predecessors. It was just much more creative. Central to this was the new importance the Greeks gave to rational, conscious inquiry about the world they lived in. The fact that many of them continued to be superstitious and to believe in magic should not obscure this. Because of the way they used reason and argument, they gave human beings a better grip on the world they lived in than any earlier people had done. Greek ideas were not always right, but they were worked out and tested in better ways than earlier ones. The Greek Miracle made an immense contribution to the development of the powers of the human mind. So intense an effort to grapple with the deepest problems of thought and life had never before been made, and there was not to be another like it for a long time.[33]

The philosopher Andrew Jeffery characterizes Greek civilization as a

> "Cambrian Explosion" of ideas, wherein both magical and rationalistic cosmological thinking, both totalitarian and democratic ideas were propounded and debated, and where individualism, capitalism, communitarian and communist ideals all received their first articulation. Nobody seriously debated such ideas before the Greeks. The dream that human beings might pry into the operation of nature and, by using their own power of reason, might learn how the universe works, originates here as well.[34]

Edith Hamilton calls the ancient Greeks "the first Westerners." "The spirit of the West, the modern spirit," she writes, "is a Greek discovery; and the place of the Greeks is in the modern world." Whether we realize it or not, she argues, "we have all been schooled by the Greeks."[35]

Thales and his conversation partners spawned a new way to make sense of the world, a freer mode of thinking, a promising way for thought to advance. When we look back on the world's first free marketplace of ideas, we see more nuanced hypotheses emerging with each new round of rational discussion and debate. One of the lessons of history deserves repeating: we make the most progress when we engage each other respectfully in a back-and-forth process of argument and counterargument (dialectic) in a setting in which we are free to think for ourselves and express our thoughts using reason, our common currency. The intellectually dormant parts of the world today remain those places where the minds and wills of the people are shackled by authoritarian governments, totalitarian religious authorities, and rigid cultural attitudes that prevent people from reasoning freely together about the fundamental questions of life.

In 470 BC, a philosopher was born who devoted his life, and ultimately gave his life, for the cause of reason, freedom, and unfettered philosophical discussion. He also contributed something of inestimable value to the emerging discipline of philosophy. His name was Socrates.

Questions for Reflection and Discussion 1.2

1. What exactly is philosophy?
2. What is a "free marketplace of ideas"? Where, if at all, do we find such a market today?
3. Who were the pre-Socratics? Why do they stand out?
4. Is politics, as it is practiced today through the mass media, a philosophical dialectic?

TWO

The Socratic Method

INTRODUCING SOCRATES

The second thing it's good to know before we dive into philosophy is the method of thought first taught by the ancient Greek philosopher Socrates (470–399 BC). Although he never wrote a book or lectured at a university, Socrates was one of the most influential individuals of all time. His unique contribution, the "Socratic method," remains a central part of philosophical inquiry twenty-four centuries after his death. And Socrates has never become outdated: new books and scholarly papers on his thoughts appear every year. We'll turn to his famous method after a brief look at his life and times, for Socrates's great contribution only comes alive and acquires its full meaning in the context of the amazing life he lived.

Socrates was born in a modest neighborhood located just outside the south entrance to Athens, Greece. In his teens, he became interested in philosophy, geometry, and theoretical physics. According to his student Xenophon (ca. 428–ca. 354 BC), Socrates and his friends met regularly to read "together the treasuries of ancient wisdom in books, and to [make]

23

extracts from them."[1] Thus, as a youth Socrates began a lifelong quest to answer the fundamental questions of life using his own powers of reason and observation. As he discussed the big questions with his friends, he came to believe that we learn best *not* when we lock ourselves away alone like a hermit on a mountaintop, but when we actively reason together with others in serious conversation, receiving and giving thoughtful feedback.

He served as an infantryman in the Athenian army from his teens into his fifties and fought on the front lines in numerous military campaigns.[2] His bravery in battle became legendary. According to all accounts, he was a fearless combat soldier. This is remarkable when you consider the nature of ancient warfare. In Socrates's day, Greek infantrymen marched across the battlefield side by side in the phalanx formation, thousands at a time. As the Athenian phalanx approached the opposing force, the men increased the pace to crash into the enemy line at the "double-quick." Blood and severed limbs would be flying everywhere. The Greek hoplite confronted the enemy in personal, hand-to-hand combat. Infantry warfare in Socrates's day was unimaginably brutal, bloody, and horrific.[3] On numerous occasions his commanders tried to decorate him for bravery, but he turned them down, suggesting the medals be given to others.

Some wonder how a philosopher can serve as a dedicated combat soldier. In his personal life Socrates opposed violence in all forms, but when he was required to defend his beloved city, he felt morally bound to answer the call of duty. He even gave a lengthy philosophical argument in defense of his commitment to the laws of Athens.[4]

According to his friends, Socrates cared little for fame, money, material possessions, or physical comforts. What mattered more to him was discussing the big questions of life with others so that he could attain the most reasonable worldview. While walking through the busy *agora* (marketplace) in downtown Athens one day, he is reported to have said, "So many things I can do without." His student Xenophon, who went on to become a war hero, writer, and famous general, described Socrates as "frugal" and said that even shoes were too much of a bother for him: Socrates was known to go barefoot all year long, even on winter military campaigns. Although he could have had more possessions, Socrates sought an uncluttered life and practiced what is today called "voluntary simplicity."[5]

Because he believed that answers to fundamental questions are best pursued on the basis of careful reasoning and in serious conversation with others, Socrates could often be found sitting in the agora of Athens discussing philosophical issues with anyone who cared to join in. According to eyewitness accounts, in these discussions he treated everyone—regardless of social standing—with equal respect. His commitment to human equality and to the intrinsic value of each individual was a novel moral attitude in his day. Those discussions in the marketplace must have been fascinating, for crowds would often gather to listen.

Socrates married late in life; he and his wife, Xanthippe, had three children (all boys). Accounts by his students suggest that the marriage was a good one.

LIFE'S MISSION FOUND

At some point around the middle of his life, in part as a result of his conversations in the marketplace, Socrates became convinced that many people *think* that they know what they are talking about when in reality they do not have a clue. He came to believe that many people, including famous politicians, military leaders, and smug experts, are in the grips of illusion. Their alleged knowledge is a mirage. Similarly, he also saw that many *believe* that they are doing the morally right thing when they are really only fooling themselves—their actions cannot be rationally justified.

At the same time, he also believed that people blinded by illusions could improve their lives by using their own powers of reason and observation more fully. As this realization sank in, Socrates found his life's purpose: he would help people use their own innate reasoning ability to discover their own ignorance and uncover their own illusions as a first step to attaining more reality-based beliefs and values. But how to proceed?

Some people, when convinced that others are deluded, want to grab them by the collar and yell at them. Others try to force people to change their minds. Many people today prefer violence and destruction. None of this was for Socrates. He felt so much respect for each individual—even those in the grips of illusion and moral error—that intimidation and violence were unthinkable. His was a completely different approach: *he asked people questions*. Not just any questions, though. He asked questions designed to cause others to look in the mirror and examine their own assumptions on the basis of rational and realistic standards of evidence.

When Socrates got through to people, these are among the questions they would be asking themselves: Why do I believe this? What is my evidence? Are my assumptions on this matter really true? Or am I overlooking something? Have I looked at all the evidence or only that which supports my preexisting view? Are my actions those of a morally good person? Or am I only rationalizing bad behavior?

Looking in the mirror in a Socratic way can be painful. For reasons perhaps best left to psychologists, it is easy to criticize others, but it is hard to question and challenge ourselves. There are also intellectual hurdles. Which standards, or criteria, should we apply when we test our basic beliefs and values?

Socrates, by his example, stimulated a great deal of research into this question. Over the years, many objective criteria for rational, reality-based thinking have been proposed, tested, and accepted as reliable guides to truth, with *truth* understood as correspondence with the facts or with reality. (We'll explore the nature of truth in chapter 3 and again in chapter 8.) These standards are studied in the field of philosophy known as *logic*—the study of the principles of correct reasoning. We'll examine some principles of logic in chapter 3.

Today we call someone whose thinking is guided by realistic and rational criteria a "critical thinker." The term "critical thinking" stems from the Greek *kritein*, "to judge, distinguish," thus a *criterion* is a standard of evaluation and means thinking by rational, objective standards. Our current notion of critical thinking grew directly out of the Socratic method. Thus, the highly respected Center for Critical Thinking begins its history of the subject with this statement: "The intellectual roots of critical thinking are as ancient as its etymology, traceable, ultimately, to the teaching practice and vision of Socrates 2,500 years ago."[6]

For this reason, many historians of philosophy consider Socrates to be the founder of critical thinking as a systematic and disciplined form of inquiry. He deserves the title because he was the first person in history to teach the subject in a systematic way and to give his life for the cause of critical thinking, as we'll see in a moment.

His unique method of thought had a huge effect on those he talked with; it has also benefited those who have applied it since his time. So many valuable insights have resulted from the example he set that it is impossible to distill his method into a few words. Here is my attempt:

Never be afraid to question your beliefs and values on the basis of rational, realistic criteria and an honest look at the evidence. When examining your beliefs on an issue, ask yourself questions like these: Why do I believe this? What is my evidence? Are my assumptions on this issue really true? Or am I mistaken? Am I only considering evidence that supports my entrenched beliefs? Am I overlooking something important? When examining your values, ask yourself questions like these: Are my character traits or habits those of a morally good person? Or am I only fooling myself and rationalizing bad behavior? Will I be proud of my actions when I look back years from now, or ashamed?

Test your assumptions frequently by discussing them with others. When you do, listen closely to what they have to say. They might see something you missed. Keep in mind that when emotions flare and things get heated, critical thinking usually suffers. So, when someone makes a statement you disagree with, don't get angry and don't automatically assume that the person is wrong. In a respectful manner ask for a supporting argument. Listen calmly and try to understand where the person is coming from. He or she might have something to teach you. Just as you bring a body of knowledge to the discussion and see the matter through your own worldview lens, others see the world through their own lens and contribute their own knowledge. This is *not* to say there is no objective truth of the matter. But both of you are more likely to reach it if you listen to each other and look for the value in the other's point of view. Together you might see further than you see separately.

The Socratic point is that if the two of you will listen to each other and look for the value in the other person's point of view, and if you will both evaluate your assumptions on the basis of rational standards, you both might learn something. The other person's information might broaden your view, and your information might broaden the other person's view.

Finally, sometimes we are not clear when we express ourselves. If the other person's thinking is vague or disorganized, don't assume that he is hopelessly mixed up. Ask him to clarify his ideas and help him by asking good questions. Again, the other person might just have something to teach you. The reverse, of course, is also true.

Over the centuries, many have discovered that they can improve their lives by looking in the mirror and asking themselves Socratic questions. Doing so requires courage, however, for often one of the first things a critical thinker uncovers is his or her own personal failings, and it is hard to face one's shortcomings with honesty and then change. Yet honest self-examination is a prerequisite for moral, spiritual, and intellectual growth, as Socrates argued and as life experience confirms.

The Examination of Conscience

Parallels to the Socratic method can be found in many religions. In the Christian tradition, an "examination of conscience" occurs in a quiet moment when a person of faith looks in the mirror and reflects critically on his or her past choices and sins before seeking forgiveness and vowing to improve. Some Christians use the Ten Commandments as a criterion when they examine their behavior, others meditate on the Beatitudes, the Psalms, or the lives of the saints. In Islam, the practice is called *Muhasaba* ("self-reflection"). The Socratic method fits seamlessly within almost any religious life.

As the pervasiveness of human ignorance sank in, his conversations in the marketplace shifted from the big questions of cosmology (Greek *kosmologia*, "the study of the universe as a systematic and beautiful whole") to questions about the human condition and the proper care of one's soul.

As we have seen, the Socratic method requires honesty. The reason is plain. If you are not honest with yourself, you will not be led to examine with some degree of objectivity your *own* beliefs and values. But that's the real point—improving your *own* thinking. Thus, if you do not look in the mirror, you will not advance. For Socrates, honest self-examination guided by objective reasoning tied to reality was one of life's most important tasks.

This explains why Socrates compared himself to a midwife. Just as the midwife helps the mother give birth but does not herself give birth, Socrates helped his interlocutors give birth to more realistic beliefs of their own, truths they discovered using their own power of reason. The philosopher Ronald Gross writes that when Socrates is depicted in Plato's dialogues acting as an intellectual midwife, we can almost hear him saying, "Push! Push! You can bring forth a better idea!" The Socratic process of giving birth to a better idea, Gross observes, can be "painful." Yet at the same time, it can be "immensely gratifying."[7]

Socratic Suggestion. If someone says something that angers or upsets you, resist giving an immediate response. Instead, wait, cool down, think calmly about what you want to say, edit it, and then offer a more reflective reply. When emotions flare, critical thinking generally declines.

I mentioned earlier that Socrates never wrote a book. Many find this fact surprising. How, they ask, do we know so many details about a man who left behind no written works? The answer is that we know about him thanks to the writings of his students. After his execution in Athens in 399 BC (for reasons we'll examine), at least *eleven* of them wrote entire books in which they tried to preserve their remarkable conversations with their teacher.[8] The writings of his most famous student, Plato (429–347 BC), stand out. After Socrates died, Plato spent the rest of his life memorializing his teacher in a series of dramatic dialogues that re-created the Socratic conversations many of which he witnessed.

Plato's dialogues (as many as thirty-six or thirty-seven, depending on who's counting) total more than 2,000 pages and are considered by scholars to be among the most beautifully written works of philosophy and literature in world history. In all but one, Socrates is the central character, challenging others to think more deeply about fundamental questions concerning knowledge, objective truth, justice, morality, God, the soul, and how to live the best life possible on earth in preparation for a life to come after bodily death.

In many of his dialogues, Plato introduces new theories of his own — new ideas inspired by and based on the thoughts of his teacher. The philosophy of Plato is one of the most influential systems of ideas in world history and it remains influential today. The noted English philosopher and mathematician Alfred North Whitehead (1861–1947) famously quipped, "The safest general characterization of the European philosophical tradition is that it consists of a series of footnotes to Plato."[9]

There are scholars who spend their entire careers studying Plato's complex arguments and gaining new insights as a result. The proof is that scholarly studies of Plato's philosophy are published every year. Plato has never gone out of style.[10]

CARE FOR YOUR SOUL!

Socrates argued that when we look inside ourselves, we find that our soul, or inner self, contains three distinct parts: reason, emotion, and desire:

- Reason is the thinking part that seeks knowledge and wisdom by reasoning from evidence to conclusion.
- Emotion is the source of anger, happiness, sadness, joy, love, hatred, jealousy, revenge, envy, and the like.
- Desire contains the bodily appetites aimed at sensual enjoyments, such as those derived from food, drink, sex, and drugs.

We know that reason, emotion, and bodily desire are distinct parts of the soul, Socrates argued, because when we engage in introspection we experience conflicts among them, and things that can stand in conflict must be distinct from each other. For example, sometimes our reason recommends one course of action, while our bodily desires push us in a different direction. Or our emotions say one thing while reason says another. Reason, emotion, and desire do not always function in harmony.

When we are going back and forth between reason, emotion, and desire, Socrates argued, anarchy exists within our soul. Life experience teaches that when none of the three parts is in charge, the result is usually bad decisions, regrettable actions, and misery. In particular, life teaches several lessons:

- When our emotions overrule our firmest reasons, the result is often something we later realize, using our best reasoning, was harmful. In such cases, we look back and wish we had followed the prompts of reason rather than raw or unexamined emotion. Road rage is a contemporary example.
- When our bodily desires overcome our reason, the result is usually something we later realize, again using our best reasoning, was un-

healthy. In such cases, we look back and wish we had followed reason rather than uncontrolled bodily desire. Overeating and overdrinking are examples.

- Life problems usually magnify when either the emotions or the bodily desires rule the soul unchecked by careful reasoning.
- We live better, more fulfilled lives when our soul is ruled by reason than when it is ruled by unexamined emotion or uncritical desire.

Have you ever done something out of pure anger (an emotion) only to wish later you had acted more reasonably? Have you ever acted out of raw desire only to later wish you had followed the prompts of reason instead? Common experience confirms that emotions and desires, when not governed by reason, can lead to actions we later regret. Of course, our faculty of reason can be distorted and sometimes also leads us astray. Reason only functions at its best when it follows realistic and rational criteria, namely, the objective standards of critical thinking studied in the subject of logic.

Reason ought to have the ultimate say, Socrates argued, because it is the one part of the soul whose built-in purpose is to seek truth and real goodness on the basis of objective and realistic standards that are self-evident. Reason is also the only part of the soul capable of self-criticism and correction on the basis of those objective standards. Emotion and desire by themselves can be wild and irrational and often lead us into unhealthy and unproductive actions. Part of reason's full-time job, argued Socrates, is therefore to keep the emotions and desires in check and balanced. The urgings of emotion and desire are fine, he argued, as long as they are governed by sound reasoning.

To those whose souls are all tangled up, Socrates says this: life does not have to be out of control and miserable. Our souls, like all things, were created by God to function in a specific way. (Socrates could make this claim as a philosopher because he gave a profound philosophical argument for God's existence, one we will explore in chapter 4.) The soul functions as it was meant to function when reason, guided by realistic, rational criteria and an educated knowledge of true goodness, governs the emotions and the desires. When reason rules wisely, the soul achieves a balance that results in a state of flourishing, a moral life that surpasses in value all worldly goods, including the alleged goods of unrestrained bodily pleasure, fame, power, glory, and material wealth.

Many people have changed their lives for the better after learning that their soul has these three parts and that they have the power within themselves to achieve harmony and moral clarity by exerting disciplined rational control over their emotions and desires.

Modern psychology recognizes many Socratic insights. Today we have anger management classes for people who — to their own detriment — let their anger rule without rational control. Professional counselors help people sort out their lives using reason and self-reflection. In both kinds of instruction, the Socratic method is employed to correct a disjointedness in the soul. Modern psychotherapy and groups such as Alcoholics Anonymous use Socratic techniques to help people discover that addictions and bad habits can be overcome and a better life can result.[11]

Socratic insights about the soul have also become part of our ordinary discourse. We naturally speak of people who have a "balanced" or "well-integrated personality," but we also observe that some people seem to be "messed up inside," "out of control," or "out of joint." As Socrates saw it, the study of philosophy can help us get our soul into balance, attain moral clarity, and achieve a more worthwhile life, a life whose well-being is independent of chance and circumstance.

Socratic Suggestion. Examine your values regularly by asking yourself: Are my character traits or habits those of a morally good person? Or am I only fooling myself? Am I rationalizing bad behavior? Sometimes we can learn by observing those we admire for their moral clarity and personal integrity. But above all, be honest with yourself. Socratic self-examination requires honesty because it is about *self-reform*.

APPLICATION

When discussing important issues with others, you can often improve the conversation by asking Socrates's two favorite questions:

1. What exactly do you mean by that?
Socrates would ask this when he believed his conversation partner's thinking was unclear or mixed up. For how can we get at the truth of a

matter if we are not even sure what we are talking about? When he asked this first question, Socrates was seeking conceptual clarification. This can be achieved partially by supplying nominal definitions for key words. A nominal definition is "an explanation of the meaning of a word or phrase." It probably goes without saying that the foggier the idea, the more detailed the nominal definition should be. But Socrates was never satisfied until the search reached an essential definition. An essential definition tells us what the thing being talked about really and essentially *is*.

2. What is your evidence or reasoning?
Socrates asked this question when he suspected that his interlocutor's claim was false. When he asked this question, Socrates was seeking an *argument* for a key claim. The word "argument" can be used in many different ways. Sometimes we use it to refer to people yelling at each other. In philosophy and in academic contexts generally, an *argument* is defined as one or more statements, called "premises," offered as evidence or reasons to believe that a further statement, called the "conclusion," is true, that is, corresponds to reality. You give an argument (in this sense of the word) every time you offer someone reasons or evidence for your belief. Many people, upon being asked either of these two Socratic questions, have come to see that their claim or belief is unrealistic and needs revision.

Questions for Reflection and Discussion 2.1

1. Is there (or has there ever been) a Socratic figure in your life? If so, describe this person, your relationship, and the difference this person made in your life. Did you make a difference in his or her life?
2. If Socrates were to be miraculously transported in time from ancient Athens to the present day, what do you think he would say about modern life?
3. What do you think he would say about U.S. politics today?
4. State a significant belief you held in the past that you do not hold today. Why did you accept the belief? What was your reasoning? Why did you give up the belief? What were your reasons?
5. Explain a situation in your life in which (a) you were going to do something, but (b) you decided not to, and (c) your decision was made on the basis of Socratic thinking.

6. What are the main steps of the Socratic method?
7. Why do we sometimes learn more in conversation with others?
8. This is a personal question. Has there ever been a time in your life when you needed, but did not get, Socratic questioning? What was the result?

DEATH OF SOCRATES

Socrates had many friends, but he also had enemies. Some Athenians believed that the Socratic method was subversive. Big shots resented him for asking them inconvenient questions in front of everyone in the public square—questions that showed them to be ignoramuses. Consequently, in 399 BC, when Socrates was seventy, his opponents talked a fool named Meletus into pressing formal charges against him in court. Here are the (trumped-up) charges, both capital offenses: "Meletus son of Meletus of Pitthos has brought and sworn this charge against Socrates son of Sophroniscus of Alopeka: Socrates is a wrongdoer in not recognizing the gods that the city recognizes, and in introducing other new divinities. Further, he is a wrongdoer in corrupting the young. Penalty, death."

As a citizen of democratic Athens, Socrates had a formal right to be tried by a jury of his peers. In accordance with the law, a jury of 500 citizens was randomly chosen from a pool of 6,000 citizens using a mechanical selection device known as a *kleroterion*. Each juror was paid from public funds and swore an oath to listen impartially and vote in accord with the written law or, if no law applies, in accord with what is just.

It is fitting to pause for a moment to note the historical significance of this legal proceeding. No other society in the ancient world at the time had formal courts of law with paid jurors selected by lot judging cases and defendants protected by enumerated rights posted publicly in written form. These procedures were part of an experiment in consensual government of historic proportions. Greek democracy was not perfect, but it was an advance on the rest of the world and the first stepping-stone on the path to our modern understanding of freedom and self-government.

Socrates was likely known everywhere he went in Athens. His trial was therefore a major public event and was probably attended by large crowds. It was held downtown in the agora, where he had questioned the rich and powerful for decades. The prosecution was given three hours to present its case. Socrates was allowed the same time for his defense, which consisted of a speech to the jury. According to Plato's account, at one point in his defense, Socrates says this to the jury:

> Suppose gentlemen, you said to me, "Socrates, you shall be acquitted on this occasion, but only on one condition. That you give up spending your time on this quest and stop philosophizing. If we catch you going on in the same way, you shall be put to death." Well, supposing, as I said, that you should offer to acquit me on these terms, I should reply:
> "Men of Athens, I am your very grateful and devoted servant, but I owe a greater obedience to God than to you, and so long as I have life and strength I shall never cease from the practice and teaching of philosophy, exhorting you and elucidating the truth for everyone that I meet." I shall go on saying, in my usual way, "My friend, you are an Athenian and belong to a city which is the greatest and most famous in the world for its wisdom and strength. Are you not ashamed that you give your attention to acquiring as much money as possible, and similarly with honor and reputation, and care so little about wisdom and truth and the greatest improvement of the soul, which you never regard or heed at all?"[12]

In the end, although the charges were phony, Socrates was found guilty.[13] The prosecution recommended death. At this point, Socrates could have saved his own life. According to law, the prosecution would propose a penalty, the defense would make a counterproposal, and the Senate would then choose between the two. If Socrates had suggested a reasonable alternative, such as a stiff fine, the Senate would probably have accepted it. His friends were prepared to raise any amount of money. Instead, Socrates suggested a penalty he knew the court would not accept: that the city provide him with free meals for life.[14] Predictably, the death sentence followed.

Socrates spent the last month of his life in a jail cell, surrounded by family and friends, doing what he loved most: discussing philosophical issues, including questions about life after death, just like in the old days. Several friends urged him to escape. The jailor would have helped. Socrates refused, justifying his decision with a philosophical argument about the nature of political obligation and our moral duty to obey the law, an argument that is still discussed profitably today.[15]

At this point in the story, some students ask a very good question. If the Greeks were pioneering the ideals of freedom, reason, democracy, and the rule of law, how could the Athenians have sentenced a leading citizen to death for thinking critically? The short answer is that the jury was thrown off track by demagoguery. A *demagogue* is an orator or leader in a democracy who moves the crowd or public opinion by appealing to unrestrained emotions, prejudice, and ignorance rather than to reason and truth. We've seen that the Athenian democracy was not perfect. The story of the trial and death of Socrates illustrates how hard it is to build institutions that fully realize our ideals. Before we judge the Greeks too harshly, though, we should keep in mind that we have not yet fully realized the democratic ideal 2,400 years later.

In the dialogue *Phaedo*, Plato tells us that when the time came to drink the poison, the jailor said to Socrates:

> To you, Socrates, whom I know to be the noblest and gentlest and best of all who ever came to this place, I will not impute the angry feelings of other men, who rage and swear at me when, in obedience to the authorities, I bid them drink the poison — indeed, I am sure that you will not be angry with me; for others, as you are aware, and not I, are the guilty cause. And so fare you well, and try to bear lightly what must needs be; you know my errand.[16]

Plato continues:

> Then bursting into tears he turned away and went out. Socrates looked at him and said: "I return your good wishes, and will do as you bid." Then, turning to us, he said, "How charming the man is: since I have been in prison he has always been coming to see me, and at times he would talk to me, and was as good as could be to me, and now see how generously he sorrows for me. But we must do as he says, Crito; let the cup be brought."[17]

In the end, even though he knew that the death he was about to experience would be extremely painful and slow, Socrates calmly drank the hemlock. You are almost there in person when you read Plato's account. Socrates has just taken the poison and is waiting for its effects when some of his friends begin to weep. Socrates stops them:

"What is this strange outcry?" he said. "I sent away the women mainly in order that they might not offend in this way, for I have heard that a man should die in peace. Be quiet, then, and have patience." When we heard that, we were ashamed, and refrained our tears; and he walked about until, as he said, his legs began to fail, and then he lay on his back, according to the directions, and the [jailor] who gave him the poison now and then looked at his feet and legs; and after a while he pressed his foot hard and asked him if he could feel; and he said, no; and then his leg, and so upwards and upwards, and showed us that he was cold and stiff. And Socrates felt them himself, and said: "When the poison reaches the heart, that will be the end." . . . In a minute or two a movement was heard, and the attendants uncovered him; his eyes were set, and Crito closed his eyes and mouth. Such was the death . . . of our friend, of whom I may truly say, that, of all the men whom I have ever known, he was the wisest, and justest, and best.[18]

SOCRATES IN RETROSPECT

Before Socrates, Greek philosophers focused on big questions such as these: What is the ultimate nature of reality? What are the elements or building blocks of the universe? By the sheer force of his personality, Socrates shifted the focus from abstract cosmological speculation to the human condition and to the following issue: What is the best life a human being can live, all things considered? The Roman philosopher and statesman Cicero (106–43 BC) put it this way: "Socrates was the first to call philosophy down from the sky, set it in the cities and even in the home, and have it consider life and morals."[19]

Gregory Vlastos, a noted expert on Socrates, calls the Socratic method "one of the great achievements of humanity":

It makes moral inquiry a common human enterprise, open to every man. Its practice calls for no adherence to a philosophical system, or mastery of a specialized technique, or acquisition of a technical vocabulary. It calls for common sense and common speech. And this is as it should be, for how man should live is every man's business, and the role of the specialist and the expert should be only to offer guidance and criticism, to inform and clarify the judgment of the layman, leaving the final judgment up to him.[20]

Socrates's claim that each of us is capable of critical thinking and self-examination was revolutionary when first proposed. Indeed, Vlastos calls the Socratic method the "first major step toward the ideal of the universal moral equality of all of humanity."[21]

Ronald Gross finds the following closely related idea to be another of Socrates's contributions: the claim that each individual has moral authority over his or her own soul. This idea, also revolutionary in its day, is one of the historical roots of the modern theory of individual freedom. It is also one of the historical precedents for the idea of universal human rights. Correlative to both notions is the Socratic claim that, as Gross puts it, "our human dignity mandates that we rule ourselves through participation in constitutional government."[22] The ideas Socrates died for were not merely theoretical.

Questions for Reflection and Discussion 2.2

1. Have you ever acted on pure emotion and done something that you later regretted? Would you have made a better choice if you had given reason more of a say?
2. Have you ever acted on mere bodily desire and as a result harmed your health or the well-being of others? Would your choice have been better if it had been guided by reason?
3. What kind of person would not learn anything at all from a conversation with Socrates?
4. What kind of person would learn from a conversation with Socrates?

THREE

And a Few Principles of Logic

WHAT IS LOGIC?

Human beings have been thinking logically (and sometimes illogically) since the earliest era of human existence. However, they have not always been aware of the general principles that distinguish logical from illogical forms of thought. Logic, as an academic subject, is the systematic study of the standards, or criteria, of correct reasoning. The logician asks, Which principles should we follow if we want our reasoning to be the best possible? A brief introduction to this fascinating subject will be helpful because philosophy, as we've seen, requires careful reasoning for and against competing philosophical claims.[1]

The Greek philosopher Aristotle wrote the first book on the standards of correct reasoning and later wrote five additional treatises on the subject. Thus, in six highly original and rigorous works of logical theory, Aristotle earned the title historians have conferred on him: founder of logic. The noted twentieth-century logician and philosopher Benson Mates writes:

We can say flatly that the history of logic begins with the Greek philosopher Aristotle. . . . Although it is almost a platitude among historians
that great intellectual advances are never the work of only one person
(in founding the science of geometry Euclid made use of the results of
Eudoxus and others; in the case of mechanics Newton stood upon the
shoulders of Descartes, Galileo, and Kepler; and so on), Aristotle, according to all available evidence, created the science of logic absolutely
ex nihilo.[2]

Logic was first taught as a course of study in the Lyceum, the university Aristotle founded in Athens during the fourth century BC. For
2,400 years, logic has been considered a core academic requirement at institutions of higher learning around the world. Logic remains a core subject today because its principles can help anyone reason more accurately,
no matter what the subject matter. Before we go further, however, a few
words about the subject's founder.

Aristotle: Plato's Most Famous Student

Aristotle was born in 384 BC in the Greek colony of Stagira, north
of Athens in the region known as Macedonia. His father, a court
physician to King Amyntas III, was interested in natural science and
encouraged his son's scholarly tendencies. However, when Aristotle
was a young boy, his father died, and Aristotle was sent to live with
an uncle. At the age of seventeen, Aristotle traveled to Athens and
enrolled in the Academy, the school Plato had founded a few years
before. Plato's Academy was the world's first independent, criti-
cal-thinking-based institution of higher learning and "the prototype
for all subsequent colleges and universities."[3]

Under Plato's tutelage, Aristotle studied philosophy, cosmology,
and mathematics for twenty years and earned a reputation as Plato's
most brilliant student.

After Plato died in 347 BC, Aristotle left Athens to visit philosophers in other Greek cities. At Assos, he met and married Pythias,
and the couple had a daughter. Aristotle later moved to the island of
Lesbos, where he set up the world's first scientific research station.

After returning to Athens around 335 BC, Aristotle founded the
Lyceum. Here he created the first system of biological classification,

taught, and wrote books on many subjects, including logic, theoretical physics, metaphysics, biology, marine biology, botany, zoology, psychology, epistemology, philosophy of religion, philosophy of language, ethics, aesthetics, political philosophy, meteorology, literary criticism, and poetics. The collected writings of Aristotle fill two 1,200-page volumes, still studied and discussed by scholars today. But many of his manuscripts have been lost over time. The historical records indicate that his complete works would require *fifty* large volumes in a modern library.[4] In addition to founding logic as an academic subject, he is considered the founder of biology, marine biology, and a number of other academic subjects that remain in today's college curriculum. By the end of his life, the library at the Lyceum was the greatest in the world at the time, and its extensive collection of natural specimens, maps, and objects is considered the first museum in history. He died in 322 BC, probably from stomach cancer.

SOME BASIC ELEMENTS OF LOGICAL THEORY

Arguments

The first elementary building block of logical theory is the notion of an *argument*. In ordinary discourse we sometimes use the word *argument* to refer to an angry or heated exchange, for instance, two people fighting or yelling at each other. In logic and in intellectual contexts generally, the word has a more precise meaning. An argument is one or more statements, called "premises," offered as evidence or reason to believe that a further statement, called the "conclusion," is true. In plainer terms, an argument is reasoning offered in support of a claim. Arguments are part of everyday life—you present one every time you put your reasoning into words to share with others. In the following example, the premises are marked P1 and P2, and the conclusion is labeled C.

P1. All songwriters are poets.

P2. Bob Dylan is a songwriter.

C. Therefore, Bob Dylan is a poet.

The second building block is the distinction, first discovered and investigated systematically by Aristotle, between deductive and inductive reasoning. Every argument can be classified as either deductive or inductive.

Deductive Arguments

A deductive argument aims to establish its conclusion with complete certainty. The word *necessarily* in the following argument indicates that the reasoning is deductive and expresses the standard deductive claim that if the premises are true, then the conclusion *must* be true:

P1. Tiny Tim played the ukulele.

P2. Anyone who plays the ukulele is a musician.

C. Therefore, it *necessarily* follows that Tiny Tim was a musician.

In the following argument, the word *certainly* indicates that the argument is also deductive:

P1. If it rains, then the roof gets wet.

P2. It is raining.

C. Therefore, *certainly* the roof is getting wet.

Deductive Indicator Words

If you want to make it clear to your audience that your reasoning is deductive, then introduce your conclusion using deductive indicator words. These are words expressing certainty, such as *necessarily, certainly, must,* and *surely.* Phrases such as "therefore, it necessarily follows that," and "it is certain that" also work.

Inductive Arguments

An inductive argument does not aim to show that its conclusion is completely certain. Rather, it aims to show that its conclusion is probable but not certain. How probable? So probable that it is reasonable to accept the conclusion. The word *probable* in the following argument indicates that the argument is inductive:

P1. Joe has eaten a Dick's Deluxe burger for lunch every day for the past month.

C. So, it is *probable* that he will have a Dick's Deluxe for lunch tomorrow.

Inductive Indicator Words
To make it clear that your reasoning is inductive, use words and phrases such as the following when you introduce your conclusion: *probably*, *likely*, and phrases such as "it is therefore probably true that" and "it is reasonable to conclude that."

TECHNICAL TERMS FOR DEDUCTIVE ARGUMENTS: VALID, INVALID, SOUND

If the premises and conclusion of a deductive argument are related in such a way that the conclusion *must* be true if the premises are true, then the argument is a *valid* deductive argument. If the premises and conclusion of a deductive argument are *not* so related, then the argument is an *invalid* deductive argument.

A valid deductive argument thus has the following feature: If its premises all are true, then its conclusion must be true. Put another way, a deductive argument is valid if it is not possible its premises are all true while at the same time its conclusion is false.[5] The following deductive argument is clearly valid because it is not possible its premises are all true while its conclusion is false:

P1. All cats are mammals.

P2. All mammals are animals.

C. Therefore, necessarily, all cats are animals.

On the other hand, a deductive argument is invalid if it *is* possible its premises are true and its conclusion is false. The following deductive argument is invalid because it is *possible* its premises are true but at the same time its conclusion is false.

P1. Nancy and Sue are cousins.

P2. Sue and Rita are cousins.

C. So, Nancy and Rita must be cousins.

Now for a surprising fact about validity. Examine the following deductive argument carefully. It is valid, yet its premises are all *false*:

P1. All students are millionaires.

P2. All millionaires drink vodka every day.

C. Therefore, necessarily, all students drink vodka every day.

This argument is valid because *if* its premises were to be true, then its conclusion would have to be true. This illustrates the surprising fact that a deductive argument can in some cases be valid and at the same time have false premises and a false conclusion.

Of course, some deductive arguments are valid and have true premises and a true conclusion. For instance, the following:

P1. All snakes are reptiles.

P2. No reptiles are warm-blooded.

C. Therefore, necessarily, no snakes are warm-blooded.

The lesson here is difficult to understand. The point is that true premises are not required for validity. Nor is a true conclusion. Again, some valid deductive arguments have true premises, others have false premises. And some valid deductive arguments have true conclusions, others have false conclusions. *Valid* does not mean "true." The one combination you will not find in a valid deductive argument is this: All true premises and a false conclusion.

Of course, the attainment of truth is the ultimate goal of reasoning. A deductive argument is *sound* if, in addition to being valid, its premises are all true. Thus, a sound deductive argument has two features: (1) it is valid, and (2) its premises are all true. It follows that if a deductive argument is sound, then its premises are all true and its conclusion is true, as in this example:

P1. All whales are mammals.

P2. No mammals are reptiles.

C. Therefore, certainly no whales are reptiles.

Valid or Invalid? How Do You Decide?

Aristotle discovered precise quantitative methods for deciding whether a given deductive argument is valid or invalid for all deductive arguments belonging to a specified category. He also developed a systematic method of precise logical proof similar to the axiomatic system of the Greek geometers. However, this is not a textbook in what is called "formal" or "symbolic" logic. The following intuitive test for validity is all we will need for our purposes. Suppose you are given a deductive argument and you wonder whether it is valid or invalid.

Step 1. Assume hypothetically that the premises all are true.

Step 2. Ask the following question: If (hypothetically) the premises are true, is it *possible* the conclusion is false? That is, are there any possible circumstances, no matter how unlikely, bizarre, or unusual, in which the premises would all be true while the conclusion is false?

Step 3. If the answer is "no," then the argument is valid. If the answer is "yes," then the argument is invalid.

Let's apply this test to the following argument.

1. Every member of the Seattle Tiny Tim fan club plays the ukulele.

2. Lorraine and Sue live in Seattle and play the ukulele.

3. Therefore, Lorraine and Sue belong to the Seattle Tiny Tim fan club.

We begin by assuming the premises are true. Next, keeping our assumption in mind, we ask, Is it *possible* that the conclusion is false? (Answer this for yourself before moving on.) Certainly it is. For isn't it *possible* that, although all members of the fan club play the ukulele, not all who play the ukulele belong to the club? And isn't it possible that Lorraine and Sue are among those ukuleleists who do *not* belong to the club? This easily conceivable possibility shows that the argument is deductively invalid.

It is extremely important to notice something here. We classified this argument as invalid *without knowing whether its premises are actually true.* We did not know whether it is true or false that Lorraine and Sue "live in Seattle and play the ukulele." We proceeded without this information, simply by considering possibilities in the abstract. Thus, two questions were kept separate:

1. Are the premises true?

2. Is the argument valid or invalid?

We answered question 2 without having answered question 1. Indeed, the information we might have uncovered by answering question 1 would not have contributed in any way to answering question 2. And, of course, the reverse is also true. The two questions are logically independent.

Now consider the following deductive argument:

1. Frasier is taller than Niles.

2. Niles is taller than Mr. Crane.

3. So, Frasier must be taller than Mr. Crane.

Is this argument valid? First, we assume the premises are true. Next, we ask, Is it possible the premises are true while the conclusion is false? Is there any possibility of this, no matter how unlikely or remote? Clearly not! If the premises are true, then the conclusion *must* be true too. The argument is therefore deductively valid. Incidentally, are the premises true? That's a completely separate issue! To answer that question, we would have to measure the members of the TV show *Frasier.* So, without knowing anything about the actual heights of the cast, we can see that the argument is valid. Of course, if we do not know the heights of the cast, we cannot tell whether the argument is *sound.*

TECHNICAL TERMS FOR INDUCTIVE ARGUMENTS: STRONG, WEAK, COGENT

If the premises and conclusion of an inductive argument are related in such a way that the conclusion is probable (but not certain) if the premises are true, it is a *strong* inductive argument. An inductive argument that is not strong is a *weak* inductive argument. Thus, a strong inductive argument has the following feature: if all its premises are true, then its conclusion is probable, but not certain. The following inductive argument appears to be quite strong.

P1. We interviewed one thousand people from all walks of life in Seattle during a ten-week period, and 90 percent said they drink coffee.

C. Therefore, it is likely that about 90 percent of Seattleites drink coffee.

For contrast, the following inductive argument is clearly weak.

P1. We interviewed one thousand people from all walks of life as they exited coffee shops in Seattle, and 98 percent said they drink coffee.

C. So, probably about 98 percent of all Seattleites drink coffee.

Now for a surprising fact about inductive strength. Consider the following inductive argument carefully. It is strong, yet its premises happen to be *false*:

P1. It has been snowing for 300 days straight in Phoenix, Arizona.

P2. All the Phoenix weather reports predict snow for tomorrow.

C. Therefore, it will probably snow in Phoenix tomorrow.

This argument is inductively strong by virtue of the fact that *if*, hypothetically, its premises *were* to be true, then its conclusion would very probably be true. Yet its premises are obviously false and its conclusion is false. This illustrates the surprising fact that an inductive argument can be strong and at the same time have false premises and a false conclusion. *Strong*, in short, does not mean "true." Of course, an inductive argument can also be strong while having true premises and a true conclusion. Consider the following example.

P1. In all of recorded history, it has rained at least once a year in Seattle.

C. Therefore, next year it will probably rain at least once in Seattle.

As we have noted, the attainment of truth is the ultimate goal of reasoning. An inductive argument is *cogent* if it is (1) strong and (2) all its premises are true. For example:

P1. NASA announced that it found evidence of water on Mars.

P2. NASA is a reliable scientific agency.

C. Therefore, it is reasonable to conclude there is or was water on Mars.

Strong or Weak? How Do You Decide?

Logicians and mathematicians have discovered precise quantitative methods for evaluating those inductive arguments in which the total number of possibilities can be counted or otherwise dealt with mathematically. For example, using the classical theory of probability — founded in the seventeenth century by the French philosopher and mathematician Blaise Pascal (1623–62) — the probability that someone draws a king from a shuffled deck of cards is 4 out of 52. This makes sense because the total number of cards is 52 and the number of kings is exactly 4. Actuaries at insurance companies use other quantitative methods for determining life expectancies for various groups of people. Some of the quantitative methods for evaluating inductive arguments take us into the branch of math called "statistics."

However, not all inductive arguments can be evaluated quantitatively using statistical methods. Common sense and ordinary experience are all that is needed to decide most of the inductive arguments we encounter in everyday life and in philosophy. Here is an inductive argument from everyday life:

1. The meatloaf I left in the refrigerator last night is no longer there. (This is the data needing an explanation.)

2. My roommates are all vegetarians except Joe.

3. Joe often eats other people's food.

4. The cat likes meatloaf but it can't open the refrigerator.

5. The best explanation of the data is that Joe ate my leftover meatloaf.

6. Therefore, Joe probably ate my leftover meatloaf.

No special training in statistics or quantitative logical methods was needed to solve this mystery. Likewise, mathematics and statistics cannot decide the classic issues of philosophy; the big arguments call for nothing more than careful critical thinking and some life experience.

INFORMATION SPILLOVER

The history of ideas is fascinating because often one idea leads to another, which leads to a completely unexpected discovery. Aristotle discovered logical principles so exact they could be expressed in symbols, such as those used in mathematics. Because those principles could be expressed and organized mathematically, he was able to develop a system of deductive logic similar to, and as definite as, geometry.

Some claim that the exact rules of Aristotle's logic are too mechanical and abstract to be of practical use. They are mistaken. His logical system was actually the first step on the path to the digital computer. It is not widely known, but the first person to design a computing machine was a logician who, after reflecting on the exact nature of Aristotle's logical principles, asked one of the most seminal questions ever: Is it possible to design a machine that can receive information in the form of symbols and whose gears, designed to obey the laws of logic, compute for us the exact, logically valid conclusion every time?

The logician who first asked the question that connected logic and computing was Raymond Lull (1232–1315), a philosopher, Aristotelian logician, and secular member of the Franciscan Order of the Catholic Church. Lull moved from theory to practice when he designed a calculating mechanism consisting of rotating cogwheels inscribed with logical symbols from Aristotle's system and aligned to move in accord with the rules of Aristotle's logic. In theory, the operator would enter the premises of an argument by setting the dials, and the machine's gears would then accurately crank out the valid conclusion. Aristotle's logic was the model for the first mechanical computer.

Lull's design may have been primitive, but for the first time in history someone had the idea of a machine that takes inputs, processes them mechanically on the basis of exact rules of logic, and outputs a logically correct answer. Since he was the first to conceive and design a computing machine,

Lull has been called the "father of the computer." We usually associate computing with mathematics, but the first design for a computer was based not on math but on logic — the deductive system of Aristotle.

Ideas have consequences, and sometimes theoretical ideas that seem impractical at first have results that are quite practical. Lull was the first in a long succession of logical tinkerers, each seeking to design a more powerful computing machine. You have a cell phone in your hand right now thanks to the efforts of these innovators, each trained in Aristotle's logical theory. In addition to Lull, the list of pioneers in computing includes Leonardo da Vinci (1452–1519), William Oughtred (1574–1660), Wilhelm Schickard (1592–1635), Pascal, Gottfried Leibniz (1646–1716), Charles Babbage (1791–1871), Vannevar Bush (1890–1974), Howard Aiken (1900–1973), and Alan Turing (1912–54).

A continuous line of thought can thus be traced from Aristotle's logic to the amazing advances in computing of the nineteenth and twentieth centuries, which led eventually to the completion of the world's first working digital computer (at Iowa State College in 1937) and from there to the much smaller yet more powerful laptops and tablets of today. It is no coincidence that the circuits inside every digital computer are called "logic gates." In the logic classroom, this is my answer to those who suppose that abstract logical theory has no practical applications.

Today, logic is one of the main branches of philosophy. It is also a fundamental branch of computer science.

But computer science is only one spin-off of logic; many more could be cited. The subject Aristotle founded remains as vital today as it was in ancient Athens. Aristotle probably had no idea how important his new subject would be — or how long the spillover and information overflow would continue.

What does all of this have to do with anything? In philosophy, as in everyday life and indeed as in every academic subject, reason is our common currency. It follows that the ability to reason well is an essential life skill and an important academic skill. But skills require theory in addition to practice. A familiarity with elementary logic can therefore help anyone improve their thinking. Some people suppose logic is a useless subject; the truth may be the reverse — it may be the most useful subject of all. In the rest of this book, we'll follow principles of logic as we reason carefully about the most fundamental questions of all, questions that help us define our worldviews, our lives, and thereby ourselves.

Logic Exercise 1. In each case, is the argument deductive or inductive? Hint: look for deductive and inductive indicator words.

1. Every human being deserves to be treated with equal respect and dignity. Homeless people are human beings. Therefore, certainly every homeless person deserves to be treated with equal respect and dignity.

2. Some cats are pets. All pets are social creatures. So, surely some cats are social creatures.

3. Every time I've taken the freeway during rush hour, it has been clogged. I'm about to take the freeway during rush hour. So, it will probably be clogged.

4. All dogs are mammals. All mammals are animals. Therefore, necessarily, all dogs are mammals.

5. If Anna swims today, then Eddy will swim today. But Eddy won't swim today. Thus, necessarily, Anna won't swim today.

6. If Anna swims today, then Eddy will swim today. But Anna won't swim today. So, certainly Eddy won't swim today.

7. If Anna swims today, then Eddy will swim today. Eddy will swim today. Therefore, certainly Anna will swim today.

8. Abby and Tan are not both home. But Tan is home. Therefore, Abby must not be home.

9. The sun has risen every day for thousands of years. Thus, it will likely rise tomorrow.

10. Figure ABCD is a square. Therefore, necessarily, it has four equal sides.

11. Most feral cats won't let you hold them. Oscar is a feral cat. So, Oscar probably won't let you hold him.

12. If Mika swims, then Pranav swims. Mika swims. Therefore, Pranav surely swims.

13. If Maria swims, then Amha swims. If Amha swims, then Darmon swims. Thus, surely if Maria swims, then Darmon swims.

14. Either Yeo has the book or Yang Ting has the book. Yeo does not have the book. Thus, necessarily, Yang Ting has the book.

15. Marta has eaten lunch every day for the past year at Spud Fish & Chips, a venerable Seattle institution since 1935. Therefore, it is reasonable to conclude that she will eat there tomorrow.

Logic Exercise 2. The following arguments are deductive. In each case, is the argument valid or invalid?

1. José is older than Maria. Maria is younger than fifty. Therefore, José must be older than fifty.

2. José is younger than Maria. Maria is younger than fifty. Therefore, José certainly is younger than fifty.

3. José is taller than Maria. Maria is taller than Pablo. Therefore, necessarily, José is taller than Pablo.

4. All chemists are Lutheran. Rita is Lutheran. So, Rita must be a chemist.

5. All cats love fish. Peter is a cat. Therefore, Peter certainly loves fish.

6. Every time Sue swims, Joe swims, no exceptions. Sue is swimming. Therefore, Joe must be swimming.

7. Cream was one of the great rock bands of the 1960s. Jack Bruce was a member of Cream. Therefore, it is certain that Jack Bruce belonged to one of the great rock bands of the 1960s.

8. All birds have wings. Your pet does not have wings. So, your pet certainly is not a bird.

9. No birds have gills. My pet has gills. Therefore, necessarily, my pet is not a bird.

10. Biological parents are always older than their children. Lauren is the biological mother of Lucca. So, Lucca must be younger than Lauren.

Logic Exercise 3. The following arguments are inductive. In each case, is the argument strong or weak?

1. Sue has eaten lunch at Ivar's Fish & Chips (a Seattle institution since 1938) every day for the past five years. Therefore, it is likely she will eat lunch there tomorrow.

2. Jan ate lunch at Ivar's for the first time yesterday. Therefore, she will likely eat lunch there again tomorrow.

3. Kramer hasn't worked a day in the past two years. Therefore, it is probable he won't be working tomorrow.

4. It has been snowing in Tampa, Florida, for thirty days in a row. The sky is full of snow clouds, and the prediction is for more snow tomorrow. Thus, it will likely snow in Tampa tomorrow.

5. We surveyed a thousand people, asking them if they believe in God, and 99 percent answered yes. Our survey was conducted outside churches in the Seattle area on a Sunday morning, and the people we interviewed were exiting church services. Therefore, most Seattleites believe in God.

6. We surveyed a thousand people, asking them if they like broccoli, and 80 percent answered yes. We surveyed people randomly, from all walks of life and from all demographic and social groups. Therefore, around 80 percent of all people probably like broccoli.

7. Unless there is some sort of emergency, Denny's restaurant never closes. I see the lights on and the door open at the local Denny's. Therefore, the local Denny's is probably open.

8. Ben is a vegetarian. Meat is all they serve at Joe's Meathouse restaurant. Therefore, it is probable that Ben is not a regular at Joe's restaurant.

9. We carefully tested a drug for liver disease on a group of one hundred monkeys with liver disease, and the drug cured the disease in all cases. Humans and monkeys have very similar livers. The drug is not known to not work in humans. Therefore, the drug will probably cure liver disease in humans.

10. We observed one hundred bats, and all were black. Therefore, the next bat we observe will probably be black.

11. The bank was robbed by a seven-foot-tall man who had a red beard and long red hair. The dye pack exploded all over his clothes as he ran from the bank carrying $10,000 in his hands. Joe Doakes was found hiding in an alley an hour later. He is seven feet tall, has a red beard, long red hair, and red dye all over his clothes. In addition, he is carrying $10,000 in his backpack. The best explanation of all the facts is that Doakes is the bank robber. Therefore, Doakes probably robbed the bank.

12. For fifty years, Dad's cars have always been Chevrolets, and they have always been mechanically sound. This car is a Chevy. Therefore, this car is probably mechanically sound.

13. The first car I owned was a brand X. It was a lousy car. This car is a brand X. I conclude that it is probably also a lousy car.

14. Lorraine is a member of the Tiny Tim fan club. Tiny Tim played the ukulele. Therefore, Lorraine probably plays the ukulele.

15. Susan emigrated from the country of Ruritania. Ninety percent of the inhabitants of Ruritania are chess players. Therefore, it is probable that Susan plays chess.

Answers to Logic Exercises

Logic Exercise 1
D = Deductive I = Inductive

1. D	6. D	11. I
2. D	7. D	12. D
3. I	8. D	13. D
4. D	9. I	14. D
5. D	10. D	15. I

Logic Exercise 2
I = Invalid V = Valid

1. I	6. V
2. V	7. V
3. V	8. V
4. I	9. V
5. V	10. V

Logic Exercise 3
S = Strong W = Weak

1. S	6. S	11. S
2. W	7. S	12. S
3. S	8. S	13. W
4. S	9. S	14. W
5. W	10. S	15. S

UNIT II

Philosophy of Religion

FOUR

The Design Argument

NATURE'S CYCLES

On the first morning of summer in the year 430 BC, the sun is coming up and Socrates is sitting on a hill above Athens, Greece. Observing. Listening. Reflecting on the cycles of life. The sun continues to rise, revealing the flowers in bloom. On a nearby hill, a sheep gives birth. A small stream gently makes its way to the sea. As he has observed many times before he thinks again:, "Each thing within nature has its own unique role to play within the overall order of things."

He reflects on the overall order: "The many parts are intertwined and balanced like the notes of a song. The universe is a system of interconnected parts functioning in harmony." The universe certainly does have an underlying order. We make predictions based on that order every time we take a step, sit on a chair, drink a cup of water, or take a breath of air.

Socrates now looks at the city below. Athens is beginning to awake. Farmers are transporting their produce along roads leading into the city. People are gathering in the center of town, waiting for the marketplace to open. His thoughts continue: "Each part of Athens has its own unique role to play within the overall economy of the city-state. Roads lead into the city so that farmers and merchants can transport their goods into and out of town; the marketplace serves people buying and selling; public speeches are given at city hall. The whole wouldn't function properly if each part within the whole did not serve its intended purpose."

As Thales asked before him, Socrates wonders what holds it all together: "Like nature, Athens has an underlying order. Day by day the city, like the system of nature, goes through its cycles, intertwined parts balanced in an overall harmony."

In a nearby grove of olive trees, a shepherd plays a flute. The melody causes Socrates to think: "Each note in the song contributes to the harmony and beauty of the whole. Each note is placed on purpose for the unique role it will play."

The balance and harmony of the song reminds him of a recent experience. As he was standing in front of the Parthenon, he was deeply moved by its beauty: "Each column, each piece of marble, each statue, each of the temple's architectural elements makes its own contribution to the overall harmony of the whole; the beauty of the structure emerges from the way in which the parts are arranged."[1]

While discussing the existence of God or a supreme being with friends in the marketplace the next day, Socrates summed up his reasoning with an argument that went about like this:

> Nature, like a magnificent temple, a beautiful song, or a city plan, is a system of intertwined, balanced parts functioning in harmony. We know through observation the cause of the temple's order: it was designed by an architect to reflect a purpose. Similarly, the orderly arrangement of Athens is due to the work of city planners. The harmony in a song is crafted by the composer. In each case, when we trace cause and effect, the ultimate cause of order is an intelligent designer existing prior to the order we observe. Since the deep order we see in nature is similar in form and since it is common sense that similar effects probably have similar causes, the cause of nature's order—like the cause of the order displayed by a temple, city plan, or a song—is probably also an intelligent designer, although one great enough to have crafted the entire cosmos. The most reasonable conclusion to draw is therefore that the universe owes its deep order to a supreme mind, an intelligent designer.[2]

The word *cosmos* is significant here. To the ancient Greeks the word meant not simply the "universe" but "the universe understood as an orderly, harmonic, and beautiful system." Our modern word *cosmetics* is derived from the same Greek root. It was the majestic order observable in every part of the universe that caught Socrates's eye and pointed his thoughts to a divine, presiding intelligence existing above it all.

Upon hearing a philosophical argument, the first thing to do is to understand it. Recall that an inductive argument aims to show that its conclusion, although not completely certain, is so probable that it is the most reasonable conclusion to draw based on the premises. The placement of the word *probable* preceding the conclusion of Socrates's argument indicates that it is inductive. Socrates's claim is therefore that the conclusion, although not mathematically certain, is so likely that it is the most reasonable conclusion to draw. But there are different kinds of inductive argumentation. Logicians call Socrates's argument an "analogical" induction because it starts with an analogy, or similarity, between two or more things. Let's pause to clarify the structure of this common pattern of reasoning.

Boiled down to essentials, an analogical inductive argument follows this general format:

1. A and B have many properties, or characteristics, in common.

2. A has property x.

3. B is not known *not* to have property x.

4. Property x is related statistically or causally (by cause and effect) to the common properties.

5. Therefore, B very probably also has property x.

6. Therefore, the most reasonable conclusion to draw is that B has property x.

Of course, the larger the number of common properties related to x, and the closer the relation, the higher the probability that the conclusion is true.

Here is an example of analogical reasoning from medical science:

1. Monkey hearts are very similar to human hearts.

2. Vaccine X cures heart disease in monkeys.

3. Vaccine X is not known *not* to cure heart disease in humans.

4. Therefore, vaccine X will probably cure heart disease in humans.

5. Therefore, the most reasonable conclusion is that X will cure heart disease in humans.

This example is perhaps more familiar:

1. I've taken three of Professor Smith's classes, and I learned a lot in each one.

2. Professor Smith has a new class scheduled for next quarter.

3. I have no reason to think his new class will be different in quality from his other classes.

4. Therefore, I will probably learn a lot if I take his new class.

5. Therefore, the most reasonable conclusion is that I will learn a lot if I take his new class.

Here is Socrates's analogical inductive argument translated into textbook (step-by-step) form with comments:

1. The deep order we observe in the universe is similar in form to the deep order we observe in songs, buildings, city plans, and works of art, namely, many parts fit together to form a highly improbable, interrelated, functioning, intelligible system.
Comment: The orderly and functional nature of the cosmos is evident in the predictable events, natural cycles, and complex but stable systems that characterize the universe from the smallest to the largest scales. Thanks to the discoveries of the Greek mathematician and philosopher Pythagoras (570–495 BC), the ancient Greeks were aware that orderly mathematical substructures exist even at levels of reality too abstract to observe, such as the mathematical order underlying the intervals of the musical scale.[3]

2. The root cause of the underlying order we observe in buildings, cities, songs, works of art, and such is always found to be an intelligent designer existing prior to the order observed.
Comment: The ultimate source of a building's design plan is the chief architect; the composer is the source of a song's melody; the artist is the cause of the painting's order, and so forth.

3. The deep, functional, and intelligible order of the universe is not known *not* to be the result of intelligent design.

4. Therefore, the cause of nature's deep order is probably also an intelligent designer, although this must be an intelligence great enough to have imposed order on the entire cosmos.

5. Therefore, the most reasonable conclusion is that the source of nature's order is an intelligent designer. The order of the cosmos, in short, is the expression of a mind.

We noted that this is an analogical argument. We reason by analogy all the time. Suppose that Lucca gets sick and has a specific set of symptoms. The next day his brother Ben gets sick and shows the same symptoms. When the doctor discovers the cause of Lucca's illness, she naturally concludes by analogy that Ben's illness probably has the same cause.

Is analogical thinking the "fuel and fire" of all thought?

In their fascinating book, *Surfaces and Essences: Analogy as the Fuel and Fire of Thinking*, Douglas Hofstadter and Emmanuel Sander argue that "analogy is the core of all thinking." From an advertisement for the book on Amazon.com:

> Why did two-year-old Camille proudly exclaim, "I undressed the banana!"? Why do people who hear a story often blurt out, "Exactly the same thing happened to me!" when it was a completely different event? How do we recognize an aggressive driver from a split-second glance in our rearview mirror? What in a friend's remark triggers the offhand reply, "That's just sour grapes"? What did Albert Einstein see that made him suspect that light consists of particles when a century of research had driven the final nail in the coffin of that long-dead idea? The answer to all these questions . . . is analogy-making—the meat and potatoes . . . the fuel and fire . . . of thought. Analogy-making, far from happening at rare intervals, occurs at all moments, defining thinking from . . . the most fleeting thoughts to the most creative scientific insights.[4]

Or a teenager prepares to buy his first car. He doesn't have much money, but he wants it to be reliable. He reasons analogically: "Dad's car is a Chevrolet, and it's reliable. Mr. Cooper's car is a Chevrolet, and it's reliable. The car for sale down the street is also a Chevrolet, so it's probably also reliable." Analogical reasoning is part of our shared common sense. Applied to the order we observe in nature, this common reasoning points to the existence of an intelligent designer. So argued Socrates.

INTRODUCING THE DESIGN ARGUMENT

Socrates's argument is known in philosophy as the "argument from design" (or the "design argument"). It is also called the "teleological argument" (Greek *telos*, "end" or "purpose at which something is aimed") since it claims that the order of the universe appears purposeful or intentionally aimed. An argument from design is usually defined as a philosophical argument that begins with the deep order of nature and reasons from there to the conclusion that an intelligent designer existing above the universal order is its ultimate source.

In one form or another, a design argument can be found presented and defended in the writings of most of the pre-Socratic philosophers as well as in the writings of Plato, Aristotle, the Greek and Roman members of the Stoic school of philosophy, Augustine of Hippo (354–430), Thomas Aquinas (1225–74), Gottfried Wilhelm Leibniz (1646–1716), and David Hume (1711–76). Versions of the design argument can also be found in the Jewish, Hindu, and Muslim philosophical traditions. Many of the founders of modern science presented and defended a design argument in their scientific treatises. In addition, the list of recent scholars East and West who have defended the argument is long and includes many of the most eminent philosophers and scientists of our time. In short, almost every major philosopher of the ancient, medieval, and modern periods has endorsed this argument. The argument from design is not only historically significant and mainstream, it is also very contemporary.

Some may object at this point: Why just one designer? Why not many? After all, it takes many architects to design a skyscraper, and sometimes two artists jointly compose a song. From ancient times, defenders of the design argument have replied that the highly integrated unity of the cosmos points to one supreme designer, not many.

Let's consider this for a moment. Physicists have discovered that the behavior of matter and energy can be described using differential equations that fit together into a unified system of interconnected formulas. Furthermore, in *Dreams of a Final Theory*, the theoretical physicist and Nobel Prize recipient Steven Weinberg, one of the greatest physicists of our time, writes:

> Think of the space of scientific theories as being filled with arrows, pointing toward each principle and away from the others by which it is explained. These arrows of explanation have already revealed a remarkable pattern: They do not form separate disconnected clumps, representing independent sciences, and they do not wander aimlessly— rather they are all connected and if followed backward (to deeper levels) they all seem to flow from a common starting point.[5]

Weinberg's statement is worth pondering. All the evidence of astrophysics indicates that the universal order stems from a single cause. But physicists—in their capacity as physicists—have never explained why this mathematically expressible, unified order exists. Why isn't motion entirely random or unpredictable all the way down to the subatomic level? Of course, if the universe were to be unpredictable, we would not exist (for no structures at all would likely exist for more than a nanosecond). But we can imagine the possibility and ask the question.

If you reject the conclusion of the design argument, then you face an extremely difficult philosophical question. How do you explain the fact that the material universe as a whole is orderly, unified, and predictable rather than disorderly and unpredictable? More specifically, how do you explain the fact that the trillions and trillions of particles of matter and quanta of energy that compose our universe are not randomly and aimlessly flitting about with no predictable pattern but instead exhibit a unified and intelligible order that can be described with mathematical equations that can be grasped by a rational mind?

Look at a college physics textbook and you'll see hundreds of formulas describing the predictable behavior of matter and energy across every domain in the universe. What you *won't* see is even an attempt at explaining— within physics—*why* matter obeys an intelligible system of laws rather than no laws at all. Even the technical condition scientists call "chaos" is governed by laws that can be expressed with equations (fractal mathematics).

So, how are we to explain the fact that the universe is orderly? The question suggests a different kind of design argument, one that takes the form logicians call "inference to the best explanation." This kind of argument is also inductive, but it is not based on an analogy. Rather, an inference to the best explanation proceeds as follows:

1. D is a collection of data (facts, observations) in need of explanation.

2. Hypothesis H, if true, would explain D.

3. No other hypothesis can explain D as well as H does.

4. Thus, D is the best explanation available.

5. Therefore, it is probable that H is true.

6. Therefore, H is the most reasonable conclusion to draw.

But how do we decide which of two competing explanations is best? We choose the best based on rational criteria, including the following:

- A good explanation is consistent with already known facts.
- A good explanation is internally consistent; that is, it is not self-contradictory.
- One explanation is better than another if it explains a wider array of facts.
- If two explanations explain the very same set of facts, then the simpler explanation—the one that makes fewer assumptions or posits fewer entities or both—is the more reasonable choice.

Here is Socrates's design argument translated into an inference to the best explanation format.

1. Careful observation indicates that the universe from the smallest to the largest scales is orderly, unified, functional, and intelligible.

2. One possible explanation of the data is that the universal order is the product of a superintending mind or intelligent designer.

3. A second possible explanation is that the universal order is the product of absolute, blind, unstructured, undirected random chance.

4. No one has suggested a plausible alternative to these two hypotheses.

5. The design hypothesis is the best available explanation of the data.

6. Therefore, the most reasonable conclusion to draw is that the intelligible order of the universe is the product of an intelligent designer.

Argument for premise 5. Imagine that you walk into class one day to find one hundred colorful leaves arranged on the floor in the form of the following English sentence: "The professor is sick today; class is canceled." Suppose in addition that the professor is nowhere to be seen. Which hypothesis makes the best sense of the data?

H1. The wind blew the leaves in from outside, and they happened to form the perfectly structured sentence by sheer, blind, random chance.

H2. An intelligent being with a knowledge of the professor's illness arranged the leaves intentionally to convey a message.

Does hypothesis H1 make any logical sense of the data? Isn't H2 the more reasonable explanation? Similarly, when we evaluate the design argument, isn't design the better explanation?

What are we to make of this version of the design argument? The first thing to note is that it is inductive. Inference to the best explanation arguments are always inductive.

Next, this kind of reasoning is common—we give best explanation arguments all the time in everyday life. For example, Jan comes home hungry and finds that the leftover cauliflower soup is gone. She reasons, "My roommate Joe hates soup. My roommate Sue can't stand cauliflower. The cat would eat it, but he can't get into the refrigerator. However, my roommate Chris loves cauliflower soup, and he has done this before. The best explanation is that Chris ate the leftover soup. The most reasonable conclusion to draw is therefore that Chris is the culprit."

Best explanation arguments are also common in civil and criminal courts of law. When a jury finds the defendant guilty, it is usually because the hypothesis—that the defendant committed the offense—best explains the verified facts presented by the prosecution.

Inference to the best explanation is also routinely employed in the physical sciences, the social sciences, and the humanities. The arguments

Einstein gave for his general and special theories of relativity, for example, are best explanation arguments. The case for every large-scale theory in science ultimately boils down to the claim that the favored theory best explains the data as a whole.

So, reject best explanation reasoning and you will have to give up most of what you believe about the world—if you are consistent. Many philosophers believe that the design argument is more compelling when stated as an inference to the best explanation rather than as an analogy. Compare the two versions of the design argument and decide for yourself.

One thing is certain: in either form—analogical or best explanation—the conclusion of the design argument contradicts nothing in physics. Indeed, the argument complements physics and science in general because it adds a level of depth to all explanations. But is intelligent design really the best explanation of the universal order? Let's turn to the first known criticism.

DOES BLIND CHANCE MAKE BETTER SENSE OF THE DATA?

In the fifth century BC, the Greek philosopher Leucippus of Miletus founded the school of philosophy known as "atomism" based on the hypothesis that every observable object is composed of tiny, indivisible particles too small to be seen, which he named "atoms" (from the Greek word for "uncuttable"). Leucippus's atomic hypothesis anticipated modern physics by more than two thousand years.

Leucippus was aware that the universe is orderly and highly integrated. However, he rejected intelligent design and proposed an alternative hypothesis, which I paraphrase: "There is no intelligent designer. The most reasonable explanation of the unified order of nature is that it is all just one giant accident. Long ago, billions and billions of primeval atoms falling through the void (empty space) happened by sheer chance to fall into the predictable order we call nature—for no reason at all. Blind random chance is the ultimate explanation of all things."[6]

Leucippus's critique targets premise 5 of the best explanation design argument as we have stated it. Let's reflect on his proposal for a moment. Suppose that we are playing five-card stud poker and I am dealing. Imagine that I deal myself a royal flush ten times in a row and win every game. When you question my honesty, I reply, "It was just an amazing run of pure, dumb luck—one big chance accident." Would that be an intellectually satisfying explanation? Would that make sense of the highly improbable pattern of the hands I dealt? (The odds against drawing one royal flush in five-card stud are 649,000 to 1.) Or would intelligent design—in this case the hypothesis that I cheated—make better sense of the data? [7]

But if blind, random chance is not a good explanation for a small-scale order, such as a winning streak in a crooked game of cards, why is it a reasonable explanation for the largest order of all, the universal order that has persisted for billions of years?

Here is a further issue. The ancient atomists knew that even a single atom must be an extremely complex and functional entity. For they argued that each atom must have hooks, flaps, and buckles that allow it to attach to other atoms in patterned ways. Today we know that a single atom has an astonishingly complicated internal structure—an order that can be expressed using advanced differential equations belonging to gigantic physical theories. Socrates's question remains as vital today as it was in ancient Athens: Does raw, unstructured, purely random chance really explain all order all the way down to the deepest level of the universe?[8]

And we are back to where we started. Socrates would ask, If you do not believe that intelligent design is the best explanation, then how do you explain the fact that the universe is orderly and unified from the largest to the smallest scales? Why isn't it all just a completely random chaos? Thales would ask, What holds it all together? What is the One over the Many that makes this a *uni*verse rather than a *multi*verse?[9]

A SURPRISING BOOST FOR THE DESIGN ARGUMENT

Thomas Nagel, University Professor of Philosophy and Law, Emeritus, at New York University, is the author of numerous influential works of philosophy. He is one of the leading philosophers of our time. He has stated that he is an atheist; however, he has also stated that his atheism is based not on philosophical argument or reason but on emotion. In *The Last Word*, Nagel writes:

In speaking of the fear of religion, I don't mean to refer to the entirely reasonable hostility toward certain established religions and religious institutions, in virtue of their objectionable moral doctrines, social policies, and political influence. Nor am I referring to the association of many religious beliefs with superstition and the acceptance of evident empirical falsehoods. I am talking about something much deeper — namely, the fear of religion itself. I speak from experience, being strongly subject to this fear myself: I *want* atheism to be true and am made uneasy by the fact that some of the most intelligent and well-informed people I know are religious believers. It isn't just that I don't believe in God and, naturally, hope that I'm right in my belief. It's that I hope there is no God! I don't want there to be a God; I don't want the universe to be like that.[10]

After having made statements like this, Nagel's latest book surprised the philosophical and scientific worlds. In *Mind and Cosmos: Why the Materialist Neo-Darwinian Conception of Nature Is Almost Certainly False*, Nagel presents an argument that adds scientific as well as philosophical support to the argument from design. Here is my summary:

1. The success of contemporary theoretical physics, including the surprising revelations contained in general relativity theory, special relativity theory, quantum theory, and evolutionary biology, indicates that the material universe at the deepest level discernable by science is governed by a complex but unified system of laws that is intelligible to rational minds.

2. If the universe at the deepest level discernable by science is governed by a complex but unified system of laws that is intelligible to rational minds, then the universe at the most fundamental level must be related in some significant way to mind, rationality, and intelligence.

3. Therefore, the universe at the most fundamental level is related in some significant way to mind, rationality, and intelligence.[11]

This raises the question: What is the relation between the fundamental laws of the cosmos and mind? Nagel admits that theism supplies the most obvious explanation: the laws of nature at the basic level are intelligible because they are the product of a mind. However, Nagel stops short of endorsing theism for the emotional reasons quoted above. That doesn't stop theistic philosophers from extending his reasoning as follows.

1. The laws of the material universe at the most fundamental level appear to be related in a significant way to mind, reason, intelligence. This is the data to be explained.

2. The data makes sense on the hypothesis that the universe is the product of an intelligent mind.

3. The data makes no sense on the atomist or chance hypothesis.

4. Therefore, intelligent design is the best explanation of the data.

5. It is therefore reasonable to conclude that the material universe is the product of a superintending intelligence.

In support of premise 3, theists might argue that intuitively the probability that an orderly, intelligible universe like ours arises from a completely random, unstructured, and unintelligible void is almost infinitely smaller than the probability that a supergun blindly aimed at random from earth hits a target the size of a pea sitting 13 billion light-years across the universe. On the other hand, if the universe is the product of a mind, the data is just what you would expect.

Going Deeper. A more rigorous argument can be given for the proposition that design rather than chance is a better explanation of the data. First, the following is an additional criterion commonly used in science and philosophy when choosing the best explanation of a set of data: If the data is more expected on one possible explanation or hypothesis (H1) than on another (H2), then H1 is the more likely explanation.

For example, suppose that a jewelry store owner is shot during a robbery. Using video footage from the store's cameras, detectives focus on Sam Smith, a career criminal who lives nearby. The stolen jewels are found in Smith's possession immediately after the crime, and Smith's fingerprints are all over the murder weapon that was left behind. This is the data in need of explanation. Now consider two hypotheses:

H1: Smith robbed the store and shot the owner.

H2: Someone else robbed the store and shot the owner.

If we assume H1 is true, the evidence is expected (Smith's fingerprints on the gun and the jewelry found in his possession shortly after the crime). For if Smith robbed the store, we would expect to find his fingerprints on the gun left behind, and we would not be surprised to learn that the jewels were found in his possession shortly after the crime. However, if we suppose that H2 is true, the evidence is not expected at all. For if someone else committed the crime, it would be highly unlikely that Smith's fingerprints would be found on the murder weapon. It would also be unlikely that the jewels would be found in Smith's possession shortly after the crime. The data is therefore more expected, more likely, on the basis of H1 than on H2. If the data is expected on the first hypothesis and is not expected on the second, this is a reason to suppose that H1 is the more likely explanation.

Now, let H1 and H2 be defined as follows:

H1: The universe is the product of an intelligent mind.

H2. The universe is the product of blind, unstructured, purely random chance.

On the basis of H1, the data (the intelligible order of the cosmos) is expected; based on H2 the data is not expected at all. Therefore, H1 is the more probable hypothesis.

To test your intuitions here, suppose that one morning fifty white rocks are observed scattered randomly on the ground in front of Judy's house at 5133 Kensington Avenue. The next morning, they are observed in an arrangement that spells out in perfectly formed letters Judy's address, "5133." One possible explanation is that during the night a blind, random gust of wind picked up the rocks and then they accidentally dropped into the observed pattern — an arrangement that by blind chance just happened to give the correct address. In this case, the explanation is random chance. A second hypothesis is that during the night, the rocks were arranged by an intelligent agent on purpose (to display the correct address).

Isn't the fact in need of explanation — the orderly and correct arrangement of the rocks — expected if we suppose that an intelligent agent arranged them on purpose? Wouldn't the arrangement be unexpected if we suppose that the only agent at work the night before was the wind? Isn't it highly unlikely that a random, mindless, unguided gust of wind with no goal in mind blew the rocks into the correct arrangement by accident? The reason is obvious: the direction the mindless wind blows has no cause-and-effect relation to the address of the house.

Recently an impressive number of scientists, philosophers, and mathematicians, including Stephen Meyer (a philosopher of science), Michael Behe (a molecular biologist), and William Dembski (a mathematician), have developed new versions of the design argument.[12] Despite the rigorous nature of their arguments, these "intelligent design theorists" (as they are called) have been ridiculed by powerful elites within the scientific and intellectual establishments. Nagel angered these elites when he criticized them:

> I believe the defenders of intelligent design deserve our gratitude for challenging a scientific world view [scientific naturalism that includes the denial of God's existence] that owes some of the passion displayed by its adherents precisely to the fact that it is thought to liberate us from religion. That world view is ripe for displacement.[13]

And:

> In thinking about these questions I have been stimulated by criticisms of the prevailing scientific world picture . . . by the [theistic] defenders of intelligent design. Even though writers like Michael Behe and Stephen C. Meyer are motivated at least in part by their religious beliefs, the empirical arguments they offer against the likelihood that the origin of life and its evolutionary history can be fully explained by physics and chemistry [i.e., without reference to God or anything supernatural] are of great interest in themselves. . . . The problems that these iconoclasts pose for the orthodox scientific consensus should be taken seriously. They do not deserve the scorn with which they are commonly met. It is manifestly unfair.[14]

Questions for Reflection and Discussion 4.1

1. In your own words, explain Socrates's design argument. Is your argument analogical, or is it an inference to the best explanation?
2. Give an example of a situation in your life when you employed analogical reasoning.
3. Give an example of a situation in your life when you employed inference to the best explanation.

4. In your own words, explain and evaluate the atomists' objection to design.
5. If you reject the conclusion of the design argument, state which premise you reject and then give a step-by-step argument against that premise. State which version of the design argument you are objecting to.
6. If you reject the conclusion of the design argument, how do you explain the fact that the universe is orderly rather than chaotic? State your alternative hypothesis and give an argument for it.
7. Explain a consideration of your own that supports the design argument.

THE DESIGN ARGUMENT DURING THE RISE OF MODERN SCIENCE

Modern experimental science was born in the universities of Europe between the thirteenth and eighteenth centuries.[15] I am speaking of science based on hypothesis testing and applied mathematics, with laboratories containing specialized scientific instruments, such as the microscope and telescope, textbooks, university courses in science and math, and experimental results disseminated widely by scientific societies publishing technical journals. This was a remarkable age that also saw the birth in Europe of modern mathematics (including analytic geometry, calculus, advanced number theory, and statistics), the first social sciences, and dozens of other new academic fields. In this period in European history, we also see the first application of modern science to agriculture, industry, technology, medicine, public health, transportation, communications, business, and information technology.[16]

Everywhere scientists pointed their new instruments and employed their new methods, they discovered previously unknown dimensions of intelligible order of stunning complexity. Microscopes revealed that a drop of pond water contains tiny living creatures with amazingly complex bodies. Telescopic observations, combined with advances in theoretical mathematics made by Galileo, Kepler, Descartes, Newton, and Leibniz, revealed that the cosmos in the large scale operates according to exact mathematical formulas. To the first modern scientists, it seemed that no matter how deeply they probed the cosmos, their instruments revealed intricate functional subsystems of increasing complexity.

The pioneers of modern science generally interpreted the new dimensions of intelligible order as empirical (observable) evidence that the universe is governed by a supreme mind or intelligence fittingly called "God." Where else could structures on this scale come from? Many included a philosophical design argument within their *scientific* works.

For example, in *The Wisdom of God Manifested in the Works of Creation*, John Ray (1627–1705), the founder of modern botany and a pioneer of ecology and modern zoology, argues that the order of nature is best explained by reference to a designer: "The bee, a creature . . . [such] that no man can expect it to have any considerable measure of understanding . . . yet makes her combs and cells with that geometrical accuracy that she must needs be acting by an instinct implanted in her by the wise author of Nature."[17] In 1665, Thomas Hooke, the first great microscopist, published the first textbook containing sketches of microscopic creatures. In his greatest work *Micrographia*, Hooke interprets the intricate wonders of life seen in a drop of pond water as signs of "God's handiwork."[18]

Robert Boyle (1627–91), one of the pioneers of modern chemistry, was fascinated by the structure of an insect's eye. His microscope revealed "hundreds of little round protuberances curiously ranged on the convexity of a single eye" of a common housefly. When Boyle discovered their function, he called the engineering of the fly's eye "a tribute to the wisdom of the creator." Boyle also argues: "[The universe as a whole] is like a rare clock . . . where all things are so skillfully contrived that the engine being once set moving all things proceed according to the artificer's design. . . . The excellent contrivance of that great system of the world [has] been . . . the great motive that in all ages and nations induced philosophers to acknowledge a Deity as the author of these admirable structures."[19]

Sir Isaac Newton (1643–1727), the founder of modern, mathematical physics, deserves special mention. His *The Mathematical Principles of Natural Philosophy* (1687) is considered one of the two or three greatest masterpieces of science ever written. I. Bernard Cohen, the noted historian of science, calls Newton's treatise "the culmination of thousands of years of striving to comprehend the system of the world, the principles of force and of motion, and the physics of bodies moving in different media."[20]

No one in his day was surprised that Newton included in his great treatise an inference to the best explanation argument for God's existence. "This most beautiful system of the sun, planets, and comets," he wrote, "could only proceed from the counsel and dominion of an intelligent and powerful being." We can make rational sense of the deep order of nature, he believed, only if we suppose that it is the expression not of blind chance but of a rational mind.

Deductive Arguments for Design

Recall that inductive arguments aim to show that their conclusions are highly probable (but not certain), while deductive arguments aim to show that their conclusions are completely certain. We have been examining inductive design arguments. Some versions of the design argument are deductive, such as this one:

1. All ordered complexity is ultimately the result of intelligent design.
2. The universe is an ordered complexity.
3. Therefore, the universe is most certainly the result of intelligent design.

Here is a commonsense (and inductive) subargument in support of premise 1. Every time we have searched and found the source of a complex and orderly system, that source has been an intelligent designer. Seattle's Space Needle originated in the mind of an architect; the first automobile was designed by an engineer, and so forth. Therefore, premise 1 is very probably true.

DAVID HUME'S CRITIQUE OF
ALL DESIGN ARGUMENTS

By the middle of the eighteenth century, the argument from design was accepted by most scientists, and nearly everyone agreed that belief in God and in science fit together logically. This consensus, however, did not last. Two major events popped the bubble. The first was the publication in 1778 of *Dialogues concerning Natural Religion* by the Scottish philosopher David Hume (1711–76). The second was the publication in 1859 of Charles Darwin's *The Origin of Species by Means of Natural Selection, or the Preservation of Favoured Races in the Struggle for Life*. We'll begin with

Hume's *Dialogues*, the book that contained the first systematic philosophical criticism of the design argument. Darwin's objection to the design argument is the topic of chapter 5.

Many in the New Atheist movement today believe that the objections raised by Hume demolished the design argument and showed that theism and science stand in logical conflict. Siding with science, they conclude that belief in God is irrational. Let's test their claim by examining several of Hume's famous criticisms.

Objection 1. Why Not a Big Hairy Spider?

Hume wrote the *Dialogues* in the form of a fictional conversation between three characters debating the existence of God. Philo, the first character, has a skeptical attitude toward religion; Cleanthes argues that we have good reason to believe in God; Demea is religious but he is a *fideist*—he believes that reason has nothing to do with religious belief.

In their discussion, Hume puts an interesting objection to the design argument into the mouth of Philo. Here is my summary. If we must posit a designer, why assume that the designer is intelligent and personal? Why suppose it is a divine being we would want to worship? Why not suppose it is an unintelligent source? Consider a spider web. Seen glistening in the morning light, it has a complex and beautiful geometrical order. Yet this complex order is produced by an unintelligent beast. Complex order therefore does not always come from intelligence. Thus, it is just as reasonable to conclude that the order of the universe was produced by a gigantic, unintelligent spider or something similar.

Philo continues: "The [Hindu] Brahmins assert that the world arose from an infinite spider, who spun this whole complicated mass from his bowels, and annihilates afterwards the whole or any part of it, by absorbing it again, and resolving it into his own essence."[21]

This is a clever objection. But is Hume's alternative hypothesis—that an unintelligent being such as a large spider created the universal order—a reasonable explanation for the fundamental order of the entire cosmos, including the mathematical equations discovered by modern physics and the formulas discovered by modern chemistry? A defender of Hume might reply, Why not? Although the spider may not be aware of the fact, its web follows complicated principles of geometry.

Does this reply work? In reply, theists argue that although it is unintelligent, a spider possesses an enormously complicated organizational structure. Anything *that* complex yet lacking intelligence, they argue, only makes sense when understood as the product of a higher intelligence.

Put another way, an unintelligent spider would be complex yet nonrational. But it is astronomically improbable that an intelligible order as vast and systematic as that of this universe would burst forth and persist from any nonrational source. A nonrational spider is not plausible taken as an unexplained or surd fact.

Objection 2. Why Not Many Designers?

We touched on this question earlier in this chapter. When scientists and philosophers of Hume's day presented the design argument, they typically argued that one supreme designer exists. In other words, they believed that the argument supports monotheism. Essentially, Philo replies, Why not postulate many designers, instead of one? After all, a machine, a temple, or a complex mechanism is typically the product of a committee. "A great number of men join in building a house or a ship," says Hume, "why may not several deities combine in framing a world?"[22] This is polytheism (belief in many gods).

Traditional theists have a strong reply. Philosophers and scientists from the earliest times have tested their hypotheses on the following assumption: when two hypotheses equally explain the same data, the simpler hypothesis (the one making the fewest assumptions or positing the fewest entities) is the more reasonable choice. Since the fourteenth century, this principle has been called "Ockham's razor" in honor of William of Ockham (1287–1347), a medieval logician and scientific pioneer who was the first to state it explicitly and defend it. Ockham's razor is an integral part of scientific practice because scientists discovered that (1) for every set of data, an infinite number of possible explanations, each of increasing complexity, exist, and (2) it is impossible to choose one explanation over another without assuming Ockham's razor.

But Ockham's razor is also common sense. Suppose that detectives find sixty identical shoeprints at the scene of a crime. One hypothesis is that one person left all sixty prints. A second hypothesis is that two people, each wearing identical shoes with identical wear patterns, each left thirty prints. Another hypothesis is that three individuals, each wearing identical shoes, left twenty prints each, and so forth. Each hypothesis explains the same data. How do we decide which one makes the best sense? In the absence of any evidence pointing to more than one culprit, such as shoeprints in two or more sizes, we employ Ockham's razor and choose the simplest hypothesis: one individual left all sixty prints. Without Ockham's razor, it is impossible to ever settle on one explanation—in science, in the courtroom, or in everyday life.

The application to the design argument is obvious. Compare the hypothesis that one designer exists with the hypothesis that two independent but cooperative designers exist. Both explain the same data set, yet the first is simpler (makes fewer assumptions and posits fewer entities). Ockham's razor as well as common sense thus support monotheism over polytheism.

Big bang astrophysics also offers evidence supporting the simpler design hypothesis. Recall the words of Steven Weinberg, one of the leading theoretical physicists of our time. Scientific explanations "are all connected and if followed backward (to deeper levels) they all seem to flow from a common starting point."[23]

And in *The Little Book of the Big Bang: A Cosmic Primer*, the astrophysicist Craig Hogan presents the now-standard model of the universe in the form of a single, unified chain of causes and effects that trace back through many cosmic epochs to a single source.[24] Although they could not have known it, Thales, Socrates, and the pioneers of modern science were in line with contemporary big bang physics when they argued for a single source of order—a One over the Many—to explain the overall structure of the cosmos.

Objection 3. Blind Chance Is a Better Explanation

Philo next recycles an idea similar to the ancient atomist hypothesis. Blind chance, he suggests, rather than an intelligent designer, is a better explanation of the universal order:

> Let us suppose [matter] is finite. A finite number of particles is only susceptible of finite transpositions: And it must happen, in an eternal duration, that every possible order or position must be tried an infinite number of times. . . . Suppose . . . that matter were thrown into

any position, by a blind, unguided force, it is evident that this first position must in all probability be the most confused and disorderly imaginable . . . Thus the universe goes on for many ages in a continued succession of chaos and disorder. But is it not possible that it may settle at last? . . . may we not . . . be assured of it . . . [settling into an orderly system] . . . and may not this account for all [order] in the universe?[25]

This hypothesis also has a problem. There is no reason to suppose that pure, unguided, random chance, even if given an eternity of time, *must* result in the appearance of every possible combination of some randomly interacting objects. Hume's hypothesis requires that the universe is a revolving system that tries out one chance configuration after another while making sure that every possibility is tried over time. Any such system would have to be governed by a complex and highly functional background order that holds the whole together while making sure that no possibility is overlooked. This doesn't eliminate design; it presupposes design! Here is an analogy. Imagine that a large roulette wheel gives every possible number an equal chance. Wouldn't the underlying mechanism have to be quite complex? Wouldn't it have to be constructed and adjusted with precision? Wouldn't that require intelligent design? Aren't the roulette wheels in Las Vegas casinos governed by complex computer programs written by intelligent designers with a knowledge of probability theory?

The point is that any continuous chance process that tries out every possibility over time—without accidentally leaving anything out—requires a background order as designed as a roulette wheel in Las Vegas. These thoughts challenge Hume's claim that "it must happen, in an eternal duration, that every possible order or position must be tried an infinite number of times."

Does Hume's random chance hypothesis really reduce all order to pure chance? Or does it require an underlying level of immense design? This point will come up again in chapter 5, when we examine the New Atheist idea known as the "multiverse."

Objection 4. The Argument from Lack of Order

Expressed as an inference to the best explanation, the design argument ends with the claim that the order of nature is best explained as the product of a mind. But the universe also contains evidence of a *lack* of order. Think about hurricanes, earthquakes, cancers, and swamps. Add to this the poor "design" of the human spine—so prone to malfunction and pain. We also know that the universe contains "chaotic" systems in which a small change in one region leads to a massive and seemingly disconnected change in a remote area. For instance, a flea falls off a mouse in Pakistan causing a tornado in Kansas. Hume's objection from disorder is that if order is evidence of a designer, then disorder is evidence *against* the existence of a designer. The design argument, expressed as an inference to the best explanation, needs to weigh *both* the evidence of order *and* the evidence of disorder before concluding that an intelligent designer exists. Perhaps the disorder present in the world exceeds the order and shows that there is likely no intelligent designer.

The defender of the design argument is not without a reply. First, *any* amount of order suggests an orderer. Therefore, "some things don't seem ordered" doesn't counter the claim that other things do.

Next, hurricanes are studied within the field of meteorology. Earthquakes and swamps are studied by geologists. Cancer is studied in oncology, and chaotic systems are examined within chaos theory, a branch of mathematics. Hurricanes, swamps, and so forth must therefore be orderly at some level if each can be studied scientifically. The word *chaos* sounds as if it connotes disorder, but chaos theorists have discovered that chaotic systems are governed by mathematical laws reflecting deep underlying regularities. The point is that, far from being examples of disorder, hurricanes, cancer, and such are orderly, intelligible, and interconnected parts of the overall system of universal order. Intelligible order appears to extend all the way to the bottom.

Objection 5. Why Not a Finite Deity?

Design arguments have often been used to support more than the claim that an intelligent designer exists. They have often been offered as evidence that God, *conceived within the Judeo-Christian religious tradition as a perfect and infinite being, exists.* Isaac Newton, for instance, offered his design argument to support his Christian belief in an all-knowing, all-powerful, and all-good God. In *An Enquiry concerning Human Understanding* (1751), Hume offered this objection:

When we infer any particular cause from an effect, we must propor-
tion the one to the other, and can never be allowed to ascribe to the
cause any qualities, but what are exactly sufficient to produce the
effect. . . . Allowing, therefore, the gods to be the authors of the existence or order of the universe; it follows, that they possess [only]
that . . . degree of power, intelligence, and benevolence, which appears
in their workmanship.[26]

So, just as we cannot infer an infinite cause from a finite effect and just
as we cannot infer a perfect cause from an imperfect effect, we cannot infer
that the cause of the world is either infinite or perfect since the world appears
to be finite and imperfect. If we must hypothesize an intelligent designer, we
should attribute to it only *finite* power, intelligence, and limited goodness.

Hume makes a strong point here. However, philosophers have given
separate arguments—apart from the design argument—for the conclusion that the designer must be all-powerful (omnipotent), all-knowing
(omniscient), and all-good (omnibenevolent). These arguments supple-
ment the design argument and are typically covered in advanced courses in
philosophy of religion and philosophical theology. Philosophical theists are
not limited to one particular argument. Like anyone else, they may appeal
to multiple arguments when supporting their belief system.

Objection 6. Who Designed the Designer?

With this question Hume seems to have the theist in a logical bind. If the
theist replies, "A designer of the designer," then the question arises again,
"Who designed that?" If the theist replies, "A designer of the designer of
the designer," the question again recycles. If the theist says, "It's designers
all the way back to infinity," then he is positing an infinite regression of
designers. An *infinite explanatory regression* is an unending series in which
one item is explained in terms of a prior item, which is explained in terms
of a prior item, and so forth back and back without end.

Philosophical theists have a deep answer to this question; however, the
full explanation requires a foray into modal logic, the notion of divine
simplicity, and the metaphysics of necessary existence—subjects best reserved for advanced discussions. Nevertheless, some elementary ideas can
be considered at the introductory level. Philosophers and logicians have
agreed since ancient times that infinite explanatory regressions explain

nothing. (In chapter 6 we'll see exactly why infinite regressions fail to explain, when we probe the cosmological argument for the existence of God.) Given that infinite regressions explain nothing, and given that the universe is intelligible, it seems to follow that the regression of designers is not infinite, in which case any regression of designers ends with one *ultimate* designer. For not only does the addition of an infinity of designers explain nothing more (and hence is not needed), it undermines the intelligibility of the whole. But if there is one ultimate designer, then that being's intrinsic order is not explained in terms of a prior designer. Again, we'll take up the issue of infinite regression in chapter 6.[27]

HUME'S SURPRISING CONCLUSION

Surprisingly, after the conversation between Philo, Cleanthes, and Demea ends, Hume editorializes and sides with the theist Cleanthes. The order we observe in nature, Hume states, is indeed good evidence that the universe was designed by a superintending mind of immense magnitude. Hume writes: "Cleanthes and Philo did not pursue this conversation much further; and as nothing ever made greater impression on me than all the reasonings of that day, so I confess that on carefully looking over the whole conversation I cannot help thinking that Philo's principles are more probable than Demea's, but that those of Cleanthes approach still nearer to the truth."[28]

> Don't you remember, said Philo, the excellent saying of Lord Bacon on this topic? That a little philosophy, replied Cleanthes, makes a man an atheist: a great deal converts him to religion.
> —David Hume, *Dialogues concerning Natural Religion*[29]

Questions for Reflection and Discussion 4.2

1. Explain and evaluate one of the design arguments given during the rise of modern science.
2. In your own words, explain one of Hume's criticisms of the design argument. How do you think Socrates would reply?
3. Do any of Hume's criticisms succeed? Offer the most intelligent and strongest reasons you can for your position.

FIVE

Design and Evolution

PALEY UPDATES THE DESIGN ARGUMENT

Hume's criticisms of the design argument did not convince everyone. They certainly did not convince William Paley (1743–1805), professor of philosophy at Cambridge University in England and archdeacon in the Anglican Church. In 1802, Paley wrote an entire book defending the design argument based on the latest science of his day. Paley's treatise, *Natural Theology or Evidences of the Existence and Attributes of the Deity Collected from the Appearances of Nature*, became a national best seller. His book delves into many of nature's most interesting wonders. Not only did it become one of the most influential works of philosophy of the nineteenth century, but philosophers today agree that Paley's book contains one of the clearest and most complete expositions of the design argument ever given. This explains why it still gets honorable mention in just about every introductory philosophy text.

Paley began his famous argument with a thought experiment. Suppose that you are out for a stroll and find a watch lying on the ground.

Your response would be different than if you had seen a rough stone lying in the same spot. If you were to see an ordinary, rough-shaped stone, you would not be inclined to suppose that it was shaped by an intelligent being. But if you were to see a watch, you would be strongly inclined to conclude that its parts were arranged and adjusted by an intelligent designer — by a watchmaker — and not by the blind processes of nature (wind, erosion, floods, earthquakes, etc.). Why? The answer, Paley argues, is the watch's structure, specifically the fact that it is a system of many interrelated parts arranged in a highly improbable order that functions in a specifiable way.

Like Socrates's design argument, Paley's is analogical and inductive. His "watchmaker" argument (as it is often called), minus its accompanying scientific data from physics and biology, looks about like this:

Paley's Watchmaker Argument

1. The deep order we observe when we look at biological specimens under a microscope and the order of a watch are similar in many ways. (This is the analogy to be considered.)

2. Like effects probably have like causes.

3. The cause of a watch's order is an intelligent designer (a watchmaker).

4. Therefore, the cause of nature's order is probably also an intelligent designer.

5. It is thus reasonable to conclude that nature is the product of an intelligent designer.

Paley's analogy can be condensed to the slogan "Watch is to watchmaker as nature is to a designer of nature."

Paley's *Natural Theology* contains fascinating examples of apparent design in nature. The hinge on a clamshell, for example, is similar in design to the hinge on a door made by a carpenter; the lens of the human eye embodies many of the design principles opticians use when they grind telescope lenses, and so on. With each new example of apparent design in nature, argues Paley, it becomes more and more reasonable to believe that nature is the product of a mind.

Two kinds of theology. *Theology* (Greek *theos*, "God," and *logos*, "reason," literally, "the study of God") has traditionally been divided into two branches. *Revealed theology* is the attempt to learn about God by studying sacred scripture, writings believed to be God's self-revelation. *Natural theology* is the attempt to learn about God by studying nature using our natural reasoning abilities. This is why philosophical arguments for God's existence are often called "natural theology." In Paley's day, it was often said that God had written two books: the Bible and the Book of Nature.

DARWIN REJECTS PALEY'S WATCHMAKER

The lives of famous people are sometimes connected in surprising ways. On October 15, 1827, nineteen-year-old Charles Darwin entered Cambridge University planning to study for the Presbyterian ministry. Although Paley was no longer teaching there (he had died more than twenty years before), every Cambridge undergraduate at the time studied Paley's *Natural Theology* (and his *Evidences of Christianity*) in preparation for a comprehensive exam at the end of the second year. Darwin not only studied Paley's books, he fervently agreed and defended Paley in discussions with fellow students. Like most universities, Cambridge had student housing. In an amazing coincidence, Darwin was assigned to live in Paley's old room at Cambridge.[1] There is a reason why this coincidence is surprising.

In 1831, Darwin was hired to serve as the naturalist aboard the HMS *Beagle*, a British Royal Navy vessel ordered to conduct a transatlantic scientific expedition. As the ship's naturalist, Darwin's job was to collect and catalogue specimens from nature at every port. When the ship set sail from Plymouth, England, on December 27, 1831, thanks in large part to having studied Paley's books, Darwin interpreted the wonders of nature as beautiful evidence of divine design. However, when the *Beagle* returned to England five years later, he was having doubts. A new theory was forming in his mind.

At the time, two opposing views on the origin and history of life competed for allegiance.

- Creationism. In the beginning God created all the biological species at once and gave each one a fixed and unchanging nature.

- Evolutionism. The species were not created at once, and they do not have fixed natures. Rather, species have changed over time, and currently existing species developed slowly, step by step, out of very small changes in previously existing species. There are no permanent natures in nature.

Creationism was the dominant view for two reasons. First, it seemed to be implied by the Bible, at least on most interpretations. Second, no one could explain how piecemeal evolutionary change starting from simple creatures could possibly have produced the extremely complex and diverse forms of life we see today. In other words, the evolutionary hypothesis lacked an underlying mechanism.[2]

Darwin presented his new theory in 1859 in his 500-page master-piece, *On the Origin of Species by Means of Natural Selection, or the Preservation of Favored Races in the Struggle for Life.* His book contained the first systematic scientific theory of evolutionary change combined with an account of an underlying mechanism.

Unlike many large-scale scientific theories, Darwin's can be summarized without mathematics and in layman's terms. Here is my attempt. First, organisms tend to produce more offspring than their environment can support. As a result, the members of each generation compete in a struggle for survival, and many die. Next, observation reveals that inheritance is high fidelity but not perfect fidelity. That is to say, offspring resemble their parents closely but not exactly. Small variations in structure randomly occur with each new generation. (Inherited variations are random in the sense that they do not occur because they are needed for survival.)

Next, some variations will be advantageous in the struggle for existence; others will be harmful. Organisms possessing advantageous variations will tend to live longer and reproduce in greater numbers; organisms possessing harmful variations will tend to die off before reproducing. In other words, the more "fit" — those better adjusted to their environments — will reproduce in greater numbers. With each new generation, this process (called "natural selection") repeats.

Over time, ever-more adaptive life-forms will develop. So, if the process begins with one extremely simple life-form possessing the power to make close but not perfect copies of itself, over long periods of time ever-more complicated and functional life-forms will develop. In this way, nature acts like a plant or animal breeder, unconsciously selecting some forms for reproduction and rejecting others.

The most controversial aspect of Darwin's revolutionary theory, however, was not the mechanism of change that he proposed (natural selection acting on random, inherited variations). Nor was it his claim that human beings and apes have evolved from a (now extinct) common ancestor by small modifications over long periods of time. Rather, it was a separate, nonscientific, and completely unsubstantiated claim that Darwin (and other scientists) *added* to his theory after it was published. Natural selection, Darwin and others claimed, is a purposeless, unplanned process. It is not the result of, and it does not reflect in any way, intelligent design, God, or any supernatural guidance. In short, it is entirely natural—there is nothing supernatural about it. Evolution is therefore not aimed at any goal or endpoint. The intended conclusion was obvious: *we can explain the appearance of design in nature without reference to God or any intelligent designer.*

Darwin did not make this claim in his famous book. Indeed, in the conclusion of *Origin of Species* he wrote:

> I see no good reason why the views given in this volume should shock the religious feelings of anyone. It is satisfactory, as showing how transient such impressions are, to remember that the greatest discovery ever made by man, namely, the law of the attraction of gravity, was also attacked . . . as subversive of religion. A celebrated author and divine has written to me that he has gradually learnt to see that it is just as noble a conception of the Deity to believe that he created a few original forms capable of self-development into other and needful forms as to believe that he required a fresh act of creation to supply the voids caused by the action of his laws.[3]

Darwin's concluding statement actually refers to God and affirms theism: "There is grandeur in this view of life, with its several powers having been originally breathed by the Creator into a few forms or into one; and that whilst this planet has gone cycling on according to the fixed law of gravity, from so simple a beginning endless forms most beautiful and most wonderful have been, and are being evolved."[4]

However, Darwin eventually came to believe that the evolutionary process can be explained entirely in naturalistic terms. In private correspondence he wrote:

The old argument of design in nature, as given by Paley, which for-
merly seemed to me so conclusive, fails now that the law of natural
selection has been discovered. We can no longer argue that, for instance, the beautiful hinge of a bivalve shell must have been made by
an intelligent being, like the hinge of a door by a man. There seems to
be no more design in the variability of organic beings and in the action
of natural selection than in the course which the wind blows.[5]

Think carefully about this claim: natural selection is not aimed at a
goal, it has no designer, it is as purposeless as "the course in which the wind
blows." This was Darwin's *opinion*; it was not a scientific proposition derived from the observable evidence he had collected. It did not follow from
his theory, and it was not validated by any scientific experiment. (Indeed, it
was a hypothesis that could not be proven by science.)

Despite the fact that his denial of intelligent design was nothing more
than an unsubstantiated and nonscientific add-on, after 1859 mainstream
scientific thought shifted heavily in a naturalistic direction, thanks in large
part to Darwin's theory. Many contemporary biologists today add Darwin's
unsubstantiated naturalistic assumption to their *scientific* presentations.
For example, the biologist Douglas Futuyma, in his *Introduction to Evolutionary Biology*, writes that "by coupling undirected, purposeless variation
to the blind, uncaring process of natural selection, Darwin made theological, or spiritual, explanations of life superfluous."[6] And the biologist Julian
Huxley writes, "Darwinism removed the whole idea of God as a creator of
organisms from the sphere of rational discussion."[7] As we've seen, Darwin
did no such thing. But thanks to ignorant statements like these from re-
spectable scientists, generations of college students have been taught that
Darwin refuted the design argument and rendered belief in an intelligent
designer rationally unnecessary.

If we simply assume, without any argument or evidence at all, that
natural selection does not reflect intelligent design and if we simply assume
that natural selection explains all order, then *of course* there is no longer any
need to suppose that nature is the product of intelligent design. Similarly,
if we simply assume without argument that the first cars simply popped
into existence out of thin air, fully designed, by sheer accident, then there
is no longer any need to suppose that an intelligent engineer designed the
first car. Yet most contemporary biologists continue to teach that Darwin's

theory eliminated all need to refer to a designer of nature. One famous example is particularly instructive.

RICHARD DAWKINS'S "PROOF" THAT INTELLIGENT DESIGN IS OBSOLETE

In his *New York Times* best seller, *The Blind Watchmaker: Why the Evidence of Evolution Reveals a Universe without Design,* the famous biologist and New Atheist Richard Dawkins uses a computer simulation to support his claim that there is no intelligent designer.[8] Dawkins begins his argument with a question: What is the probability that *in one try all at once* a computer prints out, by blind chance alone, the following line from Shakespeare's play *Hamlet*: "Methinks it is like a weasel"? The probability can be calculated. A computer generating one random string of letters after another in a series of independent trials would almost certainly never hit the target even if it ran for trillions of years. Dawkins calls a series of independent random trials like this "single-step selection."[9]

Next, Dawkins introduces a computer program he wrote that mimics evolution by routinely executing the following steps:

Step 1. Using a random character generator, the computer types out a sequence of twenty-eight characters (the length of the target sentence from Hamlet). Since this is random, it is extremely unlikely that the computer types out in one try "Methinks it is like a weasel."[10]

Step 2. The computer "breeds" from this initial sequence of twenty-eight characters by copying it over and over again thousands of times, with one wrinkle: Dawkins wrote a rule into his program that introduces into each new copy a small chance of a random copying error (representing a random genetic mutation).

Step 3. The program scans all the thousands of copies of the original random string of twenty-eight characters. Although most are exactly like the original, a few contain minor copying errors. The program automatically selects the *one* random copy that most resembles the target sentence. In the beginning, this will be a random string with one or two letters in common with the target.

Step 4. The program repeats step 2.

Step 5. The program repeats step 3.

And so on . . .

The first time Dawkins tested his program, it produced the highly improbable yet complex and orderly sentence "Methinks it is like a weasel" in
less than an hour *while he was out of the room.* Thus, he claims, the program
produced the highly unlikely result without any intelligent design or oversight during its operation. Since natural selection operates in a similar way,
this shows that an unguided process of natural selection, operating on randomly generated entities, can produce a highly improbable yet orderly outcome *without the oversight of an intelligent designer.* Dawkins calls this kind
of chance process "cumulative selection" because order accumulates over
time as one chance result after another is fed through a filter of some kind.

Dawkins notes that evolution operates by cumulative, rather than
single-step, selection. The difference between the two kinds of selection is
large. Consider single-step selection first. If we place a monkey in front of
a computer keyboard and have him start typing random sequences of
twenty-eight letters, each time starting over from scratch, there is one
chance in 10,000 million million million million million million that he
types "Methinks it is like a weasel" within a reasonable period of time. It
would take approximately a million million million million million *years*
to get the sentence by single-step selection. However, using cumulative selection, Dawkins's computer program reached the target sentence in a few
minutes, operating on nothing but randomly generated strings of letters.

It follows, concludes Dawkins, that given sufficient time, an unguided,
naturalistic process of natural selection can begin with simple organisms formed
by accident and produce highly complex entities such as human beings.

A FLAW IN THE ARGUMENT?

A defender of the design argument has an immediate and somewhat obvious rejoinder. Dawkins's computer program is itself an intelligently designed system! Dawkins purposely designed his software to produce a predetermined result. It is simply not true that his system achieves its goal
without intelligent oversight — it *embodies* intelligent oversight. Dawkins
is the intelligent designer of his simulated evolutionary process.

But the flaw in Dawkins's reasoning runs deeper than this. His intelligently designed software program accomplishes its result only when it is running within a deeper intelligently designed system, namely, his computer's operating system. And the operating system of a digital computer is a masterpiece of intelligent design. (Most operating systems contain millions of lines of carefully chosen code.) Yet without that program running in the background, Dawkins's smartly designed simulation of natural selection would not function.

Dawkins's simulation program therefore does not show by analogy that natural selection is as blind and unplanned "as the course in which the wind blows." Nor does it show that a blind evolutionary process operating on random mutations can produce intelligent life. All it shows is that an intelligently designed system operating within a deeper intelligently designed system can mimic the evolutionary process. Which brings us to the latest design argument.

During the second half of the twentieth century, theoretical physicists discovered a complex background program functioning deep within the universe at the subatomic level. To their great surprise, they discovered that no conceivable process of evolution can even get started unless this background program, or one very similar to it, is *already* in place and running. It followed that the newly found background order operating deep within nature (and needed if any evolutionary process is to occur) cannot itself be the product of an unplanned and unguided evolutionary process.

Even more surprising was the stunning degree of organized, intelligible complexity displayed by this underground background order: it looked every bit as designed as Paley's watch.

A number of scientists and philosophers drew the obvious implication: a naturalistic theory of evolution cannot explain all of nature's amazing order all the way down to the most fundamental level. Rather, at a deep level there exists an intelligible, complex, and functional order that is not itself due to any evolutionary process. Furthermore, this order looks like the result of choice not chance. What is this newly discovered pre-evolutionary background order? Why does it look like the result of a choice? The details are contained in the latest version of the design argument, one initially given by astrophysicists during the second half of the twentieth century. The argument is often called the "fine-tuning argument." It is also known as "the new watchmaker argument."

Questions for Reflection and Discussion 5.1

1. In your own words, explain Paley's argument.
2. What is the difference between natural and revealed theology?
3. In your own words, explain Darwin's hypothesis of natural selection.
4. Imagine that Socrates is transported through time to meet Darwin. What does he say after Darwin claims that natural selection is as purposeless as "the course which the wind blows"?

THE NEW WATCHMAKER OR FINE-TUNING ARGUMENT

Since the new design argument rests on recent discoveries in atomic physics, some background will be essential.

The Nuts and Bolts of the Universe

Early in the twentieth century, physicists began uncovering the atomic details of the deep structure of the material universe. The current model is based on the properties of the fundamental particles of matter, including the following:

-   Protons and neutrons make up the nucleus of the atom.
-   Electrons gyrate around the atomic nucleus in orbitals.
-   Photons carry electromagnetic radiation.
-   Quarks exist inside protons and neutrons.

And the properties of the four fundamental forces of nature:

1. The electromagnetic force holds the negatively charged electrons in their orbitals around the positively charged atomic nucleus.
2. The strong nuclear force holds protons and neutrons together within the atom's nucleus.
3. The weak nuclear force governs radioactivity.
4. The gravitational force is an attractive force operating between all particles of matter.

The Discovery of the Universal Constants

Thanks to powerful computers and advanced telescopes, astrophysicists have discovered that no matter which region of the cosmos we study, the basic particles and the fundamental forces have the same unchanging properties. The laws of physics that hold in the local region of space also hold throughout the universe. These unchanging properties have been measured in physics labs and are represented in mathematical formulas by constants (numbers that do not change). Since these constants describe the deep structure of the entire cosmos, they are called the "universal constants."[11] The astrophysicists John Gribbin and Martin Rees write:

> Physicists have now reduced nature still further. They now believe that the basic structure of the entire physical world . . . is in principle determined by a few basic "constants." These are the masses of a few so-called elementary particles, and the strengths of the forces—electric, nuclear, and gravitational—that bind those particles together and govern their motions.[12]

Once physicists had precise values for several universal constants, they asked an intriguing question: What would the universe have been like if these constants had taken different values? For instance, what would the cosmos be like if the force of gravity had been 1 percent less or 1 percent more than it actually is? What would the cosmos be like if protons were 1 percent heavier? To their amazement, when they plugged alternative constants into their mathematical models of the universe, they discovered that if even *one* of the universal constants had taken a slightly different value, the universe would have been so disorderly that no evolutionary process of any kind would have occurred, and life in any conceivable form would not have been possible.[13]

Physicists Comment on the Constants

Writing in *Nature*, one of the most prestigious scientific journals in the world, physicists Brandon Carr and Martin Rees offer this assessment: "The basic features of galaxies, stars, planets, and the everyday world are essentially determined by a few microphysical constants . . . several aspects of our Universe—some of which seem to be prerequisites for the evolution of any form of life—depend rather delicately on apparent 'coincidences' among the physical constants."[14]

Many other respected physicists have commented on the fortuitous arrangement of the universal constants, including Paul Davies: "If we could play God, and select values for [the fundamental constants] by twiddling a set of knobs, we would find that almost all knob settings would render the universe uninhabitable. Some knobs would have to be fine-tuned to enormous precision if life is to flourish in the universe."[15]

And John Barrow:

> If we were to imagine a whole collection of hypothetical "other universes" in which all the [constants] that define the structure of our universe take on all possible permutations of values, then we find that almost all of these other possible universes we have created on paper are stillborn, unable to give rise to that type of chemical complexity that we call "life." The more we examine the other types of universe . . . the more special and unusual do the properties of the actual universe appear to be.[16]

Heinz Pagels: "The universe, it seems, has been finely tuned for our comfort; its properties appear to be precisely conducive to intelligent life. The force of gravity, for example, could hardly have been set at a more ideal level."[17]

John Gribbin:

> Our form of life depends, in delicate and subtle ways, on several apparent "coincidences" in the fundamental laws of nature which make the universe tick. Without these coincidences, we would not be here to puzzle over the problem of their existence.
>
> If we modify the value of one of the fundamental constants, something invariably goes wrong, leading to a universe that is inhospitable to life. Whenever we adjust a second constant in an attempt to fix the problem the result is generally to create three new problems for every one we "solve." The conditions in our universe really do seem to be uniquely suitable for life.[18]

The universe seems to have been set up in such a way that interesting things can happen in it. It is very easy to imagine other kinds of universes, which would have been stillborn because the laws of physics in them would not have allowed anything interesting to evolve.[19]

Barrow draws together many threads when he notes that the universe's "deep unalterable structure" forms a "cosmic environment" for evolution stretching farther and wider than Darwin ever imagined:[20]

> Before biological complexity can begin to develop, there must exist atoms and molecules with properties that permit the development of complexity and self-replication; there must exist stable environments; and there must exist sites that are temperate enough for those structures to exist. All these things must persist for enormous periods of time. Deep within the inner spaces of matter, unseen and unnoticed, exist the features that enable these conditions to be met . . . [without these features] all structures complex enough to evolve spontaneously by natural selection would be impossible.[21]

By the 1980s, astrophysicists generally agreed that no evolutionary process *of any kind* would have occurred and life *in any form* would not exist if just one of the fundamental constants had taken a slightly different value. To many of the physicists who studied the matter, the arrangement of the universal constants did not look random at all—it looked intentional.

Let's look at three of the surprising numerical relationships that many scientists and philosophers today call the "cosmic coincidences." After this we'll take up the question: Is the surprising arrangement of the universal constants physical evidence that the universe was intelligently designed?

Cosmic Coincidence 1: Electron-Proton Charges in Precise Balance

The positively charged proton (normally found in the nucleus of the atom) differs in many ways from the negatively charged electron (normally found orbiting the nucleus). For instance, the proton is about 1,836 times heavier than the electron. About a million electrons would theoretically fit inside a proton. The two particles also have different magnetic properties, and the proton participates in processes involving the strong nuclear force, but the electron does not.[22]

Given their many differences, it is amazing that the negative charge on the electron precisely balances the positive charge on the proton. The two charges could theoretically have been unbalanced. How accurate is the balance? Accurate at least to *one part in 100 billion*, according to the astrophysicist George Greenstein.[23] If the charges were to differ by just one part in 100 billion, our bodies would explode like sticks of dynamite.[24] If the balance were to be off by just one part in a *billion billion*, objects like the earth and the sun would explode.[25] It follows that if the universe is to have any structure at all, let alone an evolutionary one, the charges of electrons and protons must be finely tuned to a mind-boggling degree.

Cosmic Coincidence 2: Balance between the Electromagnetic and Gravitational Forces

The strengths of the electromagnetic and gravitational forces appear to be fine-tuned to each other to an accuracy of one part in 10^{40}. If these two forces had been out of balance by one part in a billion billion billion billion, the explosion mechanism inside large stars would not have functioned, supernova explosions would not have scattered complex elements into interstellar space, complex elements would not have been available for the evolution of life, and life in any form would not have been possible.[26] Davies writes: "In one of the categories of stars, the 'red' stars, the stars do not become supernovas and so do not scatter heavy elements into the interstellar medium. In another category of stars, the 'blue' stars, the stars burn too fast for life to form. To prevent all stars from crowding into one or the other category, the relative strengths of the electromagnetic force and the gravitational force must be balanced to one part in 10^{40}."[27]

Cosmic Coincidence 3: Initial Expansion Rate of the Universe

We now know that the material universe began a finite time ago in an explosive event astrophysicists call the "big bang." (See the Interlude following chapter 6 for an explanation.) When astrophysicists calculated the initial expansion rate of the universe, they discovered that if that rate had been different by one part in a billion billion billion billion billion billion, evolution in any form would not have occurred and life of any kind would not have been possible.[28]

Specifically, if the initial expansion value had been higher by just one part in a billion billion billion billion billion billion, the universe would have expanded too fast for stars to form, and the universe would be unfit for any kind of life. But if the initial expansion value had been less by the same infinitesimal amount, the expanding universe would have collapsed before stars could form, also producing a lifeless universe. Gribbin and Rees write: "The implication is that the relevant number, the so-called 'density parameter,' was set, in the beginning, with an accuracy of one part in 10^{60}. Changing that parameter, either way, by a fraction given by a decimal point followed by 60 zeroes and a 1, would have made the universe unsuitable for life as we know it."[29]

These two astrophysicists add that the density parameter is "the most accurately determined number in all of physics, and suggests a fine-tuning of the universe, to set up conditions suitable for the emergence of stars, galaxies, and life, of exquisite precision."[30]

Speaking of the universe's initial rate of expansion, the astrophysicist George Seielstad writes: "In some way, by chance or otherwise, our universe managed to thread the narrow line between these two extremes [an expansion that is too fast for stars to form and one that is too slow for stars to form], a circumstance without which we would never have been."[31]

These are just three of more than *one hundred* cosmic coincidences discovered by astrophysicists, each an example of fine-tuning at the atomic level.[32]

Physicists Interpret the Data

Freeman Dyson, one of the twentieth century's leading physicists, writes: "The more I examine the universe and study the details of its architecture, the more evidence I find that the universe in some sense must have known that we were coming."[33] Dyson also speaks of the "numerical accidents [among the fundamental constants] that seem to conspire to make the universe habitable" and the "peculiar harmony between the structure of the universe and the needs of life and intelligence."[34]

Davies sounds almost like a pre-Socratic philosopher when he writes:

It is hard to resist the impression of something — some influence capable of transcending space-time and the confinements of relativistic causality — possessing an overview of the entire cosmos at the instant of its creation, and manipulating all the causally disconnected parts to go bang with almost exactly the same vigor at the same time, and yet not so exactly coordinated as to preclude the small scale, slight irregularities that eventually formed the galaxies, and us.[35]

Stephen Hawking, perhaps the most famous physicist of our time, writes in *A Brief History of Time*: "The laws of science, as we know them at present, contain many fundamental numbers, like the size of the electric charge of the electron and the ratio of the masses of the proton and the electron. . . . The values of these numbers seem to have been very finely adjusted to make possible the development of life."[36]

The Best Explanation?

All of this leads us to the fundamental question, What best explains the surprising arrangement of the universal constants? If the question reminds you of the problem of the one over the many first raised by Thales at the dawn of philosophy, then you are connecting this chapter with chapter 1. Two thought experiments will help us proceed.

Imagine that the pizza maker Vincenzo Ramaglia invents an automatic pizza machine. When dough, vegetables, seasonings, sauce, cheese, and other ingredients are fed into one end of the machine, intricately formed pizzas come out the other end—but only if the machine's fifty dials are set properly. The machine is so sensitive that all fifty dials must each be set within a tolerance of one-millionth of an inch, or the product that comes out will not be edible.

Now, imagine walking into Vincenzo's shop and seeing his famous machine cranking out intricately formed pizzas. Which hypothesis would make the best overall sense of the observed data?

1. The fifty dials are loose and were set by the wind—a blind, unconscious process that has no goal.

2. The dials were set on purpose by an intelligent being who intended to make intricately formed pizzas.

Our second thought experiment involves an imaginary computer game that allows you to design a possible universe on your laptop. After loading *Sim Universe* onto your computer, you design a model universe by typing in fifty mathematical equations, each containing a constant that must be entered to sixty decimal places. Together these constants determine the way your universe will function. Once you have typed in your numbers, the background order is in place, and *Sim Universe* cranks out a simulation of your "possible universe."

The goal of the game is to design a functional world containing an evolutionary process, diverse life-forms, and interesting activity. However, such a universe will not result unless the constants are set within very narrow limits.

On the first day, you load *Sim Universe* onto your laptop and begin typing in all fifty mathematical equations with your choice of fundamental constants. You are operating blindly because you lost the instruction manual and therefore have no hints at all. After you give the command, your universe starts to operate. But after one hour, you're bored—it isn't doing anything. It is just a disorderly blur.

This is a letdown because at the software store, the demo showed stars forming, galaxies coalescing, supernovas spewing out complex elements into space, and weird life-forms developing on planets with stable environments. After several weeks of effort, you give up. This was smart, because out of millions of billions of trillions of possible combinations of values for the fundamental constants, a vanishingly small fraction produces an active universe containing life-forms.

Now suppose a friend comes over and asks if she can give the game a try. She sits down and begins typing constants into the equations, each to sixty decimal places. Soon, a complex, stable, interesting universe is developing, complete with stars, galaxies, and an evolutionary process leading to complicated life-forms. Would you believe your friend if she told you that she hit the right numbers by blind luck? Or would you be strongly inclined to suppose that she chose those numbers on purpose based on a preexisting knowledge of what it takes to produce the background order needed for a life-sustaining universe?

In light of our thought experiments, which hypothesis makes the best overall sense of the fine-tuning of the universal constants—intelligent design or blind chance? This gives us a best explanation version of the fine-tuning argument, an inductive argument for intelligent design.

Summary of the Fine-Tuning Argument

1. The values of the universal constants of physics are fine-tuned to each other in such a way that if even one were different by an astronomically small amount, no evolutionary process would have occurred and life in any form would not have been possible. (This is the data to be explained.)

2. The arrangement of the fundamental constants is astronomically unlikely on a chance hypothesis.

3. The arrangement of the fundamental constants is expected on an intelligent design hypothesis.

4. No one has suggested a plausible alternative to these two hypotheses.

5. The best explanation is therefore intelligent design.

6. Therefore, it is reasonable to believe that the order of the universe is the product of a rational mind existing above the fray, in short, an intelligent designer.

A Confusion to Avoid

The fine-tuning argument is not directed against the scientific findings on evolution covered in standard biology textbooks. The argument does not claim that evolution has not occurred. To avoid possible confusions, three views must be distinguished. 1. *Naturalism* is the claim that nothing supernatural exists. The natural world recognized by science is all that exists. Naturalism is a metaphysical rather than a scientific thesis. Darwin seems to have held this view at some point in his later life. 2. *Naturalistic Darwinism* is the combination of naturalism and the purely scientific theses of evolutionary theory, including the theory of natural selection. 3. *Theistic evolution* is the conjunction of theism with the scientific theses of evolutionary theory. Advocates of theistic evolution believe that a guided evolutionary process was God's way of bringing about the living world. One can reject naturalism (and accept theism) without rejecting the purely scientific part of evolutionary theory. The fine-tuning argument is only directed against *naturalistic* Darwinism—it is not a wholesale rejection of evolutionary theory.

THE BIGGEST OBJECTION: THE MULTIVERSE HYPOTHESIS

Victor Stenger, a physicist and prominent New Atheist, agrees with theists that the intricate and hugely improbable arrangement of the universal constants *looks* designed. He also agrees that the fortuitous (for us) arrangement of the constants needs an explanation. However, the best explanation, he argues, is not an intelligent designer; rather, it is the multiverse hypothesis (MH), also called the "many worlds hypothesis" and the "many universes hypothesis."

His proposal has three parts. First, let's suppose there is no intelligent designer, no creator, no god, and nothing supernatural in any sense. Second, suppose that the material universe we inhabit is just one universe embedded within a hyperspace containing an infinite number of other material universes, each spatially and temporally discontinuous from the others.[37] Third, let's suppose that the fundamental constants vary randomly from one universe within the hyperspace to the next, for no reason at all, without any intelligent designer responsible for the variations. The differences between universes are the result of nothing but blind chance. Stenger's hypothesis suggests the following image: the many universes exist within the hyperspace, or multiverse, somewhat like raisins within a giant plum pudding.

Next, Stenger argues, *if* our universe is just one universe within a multiverse containing an infinite number of other universes, and if the fundamental constants vary randomly from one universe to the next, there is bound to be a universe or two like ours just by blind chance alone. We just happen to exist in one of the few random universes accidentally fit for life.

So, Stenger claims, if we adopt MH, we can explain the fine-tuning coincidences without reference to a higher intelligence, by arguing like this:

1. Suppose MH is true: There is no creator, no intelligent designer, no God, nothing supernatural exists. Our cosmos is just one universe within a multiverse containing an infinite number of universes each spatially and temporally discontinuous from the rest, with the fundamental constants varying randomly from one universe to the next.

2. Out of an infinity of different universes, there is almost certain to be one or two like ours just by blind chance alone.

3. We simply happen to live in one of the few universes accidentally suited for life.

4. This explains the surprising arrangement of the constants and it does so without reference to intelligent design.

5. Since MH eliminates reference to a supernatural intelligent designer and refers only to material entities, it is simpler than the intelligent design hypothesis.

6. If two hypotheses explain the same data, the simpler is the more reasonable choice.

7. The best explanation of the cosmic coincidences is therefore the multiverse hypothesis.

8. MH is therefore the most reasonable conclusion to draw from the fine-tuning data.

Similarly, if we assume large amounts of time and zillions of flips of billions of coins, we can expect that occasionally, once every few trillion trillion trillion years, a coin flipped over and over again somewhere will come up heads one thousand times in a row by random chance alone. Stenger writes:

> The multiverse provides a very simple, purely natural, solution to the fine-tuning problem. Suppose our universe is just one of an unlimited number of individual universes that extend for an unlimited distance in all directions and for an unlimited time in the past and future. If that's the case, we just happen to live in that universe that is suited for our kind of life. . . . The multiverse explanation is adequate to refute [the fine-tuning design argument].[38]

Stenger thus rejects premise 4 of the fine-tuning argument: "no one has suggested a plausible alternative to these two hypotheses" (chance or design). However, as attractive as his naturalistic explanation seems at first glance, there are severe problems.

QUESTIONING THE MULTIVERSE HYPOTHESIS

First, according to Stenger's MH (and to any similar hypothesis), no signals or information can pass from one universe to the next. Thus, if MH is true, the other universes cannot be observed or detected empirically from our universe. It follows that no strictly *scientific* evidence could ever prove MH true. In short, Stenger's hypothesis is metaphysics, not science. Of course, it does not follow from this that the theory is false. However, MH will not be acceptable to those who seek a purely scientific explanation of the fine-tuning data.

The second problem concerns Stenger's claim in premise 5 ("Since MH eliminates reference to a supernatural intelligent designer and refers only to material entities, it is simpler than the intelligent design hypothesis"). The intelligent design hypothesis explains the arrangement of the fundamental constants in terms of one single underlying cause—an intelligent designer. In contrast, MH posits (for the most basic level of explanation) an *infinity* of empirically undetectable universes existing beyond our universe. Both hypotheses explain the same data, but intelligent design actually posits fewer entities at the most fundamental level. Intelligent design, not MH, is therefore the simpler explanation. Premise 5 is therefore false. Ockham's razor actually favors intelligent design over MH.

This observation led physicist Paul Davies to say that "to explain the [fine-tuning] coincidences by invoking an infinity of useless universes seems like carrying excess [explanatory] baggage to the extreme."[39]

MH also has internal logical problems. The philosopher C. Stephen Layman writes: "Even if we suppose that there are infinitely many universes, we do not have a guarantee that at least one will support life. Consider this simple mathematical fact: There are infinitely many even numbers. So we can have an infinity of possibilities without covering every possibility."[40]

Layman's point is that the advocate of MH cannot simply posit an infinity of other universes and be done with it, for an infinite number of *lifeless* universes is theoretically possible. Rather, the advocate of MH must posit a very special infinity of universes.

If Layman's point is not obvious, consider the following infinite sequences, each of which leaves out an infinite number of positive integers:

2, 4, 6, 8 . . .
1, 3, 5, 7 . . .

So, the advocates of MH cannot simply posit a generic infinity of separate universes and leave it at that. They must posit a specific kind of infinity out of an infinity of infinities—one containing a sufficient number of life-supporting universes. From a mathematical point of view, then, Stenger's multiverse looks as designed as Vincenzo's pizza machine. Contrary to

Stenger, it seems we need to infer an intelligent designer *even if we hypothesize a multiverse.*[41]

A new objection to MH has emerged recently in the philosophical literature. According to the "this-universe reply" first developed by Alvin Plantinga, the existence of a multiverse might explain why *some* universe or other (out of an infinity) is fit for life; it would not, however, explain why *this* specific universe — the one we inhabit — is fit for life. Plantinga writes:

> Here is one response to this many-worlds objection. True, given many universes displaying different sets of parameters [constants], the probability that one or another of them will be fine-tuned, display a life-permitting set of parameters, is high. . . . But how does that affect the probability that our universe, this particular universe is fine-tuned? Return to the Old West: I'm playing poker, and every time I deal, I get four aces and a wild card. The third time this happens, Tex jumps up, knocks over the table, draws his six gun, and accuses me of cheating. My reply: "Waal, shore, Tex, I know it's a leetle mite suspicious that every time I deal I git four aces and a wild card, but have you considered the following? Possibly there is an infinite succession of universes, so that for any possible distribution of possible poker hands, there is a universe in which that possibility is realized; we just happen to find ourselves in one where someone like me always deals himself only aces and wild cards without ever cheating. So put up that shootin' arn and set down'n shet yore yap, ya dumb galoot." Tex probably won't be satisfied; this multi-game hypothesis, even if true, is irrelevant. No doubt someone in one of those enormously many poker games deals himself all the aces and a wild card without cheating; but the probability that I (as opposed to someone or other) am honestly dealing in that magnificently self-serving way is very low. (In the same way, it is not probable that I will live to be 110 years old, although it is very likely that someone or other will.) It is vastly more likely that I am cheating; how can we blame Tex for opening fire? And doesn't the same go for the many-worlds objection to [the fine-tuning argument]?[42]

Notice that the card dealer's multigame hypothesis doesn't explain his winning hands *even if his game is one of an infinity of games being played at the time.* Likewise, Stenger's multiverse hypothesis does not explain why *this* universe is orderly.

Where does this leave us? As we saw, MH is not science, it is meta-physics. Furthermore, theism is simpler and yet explains the same data. In addition, the multiverse hypothesis does not explain the data, for it does not explain why our particular universe is orderly.

No one within science has ever given a *scientific* explanation for the fundamental fact that the universe is orderly rather than not orderly. And no one in science ever will, for as we saw in chapter 4, every large-scale scientific explanation presupposes the intelligibility and orderly nature of the universe. It follows that science by itself cannot explain why the uni-verse is orderly rather than not orderly in the large scale — that question is too fundamental for science to handle.[43]

However, the question is not too fundamental for philosophy. Philoso-phers from the start have addressed the question, and no hypothesis that does not involve mind at a fundamental level has ever succeeded in making deep sense of the fact we have been considering, that the universe appears to be both orderly and intelligible at a most fundamental level. What is the best explanation of the data? We've examined many arguments pro and con. You decide.

CONCLUDING REFLECTIONS

In *Origin of Species*, Darwin notes that when a single hypothesis explains and unifies widely divergent facts, this is a good reason to adopt it. He then argues that the main evidence for his theory of natural selection is that it explains and unifies widely divergent facts from biogeography, the fossil record, and natural history — facts that had not previously been explained or linked. Darwin supported his theory with an inference to the best explanation.

The intelligent design hypothesis explains and unifies an even wider array of divergent phenomena, for it links together facts from astrophysics, chemistry, biology, geology, and many other fields, facts that cannot be explained and unified on the basis of evolution alone. Does reason ulti-mately point us toward an intelligent designer? Is there a better explanation for the deep order of the cosmos reflected in the fortuitous arrangement of the fundamental constants?

As we saw in chapter 1, Thales and other ancient Greek philosophers had a term for the source of all order. They called it the *arche*. One of the great debates in the history of thought has concerned the question, Is the *arche* of the universe a chaos or a logos? That is, is the fundamental basis of all pure blind chance? Or is it a reasoning mind? Many of the greatest scientists of history, including Charles Darwin himself at one time in his later life, have stated that when they look deeply into the systemic order of the material universe, they sometimes experience an overwhelming inclination to see it as the expression *not* of blind chance but of a *mind*.[44] The philosopher Peter van Inwagen suggests one reason why many people resist the theistic option:

> If the Arche is a chaos, our existence has no meaning; if the Arche is a Logos, our existence has a meaning. If the Arche is a chaos, then we are just one of those things that happen from time to time. If the Arche is a Logos, then we exist for a purpose, and that is the only sense in which the existence of anything can have a "meaning." . . . If my life has no purpose, if I and everyone are the results of a series of accidents that are not part of the purpose of anyone or anything, then I am free to live my life according to my own desires. . . . If, however, there is a rational being who has designed the universe for a purpose, who could say whether that being's plans and mine were compatible? . . . Chaos won't make demands on me—a Logos might have a plan for me.[45]

Questions for Reflection and Discussion 5.2

1. How does the fine-tuning argument differ from Paley's argument?
2. What is a cosmic coincidence? Give an example.
3. Describe the deep background order said to be required for any evolutionary process.
4. In your own words, explain the main steps of the fine-tuning argument.
5. Does MH provide a better explanation of the data? Why or why not? Argue for your position.
6. Is the arrangement of the fundamental constants evidence for an intelligent designer? Offer the most intelligent and strongest reasons you can for your position.

The Cosmological Argument

PERHAPS THE BIGGEST QUESTION OF ALL

Have you ever looked up at the night sky and wondered, "Why does it all exist?" "Why is there a universe rather than nothing at all?" In chapter 5, we reflected on the fact that the universe is orderly. The question in this chapter concerns the *existence*, rather than the order, of the cosmos. The question "Why does the universe exist?" is the most fundamental question of *cosmology*, the study of the universe as a systematic whole. Cosmological questions have intrigued human beings since the dawn of history, and they continue to interest us today.

Jim Holt is a journalist who travels around the world interviewing famous thinkers and then writing books about his fascinating conversations. In *Why Does the World Exist? An Existential Detective Story*, he writes:

> Of all the mysteries that humankind has encountered, the deepest and most persistent is the mystery of existence. Why should there be a universe at all and why are we part of it? Why is there Something

rather than Nothing? . . . I vividly remember when the mystery of existence first swam into my ken. I was a callow and would-be rebellious high school student in rural Virginia. As callow and would-be rebellious high school students sometimes do, I had developed an interest in existentialism, a philosophy that seemed to hold out hope for resolving my adolescent insecurities. . . . One day I went to the local college library and checked out some impressive-looking tomes: Sartre's *Being and Nothingness* and Heidegger's *Introduction to Metaphysics*. It was in the opening pages of the latter book . . . that I was first confronted by the question, Why is there something rather than nothing at all? I can still recall being bowled over by its starkness, its purity, its sheer power. Here was the super-ultimate why question. . . . Where, I wondered, had it been all my (admittedly brief) intellectual life?[1]

Why is there something rather than nothing at all? Many scientists and philosophers have acknowledged the deep feelings of awe, wonder, and a craving to know that this ultimate question arouses. The physicist Heinz Pagels writes: "I feel anxiety as I imagine the unfathomable, silent abyss of nothingness which might have been and I experience open wonder as I acknowledge the mysterious yet simple fact that the universe exists."[2]

Ludwig Wittgenstein (1889–1951), one of the twentieth century's most influential philosophers, says this of a peculiar experience he would have from time to time: "I believe the best way of describing it is to say that when I have it I wonder at the existence of the world. And I am inclined to use such phrases as 'how extraordinary that anything should exist.'"[3]

Some people say that the ultimate cosmological question doesn't interest them. They will not find this chapter interesting. (These individuals should avoid a university course in cosmology, usually taught in the astronomy department, for the question is taken seriously there.) Others say that the ultimate cosmological question makes no sense at all. It is literally nonsense, gibberish, they claim, like the question, "What color is up?" These individuals should also skip the college course on cosmology, where the question is considered meaningful by physicists and mathematicians working on the cutting edge of big bang astrophysics.

Socrates once observed that "philosophy begins in wonder." Aristotle stated that it was wonder that led the first seekers of wisdom to philosophy.[4] Nearly every major philosopher has echoed their sentiments. The cosmological argument, which we'll examine in this chapter, is inspired by the same sense of wonder.

CAN SCIENCE ANSWER THE ULTIMATE QUESTION?

Recently, a number of prominent scientists have written popular books in which they claim to explain in scientific terms alone, without reference to God, religion, or anything supernatural, why the universe exists. If these scientists are right, science by itself has answered the ultimate cosmological question, and there is no longer any need to refer to God or to anything supernatural in order to explain where the universe comes from or why it exists.

This is what the physicist and New Atheist Lawrence Krauss claims in his 2012 *New York Times* best seller *A Universe from Nothing: Why There Is Something Rather Than Nothing.* Steven Hawking (1942–2018), the famed cosmologist and theoretical physicist who taught for many years at Cambridge University, makes the same claim in his book *The Grand Design*, coauthored with the physicist Leonard Mlodinow. Hawking's book was also a *New York Times* best seller.[5]

However, neither book delivers. Let's begin with Krauss. Why is there something rather than nothing? At the start of his book, Krauss presents the hypothesis suggested by the title of his book: the universe just popped into existence out of absolutely nothing for no reason at all—and that explains its existence. However, later in the book, perhaps because he realizes that this is not actually a scientific explanation, Krauss shifts to another explanation.[6] The material universe, he claims, *may* have come into existence out of a "quantum haze." What is this? It is a gigantic field of energy governed by the complex equations of quantum physics.

Noting the title of Krauss's book (*A Universe from Nothing*), critics were quick to point out that a quantum haze full of energy is not nothing; it is a very big something governed by physical laws. David Albert, professor of physics and philosophy at Columbia University, who holds doctorates in both fields, slams Krauss's claim that science by itself has now explained why something rather than nothing exists. Quantum physics "has nothing whatsoever to say on the subject of where [the quantum haze] came from, or of why the world should have consisted of the particular kinds of fields it does, or of why it should have consisted of fields at all, or of why there should have been a world in the first place. Period. Case closed. End of story."[7]

If Krauss does not succeed in answering—in scientific terms alone—the ultimate cosmological question, perhaps Hawking, then the most famous physicist in the world, does better. The answer, Hawking and his coauthor claim, is simple: the universe was brought into existence by the law of gravity acting within a quantum field. "Because there is a law like gravity, the universe can and will create itself from nothing." Thus, "the beginning of the universe was governed by the laws of science and doesn't need to be set in motion by some god."[8] It follows that it "is not necessary to invoke God to light the blue touch paper and set the universe going."[9] Is Hawking's logic correct?

Think critically here. Has he explained—in strictly scientific terms alone—why there is something rather than nothing? Has he explained how the universe came to be out of absolutely *nothing*?

Of course not. Critics quickly noted that Hawking's explanation for the fact that the universe exists—preexisting gravity acting within a preexisting quantum field brought everything into existence—is no better than Krauss's. The reason is plain. Gravity acting within a quantum field is not nothing—it is a definite something. Hawking and Mlodinow do not even attempt to explain why the original force of gravity exists, let alone why the first quantum field exists, why the laws of nature exist, and why the laws of nature take their existing form. Thus, all three physicists leave the most fundamental questions unanswered, including these:

- Why is there a law of gravity rather than no law of gravity at all?
- Why does the law of gravity assume an inverse square form rather than some other?
- Why are there laws of physics rather than no laws at all?
- Why is there a quantum haze rather than no haze?
- What accounts for the existence of the initial quantum field? Why not a *non*quantum field? Why are there any fields at all?

And, of course,

- Why is there something rather than nothing?

Despite the grand promises made in their best-selling books, these famous scientists simply do not deliver.

Going Deeper. Logicians say that the equations of quantum mechanics and universal gravitation are logically contingent. By this they mean that the equations could have been different than they are. But if they could have been otherwise, the question arises, Why are they just so and not otherwise? Contingent structures never provide an intellectually satisfying stopping point for a series of explanations. Steven Weinberg, one of the twentieth century's greatest theoretical physicists, writes:

> I have to admit that, even when physicists will have gone as far as they can go, when we have a final theory, we will not have a completely satisfying picture of the world, because we will still be left with the question "Why?" Why this theory, rather than some other theory? For example, why is the world described by quantum mechanics? Quantum mechanics is the one part of our present physics that is likely to survive intact in any future theory, but there is nothing *logically inevitable* [i.e., logically necessary] about quantum mechanics; I can imagine a universe governed by Newtonian mechanics instead. *So there seems to be an irreducible mystery that science will not eliminate.* (Emphasis mine)[10]

Weinberg is expressing the sense of incompleteness that many feel when they contemplate the final answers physicists such as Krauss, Hawking, and Mlodinow give to the ultimate cosmological question.

WHY SCIENCE CAN'T EVEN IN PRINCIPLE ANSWER THE QUESTION

There is a theoretical reason why science alone cannot, even in principle, explain why there is something rather than nothing. The reason, in a nutshell, is that science explains how the universe works, not why it exists. To elaborate, the most fundamental scientific theories explain how *already existing* space, time, matter, and energy interact, how they behave, and what predictions can be made by observing objects within the universe. Those theories do not explain why matter, energy, time, and space exist in the first place. Nor do they explain why the laws of nature exist. Examine the explanations in any standard physics, chemistry, or biology textbook for confirmation.

Here is an example to help make the point more concrete. When I was a child, I was fascinated by the amazing chemical phenomena I observed using my 1960 Lionel-Porter chemistry experiment set. I especially remember the reaction that occurred when I mixed vinegar and baking soda to produce a foaming chemical volcano. The scientific explanation goes about like this:

1. It is a law of chemistry that when vinegar (acetic acid) and baking soda (sodium bicarbonate) combine, carbon dioxide is released in accord with the following equation:

$$NaHCO_3(s) + CH_3COOH(l) \rightarrow CO_2(g) + H_2O(l) + Na^+(aq) + CH_3COO^-(aq)[11]$$

2. I mixed vinegar and baking soda.

3. Therefore, carbon dioxide was given off.

Notice that the existence of the chemical elements is not explained; it is presupposed. The explanation also presupposes the prior existence of the laws of chemistry, chemical compounds (vinegar and baking soda), and my laboratory apparatus. But every scientific explanation is like this.

Here is an analogy. Suppose that I have a watch in my hand, and I am explaining how it works. I tell you that this part moves that part, which moves this part, and so forth. When I finish explaining how the watch works, have I explained why the watch *exists*? Of course not. Won't I need to refer to a watchmaker to answer that question? Notice that the *maker* of the watch exists before the watch exists. To attempt to explain, in purely scientific terms, the fact that the material universe exists—without reference to something beyond space, time, matter, energy, and the laws of physics—would be like attempting to explain the existence of a specific watch by explaining how the gears and springs *inside* the watch function.

In an earlier book, Hawking seems to be aware of this point::

Even if there is only one possible unified theory [of physics], it is just a set of rules and equations. What is it that breathes fire into the equations and makes a universe for them to describe? The usual approach of science of constructing a mathematical model cannot answer the question of why there should be a universe for the model to describe. Why does the universe go to all the bother of existing?[12]

Exactly. This, in brief, is why science will never, by itself, answer the fundamental cosmological question.

This is not to say that science is invalid or that science is all wrong. Science explains many things. Science has deepened our knowledge of the world. This is only to say that the ultimate question of cosmology is beyond its theoretical reach. The point is not new. About 2,400 years ago, Socrates, Plato, and Aristotle argued that the physical sciences alone cannot explain everything. In this book, we'll examine many other aspects of our world that cannot be explained by science alone, including the nature of truth, knowledge, consciousness, free will, morality, and social justice. These thoughts indicate that we'll have to go deeper than science if we're going to answer the most fundamental questions of all. We are now ready for the cosmological argument.

Questions for Reflection and Discussion 6.1

1. Was there a time in your life when you asked, and thought about, the ultimate question, "Why does the universe exist?" If so, can you describe the experience?
2. In your own words, explain either Krauss's argument or Hawking's argument. Does either succeed in answering the ultimate question? Offer the most intelligent and strongest reasons you can for your position.
3. In your own words, explain the argument for the claim that science alone cannot answer the fundamental cosmological question.

INTRODUCING THE COSMOLOGICAL ARGUMENT

Philosophers use the term *cosmological argument* to refer to any philosophical argument that reasons from the fact that the universe exists or from some elemental aspect of its existence to the existence of God or a supreme being understood as the creator of the material universe. Hundreds of variations have been developed by philosophers over the centuries. Although versions of the cosmological argument can be found in the writings of Plato, Aristotle, and most major philosophers up to the twentieth century, several of the most influential statements were given by Thomas Aquinas (1225–74), arguably the greatest philosopher of the Middle Ages. His most famous argument will be our focus.

So, in the second question of his 4,000-page masterpiece, *Summa theologica*, Aquinas states that there are five general ways to establish the existence of God through reason and observation alone, thus without reference to sacred scripture, feelings, faith, or religious authority.[13] Aquinas presented each of the "Five Ways" (as they are called) as an argument in a step-by-step format. However, each argument is only a paragraph long, and all five can be read in half an hour. This causes some to ask, "Can God's existence really be proved that quickly?" In addition, each of the five arguments contains one or more logical gaps—holes that critics invariably point out.

Why are the Five Ways so short? And why are they incomplete? There is a logical reason. Aquinas wrote the *Summa theologica* for teachers and scholars, not for the average layman, who at the time was most likely a farmer working long days on a medieval manor. Few farmers in the thirteenth century—anywhere in the world—had time to read a 4,000-page book. The Five Ways are summaries of well-known lines of reasoning, rather than complete arguments, written as guides for teachers and college students who, Aquinas assumed, would fill in the gaps and complete the reasoning themselves.

It is therefore the job of each philosopher to flesh out the Five Ways as he or she sees fit, as reasonably as possible, as part of his or her teaching assignment. The single argument we're about to examine step-by-step is one way to fill in the second of Aquinas's Five Ways. Here's the big point: If the conclusion of Aquinas's argument is true, then the question with which we began this chapter—the ultimate cosmological question—has a definite answer. An answer reached by careful reasoning.

Aquinas's Second Way

We begin with Aquinas's summary statement:

> The second way is from the nature of the efficient cause. In the world of sense we find there is an order of efficient causes. There is no case

known (neither is it, indeed, possible) in which a thing is found to be the efficient cause of itself; for so it would be prior to itself, which is impossible. Now in efficient causes it is not possible to go on to infinity, because in all efficient causes following in order, the first is the cause of the intermediate cause, and the intermediate is the cause of the ultimate cause, whether the intermediate cause be several, or only one. Now to take away the cause is to take away the effect. Therefore, if there be no first cause among efficient causes, there will be no ultimate, nor any intermediate cause. But if in efficient causes it is possible to go on to infinity, there will be no first efficient cause, neither will there be an ultimate effect, nor any intermediate efficient causes; all of which is plainly false. Therefore it is necessary to admit a first efficient cause, to which everyone gives the name of God.[14]

I will now restate and flesh out Aquinas's reasoning in the form of a numbered sequence of premises leading to an ultimate conclusion, with each premise supported by a subargument. Here are the basic premises.

1. When we carefully observe the material universe, we find it to be one large series of orderly causes and effects.

2. It is impossible that some individual thing is the cause of itself.

3. An orderly series of causes and effects, with each cause explained in terms of a prior cause, cannot go back infinitely far.

4. Therefore, necessarily, the universal series of causes and effects has a First Cause, which everyone calls God.

The word *necessarily* indicates this is a deductive argument (an argument claiming that the conclusion *must* be true if the premises are true). Next, the argument clearly is deductively valid—that is, if the premises are true, then the conclusion indeed must be true. Since the argument is valid, the only question is, Are the premises all true? And if the premises are all true, then the conclusion is certain. However, before we turn to this matter, we must understand Aquinas's terminology. What does he mean by a system of "orderly causes and effects"?

We all understand in an intuitive sense the ordinary meaning of *cause and effect*. Leaving milk out on a hot day causes it to sour. Dropping an ordinary wine glass onto a concrete patio causes it to shatter. Baking bread dough causes it to rise. In general, if A is the cause of B, then B must happen once A has happened in the same sense that milk must sour if it is left out on a hot day, an ordinary glass must shatter if it is dropped onto concrete, and so on. Aquinas intends our ordinary meaning of cause and effect.

Next, we all know that causes and effects can be arranged in an orderly series in which A causes B, B causes C, and so forth. The horse's motion causes the coach to move, the moving coach causes the passengers to move, and so forth.[15]

Next, a series of causes that goes back infinitely far (and thus has no first member) is called an "infinite regression." Imagine that I borrow a book from A, who previously borrowed it from B, who previously borrowed it from C, and so forth back and back. If we suppose that the book is infinitely old and if we assume that the series of borrowers—each borrowing a book from a previous borrower—goes back infinitely far, with no book creator, no first borrower, and no beginning, *that* would be an infinite regression. In general, an infinite regression is a series of objects in which each object depends in some way on the previous object in the series, back and back without end. With the basic terms defined, we turn to the subarguments supporting the major premises.

Argument for Premise 1

Plain observation reveals the many causes and effects operating within the universe. Next, like scientists today, scientists in Aquinas's day saw the universe as one interconnected system of causes and effects ultimately constituting a single overall causal regress. This insight, which goes back to the ancient Greeks, has been confirmed by the latest scientific discoveries. For example, in *The Little Book of the Big Bang: A Cosmic Primer*, the astrophysicist Craig Hogan condenses the history of the material universe into a single overall chain of causes and effects tracing back to a single creation event.[16] And we have already considered the words of the physicist Steven Weinberg:

> Think of the space of scientific theories as being filled with arrows, pointing toward each principle and away from the others by which it is explained. These arrows of explanation have already revealed a remark-

able pattern: They do not form separate disconnected clumps, representing independent sciences, and they do not wander aimlessly — rather they are all connected and if followed backward (to deeper levels) they all seem to flow from a common starting point.[17]

Aquinas was thus in line with today's big bang astrophysics when he began his argument with the fact that causes and effects can be organized by the scientist into a single overall cause and effect regression.

Argument for Premise 2

Aquinas writes that ". . . for so it would be prior to itself, which is impossible." Let's clarify his idea. The cause exists independently of the effect: the baker (the cause of the bread) exists before the bread exists, the factory exists before the car exists, and so forth. Now, for an entity to cause itself to exist, it would have to exist independently of its own existence, and then bring itself into existence. This is self-contradictory. But self-contradiction is the mark of the impossible. It is therefore impossible that something caused itself to exist. Of course, given this premise, Aquinas will not be able to claim later that God caused himself to exist. But this is fine, for Aquinas never claims — and no serious philosopher has ever claimed — that God caused himself to exist. Premise 2 seems eminently logical.

Argument for Premise 3

Aquinas gives an argument for this premise, but many philosophers believe that his argument has a flaw. As we saw, he writes:

> Because in all efficient causes following in order, the first is the cause of the intermediate cause, and the intermediate is the cause of the ultimate cause, whether the intermediate cause be several, or only one. Now to take away the cause is to take away the effect. Therefore, if there be no first cause among efficient causes, there will be no ultimate, nor any intermediate cause. But if in efficient causes it is possible to go on to infinity, there will be no first efficient cause, neither will there be an ultimate effect, nor any intermediate efficient causes; all of which is plainly false.[18]

Critics have objected as follows. If we assume that the regression of causes is infinite rather than finite, we are not "taking away," or removing, a first cause or any particular cause. Rather, we are simply noting that the series has no first member. Of course, in any linear series of causes, if we reach in and remove a specific cause from the series, leaving a gap, then no subsequent causes will operate. But we do nothing of the sort when we deny the existence of a first cause and posit an infinite regression. That is, we do not remove a cause and leave a gap—an infinite regression has no gap.

This criticism of Aquinas is correct on a surface reading of the text, but I believe that it is based on a mistaken interpretation of the subargument Aquinas intended for premise 3. There is a more reasonable—and therefore more charitable—interpretation of Aquinas's words. I believe that Aquinas is assuming at this point that the universe is intelligible. As we have seen, this assumption has been an integral part of philosophical and scientific explanation since the days of Thales, and it is a principle philosophers and scientists rely on today. Indeed, the thesis of the intelligibility of the universe not only guides research at every level in every academic subject, it is confirmed anew every time science makes an advance to a more fundamental level. The point deserves emphasis: every scientific advance confirms the thesis of the fundamental intelligibility of the universe.

But if the universe is intelligible, then there is an explanation, known or unknown, for everything that exists, for an existing object lacking any explanation at all of its existence would be a partially unintelligible object.

With the intelligibility thesis as background, I believe that Aquinas intended the following subargument. If we hypothesize that a currently active causal series regresses to infinity, then there is no explanation at all for the fact that the series as a whole exists, for the hypothesis of an infinite regression explains nothing. If so, then the universe is not intelligible. But the universe is intelligible. Therefore, the ultimate explanation is not an infinite regression. If the regression is not infinite, then cause and effect trace back to a First Cause.

But why suppose that an infinite regression explains nothing? First, an infinite regression, if one were to exist, would be a series of entities each caused or explained by a prior entity in the series, back and back without end. If the history of the universe is an infinite regression, then each thing in existence was caused by a previous thing, which was caused by a previous thing, back infinitely far. To anyone attempting to explain why the universe exists, this idea sounds promising at first glance because if each thing was caused by a prior thing, infinitely far back, then it seems that nothing lacks an explanation. (This assumes that one way to explain the existence of a thing is to cite its cause.)

To see why this won't work, consider this analogy. Suppose that person A is holding a book in her hands, and someone asks, "Why does the book exist?" The questioner means, "What explains the fact that the book exists?" Suppose that A replies, "I borrowed the book from B." Would that explain why the book exists? Certainly not. Suppose that A replies, "I borrowed the book from B, who borrowed it from C, who borrowed it from D." Would that explain why the book exists? Obviously not. For borrowers pass on already existing books; they do not create books.

Now suppose that A proposes an infinite regression explanation: "The series of book borrowers goes back forever. The book is thus infinitely old—for an eternity of time it has been passing from one borrower to another, back and back without end." Would that hypothesis explain the book's *existence*? It would not. That would explain how *old* the book is. It would also explain how A came to possess the book, how B came to possess the book, and so forth. However, an infinite regression hypothesis would not explain the fact that the book *exists*.

To put the point another way, an infinite regression of book borrowers would not explain the fact that a preexisting book has been passing from one borrower to another along an infinite series of borrows forever. The question left unanswered would be, Why does the infinitely old book exist rather than not exist?

Similarly, an infinite regression hypothesis won't explain the fact that the universe—understood as an arena of active causes and effects—exists. Infinite regression simply shifts our thoughts to the question, Why does an infinitely old universe exist? This, in brief, is why the mainstream view in philosophy, from ancient times to the present, has been that an infinite regression of causes ultimately explains *nothing*. If the universe is intelligible, then its history is not an infinite regression.

INTRODUCING THE PRINCIPLE OF SUFFICIENT REASON

During the rise of modern science, the background assumption employed by Aquinas (and every philosopher going back to Thales) that the universe is intelligible was named the *principle of sufficient reason*. Since we'll be referencing this principle many times, let's use its common abbreviation PSR.

The PSR has been stated in many different ways, some quite technical. Here is one precise way to state it. For every fact F there is a sufficient reason, known or unknown, that explains why F is the case. According to this version of the PSR, if it is a fact that my car broke down yesterday at noon, there is a sufficient reason why it broke down at exactly that time. If it is a fact that the dog Rover has twenty-three fleas on his back, there is a sufficient reason why his back contains twenty-three fleas. The claim that the universe is intelligible is a form of the PSR. The following idea seems to be what Aquinas had in mind:

> PSR: For each existing being and every collection of beings, there is a reason, or explanation, known or unknown, accounting for the fact of its existence.

Imagine that one morning while you are having breakfast, a baby aardvark pops into existence out of thin air on the table in front of you. Nothing caused it to exist. It has no parents. It came from nowhere. It simply popped into being, fully formed, out of absolutely nothing, from no cause and for no reason at all. Is that even a coherent idea? According to the PSR that I attribute to Aquinas, such an event is not physically possible. Now, if the PSR in this form is true, then Aquinas's third premise seems eminently reasonable, for if the regress of causes is an infinite regression, then there is no explanation for the fact that the universe exists. But is the PSR true?

The PSR—stated in one form or another—has been accepted and employed by every major philosopher from the start of the discipline. Is that at least a partial reason to accept the principle? Perhaps. But the mere fact that the PSR has been employed by major philosophers and scientists throughout history doesn't prove the principle true.

Some philosophers have defended the PSR by arguing that "it is . . . a basic assumption that rational people make, whether or not they reflect sufficiently to become aware of the assumption."[19] This argument also fails, argues philosopher William Rowe, for even if the PSR is a shared assumption so basic to our conceptual framework that most of us are unaware it is present, the principle might nevertheless be false. For "nature," he writes, "is not bound to satisfy our presuppositions."[20]

Can something more be said in favor of version of the PSR that I attribute to Aquinas? Yes. The philosopher Richard Purtill has given an empirical argument. Here is my summary:

> If the PSR is true, then it is not possible that something pops into existence out of nothing for no reason. If the PSR is false, then we should expect that at least occasionally a macroscopic object simply pops into existence out of nothing for no reason. For instance, a purple elephant wearing a yellow raincoat and green shorts just materializes out of thin air in front of you as you walk down the street. But this sort of thing has never been observed. Not one counterexample to the principle has ever been confirmed. The best explanation is that the PSR, in the form attributed to Aquinas, is true. This is a sufficient reason to accept the principle.[21]

Purtill's argument dovetails with an argument we examined in chapter 4, namely, Nagel's argument for the claim that the success of deep physics indicates that the universe is fundamentally intelligible. If his argument is cogent, that is another reason to accept the version of the PSR I am attributing to Aquinas. But if the PSR is reasonable, Aquinas's third premise is reasonable too. Is the PSR a reasonable proposition? Important questions for any philosophical account of the world. You decide.

BEFORE WE GO FURTHER

This concludes my interpretation of Aquinas's argument. Some advice before we proceed. When reading a philosophical argument, it's a good idea to try to understand it before judging it. The reason is obvious. How can you effectively criticize an argument if you haven't first understood it? There will be time to criticize after it has been understood. We'll consider objections in a moment.

Keep in mind that there are two ways a deductive argument can be flawed. First, one or more premises might be false. Second, the conclusion might not validly follow from the premises, even if they are true. It follows that if you reject the conclusion of a deductive argument, it is incumbent on you as a critical thinker to either provide an argument showing that one or more of the premises are false or provide an argument showing that the conclusion does not validly follow from the premises even if they are true.

So, if you reject the conclusion of Aquinas's Second Way as presented here, you have a philosophical duty to either provide an argument showing that one of the premises is false or provide an argument showing that the argument is invalid, that is, that the conclusion does not validly follow from the premises. (Remember that a valid deductive argument has this feature: If the premises are true, then the conclusion *must* be true.)

Finally, a couple of additional points bear repeating. Aquinas's Second Way, as we have filled it in, contradicts nothing in science. In addition, although it reaches deeper than science reaches, it proceeds through a reasoned examination of cause and effect, which is standard practice in science and in everyday life. For example, the noted science writer and physicist James Trefil suggests that tracing cause and effect back and back is the strategy of modern scientific cosmology: "Since the discovery of the expansion of the universe in the 1920s, one goal of cosmology has been to trace the history of the universe—in effect, to run the film backward until we can see and understand how the universe came into being."[22]

Aquinas's cosmological argument gives expression to the universal human desire to make sense of the universe as a whole—a rational desire to go beyond the partial explanations given by physical science alone. Like the broader discipline in which it is situated, the argument begins in wonder— the wonder of it all.

Questions for Reflection and Discussion 6.2

1. Summarize Aquinas's argument in your own words, as if you are talking to your neighbor or the typical "person on the street."
2. If you do not accept the conclusion of the Second Way, then how do *you* explain the fact that the universe exists? What is your alternative explanation?
3. If you do not accept the conclusion of the Second Way, then which specific premise do you reject, and what is your argument against that premise? Make your case.
4. Whether or not you believe in God, what do you mean by the word *God*?

COMMON MISUNDERSTANDINGS
OF AQUINAS'S LOGIC

"There's nothing wrong with infinite regression"

The question of infinite regression is one of the most important in all of philosophy. We met the Scottish philosopher David Hume (1711–76) in chapter 4. In *Dialogues Concerning Natural Religion* (published posthumously in 1778), Hume gives what some believe to be the most powerful objection ever made to the cosmological argument. Hume argues that the hypothesis of an infinite regression would, contrary to Aquinas's claim, fully explain the fact that the universe, with all of its causes and effects, exists. If so, then there is no need to suppose that there is a First Cause. Here is his argument in full:

> In tracing an eternal succession of objects, it seems absurd to inquire for a general cause or first author. . . . In such a chain . . . or succession of objects, each part is caused by that which preceded it, and causes that which succeeds it. Where then is the difficulty? But the WHOLE, you say, wants a cause. I answer, that the uniting of these parts into a whole, like the uniting of several distinct members into one body, is performed merely by an arbitrary act of the mind, and has no influence on the nature of things. Did I show you the particular causes of each individual in a collection of twenty particles of matter, I should think it very unreasonable, should you afterwards ask me, what was the cause of the whole twenty. This is sufficiently explained in explaining the cause of the parts.[23]

Hume's reasoning is not easy to grasp. Here is one way to break it down:

1. In ordinary circumstances, to cite the cause of a material object is to explain its existence.

2. If each part of a whole has an explanation, then nothing is left unexplained.

3. If nothing is left unexplained, then no further explanation is needed.

4. Each cause in an infinite series of causes has a cause.

5. Therefore, each part of an infinite series of causes has an explanation.

6. So, an infinite series of causes leaves nothing unexplained.

7. Thus, if we suppose that the series of causes and effects goes back forever, then nothing is left unexplained.

8. If there is nothing left to explain, there is need to suppose that a first cause exists.

9. Therefore, if we posit an infinite regression, there is no need to believe in God or a first cause.

What are we to make of this intriguing argument? Was Aquinas wrong? Does an infinite regression of causes explain everything with no remainder? Is there no need to posit a first cause? Or did Hume miss something important? The consensus among philosophers who specialize in the philosophy of religion today is that Hume missed something extremely important. Let's investigate.

Hume was clearly right to note that every cause in an infinite series of causes has a preceding cause. Therefore, every cause in an infinite regression has an explanation. However, it does not follow from this that the series *as a whole* is completely explained. This is the point Hume missed. Consider a new example.

Imagine a long line of railroad boxcars rolling along railroad tracks up a hill. Why are the cars moving rather than standing still? The question arises because a boxcar, lacking a motor or any other internal source of motion, doesn't move itself. Suppose someone offers the following explanation: "The boxcar in front — boxcar 1 — is moving because it is being pushed by the boxcar behind it — boxcar 2."

This explains why boxcar 1 is moving, but it doesn't explain why boxcar 2 is moving. It also doesn't explain why the series as a whole is moving (rather than standing still).

Now suppose that someone says, "Boxcar 2 is moving because it is being pushed by the car behind it, boxcar 3." This explains why boxcar 2 is moving, but it doesn't explain the motion of boxcar 3. It also doesn't explain why the series as a whole is in motion.

Now imagine that the series of boxcars stretches as far as the eye can see. We stand before the tracks with the question still unanswered: Why are they all moving rather than standing still? Since we have entered the realm of science fiction, let's suppose that Hume suddenly appears in front of us, having stepped into a time-travel machine back in 1775. Upon seeing our puzzlement, he offers the following explanation:

> The series is infinite. Each boxcar is moved by the one behind it, which is moved by the one before it, without end. There is no First Mover or First Cause. But this is not a problem. The motion of each boxcar has an explanation (in terms of the motion of the car before it). So, no individual car's motion lacks an explanation. Therefore, each part of the series has an explanation. It follows that there is nothing left to explain—and no reason to posit a first boxcar pushing all the others.

So Hume might say. But does his infinite regression explanation work? Does it explain what it is meant to explain? The consensus in philosophy is that it does not. Hume's infinite regression hypothesis leaves unanswered the following clearly meaningful question: Why are the (infinitely many) boxcars moving rather than standing still? Put another way, Why is the series in motion rather than idle? Infinite regression doesn't touch that question. (Think carefully about this before moving on.) It follows that there is a fact that the infinite regression hypothesis doesn't explain: *the motion of the series as a whole.* Contrary to Hume's general principle, then, although the motion of each part of the series has an explanation, the motion of the series as a whole remains unexplained. Hume's sixth premise does not follow from the previous five, and his seventh premise does not follow from the previous six.

Let's now suppose that the series of boxcars is not endless. The series stretches back a finite distance to a first boxcar. Furthermore, suppose that behind the first boxcar is a locomotive pushing it and thereby imparting motion to it, which the first boxcar then transmits to the next car, and so on down the line to the one in front of us. The motion of the series of boxcars as a whole has now been explained.

Notice that a locomotive is not a boxcar. It exists outside the series of moving boxcars needing explanation. Furthermore, a locomotive is a different kind of entity altogether. For a locomotive, unlike a boxcar, is a self-moving object—it generates its own motion from within itself. Put another way, a locomotive is not being pushed—it pushes.

This is a philosophically attractive solution. The locomotive hypothesis explains the data—the motion of the boxcars—in a complete, or categorical way, in the sense that it does so without referring to any prior *motion*. The locomotive explanation, unlike Hume's explanation, puts the initial question to rest, for once we hypothesize a self-moving locomotive as the first cause, the motion of the whole is explained, *including the motion of the locomotive*.

Are Circular Regressions Better?

Some people try to support infinite regression in a different way. They claim that if the series of causes and effects travels in a closed circle instead of a linear regression, then a complete explanation is achieved. However, an example suggested by the philosopher Richard Purtill shows the mistake in their argument. Suppose you do not understand the meaning of the word *abab*. Fortunately, you are told that *abab* means "glog." But the word *glog* has no meaning to you. Luckily, someone tells you that *glog* means "wlog." But *wlog* means nothing to you. Now, suppose that the series of explanations circles around on itself: *wlog*, you are told, means "abab." Does the closed circle of explanations explain the meaning of *abab*? It does not. Does a circular regression shed any more light than an infinite linear one? Aristotle gave a similar argument for the claim that not every word can be defined.[24]

Going Deeper. Exactly why does an infinite regression fail to explain? Philosophers and mathematicians since Aquinas's time have thought a great deal about this question and about the nature of infinity. Today they have a fuller understanding of the problem. In a nutshell, an infinite regression fails to explain anything because each of the linked explanations within the infinite series is only a hypothetical (if, then) explanation. Not a single one is categorical, or complete in itself, but only a categorical explanation can complete an explanatory series.

Consider the boxcars again. The motion of boxcar 1 is explained *only if* the motion of boxcar 2, which is pushing it, has already been explained. But the motion of boxcar 2 is explained *only if* the motion of boxcar 3 has been explained, and so on. Each explanation passes the explanatory bill to the previous explanation, like one flat broke concertgoer after another in an infinite line of concertgoers outside a venue telling the ticket-taker that the person behind him will pay. No one explanation in an infinite series is categorical, or fully explanatory in its own right (no concertgoer ever pays). Thus the question that generated the regress is never answered (the venue never receives any money).

But why suppose that a hypothetical explanation is incomplete? Imagine that a bank has been robbed. Shortly after the crime, the police spot the infamous bank robber Joe Doakes carrying a thick wad of $100 bills marked with the bank's red dye. When they ask for an explanation, he replies, "*If* I received this money through a legal transaction from someone who legally owned it, then I possess it legally and did not rob the bank." Doakes has given the police a hypothetical explanation. Does his reply explain why he is actually holding the money? Clearly not. The police are going to ask, "Who gave it to you?" Suppose they discover that Joe received the money from Herman Snodgrass. Upon being questioned, Mr. Snodgrass replies, "*If* I received this money through a legal transaction from someone who legally owned it, then I possess it legally and did not rob the bank."

Isn't it clear that no matter how many hypothetical, or "if-then," explanations are given, the police are never going to have the answer they are seeking? The police are looking for a categorical explanation, one that is complete without reference to a prior explanation. Notice that they will have the answer they are seeking if they find someone who says, categorically, "I robbed the bank." In short, they won't find an answer until they reach a categorical explanation.

Since the question of infinite regression is so crucial and yet so often misunderstood, here is one more analogy for you to ponder, this one adapted from an idea suggested by the philosopher Robert Martin.[25] A group of extremely shy people have all been invited to the same party. Suppose that A will go *if* B will go but not otherwise. Suppose that B will go *if* C will go but not otherwise. Suppose that C will go *if* D will go, and so forth. Each will *hypothetically* go, that is, each will go *if* someone else goes. Now, if no one in the series categorically will go, that is, if no one will simply go with or without the others going, then no one goes — no matter how many shy people are added to the series.

The flaw in Hume's reasoning should now be evident. He failed to notice the distinction between hypothetical and categorical explanations. Had he recognized the difference, he would have realized that an endless explanatory regression contains only hypothetical explanations and for that reason explains nothing.

"It's always existed, so there's nothing for a Creator to have done"

This misunderstanding is closely related to Hume's mistake. "The danger that science poses for theism," the philosopher Keith Parsons argues, "is that as science progresses, God seemingly becomes increasingly irrelevant. A creator has to have something to do."[26] Parsons claims that if we suppose that the universe has simply always existed, then there's nothing for a creator to have done, and therefore there is no need to suppose that the universe has a creator or First Cause. Thus, he urges, let's simply assume that the cosmos is eternal.

The philosopher Derek Parfit offers the perfect response. If we assume that the universe has always existed, this just raises the follow-up question, Why does an *infinitely old* universe exist? The assumption of an eternal universe, Parfit argues, does not put the ultimate cosmological question to rest at all.

The philosopher Richard Taylor agrees and points out that "it is no answer to the question, why a thing exists, to state how long it has existed. A geologist does not suppose that he has explained why there should be rivers and mountains merely by pointing out that they are old."[27]

This may be the point the great physicist Stephen Hawking was making when he poignantly observed at the end of his *A Brief History of Time* that if physicists were to finally verify a grand unified theory of the universe, which would be a system of interrelated mathematical equations describing the overall physical structure of the cosmos, we would still need to ask, "What is it that breathes fire into the equations and makes there a universe for them to describe? The usual approach of science of constructing a mathematical model cannot answer the question of why there should be a universe for the model to describe. Why does the universe go to all the bother of existing?"[28]

The mathematician and physicist Roger Penrose, Hawking's colleague at Cambridge University, makes the same point in a different way when he writes, "Once you have put more and more of your physical world into a mathematical structure, you realize how profound and mysterious this mathematical structure is. How you can get all these things out of it is very mysterious."[29]

Theists seem to be in good company, then, when they continue to press the question of existence even in the face of Parsons's nonscientific assumption that the universe has always existed. The existence of an active universe saturated with cause and effect—no matter how old it is—is simply not explained by saying, "It has always existed."

"Why not a physical first cause within the material universe?"

This objection presupposes some context. In the *Summa theologica*, after Aquinas states his Five Ways, he goes on to argue, in a separate argument, that the First Cause must be a nonmaterial, supernatural being existing above and beyond the material universe. He also argues that the First Cause must be omnipotent (all-powerful), omniscient (all-knowing) and omnibenevolent (all-good). Although we will not examine his complex reasoning—to do so would take us far into the field known as "philosophical theology"—some plain considerations about cause and effect suggest that the First Cause is not simply a material entity within the material universe.

Consider that a cause is logically distinct from, and in some explanatory sense prior to, its effect. The cause of the bread—the baker—exists before the bread. Furthermore, the baker is not himself or herself *made of bread*. Now, the material universe is the interconnected system of causes and effects embedded in space and time and encompassing all material objects, quanta of energy, forces and fields. The First Cause is the cause of all of *that*. It follows that the First Cause must transcend space, time, energy, and matter. The First Cause, in short, must be a supernatural being. Further reflection adds that the First Cause possesses degrees of knowledge and power beyond human comprehension. The divine attributes (omnipotence, omniscience, etc.) are studied in advanced courses in philosophy of religion and philosophical theology. [30]

These thoughts suggest something of great significance for the philosophically inclined: the conclusion Aquinas reaches in the Second Way is only the first part of the ultimate explanation. For those who want to go deeper, the next step is to study theories of the nature of God proposed and defended by Plato, Aristotle, Augustine, Aquinas, and many other theistic philosophers East and West down to the present day. Philosophy, as most of the major philosophers throughout history have argued, is a spiritual journey to God, an ascent of the soul and the intellect toward what Thales first called the "One over the Many."

Introducing Mere Theism

Aquinas did not claim that his Five Ways by themselves—without additional argument—establish the existence of God as *God* is defined within Christianity or within any specific religion. He only claimed that his arguments show that the material universe was created by a supreme being whose existence and nature transcends space, time, matter, and energy. But this generic claim is the core belief common to Judaism, Islam, Christianity, and many other monotheistic world religions. Some new terminology will be helpful here. Let's call the core belief common to many monotheistic religions—that the material universe was created by a supreme being who exists beyond space and time—"mere theism." Although it is not an argument for Christianity, Aquinas's Second Way is certainly an argument for mere theism. This explains why Aquinas adds to the conclusion of his Second Way, "to which everyone gives the name of God."

"Why not millions of First Causes?"

In addition to favoring infinite regression, Hume also challenged monotheism. Why, he asked, should we postulate only one First Cause? Why not many (polytheism)? As a colleague once mockingly put it to me in a discussion during a philosophy conference, "Why one God? Why not millions? The more the merrier!"

Defenders of the cosmological argument have a strong reply here. As we saw in chapter 4, philosophers and scientists from the earliest times have agreed that when two hypotheses equally explain the same data, the simpler of the two (the hypothesis that makes the fewest assumptions or posits the fewest entities) is the more reasonable choice. Science cannot operate without this principle or one very much like it. As we saw in chapter 4, this principle of explanation is called "Ockham's razor" in honor of William of Ockham (1287–1347), a medieval logician and scientific pioneer who was the first to state it explicitly and defend it. Ockham's principle is now an integral part of scientific practice because (again) scientists discovered that (1) for every set of data, an infinite number of explanations are possible, each of increasing complexity, and (2) it is impossible to choose one explanation without assuming Ockham's principle or one like it.

The application is obvious. Consider the conclusion that one First Cause exists. Now consider the conclusion that two independent first causes exist. Both hypotheses explain the same data; however, the first is simpler. Ockham's razor supports Aquinas over Hume on this one.

Modern scientific cosmology gives us further reasons to posit one rather than many first causes. For instance, big bang astrophysicists have discovered that all chains of cause and effect—throughout the entire universe—coalesce into a single, unified series that traces back to a single starting point. As I have already noted, in *The Little Book of the Big Bang: A Cosmic Primer*, the astronomer Craig Hogan condenses the history of the material universe into one chain of causes and effects that stems from a single creation event.[31] And as we've seen, Steven Weinberg, one of the leading physicists of our time, argues the same point.

Aquinas was more correct than he could have known when he maintained that there is just one (large) cause-and-effect regression of material causes tracing back to one first cause—a fact that supports monotheism over polytheism.

Consider this defense of Ockham's razor. Suppose that two hypotheses, H1 and H2, both explain exactly the same data set, but H1 posits fewer entities. It follows that H2 posits more entities than are needed to explain the data. H2 therefore contains unnecessary explanatory elements. H2 is therefore more arbitrary. But if it is more arbitrary, then it is less intelligible. Given that the universe is intelligible, H1 is the more reasonable conclusion. The intelligibility of the universe is another reason to accept Ockham's razor.

"Who made God?"

In *Why I Am Not a Christian* (1927), the philosopher Bertrand Russell sums up and casually dismisses the cosmological argument in one often quoted paragraph:

Perhaps the simplest and easiest to understand [argument for God's existence] is the argument of the First Cause. . . . [The argument] cannot have any validity. I may say that when I was a young man, and was debating these questions very seriously in my mind, I for a long time accepted the argument . . . until one day, at the age of eighteen, I read John Stuart Mill's Autobiography, and I there found this sentence: "My father taught me that the question, Who made me? cannot be answered, since it immediately suggests the further question, Who made God?" That very simple sentence showed me, as I still think, the fallacy in the argument of the First Cause.[32]

The philosopher J. P. Moreland offers this response:

The question "What or who made God?" is a pointless category fallacy, like the question "What color is the musical note C?" The question "What made X?" can only be asked of Xs that are by definition makeable. But God, if he exists at all, is . . . the uncreated Creator of all else. This . . . is what theists mean by "God," even if it turns out that no God exists. Now, if that is what "God" means, then the question "What made God?" turns out to be "What made an entity, God, who is by definition, unmakeable?"[33]

Moreland's point is that *if* there is a First Cause—and the cosmological argument gives us a valid reason to believe that there is—then nothing caused it, for if it were to have a cause, it would not be the *first* cause. A cause cannot be first and also have a cause. If Moreland is right, Russell's question is self-contradictory. It is as self-contradictory as the question, "What color is a colorless object?" Of course, since particles of matter typically have causes, there is nothing illogical in asking, of a *material* being, "What caused it?"

Despite its logical flaw, the question asked by Russell leads us to an interesting idea. Although it is irrational to ask for the cause of the First Cause, it is not irrational to inquire into the *nature* of the First Cause. We touched on this point a few paragraphs back. If you were to ask Aquinas for advice on this course of study, he would recommend that you study philosophical theology, the field of philosophy that contains deep arguments on the divine attributes and the nature of God. Socrates, Plato, and Aristotle, and nearly every major philosopher since their time, would make the same recommendation.

FAILED ATTEMPTS TO SIDESTEP THE ARGUMENT

"Let's just say the universe popped into existence out of nothing"

We encountered this idea earlier when we looked at the books by Krauss and Hawking. Here is a question for you. Is it ever reasonable to believe that something popped into existence out of sheer and absolute nothingness? Suppose you walk into the classroom and a baby aardvark is sitting on the teacher's desk. When you ask her where the little beast came from, she replies, "Nowhere. It just popped into existence out of thin air, out of absolutely nothing, from no cause and for no reason." Would that explain the existence of the aardvark? Is "It popped into existence from nothing" an explanation of anything at all? But if it would not be an explanation of the existence of something as small as an aardvark, how can it be an explanation of something as big as the universe?

Furthermore, as we have seen, no strictly scientific evidence could ever prove that some object simply popped into existence out of nothing. The hypothesis is not scientific.

Medieval philosophers thought deeply about this attempt to sidestep the conclusion of the cosmological argument and offered a carefully considered reply. They argued *ex nihilo nihil fit*—"out of nothing comes nothing." They believed that *ex nihilo nihil fit* is a necessary truth (one that cannot possibly be false), and they claimed that it is justified the way truths of pure mathematics are justified, namely, *a priori* (i.e., on the basis of unaided reason alone without reliance on empirical data). We'll examine the nature of necessary truth and a priori justification in chapter 8. The following argument is one way to justify the *ex nihilo* principle on the basis of abstract reason alone.

A state of complete nothingness would contain no possibilities at all, for possibilities are somethings. Therefore, if there ever were to be, or to have been, a state of absolute nothingness, that state would contain no possibilities. But if there were a state with no possibilities at all, then it would contain no possibility that something comes into existence out of it. Therefore, it is not possible that something might come into existence out of absolutely nothing.

Richard Purtill suggests an empirical argument for the *ex nihilo* principle, that is, an argument based on observations. Here is my summary.

If reality were to be such that objects as big as universes can simply pop into existence out of nothing for no reason, then we should expect to occasionally observe things of various sizes just popping into existence out of sheer nothing for no reason. For instance, a green pig wearing a yellow wig just materializes out of thin air in front of you as you walk down the street. But in all of recorded history, nothing has ever been observed popping into existence out of nothing. The best explanation, Purtill argues, is that the *ex nihilo* principle is true.[34]

Some philosophers support the *ex nihilo* principle by arguing that it is a necessary presupposition of scientific investigation. They have a point. It is hard to see how science could proceed if "it just popped into existence out of sheer nothing" were an acceptable scientific explanation for anything.

"Let's just leave it unexplained"

So stated Bertrand Russell during one of the most famous debates in the history of philosophy, the Copleston–Russell radio debate on the existence of God, broadcast to the nation of England over BBC radio in 1948. Arguing for the existence of God was Fr. Frederick Copleston (1907–94), professor of philosophy at the University of London, a Catholic priest of the Jesuit Order, and the author of the most in-depth and comprehensive history of philosophy ever written. (The edition I possess is eleven volumes.) Arguing against theism and for atheism was Russell, one of the most famous philosophers in the world at the time and also the author of a (much shorter) history of philosophy.

Copleston began by stating a version of the cosmological argument, contending that we need to infer God's existence to make rational sense of the fact that the material universe exists. "The world is intrinsically unintelligible apart from the existence of God," he concluded.

Russell countered, "I should say that the universe is just there, and that's all." Russell's claim was that we should simply leave the existence of the cosmos unexplained. Many have responded to the cosmological argument as Russell did in 1948.

But is this a reasonable position? Imagine that a famous painting has been stolen and detectives find it in the home of the suspected art thief Joe Doakes. When they ask him to explain the presence of the stolen art hanging on his wall, he replies "There is no explanation; it's just there, end of story, no explanation needed." Would that work? But if Russell's gambit does not work in the case of a small object such as a painting, why suppose it works for an object as big as the cosmos?

OCKHAM'S RAZOR AND MONOTHEISM

Suppose that you find the design argument (from chapter 5) rationally compelling and you also find the cosmological argument reasonable. Given this, which of the following two hypotheses is more reasonable?

H1: The Designer and the First Cause are two different beings.

H2: The Designer and the First Cause are one and the same being.

Ockham's razor points us to H2, for H2 explains the same data explained by H1 but with fewer assumptions. The second hypothesis thus knits the design and cosmological arguments into a single intertwined case for monotheism over polytheism.

CONCLUDING REFLECTIONS

Ever since Thales of Miletus circulated the first philosophical theory of the cosmos for critical comments in the early sixth century BC, philosophers have sought a rational explanation of the fact that the universe exists. Aquinas's Second Way, with its roots in ordinary explanatory reasoning, is a logic-based response to this age-old explanatory demand. If the conclusion of his venerable argument is true, there is a rational answer to the fundamental question of cosmology.

Should we accept Aquinas's conclusion? One consideration worth keeping in mind is this: when seeking to explain something, it is rational to seek the best explanation. This is the driving force behind science, the maxim of every courtroom, and the spirit of every academic subject. Seeking the best explanation is not only common sense, it is the spirit of philosophy. If, after exploring all the available ways to make sense of a phenomenon, one hypothesis stands out as the best or the only explanation, that is a good reason to accept the hypothesis.

There is something elemental in all of this. Children often ask strings of "why" questions. Why is the sky blue? Why does the sun move across the sky? Their natural curiosity sometimes draws their parents into a philosophical regress. It is very human to ask why. People of all cultures and all times have asked the ultimate cosmological question. The cosmological argument gives expression to the universal human desire to make sense of things as a whole. If the cosmological argument is sound, the material universe was created by a being existing beyond space, time, matter, and energy—a supernatural being many naturally, and with good reason, call "God." The philosopher William Lane Craig writes:

> We ought to ponder long and hard over this truly remarkable conclusion, for it means that transcending the entire universe there exists a cause which brought the universe into being . . . this conclusion ought to stagger us, ought to fill us with a sense of awe and wonder at the knowledge that our whole universe was caused to exist by something beyond it and greater than it.[35]

Uniting the design and cosmological arguments brings the issue close to home: if God created the universe for a purpose, then God created *you* for a purpose. And that is an amazing thought.

One final consideration. Perhaps the cosmological argument by itself doesn't take us all the way to the God of the Bible or the supreme being worshipped in any particular religion. Perhaps, in this argument, reason elevates our minds above matter, space, energy, and time, and then gestures silently toward a majestic supernatural agency who created it all. Perhaps reason stops there and leaves the last step to each of us, as if to say, "This is as far as I can take you, but the journey is not finished. The next step must be your own." Perhaps the last step is faith.

In his first work of Christian apologetics, *Pilgrim's Regress*, a novel published in 1933, C. S. Lewis (1898–1963), professor of Renaissance and Medieval Literature at the Universities of Oxford and Cambridge, describes in allegorical form the human quest for meaning. As his story unfolds, the reader is presented with a vision of life as a continuing search for God, with reason leading the seeker from one false material idol to another, and finally to a brink, where it gently points the way to a source beyond the material world, as if to leave the final step to the person's free will, and to God's response by grace to the person seeking him.[36]

George Harrison, the lead guitarist for the Beatles, wrote a song expressing the Lewisian theme of life as one long search for God: "Long, Long, Long" can be found on the Beatles' *White Album*.

Questions for Reflection and Discussion 6.3

1. Explain what is meant by "mere theism." How does mere theism differ from biblical theism?
2. Do you agree with Hume that an infinite regression explains everything, leaving nothing unexplained? Offer the most intelligent and strongest reasons you can for your position.
3. In your own words, explain one of the common misunderstandings of the logic of the cosmological argument.
4. If we assume that the material universe is eternal, does that answer the fundamental question of cosmology? Does that put the question to rest?
5. In your own words, explain Moreland's answer to the question "What caused God?" Is his reply successful? Argue for your position.

APPENDIX: THE LIFE OF THOMAS AQUINAS

Thomas Aquinas ranks with Socrates, Plato, and Aristotle as one of the greatest philosophers of all time. In treatises that will fill more than fifty volumes when his collected writings is published in one series by the scholars of the Leonine Commission in Paris, he raises some of the most difficult philosophical questions ever stated, critically examines answers from just about every school of thought in his day, and offers original arguments ranging over almost every area of philosophy. At the height of his productivity, he was writing four manuscripts at a time, dictating to four different secretaries. Today, nearly 800 years after his birth, some scholars still spend their careers drawing new insights from his writings. New research into his thought is published every year. Aquinas was a serious philosopher whose ideas deserve careful consideration.

He was born in 1225 in a tiny Italian village of Roccasecca, about seventy-five miles south of Rome and just twelve miles from the present-day city of Cassino. When he was five years old, his parents sent him to the abbey school at the Benedictine monastery of Monte Cassino, founded in 529 by Saint Benedict, on the hill high above the town. The rich intellectual life within the monastery has been described as a "theocentric humanism": philosophy, science, math, and the humanities were studied rigorously as knowledge valuable for its own sake. At the same time, all subjects were understood to be related to God as the source of all being, the One over the Many. As a young boy at Monte Cassino, Thomas was fascinated with philosophical questions about the existence and nature of God.

After his studies there, Aquinas transferred to the University of Naples and, against the wishes of his parents, joined the Dominican religious order of the Catholic Church. Aquinas's work so impressed his teachers that they sent him to the University of Paris, the most prestigious center of learning at the time, to study under Albert the Great (1200–1280), one of Europe's leading scholars and in many ways the Einstein of his day.

It was a time of great intellectual excitement and broad-based critical thinking. The debates taking place at the University of Paris and at the other European universities not only led to the birth of modern experimental science, modern mathematics, and the social sciences, they laid the foundations for the emergence of modern thought in general. No one then could have known it at the time, but the discussions taking place in the universities of Europe during the thirteenth century would one day change the world.[37]

Aquinas was a large man and probably overweight. While serving as Albert's teaching assistant, some of the other graduate students ridiculed him, nicknaming him the "Dumb Ox"—that is, a big guy who didn't say much. When Albert heard this, he reportedly said, "Call him a dumb ox if you wish, but the bellowing of this ox will one day be heard around the world." Albert saw Thomas's potential.[38]

In early March 1274, Aquinas, by this time one of the greatest scholars in Christendom, fell gravely ill while traveling from Naples to an important Church council in Lyon, France. He was carried into a small monastery near Fossanova, Italy, about sixty miles south of Rome. As he neared his final hour, surrounded by the local monks, he is said to have prayed, "I receive Thee, ransom of my soul. For love of Thee have I studied and kept vigil, toiled, preached and taught."[39] Thomas Aquinas died on March 7, 1274.

In their excellent textbook, *The Philosophy of Aquinas*, Robert Pasnau and Christopher Shields write: "The philosophy of Thomas Aquinas is animated by a kind of creative intellectual dexterity rarely equaled in the long history of the subject. If for this reason only, his works merit careful study. . . . [Aquinas deserves to be read] alongside other towering figures of philosophy, including Plato, Aristotle, Descartes, Leibniz, and Hume."[40]

A Survey of Modern Cosmology

INTRODUCTION

Enormous advances in astronomy became possible with the invention of the telescope in Europe in the seventeenth century.[1] Thanks to a string of constant improvements by European opticians and telescope makers over the next one hundred years, new discoveries occurred at a rapid pace. Only about 4,000 stars are visible to the naked eye, but millions are visible through astronomical telescopes because they gather far more light than the human eye can gather.

By the middle of the eighteenth century, astronomers in Europe were investigating smudgy specks of light called *nebulae* (Latin for "clouds"), most visible only through telescopes. Were the nebulae stars? Or were they some other kind of object? At the time, no one knew for sure. In 1755, in *A General History of Nature and Theory of the Heavens*, the German philosopher Immanuel Kant (1724–1804) raised the question: Are all the stars in the night sky part of *one* system of stars, the one we call the Milky Way? Or are there other systems of stars, separate from the one our Sun belongs to, located far off in space?

Kant hypothesized that the nebulae are not stars at all; rather, they are separate star systems — "island universes" — that look like fuzzy blobs only because they are so far away. However, since telescopes before 1917 were not powerful enough to adequately resolve their details, the nature of the nebulae was still a mystery at the start of the twentieth century.[2]

The slow but steady advance of discoveries in astronomy increased dramatically in the early twentieth century after Einstein presented his theory of general relativity. Einstein's theory changed forever our understanding of the nature of space, time, and the cosmos.

EINSTEIN'S GENERAL THEORY OF RELATIVITY

At the beginning of the twentieth century, three assumptions were taken for granted by most physicists and astronomers:

1. Euclidean geometry — the geometry of a flat surface — correctly describes the structure of the universe.
Comment: In Euclidean geometry, parallel lines never meet. In a Euclidean universe, two objects traveling along exactly parallel paths could theoretically keep moving forever without ever meeting. On this lens, space was thought of as a void in which objects move, but not as a positive something that could be affected by the objects moving through it. In addition, space was not thought to have a shape or a relation to time.

2. The universe is eternal: it has neither a beginning nor an end.
Comment: This was a working assumption for most scientists, but in the nineteenth century, the German scientist and philosopher Hermann von Helmholtz (1821–94) and the German physicist and mathematician Rudolf Clausius (1822–88) had argued, on the basis of the newly discovered second law of thermodynamics, that the universe must have had a beginning in time.[3] They also argued, also on the basis of the second law, that the universe is heading inexorably to "heat death" — a state in which all motion has stopped and the temperature of the universe is absolute zero. Their arguments were largely ignored, however, and the eternal existence of the universe remained a working assumption among physicists.

3. The universe is static in the large scale.

Comment: Most scientists did not believe the universe as a whole is, or could be, expanding or contracting, or otherwise evolving in a direction.

Einstein accepted these governing assumptions as he developed his general theory of relativity, which he completed and published in 1915. His general theory is a theory of gravity offered as an advance on the theory of gravity proposed by Newton in the seventeenth century. Unlike Newton's theory, which was expressed in algebraic terms, Einstein's was expressed in geometrical terms.

The new theory contained many surprises. The geometry of the universe, Einstein claimed, is not the familiar Euclidean geometry of a flat surface that we all learned in junior high. Rather, it is Riemannian geometry, the geometry of a positively curved surface such as that of a globe. Furthermore, claimed Einstein, the presence of matter causes space to curve. Because space with matter is curved, objects move through space in curved rather than straight paths. Space isn't just an empty void through which objects move; it is flexible and has a *shape*. Einstein thus directly rejected the first widely accepted assumption in physics — that the geometry of the universe is Euclidean. Since the force of gravity is universal, the differential equations of general relativity theory constituted a new blueprint for the overall structure of the universe.

In 1917, Einstein plugged the latest astronomical data into the equations of his yet-to-be-tested theory. The result troubled him. His equations indicated that the universal force of gravity is causing the universe to implode like a collapsing building. Einstein immediately saw that *if* this is right, then the universe is not static in the large scale; rather, it is changing in a direction. This bothered him because it contradicted the third governing assumption of physics.

Moreover, if the universe is collapsing, this suggests that it began a finite time ago, for (1) no known force could stop a universal gravitational collapse and (2) the collapse has obviously not yet run its course. Einstein wanted to avoid a universal beginning and a universal end, for both would violate the second assumption — that the material universe is eternal.

It is noteworthy that the three guiding assumptions were not derived from science or based on scientific data, as Einstein himself later admitted. They were (unproven) *metaphysical* assumptions.

To avoid the two unwelcome conclusions—that the universe is evolving in the large scale and that it all began a finite time ago—Einstein tinkered with his equations. Specifically, he added a new term to the left side, which he named the "cosmological constant." Denoted by the Greek letter Λ (lambda), this constant represented a hypothetical antigravity force that, if it were to exist, would exactly oppose and balance the force of gravity, prevent a cosmic collapse, and hold the universe in equilibrium in the large scale for eternity.

Einstein inserted lambda into his equations even though no corresponding antigravity force had ever been discovered and despite the fact that the natural solution to the equations of general relativity indicated an evolving universe with a finite age rather than a universe that is static and eternal. The cosmological constant was inserted for one reason only: to prevent his theory from predicting a dynamic universe with a finite age.

The same year, 1917, the Dutch astrophysicist Willem de Sitter (1872–1934) discovered a different but mathematically consistent solution to Einstein's equations that surprised everyone. The solution derived by Sitter described "a static universe that was completely devoid of matter."[4] The Sitter solution was anathema to Einstein: the very possibility of empty space was inconsistent with a number of assumptions he had made. In the context of his general theory, it seemed impossible that pure space could exist without matter.

It is worth noting that Einstein's disagreement with Sitter was not based on physical data or pure mathematics—it was based on assumptions brought in from outside science. Sitter's math was correct in the sense that his solution was mathematically and logically consistent. In other words, Einstein's disagreement was based (again) on a metaphysical assumption.

However, like any good scientific theory, the general theory did generate observational predictions. Einstein calculated that if his theory is true, then a heavy mass such as the sun will cause space to curve, which will bend the path of light passing nearby. Using some amazing mathematics, Einstein predicted the degree by which light will be bent when it passes near the sun.

The first test of Einstein's prediction was conducted four years later, in South Africa in 1919, by Sir Arthur Eddington (1882–1944), one of Britain's greatest astrophysicists. After making careful telescopic measurements during a solar eclipse visible only from the southern tip of the African continent, Eddington announced to the world press that light passing near the sun was found to have been bent to the exact degree predicted by Einstein's theory. Astronomers and physicists were stunned. Almost overnight Einstein became an international superstar in the world of science.

Then, in 1922 the Russian mathematician and physicist Alexander Friedmann (1888–1925) made a surprising discovery: a mathematically consistent solution to Einstein's field equations exists for an *expanding* universe. This was one more hint that the universe might be dynamic rather than static in the largest scale.

Einstein quickly dismissed Friedmann's result, however, claiming that the mathematician must have made a mistake in his calculations. It later turned out that it was Einstein who had made the mistake. The stage was now set for the next big step in cosmology, a gigantic discovery that would come from an unlikely source: an unknown Catholic priest in Belgium who was also a high-powered mathematician and a professor of physics.

GEORGES LEMAÎTRE, FATHER OF THE BIG BANG

Georges Lemaître (1894–1966) was born in Belgium into a devout Catholic family. From an early age, he showed signs of mathematical genius. As a young man, Lemaître was attracted equally to the Catholic priesthood, theology, mathematics, engineering, and physics. The life path he chose allowed him to pursue all five. While studying for the priesthood, he took courses in higher math, engineering, and theoretical physics in preparation for the academic part of his vocation. In 1914, when World War I began, Lemaître and his brother left college to serve on the front lines. Georges actually carried math and physics textbooks into the trenches and studied between ferocious and bloody battles.

After the war, Lemaître was admitted to Cambridge University, where he did research in physics under Eddington, at the time one of the most famous scientists in the world. Next came studies at Harvard and MIT, supervised by Harlow Shapely (1885–1972), one of the greatest American astronomers of the day.

Between 1920 and 1925, Lemaître earned doctorates in mathematics and physics, was ordained to the Catholic priesthood, and was appointed professor of physics at the prestigious Catholic University of Louvain, Belgium. While meeting his duties as a diocesan priest, Lemaître taught courses in physics and mathematics and conducted advanced research in general relativity and quantum mechanics.

Lemaître's First Scientific Paper

In 1925, Lemaître published his first scientific paper. In this now historic work, he showed that Sitter had made an error in his calculations: a Sitter universe would indeed be empty of matter, but it would not be static—*it would be expanding.* This was an amazing result at the time, coming two years before the discovery by astronomers of the expansion of the universe.

Lemaître's discovery was one more hint that the universe is not static in the large scale. Einstein was puzzled. How, he asked, could empty space *expand?* Why would it expand? How could space do anything without the presence of matter? This made no sense in the context of his general theory with lambda added.

At this point, Lemaître was still assuming an eternal universe. The model universe he derived using Einstein's equations was expanding in the future but was static (and thus eternal) in the past.

Lemaître's Second Paper

In 1927, Lemaître published his second scientific paper. Using astronomical data received in private correspondence from the leading astronomers of the day, Edwin Hubble (1889–1953) and Harlow Shapely, and the field equations of general relativity, Lemaître proved that a model universe containing matter that starts "from a static Einstein state stretching back into the indefinite past" *must be expanding in the future.* This result was even more amazing than the result obtained in his first paper. Astronomers had not yet proved that the universe is expanding—everyone still assumed (and wanted to believe) that the universe is static in the large scale.

Lemaître's second paper contained the first complete solution to Einstein's field equations that was based on empirical data and that *required* an expanding universe. Again, this result came two years before astronomers finally had the data to prove that the universe is indeed expanding. By solving gigantic systems of equations in differential geometry on paper, the young priest had previsioned one of the greatest astronomical discoveries of all time—a discovery which we'll turn to in a moment.

At this point Lemaître was still assuming an eternally old cosmos. His 1927 model of the universe started from an initial static state and expanded only in the future.[5] But Lemaître had shown something remarkable: even if we posit a past-eternal static Einstein universe, the whole thing, *space-time included*, must now be expanding. In this same paper, Lemaître also derived the principle known today as "Hubble's law," which states that the nebulae are receding from us and from each other at velocities directly proportional to their distances. Lemaître also gave the first estimate for the number known today as the "Hubble constant," a number astrophysicists use today to estimate both the size and age of the universe. Lemaître was also the first to attribute the recession of the nebulae to the actual expansion of space itself—an idea that is as mind-boggling today as it was in 1927.[6]

Lemaître's theory attracted little attention, even though it raised enormous problems for the reigning assumption of a static, eternal universe. For instance, if the universe is past eternally static, why would it wait until *now* to start expanding? How could a universe be static for an infinite number of years and then all of a sudden start expanding?

A short time after his second paper was published, Lemaître met Einstein at an international physics conference in Brussels. Over a period of several days, the priest discussed his calculations with the great physicist. The two men even traveled to England together to visit Eddington's laboratory—followed everywhere they went by the world press. Still Einstein was not convinced. He told the young physicist, "Your mathematics is perfect, but I find your physics abhorrent." By this Einstein meant that Lemaître's math was correct, but he could not emotionally stand the idea of an evolving universe, even one that is static and eternal in the past and expanding only in the future. Einstein was still wedded to the metaphysical assumption of an eternally static universe.

The next big discovery in cosmology would come from another unlikely source, a man who had been a boxer before becoming a professional astronomer. Many recognize Edwin P. Hubble as the man for whom the space telescope is named. Astronomers recognize him as the scientist who made the biggest cosmological discovery of the twentieth century. We'll return to Lemaître after we look at Hubble's amazing find.

HUBBLE SOLVES THE MYSTERY OF THE NEBULAE

In 1919, when Edwin Hubble began observing the heavens with the 100-inch Hooker telescope at Mount Wilson, near Los Angeles, the largest telescope in the world at the time, it was generally believed that the Milky Way is the whole universe; that is, it was believed that all the stars and objects in the heavens belong to one star system, the Milky Way. It was also believed, of course, that this system of stars is static in the large scale.[7]

By 1925, Hubble had managed to resolve individual stars within the Andromeda nebula. When he inspected the photographic images under a magnifying glass, he discovered that the stars were Cepheid variable stars, a type known to brighten and dim periodically, with the period of variation a mathematical function of the star's intrinsic (internal) brightness. After measuring the period of variation, Hubble was able to determine the total amount of intrinsic light they emitted. Using this value, and the law of physics stating that light decreases with distance according to a mathematical formula first discovered by Newton, Hubble was able to calculate the distance to the Andromeda nebula.

To his surprise, he found that the Andromeda nebula is a separate star system, an "island universe," located outside the Milky Way. The Milky Way is therefore not the whole cosmos. Within a few years, Hubble was able to show that the heavens contain millions of separate star systems, now called *galaxies*. Astronomers today count more than 200 billion galaxies, each containing hundreds of billions of stars on average.

You need to understand the Doppler effect to understand Hubble's next discovery, one of the greatest cosmological discoveries of all time. As a speeding train approaches, the pitch of its whistle increases, and as it speeds away, the pitch drops. The explanation for the change in pitch was discovered in 1842 by Christian Doppler (1803–53), an Austrian physicist. If a source emitting sound waves is moving toward an observer, the waves are bunched up, which increases their frequency and hence the pitch. If a source of waves is moving away from an observer, the waves are stretched out, which causes the frequency and pitch to decrease. Hubble reasoned that since light is a wave phenomenon, it must also display a Doppler effect. If a light source is moving toward us, its light waves should be crunched up and hence shifted toward the higher frequency (blue) end of the spectrum. If the source is moving away, its light should be spread out and therefore shifted to the lower frequency (red) end of the spectrum.

Hubble analyzed the light from the galaxies and found it to be shifted toward the red end of the spectrum. After measuring the degree of the shift, he concluded that other galaxies are moving away from our galaxy and from each other at great speeds. In 1929, he published his data and made the announcement that shook the world of science: the *best explanation* of the redshift data is that the universe is expanding. We live in a dynamic, not a static cosmos.

However, astronomers still assumed that the universe is past-eternal. The question now became, How can the universe be both past-eternal and expanding? It was Lemaître who finally solved the problem.

THE BIG BANG THEORY

Between 1927 and 1930, Lemaître found new problems with expanding, past-eternal Einstein model universes. By the end of 1930 he began to see that any universe that satisfies the field equations of general relativity and Hubble's data *cannot have existed forever*. After verifying that the model cannot be altered to allow for an eternally old universe, Lemaître drew his momentous conclusion: The universe does not have an eternal past. *The physical universe had a beginning.* The best relativistic model of the universe indicated a "beginning of all physical processes."[8]

When Lemaître published his findings in 1931, the scientific community immediately rejected his conclusion. Eddington said in an address, "Philosophically, the notion of a beginning . . . is repugnant to me."[9] Einstein could not accept the theory "because of its metaphysical implications."[10] The first time Lemaître tried to speak to Einstein about the matter, Einstein said, "No, not that, that suggests too much creation."[11] Most scientists also rejected Lemaître's conclusion, but not on the basis of scientific evidence: they rejected it on the basis of metaphysical assumptions to which they were emotionally wedded.

Despite the hostile response, in 1933, Lemaître was invited to Cal Tech, in Pasadena, California, one of the foremost scientific research institutes in the world, to conduct a series of seminars on his solutions to Einstein's field equations and on his theory of cosmic rays. Einstein was in the audience when Lemaître lectured on his 1927 paper. After the lecture, the great physicist stood up and called Lemaître's theory "the most beautiful and satisfying interpretation [of the data] I have listened to."[12] Lemaître's argument had convinced the greatest physicist in the world.

Each day now, Lemaître and Einstein walked the grounds of Cal Tech discussing their theories, followed everywhere by reporters from around the world. Everyone was speculating on what the two scientists might be saying about *little lamb*—the world press's term for Einstein's lambda symbol. After attending Lemaître's seminars, Einstein called his own decision in 1917 to insert the cosmological constant (lambda) into his equations "the biggest blunder of my life."

Lemaître's latest calculations indicated that all the physical processes in the universe started from an initial "super dense state" containing the entire mass-energy of the universe packed into a single point too small and dense for the equations to describe. Lemaître named this initial state the "primeval atom." As the universe emerged out of this point, it expanded, and space, time, and matter all came into existence and took form.

Lemaître also derived theoretical implications that anticipated discoveries that would be made years later by others. For instance, he hypothesized that cosmic rays are leftover energy from the initial "fireworks" at the beginning of the universe. He also suggested that the universe expanded quickly and then slowed down to its present level of expansion.

Lemaître as a Critical Thinker

Finding errors in reasoning had always come naturally to Lemaître. While serving in an artillery unit during World War I, he upset his commanding officer by finding an error in a mathematical equation in the ballistics manual. When he found errors in Sitter's solution to Einstein's field equations, "Lemaitre was doing what he had always done—noticing mathematical inconsistencies and flaws and seeing how their correction opened up new ways to look at the problem."[13] Just like Socrates had before him.

Lemaître named the initial explosion that resulted in the expanding universe the "big noise." The English astronomer Fred Hoyle (1915–2001), an atheist at the time, disliked Lemaître's hypothesis so intensely that he mockingly named it "the big bang." Although he was making fun of

Lemaître's idea, the new name stuck. Astronomers now estimate that the material universe, and all physical processes, began about 13.8 billion years ago in one initial event. Lemaître received a number of prestigious awards for his work. He is known as the "father of big bang theory."

GOD AND THE BIG BANG

Although Lemaître was a devout Catholic priest, he did not promote his theory as scientific proof that God exists. Nevertheless, a number of scientists, including the Russian physicist George Gamow (1904–68) and the British astronomer Fred Hoyle, openly mocked Lemaître for his religious beliefs and insinuated (dishonestly) that the priest's Catholic faith had influenced his scientific investigations. Hoyle even ridiculed Lemaître on the BBC radio show he hosted in Britain during the 1950s, proving that famous scientists can be as mean-spirited (and dogmatic) as anyone else.

But Hoyle and Gamow, both outspoken atheists at the time, were completely wrong. Lemaître's theory of the big bang was not a projection of his Catholic beliefs. Indeed, the truth was probably the reverse: Gamow's and Hoyle's opposition to Lemaître's theory probably stemmed from their dogmatic atheism and emotional resistance to anything suggesting creation, rather than from any commitment to the scientific method. For the data strongly supported Lemaître's theory and did not at all support the alternative theory they proposed, to which we now turn.

THE STEADY STATE THEORY

Despite Einstein's endorsement of Lemaître's theory, Hoyle, Gamow, and many others continued to oppose it. However, these big bang deniers faced a serious paradox: their assumptions formed an inconsistent tetrad. They believed the following.

1. The universe is expanding (the galaxies are rushing apart from each other).

2. The universe is eternal.

3. Separate galaxies are observable a finite distance away in space.

4. If the universe is eternal, then it has been expanding for an eternity (since no force exists capable of reversing a universal expansion).

But given 1, 2, and 4, it follows that

5. All the galaxies are by now infinitely far apart.

However, 5 contradicts 3, for if all the galaxies are infinitely far apart, then none should be visible relatively nearby. Since 5 logically follows from 1 through 4 but contradicts 3, it follows that 1 through 4 are logically inconsistent: they cannot all be true. These famous physicists were endorsing a contradiction. Something had to go.

In 1948, to resolve the contradiction, Hoyle and two other astrophysicists, Hermann Bondi and Thomas Gold, proposed the "steady state" theory of the universe as an alternative to the big bang hypothesis. According to their hypothesis, as the galaxies rush apart from each other, they leave behind enormous voids in space. However, these voids do not remain empty. New matter comes into existence inside the voids *out of absolutely nothing*, and it does so at exactly the rate needed to keep the average density and appearance of the universe constant forever, in other words, to keep the universe in a "steady state." The *ex nihilo* principle obviously did not impress these theorists.

Hoyle calculated that the average density of the universe would remain constant everywhere if the "creation fields" (as he called them) inside the voids left by the expanding universe produced "about one atom every century in a volume equal to the Empire State Building."[14] By adopting this assumption, one could accept the expansion of the universe, and the fact that galaxies are visible relatively nearby, while holding onto the metaphysical assumption of an eternal cosmos.[15] The steady state theory now became the main competitor to Lemaître's big bang theory.

COSMIC MICROWAVE RADIATION
PROVES HOYLE WRONG

Unfortunately for Hoyle and Gamow, the next big discovery in cosmology completely disproved their steady state theory. In 1965, Arnold Penzias and Robert Wilson, scientists at the Bell Telephone Laboratories in New

Jersey, were using a giant radio receiver to track signals from NASA's Echo communications satellites. No matter how finely they tuned their instrument, they kept hearing a static they could not explain. At first they thought the static might be caused by pigeon droppings inside their large, horn-shaped antennas. However, this was ruled out after they cleaned the antennas and the noise remained. After checking every component, they concluded that the static they were hearing was not coming from their instruments, it was coming from deep space.

The mystery deepened when they discovered that the signal was coming from every direction and at exactly the same strength. They finally realized that the static could only be low temperature microwave radiation bathing the earth uniformly from every corner of the universe. The question now became, What cosmic process could possibly generate this type of radiation?

A colleague now recalled a prediction that had been derived from Lemaître's big bang hypothesis almost twenty years before by physicists Ralph Alpher and Robert Herman. If the universe began in a dense state and then exploded, residual heat left over from the initial explosion would be detectable as microwave radiation at about three degrees above absolute zero, bathing the earth uniformly from every direction. A similar prediction had also been made by Lemaître. All of a sudden, the best explanation was clear: The microwave radiation predicted by Lemaître, Alpher, and Herman was exactly what Penzias and Wilson had detected. The two Bell scientists had discovered the heat left over from the big bang.

The discovery disproved Hoyle's hypothesis and confirmed Lemaître's, for the cosmic background radiation was predicted by the big bang theory but could not be explained at all on the steady state theory.

Almost overnight, the scientific profession shifted to Lemaître's side. Today, at least four independent lines of empirical evidence have made the big bang hypothesis one of the most well-confirmed theories in all of physics:

1. The data from the redshift of the galaxies can be explained in no other way.
2. The cosmic microwave background radiation can be explained in no other way.
3. The mixture and distribution of the elements across the universe can be explained in no other way.
4. The changes in the galaxies over past time can be explained in no other way.

Notice that the scientific argument for the big bang theory takes the form of an inference to the best explanation.

Thus, in a standard textbook on the big bang, the cosmologist Joseph Silk writes that although models for exotic universes can be drawn out on paper, "our preference must be for the simplest tenable cosmology. Practically all known astronomical phenomena can be understood in the context of big bang cosmology—if not completely, then at least to a greater degree than in any alternative framework that has yet been proposed. Thus, we shall accept the big bang model as providing a satisfactory description of the universe."[16]

On June 17, 1966, Father Lemaître was in a nursing home close to death when news of the discovery of the cosmic microwave radiation, which he had predicted in 1933, was presented to him. Georges Lemaître died three days later. In his wonderful biography, John Farrell writes that the humble Belgian priest convinced a generation of thinkers to embrace the notion of cosmic expansion and the theory that this expansion could be traced backward to a cosmic origin, a starting point for space and time that Lemaître called "the day without yesterday."[17]

THE OSCILLATING UNIVERSE THEORY

Suppose someone strongly wants to hold on to the assumption that the universe is eternal but also grants that the universe is expanding and agrees that some galaxies are only a finite distance apart. With the steady state theory refuted, how might someone reconcile these seemingly inconsistent propositions? One way is by adopting the *oscillating universe theory*, which states that the universe has been oscillating back and forth between expansion and contraction forever, like a giant accordion, and it will continue to do so forever. The current expansion will eventually reach a maximum, at which point the universe will begin collapsing until it reaches a minimum, at which point it will expand again, and so forth, like a huge bellows expanding and contracting forever.[18]

The oscillating universe model was at one time a hopeful alternative to the standard big bang model. However, the latest data strongly indicates that the model is false.[19] The philosopher Quentin Smith, although an atheist, states that "it is metaphysics, not physics, that partly motivates (against all evidence) the attraction to an infinitely old oscillating universe . . . the idea gained currency merely because it avoided the issue of divine creation—not because there was the slightest evidence in favor of it."[20] In short, according to the latest data, it is not possible that the current universe is the result of an infinite regression of bang-crunch cycles or oscillations.[21]

THE *KALAM* COSMOLOGICAL ARGUMENT

We've been discussing physics. What does any of this have to do with philosophy of religion and the existence of God? In chapter 6 we saw that philosophers have given many different versions of the cosmological argument. One version is particularly relevant in the present context. During the ninth century, Islamic philosophers of the *kalam* (Arabic for "science of discourse") school of philosophy in Baghdad stated and defended an argument known today as the "kalam cosmological argument." The reasoning they employed was derived from their studies of Aristotle and other Greek philosophers. The argument had also been stated previously by Christian philosophers, such as John Philoponus (ca. 490–ca. 570).[22] Today, the most prominent advocate of the *kalam* argument is the American philosopher William Lane Craig, who summarizes it in three steps:

1. Whatever begins to exist has a cause.

2. The material universe began to exist.

3. Therefore, necessarily, the material universe has a first cause.[23]

As we saw in chapter 6, a first cause of the universe would be a being who is the cause of space, time, matter, and all energy; thus, a supernatural being whose existence transcends the entire physical universe.

This argument is obviously deductively valid. It follows that if you don't accept the conclusion, it is incumbent on you as a critical thinker to provide an argument against one of the premises.

This is not an easy task. The *ex nihilo* principle (from chapter 6) and commonsense support the first premise. Modern big bang astrophysics supports the second premise. The *kalam* version of the cosmological argument thus has direct support from logic, common sense, and big bang astrophysics—a tough combination to beat.

Isn't the history of ideas fascinating? It is amazing the way new ideas and great advances in thought emerge from the unlikeliest of places—a boxer turned astronomer, a humble Catholic priest. One more reason why the free discussion of ideas is a good thing: history suggests that it tends to result in the advancement of thought.[24]

Questions for Reflection and Discussion, Interlude 1

1. What was Einstein's biggest blunder? How was it discovered?
2. On what logical basis is Lemaître's big bang hypothesis considered today to be the most reasonable theory?
3. Does the big bang theory support theism? Discuss philosophically.
4. If it were somehow proved that the universe is eternal, would that eliminate all need to believe in God or a supreme being?

SEVEN

The Problem of Evil

SO MUCH SUFFERING

Between 1933 and 1945, fourteen million civilians were murdered by the governments of the Soviet Union and Nazi Germany. That number does not include the millions who died from malnutrition, forced labor in concentration camps, bombing raids, and soldiers killed in battle. Fourteen million is the Yale University historian Timothy Snyder's "estimate of the number of people killed in deliberate policies of mass murder" carried out by the Soviet Union and Nazi Germany in the "Bloodlands," the territory that stretched "from central Poland to western Russia, through Ukraine, Belarus, and the Baltic states."[1] Snyder observes that "not a single one of the fourteen million murdered was a soldier on active duty. Most were women, children, and the aged; none were bearing weapons, many had been stripped of their possessions, including their clothes."[2]

The numbers are so large they almost defy human understanding. The historical record includes stories like this: during the fateful summer of

1942, "a 12-year old Jewish girl in Belarus wrote a last letter to her father: 'I am saying good-bye to you before I die. I am so afraid of this death because they throw small children into the mass graves alive.' She was among the more than five million Jews gassed or shot by the Germans."[3]

And this: in 1940 a Polish officer ended his diary in mid-sentence seconds before he was shot by the Soviet secret police. His last words: "They asked me for my wedding ring, which I . . . ."[4] Stories that can break your heart.

QUESTIONING WHY

Many people believe that the universe was created by a supreme being—commonly called "God"—and that God is personal, omnipotent (all-powerful), omniscient (all-knowing), omnibenevolent (all-good), and infinitely loving. They also believe that God loves us and cares for us. But if so, why would God, understood traditionally as infinitely loving, omnipotent, omniscient, and so forth, create persons capable of committing atrocities such as the mass murders described by Snyder? Wouldn't an infinitely loving God have created only saintly people who have a strong disposition to be loving and good?

Mass murders carried out by moral monsters such as Hitler and Stalin are not the only things that can shake a traditionally religious person's faith. Every year large numbers of people die from diseases and destructive acts of nature. Why would an infinitely loving God create a world containing cancer, hurricanes, floods, and earthquakes? Wouldn't a good God create a pain-free world that has no disease and no natural disasters?

Yet in the face of all this suffering, traditional theists, whether Muslim, Jewish, Hindu, or Christian, continue to believe that the universe was created by an omnibenevolent, omnipotent, omniscient, infinitely loving deity. Couldn't a supreme being have created a world with less suffering than this?

No matter how we think of it, the existence of a great deal of pain, loss of life, and other kinds of suffering doesn't fit well, at least initially, with the traditional claim that the universe was created and designed by an all-good, all-knowing, all-powerful, infinitely loving being.

INTRODUCING THE PROBLEM OF EVIL

These questions about God and suffering have traditionally been grouped together and called "the problem of evil" since it is puzzling why God, as traditionally conceived, would create a world containing terrible evils such as the diseases, natural disasters, and crimes just mentioned. In what follows, let's define *evil* broadly as "diseases, natural disasters, crimes, and other things that cause much suffering." And by *God* let's mean "the all-powerful, all-knowing, all-good, and infinitely loving creator and designer of the universe." The problem of evil, in turn, has given rise to a philosophical argument against the existence of God (as traditionally conceived), known as the "argument from evil." Here is an initial statement of the problem and the corresponding argument.

> The problem of evil (initial statement): Why would God, being all-good, all-powerful, infinitely loving, and so forth, allow evil to exist? It seems that God, understood in this way, would not allow *any* evil. Yet evil obviously exists.

> Argument from evil (initial statement):
>
> 1. If God exists, then evil does not exist.
>
> 2. But evil exists.
>
> 3. Therefore, necessarily, God does not exist.

The presence of the word *necessarily* makes this a deductive argument. The argument is clearly valid, for if the premises are true, then the conclusion must be true. The only question, then, is this: Are the premises true?

> Argument for premise 1: Just as loving parents do not want their children to suffer, God—being all-loving—would not want any creature to suffer. God would therefore be opposed to all suffering. Being all-good, all-powerful, all-knowing, and all-loving, God would therefore not allow any suffering to exist. Therefore, premise 1 is true.

> Argument for premise 2: Hospitals are full of people suffering from illnesses, the world is full of violence, and many die every year from natural disasters. Therefore, premise 2 is true.

Keep in mind as we proceed that the argument from evil is *not* an argument against *mere theism* (which we defined in chapter 6). Thus, it is not an argument against one of the premises of the cosmological or design arguments we examined. The existence of evil is logically compatible with the existence of a First Cause or an Intelligent Designer—as long as we do not attribute to the Creator or Designer omnipotence, omniscience, omnibenevolence, infinite love, and so forth. The problem of evil, as defined here, therefore does not arise if we simply define *God* as "the First Cause" or as "the Intelligent Designer."

The problem of evil also does not arise if we suppose that God is radically limited in knowledge, power, love, or goodness. For if God has a limited degree of knowledge, God may not know that evil exists. If God has a limited degree of power, God might be unable to prevent the evil that exists. If God has a limited degree of goodness, God might not care about the evil that exists, and so forth. The argument from evil is directed only at traditional theism—the claim that God, understood as personal, all-powerful, all-knowing, all-good, and infinitely loving, exists.

The initial statements convey the basic idea; however, in recent years the issue has become more complicated. Philosophers today distinguish two different forms of the initial problem of evil and two different variations on the initial argument from evil. The first form of the problem of evil is commonly called the "logical problem of evil," and the corresponding argument is known as the "logical argument from evil." This argument is deductive—the claim is that the conclusion *must* be true if the premises are true. According to this argument, traditional theism is self-contradictory and therefore completely absurd. If the logical argument from evil is sound, traditional theism is certainly false.[5]

The second form of the problem is called the "evidential problem of evil," and the corresponding argument is known as the "evidential argument from evil."[6] This argument is inductive—the claim is that God *very probably* does not exist. And of course, if it is highly improbable that God exists, then it is unreasonable to believe. The evidential argument also attacks traditional theism, but it is a softer critique.

In the rest of this chapter, we'll explore these two thought-provoking lines of argument. One last time: keep in mind as we proceed that *evil* is defined as "diseases, natural disasters, crimes, and other things that cause suffering," and the word *God* signifies "the omnipotent, omniscient, omnibenevolent, infinitely loving creator of the material universe." This is appropriate, for (again) the argument from evil is directed at traditional theism, not at mere theism.

THE LOGICAL ARGUMENT FROM EVIL

In 1955, the Australian philosopher J. L. Mackie (1917–81) gave an influential and detailed statement of the argument, which he introduced with a bold claim: It can be shown conclusively, by purely deductive logic alone, that traditional theism is "positively irrational, that the several parts of the essential theological doctrine are inconsistent with one another, so that the [traditional theist] . . . must be prepared to believe . . . what can be disproved from other beliefs that he also holds."[7]

In short, the essential beliefs of traditional theism contradict each other. Here is one way to summarize Mackie's famous argument.

1. It is not logically possible that God and evil both exist at the same time.

2. Traditional theism claims that God exists.

3. Traditional theism also acknowledges that evil exists.

4. Therefore, traditional theism is self-contradictory.

5. Therefore, it is certain that traditional theism is false.

The word *certain* indicates that this is a deductive argument. The claim is that the conclusion must be true if the premises all are true. The argument is clearly valid. If the premises are true, then the conclusion *must* indeed be true. Premises 2 and 3 are not controversial; the first premise is therefore the only step needing support.

Argument for premise 1:

a. If a being is all-good, it is completely opposed to all evil.

b. If a being is all-knowing, it is aware of every evil that exists.

c. If a being is all-powerful, it has the power to prevent any evil.

d. Therefore, an all-good, all-knowing, all-powerful God would not allow *any* evil to exist.

e. But God is traditionally said to be all-good, all-knowing, and all-powerful.

f. Therefore, God would not allow any evil to exist.

g. It is therefore self-contradictory to assert that God and evil both exist.

h. It is a standard axiom of logic that self-contradictions are impossible.

i. Therefore, premise 1 is certainly true.

Although at first glance Mackie's argument appears airtight, there is actually a logical gap between steps (c) and (d) in the subargument supporting premise 1. Step (d) follows validly from the previous steps only if the following assumption is inserted:

Assumption: Necessarily, an all-powerful, all-good, all-knowing being will always eliminate every bit of evil it can possibly eliminate.

With this assumption added, Mackie's argument looks invincible. But is the assumption true? To some, the assumption seems self-evident. Others disagree. They point out that if an all-powerful being were to have a *morally sufficient reason* to permit an instance of suffering S—a reason that would morally justify permitting S—then that being might permit S, and its permitting S would not be morally wrong.

Here is an analogy from everyday life. A teenager gets too many speeding tickets, and his insurance rate doubles. His parents could pay his insurance bill for him, but they stand back and let the experience be a lesson in life. They do so because they know that (1) it is important to learn to accept responsibility, and (2) we learn to accept responsibility (and we grow) by being held responsible for our choices. The young driver is unhappy for a time, but his parents did the right thing for the right reason, for a valuable life lesson was learned. The young man becomes a more responsible driver. The parents had a morally sufficient reason to allow their son to experience the unhappy consequences of his actions. They were morally justified in letting him pay the added cost.

Similarly, *if* God were to have a morally sufficient reason for permitting some instance of suffering S, then God might allow S to occur and there would be nothing morally wrong with God's allowing S to occur. God would be justified in allowing S to occur. But it certainly seems *possible* that God has a morally sufficient reason—perhaps one we have not yet thought of—to allow the evils we observe. Therefore, it is possible God would not eliminate every evil, and the needed assumption is false. But are we talking about real possibilities here?

The philosopher Alvin Plantinga offers this suggestion. Perhaps there is some enormously great good G and some evil E that is related to G in such a way that G logically cannot occur without E having occurred first. In other words, E is a necessary condition for the occurrence of G. In addition, perhaps a world containing both G and E is far better morally than a world containing neither. In a case such as this, God would have a morally sufficient reason for allowing the evil E.

With this point noted, critics of Mackie such as Nelson Pike and Plantinga argue that the mere logical possibility of goods and evils related as G and E are related shows that the assumption Mackie needs is false.[8] For if it is even *possible* that God permits some evils he could have prevented and does so for a morally sufficient reason, then Mackie's assumption that, necessarily, an all-powerful, all-knowing, all-good being will always eliminate every bit of evil it can possibly eliminate is false. But without that assumption, premise 1 of his argument is not supported.

The arguments of Pike and Plantinga carried the day. The consensus in philosophy of religion today is that Pike and Plantinga showed definitively that Mackie's logical argument from evil, and others in the same vein, fails to show that traditional theism is self-contradictory.

All of this raises a fascinating question. What reason could God possibly have for permitting a preventable instance of suffering? What reason could God possibly have for not preventing some of the horrible evils of the twentieth century, such as the Holocaust or the Rwandan genocide (1994)? Theistic philosophers have suggested several; the reasons they propose are called *theodicies*. We'll turn to the three most important ones in the next section.[9]

Questions for Reflection and Discussion 7.1

1. What is traditional theism? How does it differ from mere theism?
2. In your own words, explain the problem of evil.
3. How could the definition of God's attributes be changed so that the problem of evil would not arise?
4. In your own words, explain Mackie's argument. What is he trying to prove? Evaluate his argument philosophically.

THEODICIES

A *theodicy* is a hypothesis offered to explain why God, if he exists, permits evil. Keep in mind as we proceed that a theodicy is not an argument for God's existence. A theodicy has only one aim: to propose a plausible and morally sufficient reason God *might have had* for permitting the suffering we see around us. If at least one theodicy seems sensible, then it is logically *possible* that God and evil both exist. Theodicies are thus defensive in nature: they are offered as rebuttals of the assumption in Mackie's argument that we examined earlier that "necessarily, an all-powerful, all-knowing, all-good being will always eliminate every bit of evil it can possibly eliminate." It is true that a theodicy supports belief in God, but only in the indirect sense that it claims to ward off a premise in an argument against belief in God.

We'll now examine three theodicies: the *free will theodicy*, first put forward in a philosophical context by Saint Augustine (354–430), the bishop of Hippo, North Africa, and one of the great philosophers of the Western tradition; the *rug maker theodicy*, suggested by the philosopher J. R. Lucas (1929–2020); and the *moral qualities theodicy*, originated by Saint Irenaeus (ca. 130–ca. 202), the bishop of Lyon, France. In addition to being philosophers and churchmen, Augustine and Irenaeus were both Christian Platonists. (Their philosophies combined Plato's philosophy with the central tenets of Christianity.)

THE FREE WILL THEODICY

The seed idea emerged as Augustine reflected on the following philosophical puzzle. According to the Christian view, God is perfectly good. But a perfectly good being, it seems, would not create anything evil. But God created everything in the beginning. Therefore, everything must have been perfectly good in the beginning. These thoughts led Augustine to conclude that evil cannot have been one of the original constituents of the universe. Why, then, is there evil in the world today? How did it first arise?

As I interpret his reasoning, the first hint was the thought that God, being supremely good, is infinitely loving, since love is obviously an intrinsic good.[10] God's act of creation therefore must have been an act of love: God created us to be loved by him and to love him in return.

But love is an act of will. More deeply, Augustine came to believe that it is an act of a *free* will. For real love, by its inherent nature, is freely given; it is not coerced or determined by external circumstances or forces. It follows that God freely chose to create us. It also follows that God gave us free rather than predetermined wills, since God created us to love and to be loved, and love requires freedom. Furthermore, the possession of free will must itself be a good thing since it is a necessary condition for an act of love.

However, freedom has a dual nature. It can be used for bad and also for good. If God were to give us free will and then control us so that we only do good things, then our wills would not really be free (and we would not be capable of real love). We would be senseless robots. A truly free creature, then, must have the power to love God and do good and at the same time the power to turn from God and cause suffering.

In an early work, *On the Freedom of the Will*, Augustine deepens his theory of freedom when he argues that a person's freely undertaken action is not caused or predetermined by God or by any antecedent or external conditions, for if it is caused by outside forces, it is not really free. A free action therefore proceeds from the acting agent, or person, and not from a prior cause. Free will is thus the power to perform an action without being caused to perform just that action. It follows that when we turn from God and commit a sin and cause suffering, it is *we* who turn.

So, in the beginning, free will must have been a purely good thing, for it was necessary if human beings were to one day enter into a loving relationship with God, the ultimate source of love. However, this original freedom—pure in the beginning—included the power to rebel against God, since (again) real freedom includes the power to do both bad and good. Experience also shows that when we turn from God, the result is suffering and disorder.

The free will theodicy was now complete: evil must have entered the world after the creation, when free creatures misused their gift of free will by rebelling against their creator. This, Augustine believed, explains how evil might arise in a world that was originally created in a state of complete goodness. It also explains how suffering might enter the world *without God being its cause.*

Augustine's meditations on the nature of love and freedom suggested a morally sufficient reason God might have had for permitting the suffering we see: God allows suffering caused by the creaturely misuse of free will because the gift of free will is a necessary condition for God's ultimate goal, which, scripture assures us, is that human beings will one day freely enter into an eternal and loving relationship with their Creator in the next life, in heaven. Without free will, creatures would be robots incapable of real love since love is a free response to the goodness in another, and robots do not act freely. Freedom, then, including the freedom to misuse freedom, was a necessary precondition for God's ultimate goal—a heavenly reunion so great that its value will one day outweigh, justify, and redeem all the suffering that led up to it. Surely *that* would be a morally sufficient justification for allowing evil.

The connection to Mackie's argument from evil should be apparent. The mere *possibility* that Augustine's free will theodicy is true is a reason to reject Mackie's crucial assumption that "necessarily an all-powerful, all-good, and all-knowing being will always eliminate every bit of evil it can possibly eliminate." For if it is even possible that the free will theodicy is true, then Mackie's assumption is false. And as we have seen, if Mackie's hidden assumption is false, then his argument from evil has an unsupported premise. Does Augustine's free will theodicy provide a morally sufficient reason God *might have had* for allowing people the freedom to bring suffering into the world?[11] (We'll examine the notion of free will more closely in chapter 11.)

Incomplete Lives

Some ask: What about people whose lives are wrecked or cut short by the evil actions of others? Or those whose lives are ruined by accidents, diseases, and destructive acts of nature? In response to questions like these, the philosopher C. Stephen Layman suggests that theists add the following corollary to their worldview:

If there is an almighty and perfectly good entity who has purposes for its creatures and the creatures die before those purposes are fulfilled, then the purposes will be fulfilled (insofar as possible) after the death of those creatures [in heaven]. . . . [For] love will not accept tragedies and horrors as final if there is any alternative. . . . A God of love would seek the fulfillment of his creatures and therefore would not allow wickedness to have the last word in the long run. Being omnipotent, God would have the power to raise creatures from the dead and make a future life after death possible.[12]

THE RUG MAKER THEODICY

Many traditional theists find Augustine's theodicy inadequate because it seems to imply that God is not ultimately in control. They reject this implication because of four beliefs they consider certain. (1) Being omnipotent and omniscient, God is ultimately in control of the universe. (2) God has the power and knowledge to intervene in the natural order to bring good out of evil in the end. (3) Given the mess we human beings have made of things, God has good reason to intervene. (4) Being all-good, God will intervene to bring good out of evil in the end.

On this basis, some philosophers believe that the free will theodicy is stronger when it is supplemented with the rug maker theodicy suggested by the philosopher J. R. Lucas.[13] According to this theory, God is like a master Persian rug maker who teaches his children by letting them weave the rug from one end while he weaves from the other. When his children make mistakes, as they inevitably will because they are novices, he adjusts the weave from his side so that his plan from the beginning—a beautiful rug—is accomplished in the end. Like the rug maker, God is a supreme artist who will sometimes intervene to bring good out of bad and beauty out of ugliness in the end to complete his plan.

The rug maker analogy can be taken further. If we look at only one tiny spot on a beautiful rug, we will miss the overall beauty of the whole. Some small spots may even look ugly. God, being omniscient, sees the whole; we see only a small part of the whole. For these reasons, many traditional theists argue that the evil we see is only a small part of a whole that will be redeemed and made good by God in the fulfillment of time.

Augustine may have had a similar idea in mind when he wrote that "God did not deprive man of the power of free will because he at the same time foresaw what good he himself would draw out of evil."[14] This complement to the free will theodicy can also be found in the writings of Aquinas and many other philosophers. It can also be found in the Old Testament.[15] Theories that portray God bringing good out of evil and beauty out of ugliness in the end are called "aesthetic" theodicies.

OBJECTIONS

The Natural Evil Objection

The free will theodicy, like all philosophical theories, faces objections. The first problem is that the universe contains at least two kinds of evil: human evil and natural evil. *Human evil* is suffering caused by human beings— crimes, wars, and so forth. *Natural evil* is suffering caused by destructive acts of nature—cancer, earthquakes, and so on. A satisfactory theodicy ought to offer a sufficient reason why God would allow both kinds of evil. Although Augustine's free will theodicy as presented here offers an explanation for the existence of human evil, it offers no justification or reason why God would allow the vast amount of natural evil our world contains. How might a traditional theist respond to this counterargument?[16]

The All Saints Objection

Another objection to Augustine's free will theodicy goes like this. If God is omniscient (all-knowing), then God knows the future in complete detail. If so, then why didn't God use his knowledge of the future to make only those free creatures who have a strong tendency toward the good, such as the saints and other virtuous people? Why didn't God just *not* create the Hitlers, the Stalins, the serial killers, and the other moral monsters? By exercising intelligent foresight, God could have made a world with plenty of free will but with very little evil. Isn't this what an omniscient, omnipotent, and loving God would have done? If so, then the vast quantity of moral evil in the world remains unexplained on the free will theodicy. This objection gives expression to the fact that it is the *quantity* of evil that bothers many people, not the mere fact that some evil exists. How might a defender of Augustine respond to this objection?

The Frankenstein Objection

The free will theodicist attempts to place all responsibility for the world's evil on the free choices of human beings. However, according to theism, God is the creator of human nature. Isn't there a flaw in human nature if many humans keep doing bad things over and over again and never seem to learn? If so, isn't this flaw at least partly the fault of the creator of human nature? Doesn't Dr. Frankenstein bear some responsibility when the monster he created keeps doing monstrous things? Doesn't the creator of a flawed nature bear at least *some* responsibility for the actions of the creature? If so, then the vast amount of human wrongdoing implies a flaw in God. But God is thought to be morally perfect. Surely God could have made better creatures than us, or at least the worst of us. A loving God *would have*. How might a traditional theist answer this objection?

Augustine was the last Christian scholar of the ancient period, which ended during the fifth century AD with the decline and fall of Rome. His most important works are *Confessions* and *City of God*, but his collected writings include approximately 100 books, 300 letters, and 500 sermons that fill more than 50 volumes in a modern library. Augustine was a profound philosopher who ranks with Socrates, Plato, and Aristotle as one of the most important and influential scholars of all time.

THE MORAL QUALITIES THEODICY

This theodicy, proposed by Irenaeus in the second century AD, presupposes free will but rejects Augustine's claim that in the beginning God created perfected creatures and placed them in a perfectly good world. Irenaeus argued that God is not like a master sculptor who makes perfectly formed and completed statues. Rather, human beings begin their existence in an imperfect, immature, and incomplete state. Furthermore, the world we enter at birth is full of hardships, temptations, and hurdles. However, the hardships of this world exist for a purpose: imperfect, immature creatures will only develop and mature morally and spiritually by overcoming challenges, resisting temptations, and persevering through hardships. This, Irenaeus hypothesized, is the reason our world is full of difficulties. Our assignment, if we will accept it, is to meet and overcome life's many challenges and thereby grow morally, and spiritually, in small steps over a lifetime.

Our world, then, is like an army boot camp for moral and spiritual growth. God filled the world with hurdles to test us and help us grow. Life is a struggle, with many lessons to be learned. But it is not a meaningless struggle, for it is all preparation for something higher—for a state of being in the next life that, scripture assures us, will be so great as to redeem and justify all the suffering that came before. Different religious outlooks characterize this future life in different ways. As a Christian, Irenaeus believed that life on earth is a preparation for an eternal union with God in heaven in a realm that will be so filled with love, goodness, and beauty as to make the process leading up to it—as difficult as it is—worth the cost.[17]

Imagining a Pet Shop World

But is overcoming challenges, enduring hardships, and resisting temptations actually required for moral and spiritual growth? To test the idea, imagine a world devoid of all suffering, hardships, temptations, and moral challenges. In this semi-Edenic paradise, there is no war, crime, poverty, loneliness, hunger, pain, or disease. There are no temptations of any kind. Suffering is not even possible. Every need is instantly satisfied. Everyone is taken care of by nature like pampered pets in a luxurious pet shop. No sacrifice is ever required. Now, given these conditions, what would the inhabitants of this "pet shop world" be like?

Irenaeus would argue that many moral and spiritual character traits would not exist. For instance, in a pet shop world no one would ever have felt, or expressed, sympathy or compassion for another person. For you can't possibly feel or express sympathy or compassion for another person if no one is suffering or in need. But someone who has never felt or expressed sympathy or compassion cannot possibly develop the corresponding character traits. In short, compassion and sympathy would not exist.

In a pet shop world, no one would ever have helped another person, for no one would ever need any help. But a person can't be genuinely charitable without ever having performed a charitable action. Charity would not exist.

Other examples come quickly to mind. It seems that no one in a pet shop world would ever have faced danger or trouble. Consequently, no one would ever have the opportunity to be courageous, for courage only develops as we confront danger. The character trait of courage would also be missing.

Similar arguments can be made for such moral and spiritual qualities as loyalty, self-discipline, perseverance, responsibility, generosity, and the work ethic. Would love exist in such a world? That's a question worth thinking about. The philosopher John Hick, a contemporary defender of the Irenaean theodicy, writes:

> We can at least begin to imagine a world custom-made for the avoidance of all suffering. But the daunting fact that emerges is that in such a world moral qualities would no longer have any point or value. . . . It would be a world without need for the virtues of self-sacrifice, care for others, devotion to the public good, courage, perseverance, skill, or honesty. It would indeed be a world in which such qualities, having no function to perform, would never come into existence. . . . Perhaps most important of all, the capacity to love would never be developed; except in a very limited sense of the word, in a world in which there was no suffering.[18]

If Irenaeus's moral qualities theodicy is plausible, we have another reason to reject the crucial assumption Mackie needs if his logical argument from evil is to succeed, namely, that "necessarily, an all-powerful, all-good, and all-knowing being will always eliminate every bit of evil it can possibly eliminate." Irenaeus's point is that God might not eliminate a hardship if it is part of a necessary condition for magnificent moral and spiritual growth that outweighs the costs that led up to it. And his decision not to eliminate the hardship and the suffering that results would seem to be morally justified. However, like all philosophical theories, the moral qualities theodicy faces philosophical objections.

OBJECTIONS

The Birthright Objection

This counterargument concerns the concept of omnipotence. If God is all-powerful, then God has the power to build moral and spiritual qualities into us before we are born, just as God builds eye color or musical talent into a person before birth. But if God were to build moral and spiritual traits into each person at birth, then no one would need to confront hardship, suffering, or temptation. The world would contain no evil and no hardships, yet it would still contain the moral and spiritual character traits. A world like that would be morally better. Therefore, that is what God would have done. Since the world contains evils, hardships, and temptations, it follows that Mackie's argument is correct and God doesn't exist.

Defenders of Irenaeus's theodicy reply that moral and spiritual qualities simply can't be built in or programmed at birth, even by an omnipotent God. In support of this claim, they argue that a person can't possess moral and spiritual qualities without actually having *experienced* and *freely responded to* real challenges. In other words, the moral and spiritual qualities are logically dependent on actually lived experiences coupled with the exercise of real free will—they cannot simply be built in before birth.

Is this right? Could a person be compassionate, or even know what compassion is, without having ever experienced and freely responded to someone in need? Could a person come to be brave without ever having experienced and freely responded to real danger? Could a person be born fully compassionate, brave, and charitable prior to any lived experiences? Can moral character traits be conferred on us before birth, like hair or eye color? Or do they only develop over time as a person freely confronts real perils, temptations, and suffering? If this reply is sound, the objection fails.

The Quantity of Evil Argument

Let's grant that some challenges are necessary for moral and spiritual growth. But *this many*? Did God have to permit the Holocaust? The mass killings ordered by Lenin, Stalin, Mao Tse-tung, Ho Chi Minh, and Pol Pot?[19] The many wars of history? Cancer? Couldn't God have created an environment for moral and spiritual growth that contains a lot less evil? In the end, it is the vast *amount* of evil, not the mere existence of some evil, that deeply troubles many critics of the traditional theodicies. This thought leads us to the evidential problem of evil, which we'll examine after we consider a non-Western approach to the problem.

Questions for Reflection and Discussion 7.2

1. How does a theodicy differ from an argument for the existence of God?
2. In your own words, explain one of the theodicies examined in this chapter.

3. Is free will a requirement for genuine love? Is love by its nature freely given?
4. Could someone who had never freely responded to suffering be compassionate?
5. Would you rather live in a pet shop world?
6. Choose one of the objections to Augustine's free will theodicy. How might a traditional theist respond?
7. Choose one of the objections to Irenaeus's theodicy. How might a traditional theist respond?
8. Evaluate Lucas's rug maker theodicy.

THE HINDU AND BUDDHIST SOLUTION TO THE PROBLEM OF EVIL

The Hindu and Buddhist sages of ancient times were as aware as anyone of the miseries and suffering of this world. They argued that the doctrine of karma provides the best solution to the problem of evil. Karma is said to be a universal law of cause and effect guaranteeing that the moral consequences of our actions eventually come back to us in time, in this life or in a future life. When we do something good, something good eventually comes back to us, and when we do something bad, negative results come back. Each of us is thus the cause of whatever good and bad we experience.

Why, one might ask, does karma exist? The system of causes and effects has a purpose. By experiencing the karmic effects of our actions, we eventually learn to be good.

However logical the theory of karma seems at first glance, the doctrine has surprising consequences that are not often noted. If the doctrine is true, it follows that whenever someone is enjoying wealth, high income, power, happiness, or anything good, that person is reaping the positive results of his or her previous good actions. The wealthy therefore morally deserve their wealth and the other good things in life that they enjoy. The powerful morally deserve their power, and so forth.

Similarly, whenever someone suffers, is poor or oppressed, or experiences anything bad, that person is reaping the negative results of his or her own previous bad actions. The poor, the sick, and the downtrodden therefore morally deserve their condition.

Therefore—and this is the key point—there is no such thing as unde-served suffering anywhere in the world. In his authoritative Hindu cate-chism, *Dancing with Siva*, the Hindu philosopher and sage Satguru Sivaya Subramuniyaswami (1927–2001) writes:

> When something happens to us that is apparently unfortunate or unjust, it is not God punishing us. It is the result of our own past actions. The Vedas, Hinduism's revealed scripture, tell us if we sow goodness, we will reap goodness; if we sow evil, we will reap evil. Thus we create our own destiny through thought and action. And the divine law is: whatever karma we are experiencing in our life is just what we need at the moment, and nothing can happen but that we have the strength to meet it. Even harsh karma, when faced in wisdom, can be the greatest catalyst for spiri-tual growth. Understanding the way karma works, we seek to live a good and virtuous life through right thought, right speech and right action.[20]

> Karma is a very just law which, like gravity, treats everyone the same. Because we Hindus understand karma, we do not hate or resent people who do us harm. We understand they are giving back the effects of the causes we set in motion at an earlier time. The law of karma puts man at the center of responsibility for everything he does and everything that is done to him.[21]

> Karma is not fate, for man acts with free will creating his own destiny. The Vedas tell us that if we sow goodness, we will reap goodness; if we sow evil, we will reap evil. . . . Not all karmas rebound immediately. Some accumulate and return in this or other births.[22]

Challenges for the Doctrine of Karma

The traditional doctrine of karma has been an integral part of the religious and philosophical thought of the Indian subcontinent since ancient times. It is accepted in one form or another by Buddhists, Hindus, and Jains. However, as is the case with any philosophical theory, challenging ques-tions can be (and must be) asked. It's time to do our philosophical duty.

If all suffering and oppression everywhere is morally deserved, and if all wealth, power, and other desired things in life are also morally deserved, it logically follows that

- all who suffer caused their own suffering through their own past bad actions and deserve exactly what they get, whether they are hurting from disease, abuse, war, oppression, racial discrimination, sexual harassment, poverty, or anything else bad. In plain terms, when someone suffers, that person "brought it on him- or herself" and morally "had it coming."
- the wealthy and powerful caused their wealth and power through their own past good actions and are getting just what they deserve (and earned).

Are these implications of the theory of karma believable? Or do they contradict commonsense moral judgments that seem most certainly true, judgments we routinely make in everyday life? Doesn't it seem clearly and undeniably false that *all* victims of abuse, harassment, crime, and discrimination are the causes of their own suffering and deserve their mistreatment? The answer you give depends in part on your theory of human nature. (We'll explore the philosophy of the human person in Unit IV.) Decide for yourself. But keep this in mind: if a theory has implications that clearly seem false, that is a reason to reject it. We'll examine other theories of good and bad, right and wrong in chapter 12 when we apply reason to morality and ask one of Socrates's favorite questions: What is the best way to live, all things considered? Like the other conversations we've had so far, this one goes back thousands of years and circles around the world. It continues to enrich our thought today.

Questions for Reflection and Discussion 7.3

1. In your own words, explain the solution to the problem of evil proposed by the Satguru Sivaya Subramuniyaswami.
2. Does the theory of karma provide a reasonable solution to the problem of evil?
3. Does the theory of karma entail that there is no such thing as undeserved suffering? Does the theory imply that each of us is the cause of our own suffering and misfortune, wealth, and power?
4. Does the theory of karma entail that every society is already perfectly just? If so, is this consequence of the theory believable?

THE EVIDENTIAL ARGUMENT FROM EVIL

Moving beyond the logical argument from evil as presented by Mackie, the traditional theist faces a second major objection in the form of the evidential argument from evil. This objection focuses on the *kind* of evil that exists, not the mere fact that evil exists. This particular line of thought first appeared in the writings of the philosopher William Rowe in the late 1970s. Whereas Mackie's logical argument from evil was deductive and relied heavily on abstract logic, Rowe's evidential argument from evil is inductive and relies heavily on empirical observations. Whereas Mackie argued that it is *certain* that God does not exist, Rowe's argument concludes that God, as traditionally conceived, *very probably* does not exist. And if God very probably does not exist, it is unreasonable—though not strictly self-contradictory—to believe.

Keep in mind as we proceed that the evidential argument from evil, like the logical argument from evil, is only directed at traditional theism—belief in God with God understood as personal, omniscient, omnipotent, infinitely loving, and so forth. The argument does not touch mere theism.

Rowe's argument from evil grew out of the evidential problem of evil, which I'll summarize in the following terms. It is logically *possible* that God and evil both exist. The traditional theist is right about this, and Mackie is wrong. There is nothing self-contradictory in believing in God and at the same time acknowledging that evil exists. Therefore, the existence of some evil does not by itself prove with certainty that God does not exist, and the logical argument from evil is unsound. However, the world appears to contain a good deal of *gratuitous* evil, defined as evil that God (if God were to exist) would have no morally sufficient reason to permit. We can't be completely certain that the world contains gratuitous evil, but a great deal of evil surely *looks* gratuitous, for (1) it seems that the world would have been a morally better place if evils such as the Nazi Holocaust and Stalin's crimes against humanity had never occurred, and (2) there appears to be no morally sufficient reason why a good God would permit these and other terrible tragedies. Since God certainly would not permit gratuitous evil, it follows that very probably God does not exist.

Rowe organizes these thoughts into an inductive argument that runs about like this:

1. An instance of evil is "gratuitous" if God would have no morally sufficient reason to permit it.

2. In some cases of suffering, we cannot think of any morally sufficient reason God might have had for permitting that suffering.

3. Therefore, in some cases of suffering, it appears that there is no morally sufficient reason that would have justified God's permitting that suffering.

4. Therefore, in some cases of suffering, there is probably no morally sufficient reason that would have justified God's permitting that suffering.

5. Thus, it is very probable that some gratuitous evil exists.

6. If God were to exist, there would be no gratuitous evil at all.

7. So, it is very probable that God does not exist.

8. The most reasonable conclusion to draw is therefore that God does not exist.[23]

Rowe supports premises 2 and 6 with subarguments. In support of premise 2, he gives this example, sometimes called the "Bambi argument":

Suppose in some distant forest lightning strikes a dead tree, resulting in a forest fire. In the fire, a fawn is trapped, horribly burned, and lies in terrible agony for several days before death relieves its suffering. So far as we can see, the fawn's intense suffering is pointless, for there does not appear to be any greater good such that the prevention of the fawn's suffering would require either the loss of that good or the occurrence of an evil equally bad or worse. Nor does there seem to be an equally bad or worse evil so connected to the fawn's suffering that it would have had to occur had the fawn's suffering been prevented.[24]

However, we cannot be completely certain that no morally sufficient reason exists that would justify God's allowing the fawn to suffer, for we

are often surprised by how things we thought to be unconnected turn out to be intimately connected. Perhaps, for all we know, there is some familiar good outweighing the fawn's suffering to which that suffering is connected in a way we do not see. Furthermore, there may be unfamiliar goods, goods we haven't dreamed of, to which the fawn's suffering is inextricably connected. Indeed, it would seem to require something like omniscience on our part before we should lay claim to knowing that there is no greater good [justifying the fawn's suffering].[25]

Nevertheless, even if an investigation were to show that the fawn's suffering was not pointless because it led to a greater good that outweighed the suffering and thus justified God's permitting it to happen, it seems extremely unlikely that *all* instances of suffering all around the world lead to either some greater good that justifies permitting the suffering or to the prevention of evils at least as bad that morally justify God's permitting the suffering. So, Rowe concludes, it is reasonable to believe that premise 2 is true.

In support of premise 6, Rowe argues that God would prevent any instance of suffering unless he could not do so without thereby losing some greater good or permitting some evil equally bad or worse. In other words, God would prevent any instance of evil unless he had a morally sufficient or overriding reason to allow it. If God has no morally sufficient reason to permit an evil, he will not permit it. Therefore, premise 6 is true.

Rowe's novel argument stimulated an avalanche of replies from theistic philosophers around the world. One group of theistic critics of Rowe's argument became known as the "skeptical theists."

THE SKEPTICAL THEIST RESPONSE

William Alston (1921–2009) was one of the first theistic philosophers to respond to Rowe's evidential argument from evil. A pioneer of contemporary epistemology and one of the greats of twentieth-century philosophy, Alston taught for many years at the University of Michigan. For reasons that will become apparent, his general line of response was named "skeptical theism." Alston asked, How could we ever *know* that some particular evil E is gratuitous? That is, how could we ever know that there is absolutely *no* morally sufficient reason that would justify God's permitting some particular evil E? For, to be sure that an instance of suffering E is gratuitous, we would have to accomplish three things:

1. Grasp all the reasons God could possibly have had for permitting E.

2. Foresee all the future consequences of permitting E, good and bad, and also any good and bad that might result from preventing E.

3. Find reasons to rule out as morally insufficient each and every possible reason God might have had for allowing E to occur.

How, Alston asks, could we—with our limited cognitive abilities—possibly accomplish all three tasks? Wouldn't we have to know as much as God knows or would know? For instance, to be sure that we had accomplished 1, we would have to suppose that *if God did have a sufficient reason for permitting some instance of suffering E, we would have thought of it.* But why believe that this is true? How could we ever be certain that we had thought of all the possible reasons God would possibly have had for permitting a particular evil E and all the possible reasons God would have had for blocking E from occurring? Given the limited nature of the human intellect compared to God's, isn't it highly likely that at least *some* of the reasons God would have had would be beyond our grasp?[26]

Of course, God's reasons would not contradict human reason or morality, for traditional theism holds that God's eternal nature is the source of both reason and morality, and as such cannot stand in contradiction to either one. God's reasons could be beyond our present human comprehension without standing in contradiction to our deepest and most rational moral considerations.

A similar argument applies to the second and third tasks, suggesting that they, too, very probably outstrip our limited human cognitive abilities.

Therefore, argues Alston, our intellectual powers are likely "radically insufficient" to provide us with a good reason to accept the fourth and fifth premises of Rowe's argument.[27] Skepticism (lack of belief) with respect to those two premises is thus the correct response to Rowe's argument. Put another way, because of our human limits, we can never *know* that any particular evil E is gratuitous.[28] It follows that at least one of Rowe's premises is false, and "the inductive argument from evil is in no better shape than its late lamented cousin [the logical argument from evil exemplified by Mackie's argument]."[29]

The contemporary philosopher Stephen Wykstra was also one of the first to respond to Rowe's evidential argument from evil. Wykstra's critique made use of an unusual idea from the insect world. "No-see-ums" are pesky insects so tiny they usually bite you before you realize they are present.

Wykstra begins his argument by noting that the reasoning from step 3 to step 4 of Rowe's argument is logically equivalent to reasoning from (1) we cannot see any morally sufficient reason God might have had for permitting some of the evils around us to (2) very probably there is no morally sufficient reason.[30]

Next, Wykstra calls this form of reasoning the "no-see-um inference." In general, we make a no-see-um inference when we reason from (1) we see no x's here to (2) there probably are no x's here. Essentially, a no-see-um inference takes the absence of evidence as direct evidence of absence.

However, argues Wykstra, in some cases a no-see-um inference is falla-cious. We can reason from "we see no x's here" to "there probably are no x's here" only when x has "reasonable seeability." Something x has reasonable seeability when it is the case that *if* an x were to be present, we would rea-sonably expect to see it.[31]

For example, from "I see no elephant in the living room," I can reason-ably conclude that "there probably is no elephant in the living room." This no-see-um inference is reasonable because elephants have high seeability. (If an elephant were in the room, I would reasonably expect to see it.) However, I cannot reasonably argue from "I see no flea in the room" to "there probably is no flea in the room," for fleas have low seeability. If a single flea is in the living room, I cannot reasonably expect to see it. This no-see-um inference is fallacious.

Now, it is extremely probable, Wykstra continues, that some of the reasons God would have for permitting evil would have very low seeability. Why? Our cognitive capacities are so radically limited compared to God's that we cannot expect to be aware of *all* the reasons God might have had. Therefore, in the case of any particular evil E, if God *does* have a morally sufficient reason R for permitting E, we may not be aware of it. We may not even be able to grasp it if God were to try to explain it to us. Thus, Rowe's inference from his third to his fourth premise is a fallacious no-see-um inference. Therefore, Wykstra concludes, we should be skeptical of (withhold our belief in) premise 5 of Rowe's argument.

The philosophers C. Stephen Evans and R. Zachary Manis put the point this way:

Given that God is both omniscient and transcendent, there is every reason to believe that God is privy to a vast amount of knowledge about the relations between good and evil of which we are ignorant. We have every reason to believe, then, that for any allegedly pointless evil, if there were some justifying reason that God had for allowing it, we very likely would not be in a position to perceive it. If God exists, it is virtually certain that many of his reasons are inscrutable to us.[32]

A skeptical theist is therefore someone who maintains that (1) traditional theism is true; (2) our cognitive faculties are far too limited to allow us to know all the reasons God might have for permitting any specific evil; and therefore (3) we ought to be skeptical regarding any claim, such as Rowe's, that gratuitous or unjustified evils probably exist. If the skeptical theists are right, one of Rowe's premises is unacceptable, and his argument fails. Does skeptical theism defeat Rowe's inductive argument from evil and save traditional theism from refutation? You be the judge.

In *God, Freedom, and Evil,* Alvin Plantinga imagines an atheist asking a theist, "Why does God permit evil?" The theist replies, "I don't know." Plantinga continues:

> What follows from that? Very little of interest. Why suppose that if God does have a reason for permitting evil, the theist would be the first to know it? Perhaps God has a reason but that reason is too complicated for us to understand. Or perhaps He has not revealed it for some other reason. The fact that the theist doesn't know why God permits evil is, perhaps, an interesting fact about the theist, but by itself it shows little or nothing relevant to the rationality of belief in God. Much more is needed for the atheological argument [an argument against the existence of God] to even get off the ground.[33]

WHERE DOES THIS LEAVE US?

The argument from evil, in either its logical or evidential form, certainly gives us some reason to doubt that God, as conceived within traditional theism, exists. On the other hand, there are deep arguments for the existence of God. And we have examined only five of the hundreds that have been given by philosophers down through the ages.[34] Many philosophers contend that although the argument from evil is some evidence against theism, the many compelling arguments in favor of God's existence outweigh it, so that after we balance the total evidence, it remains eminently reasonable to believe in God. This is the conclusion the philosopher Richard Swinburne draws after examining many of the major arguments for and against God's existence in his path-breaking book *The Existence of God*.[35]

The traditional theodicies certainly give us plausible reasons God might have for permitting some of the evils of this world. Skeptical theists add another dimension to the discussion when they argue that we should be skeptical whenever someone claims that a specific instance of evil is gratuitous. Given the theodicies, the case made by the skeptical theists, and the parallel argument suggested in the book of Job, chapters 38–40, is it reasonable to hold on to faith in the face of the enormous quantity of suffering the world contains?

Questions for Reflection and Discussion 7.4

1. How do the logical and evidential arguments from evil differ?
2. Why does Rowe believe that gratuitous evils exist?
3. In your own words, explain Rowe's argument from evil, and then critically evaluate it.
4. What is skeptical theism?
5. In your own words, explain either Alston's or Wykstra's argument for skeptical theism.
6. Is skeptical theism an adequate response to Rowe's argument?
7. Do you have a theodicy of your own that you believe makes sense of the existence of evil? Can you defend it philosophically?
8. In the book of Job, chapters 38–40, from the Old Testament, does God endorse the skeptical theist solution to the problem of evil?
9. Where does the problem of evil leave us? Offer the most intelligent and strongest reasons you can for your position.

Epistemology

EIGHT

What Can We Know?

RELATIVISM, SKEPTICISM, AND
THE BIRTH OF EPISTEMOLOGY

Many people today claim that there is no such thing as objective truth. Truth, they confidently say, is relative to each person. By this they mean two things: each person has a unique perspective and each person's perspective is equally valid because there are no objective facts that might serve as a basis for saying that one person's belief is true and another's is false. For example, if Fred believes that global warming is a hoax, that is his truth. If Susan believes that global warming is real, that is her (alternative) truth, and there is no objective fact that decides the matter one way or the other.

In philosophy, this view is known as "alethic relativism" (Greek *aletheia*, "truth or disclosure"). It is also called "relativism about truth." According to the relativist about truth, those who believe in objective truth are mistaken. The real truth about truth is that truth is relative to each person. There is no such thing as an objective truth that is the same for everyone or that can be accessed by everyone. Of this the relativist is *certain*.

185

Relativism about truth sounds exciting to many today, especially to those who have an adversarial attitude toward traditional ideas. The claim that truth is relative can be found, in one form or another, in the writings of philosophers who call themselves "postmodernists." It can also be found in the writings of those multicultural theorists who copy their basic premises from relativistic postmodernist philosophy. Some of these multicultural theorists go further and relativize truth, not to each person, but to each racial or ethnic group. If one group believes X, then that makes X true for that group, and that group's belief cannot be criticized by anyone outside the group, for there is no objective fact of the matter that is the same for every group. If another group believes Y, then that makes Y true for that group, and that group's belief cannot be criticized by anyone outside that group (for the same reason). Each group has a unique perspective that cannot be assessed or criticized on objective or rational grounds by anyone outside the group.

However, whether in the individual or group form, relativism about truth has severe problems. When relativists assert that truth is relative, aren't they making an objective claim about the nature of truth? Aren't they saying that (being relative) is the way truth really is — "really is" in a non-relative way? Aren't they saying that, *in fact*, truth is relative, and we all should agree? In other words, aren't relativists, in effect, claiming that it is objectively true *for all of us* that truth is relative? If so, aren't they contradicting themselves? But if a theory cannot even be asserted without self-contradiction, why believe it?

Here is another way to think of it. The relativist about truth claims that there is no such thing as an objective truth that is the same for everyone or that can be accessed by everyone. Then he turns around and says that we should all accept relativism. Isn't that a self-contradiction?

Suppose the relativist argues for his view by giving us reasons to believe that truth is relative. Look at what he is doing. He wants us all to see the light and agree on the basis of common grounds. Doesn't that contradict his claim (that truth is relative)? Common reasons given for a view would be reasons available to all, wouldn't they? And reasons available to all — reasons all should be moved by — would have to be nonrelatively true. Relativists contradict themselves if they reason for their view. But if no good reasons can be given for the relativist theory of truth, then why believe it?

Some people today believe that relativism about truth is a new, cutting-edge idea. They are wrong; the idea is as old as the hills. In Socrates's day, alethic relativism was advocated by some members of a group of private teachers who traveled from city to city in Greece during the fifth century BC giving lessons in subjects such as public speaking, grammar, law, and poetry. They were known as the Sophists and their services were in demand because the Greek experiment in democracy — underway at the time — required educated citizens. Socrates clashed with the Sophists on many occasions. As he saw it, the relativists among them were dangerous because they taught politicians to win by appealing to emotions rather than to objective truth, and to get ahead by pandering to the prejudices of the masses rather than to what is truly just and right.[1] He argued that if such politicians gain power, the result will be injustice and cognitive error. Many contemporary philosophers hold that Socrates's argument against demagogues — politicians who pander to emotions rather than to reason and truth — are as relevant today as they were 2,400 years ago.[2]

The question, What is objective truth? is examined in *metaphysics*, the branch of philosophy that seeks a rational account of the most fundamental aspects of reality. (We'll examine the concept of objective truth in a moment.)

The concepts of truth and knowledge are closely related. When we say that someone "knows" something about the world, for instance, "Pat knows that the moon has mountains," we ordinarily mean, in part, that the claim said to be known (in this case, the proposition that the moon has mountains) is true in an objective sense. As we'll see in more detail in a moment, we also ordinarily suppose that the knower has a sufficient reason anchored in reality to believe that the claim is true. It follows that *if* objective truth does not exist, then neither does knowledge in the traditional sense of the word.

It should be no surprise, then, that those who deny the existence of objective truth usually also reject the traditional concept of knowledge. "Knowledge with a capital K is a myth," some say. "Nobody really knows anything. All we have are opinions, and one opinion is as valid as any other." Those who make this claim usually sound so confident that they give the impression they really know what they are talking about.

Time for another definition. A skeptical person is someone who is hard to convince. A skeptic with respect to a particular subject is someone who is hard to convince on that subject. A religious skeptic, for instance, is hard to convince on matters of religion. In philosophy the denial of *all* knowledge is called "absolute skepticism."

If absolute skepticism is correct, *knowledge* as we normally use the term is a total mirage. Knowledge does not exist. Which raises an interesting question. If knowledge does not really exist, then what are people doing when they claim to know something? The answer given by some postmodernist absolute skeptics echoes an idea first stated by some of the Sophists who debated the idea with Socrates. A claim to knowledge, these absolute skeptics argue, is really just a power grab. In other words, when people claim to know something, they are simply trying to bully you into agreeing with them. In most cases, they are merely attempting to gain power over you. As Sophists such as Gorgias of Leontini (ca. 485–ca. 380 BC) suggested, victory, not truth, is the hidden goal of every argument. Reason is a weapon, not a searchlight. Like relativism, absolute skepticism is as old as the hills.[3]

However, if the skeptics are right, then isn't *their* confident assertion — that a claim to knowledge is merely a disguised power grab unrelated to objective truth or reality — also a disguised power grab unrelated to objective truth or reality? When they try to convince us to agree with them, aren't they merely doing what they claim to hate? Isn't their theory also nothing but another power grab?

At the risk of overkill, one last thought on the matter. If knowledge does not exist and all we have are unsubstantiated opinions, then the claim that knowledge does not exist is itself just one more unsubstantiated opinion. In which case, why should we believe it?

I meet students every quarter who subscribe to these relativistic and skeptical postmodernist views. The traditional concepts of objective truth and traditional knowledge are under attack today in many quarters of the academic world. Knowledge and truth, many academics now believe, are collective delusions, throwbacks to primitive times, or (worse) mind-control tools imposed by the ruling class, "the man," or the Establishment. Are these critics of tradition right? Or can the traditional notions of truth and knowledge be defined in plausible terms and defended rationally in the twenty-first century? That is the question before us in this chapter. For clarification we'll begin with the underlying metaphysical question, What is truth?

WHAT IS TRUTH?

The most widely held definition among philosophers today is the account first expressed by Socrates in the dialogues of Plato and stated more formally in the logical works of Aristotle:

A proposition is true if it accurately corresponds to the facts; it is false if it does not.

Truth, in short, is correspondence with the facts. In philosophy, this is known as the *correspondence theory of truth*.

Notice the way each of the following true statements, each expressing a proposition, accurately corresponds to, or specifies, the relevant facts:

- There are craters on the moon.
- The White House is located in Washington, DC.

The fact that there really are craters on the moon makes the first statement true; the fact that the White House really is located in Washington, DC, makes the second one true.

And notice the way the following false statements fail to correspond:

- There are large cities with skyscrapers on the moon.
- The White House is located in Minnesota.

It is simply not a fact that there are skyscrapers on the moon. The second false statement is also not factual, right?

Although most philosophers throughout history have thought that the correspondence theory of truth is simply common sense made precise, two alternative theories have been proposed. According to the *coherence theory of truth*, what makes a proposition true is that it belongs to a coherent system of propositions. A system of propositions is coherent if its members are (1) logically consistent and (2) stand in a sufficient number of explanatory and logical relations to one another. A well-written novel is an example of a coherent system of propositions.

However, the coherence theory faces an objection that nearly all philosophers find decisive. It is possible to specify two equally coherent systems of propositions that are related in such a way that one contradicts the other. Since the two systems are contradictory, they cannot both be true. Yet both are equally coherent. If so, then truth cannot be mere coherence.

A second alternative to correspondence is the *pragmatic theory of truth*. According to this theory, truth is usefulness. A proposition is useful if belief in the proposition serves a human purpose. The pragmatic definition also faces an objection that most philosophers find fatal. Some propositions are useful in the pragmatic sense, even though they are clearly false. Hitler's racial theories, for example, were useful to him in his quest for power, yet his theories have been proved false. But if a theory can be useful and yet false, then truth is not simply usefulness. For many reasons, the correspondence theory remains the mainstream, and also the commonsense, view.

Is All Truth Subjective?

Some people today deny the existence of objective facts accessible to all. Every claim to objective truth, they say, is merely the unsubstantiated, personal opinion of a subject (person). Every truth claim, in short, is subjective. This view has serious problems. The claim that everything is subjective is either an objective claim or a subjective claim. If it is an objective claim, then it is self-defeating because it is self-contradictory. For it is self-contradictory to say, "It is objectively true that everything is subjective." On the other hand, if the claim is subjective—if it is merely the speaker's unsupported opinion—then why should anyone believe it?[4]

INTRODUCING EPISTEMOLOGY

Epistemology (Greek *episteme*, "knowledge") is the philosophical study of the nature, scope, and limits of knowledge. What exactly is knowledge? How (if at all) does it differ from mere opinion? What (if anything) can we know? What is the relationship between knowledge and truth? Socrates, as recorded in Plato's dialogues, was the first to ask these questions in a philosophical context and to propose answers within a systematic theory of epistemology.[5] His student Plato was the first to examine them in depth and work out a unified theory in written form. The ancient Greeks are the founders of epistemology as an academic subject. Let's clarify our thinking further by turning to the first question of this important field of philosophy.

WHAT IS KNOWLEDGE?

There are many different kinds of knowledge. We may say that a person "knows" how to drive a car. This is practical, or how-to, knowledge. We say that a carpenter "knows" how to build a house. Call this "craft-knowledge." We often say that one person "knows" a second person. This is acquaintance knowledge. There is also public knowledge (information that has been made public) and common knowledge (facts known by most people).

But we also say things like "I know that there are an infinite number of prime numbers" and "I know that the moon has craters." Epistemologists call this "propositional knowledge" because a proposition or statement (rather than a skill, a person, etc.) is what is known.[6] In many of Plato's dialogues, Socrates seems quite interested in craft knowledge (Greek: *technê*).[7] However, when he works out a strict definition, his focus is propositional knowledge. This is understandable since the context in the dialogues is intellectual. From here on, by *knowledge* we'll mean the propositional kind. So, what exactly *is* propositional knowledge?

In his dialogues, Plato portrays Socrates seeking an answer to the following question: When is it correct to say that someone "knows" something? Socrates's first observation, put in modern terms, is that we would not ordinarily say that a person knows that some proposition P is true if the person does not *believe* that P is true, that is, corresponds to the facts. (Socrates and Plato accepted the correspondence theory of truth.) So, believing P is surely a necessary condition for knowing P. If I sincerely state that I do *not* believe that whales are mammals, then it would not be correct to say that I "know" that whales are mammals.

Next, Socrates observes, we do not ordinarily say that a person knows some proposition P if, in fact, P is not true.[8] For a contemporary example, some people actually believe that the earth is flat. They claim to have credible evidence. However, the earth is not flat. This is why we do not say, "They *know* that the earth is flat." Rather, we say, "They *believe* that the earth is flat." The truth of the proposition said to be known is clearly a necessary condition for the presence of knowledge.

Finally, we do not normally call some proposition P "knowledge" unless its truth is anchored to reality by good reasoning, that is, by an argument showing that P is certainly or at least very likely true. For example, imagine that during a drawing for a door prize at a party, I believe that Ann will win the prize, and she, in fact, does. My belief was true. However, suppose that I had no reason to believe that she would win; my belief was just a lucky guess based on nothing at all. In that case, we would not say that I "knew" (beforehand) that she would win, for guesses are not justified by credible evidence connected to reality. The mere fact that a belief is true does not imply that the belief is knowledge. In general, a true belief only rises to the level of knowledge if it is anchored to reality by solid reasons, that is, by an argument making it certain or very likely that the proposition said to be known is indeed true.

In sum, three conditions need to be satisfied before we ordinarily say that a person or "subject" S *knows* that a proposition P is true:

1. S believes that P is true. (This is called the "belief condition.")

2. The proposition P is true. (This is called the "truth condition.")

3. S has an adequate justification for believing that P is true, where the justification for a claim P is "a sufficiently strong reason or justification for thinking that P is true."[9] (This is called the "justification condition.")

The epistemologists Ernest Sosa and Laurence BonJour summarize all three conditions compactly in the following words: "Ever since Plato it has been thought that one knows only if one's belief hits the mark of truth and does so with adequate justification."[10]

For example, Jane *knows* that Jupiter's atmosphere is mostly hydrogen and helium only if (1) she believes that the atmosphere of Jupiter is mostly hydrogen and helium, (2) it is true that the atmosphere of Jupiter is mostly hydrogen and helium, and (3) she has adequate justification for her belief in the form of a sufficiently strong reason anchored in reality for thinking that her belief is true.

Socrates, as Plato presents him, argued that the belief, truth, and justification conditions are *jointly sufficient* and *individually necessary* for the presence of knowledge. Some technical terminology is required before this will be precise. A condition is a sufficient condition for X if its presence all by itself guarantees X. For example, jumping in Green Lake is a sufficient condition for getting wet. A condition is a necessary condition for some X if it is a requirement for X, which means that without it, X cannot exist. For example, oxygen is a necessary condition for human life. Here's a shorthand way to think of it: a sufficient condition is a guarantee; a necessary condition is only a requirement. Notice that oxygen is necessary but not sufficient for life (you need more than oxygen), whereas jumping in a lake is sufficient but not necessary for getting wet (there are other ways to get wet).

So, the Socratic claim is that if all three conditions are satisfied, knowledge is present (the person knows that P), but if even one condition is not satisfied, knowledge is not present (since each condition is required). Because this was the first philosophical theory of knowledge, it is called the *classical account of knowledge*. It may also be called the *Socratic account of knowledge* in honor of the first philosopher to teach it explicitly.

The justification condition is the only one of the three that is difficult to understand. People can have many different kinds of reasons or justifications for holding a belief. Someone might believe a proposition simply because he finds the belief comforting. The belief serves as an emotional crutch, and that is why the person is attached to it. The reverse, of course, is also possible: someone might reject a proposition simply because he doesn't want it to be true. These would be emotional motives for belief.

Some beliefs are held for self-serving reasons. For instance, someone benefits greatly from a particular economic system, and this—rather than a reasoned argument—is the real (perhaps unconscious) reason why the person believes the system is best.

A belief might also be accepted because it is useful, even though the believer might not realize this is the unconscious reason he accepts the belief. This would be a pragmatic motive to accept a belief.

Emotional, self-interested, and pragmatic motives or reasons for belief do not satisfy the justification condition for knowledge because they are not intrinsically related to the goal of the cognitive enterprise, which is the attainment of objective truth. The fact that believing P comforts you or makes you happy does not make it likely that P is true. Just because you want P to be true, or hope that P is true, does not make it certain, or even likely, that P is true. A belief could be useful and yet false. (Hitler's racial beliefs, for instance.) In short, emotional, self-interested, and pragmatic motives for holding a belief do not satisfy the classical justification condition for knowledge because there is no intrinsic connection between unexamined emotions, feelings, ego, self-interest, or usefulness, and objective truth.

Today epistemologists call the special type of justification required for knowledge "epistemic justification." This kind of justification consists in critical reasoning that makes it either certain or at least likely to a sufficient degree that the belief said to be known is true. Epistemic justification is thus reasoning that is *truth-conducive*. As BonJour puts it, epistemic justification "increases or enhances to an appropriate degree . . . the likelihood that the belief is true."[11]

The Value of Knowledge

Reflecting on some of the lessons he had learned in life, Socrates once said: "And isn't it a bad thing to be deceived about the truth, and a good thing to know what the truth is? For I assume that by knowing the truth [we] mean knowing things as they really are."[12]

Do you agree with Socrates? Is knowledge valuable? And isn't it valuable because it puts us in touch with reality, which we all seek? Don't we value truth over falsehood, reality over illusion?

WHY ACCEPT THE CLASSICAL THEORY?

Socrates based his theory of knowledge on observations of the way we use the verb *to know* in propositional contexts. With this in mind, let's briefly examine the conditions one by one. An obvious reason to accept the belief condition is that we do not ordinarily say that someone "knows" that a proposition P is true if the person does not believe that P is true.

Why accept the truth condition? The main reason is that we ordinarily do not dignify a belief by calling it "knowledge" if the belief is false. For example, if someone claimed to *know* that George Washington is still president today, we would reply, "That may be your belief or your opinion, but it is not genuine *knowledge*." (And the reason the belief is not knowledge is that it is false, right?) Certainly, truth is a necessary condition if a belief is to qualify as real knowledge.

Turning to the third condition, imagine that a fortune-teller reads a crystal ball and predicts that it will snow tomorrow. Suppose that she believes her own prediction and her prediction, though unlikely at the time, happens to come true. Nevertheless, we would not say she *knew* in advance that it would snow. For she had no good reason connected to reality to conclude ahead of time that it would snow. She just made a lucky guess. In the language of epistemology, her guess did not rise to the level of knowledge because it was epistemically unjustified.

I mentioned but did not examine the distinction between opinion and knowledge. With the Socratic theory of knowledge in hand, that distinction can now be clarified. An *opinion* (or a *guess* or a *hunch*) is a belief that does not rise to the level of knowledge because it is not solidly grounded in reality by a sufficiently strong reason to believe it is true. In other words, an opinion is not real knowledge because it is not epistemically justified.

OBJECTIONS AND REPLIES

Some argue against the belief condition by pointing out that we sometimes say, "I know it, but I don't believe it." These critics suppose that statements such as this show that knowing does not require believing. However, when someone makes such a statement, the person normally does not intend to be taken literally. It's just a way of saying, "I'm astonished." The objection fails.

A common objection to the truth condition runs like this: "In the Middle Ages, it was common knowledge that the sun circles the earth. But the proposition (that the sun circles the earth) was false; therefore, we *can* know that which is false."

This argument is flawed. We misuse the word *knew* if we say that people in the Middle Ages "knew" the sun circles the earth. The correct thing to say is that in the Middle Ages people *claimed* to know that the sun revolves around the earth. It would be even better to say, "In the Middle Ages, it was commonly *believed* that the sun circles the earth." The objection fails.

Some have argued that the justification condition is not needed. They observe that people sometimes make lucky guesses — based on no grounds or evidence whatsoever — and then say, "See, I *knew* it!" It follows, they conclude, that justification is not a necessary condition for knowledge. The problem is that examples like this are not what we would ordinarily call "knowledge." People can *say* that they have knowledge, but saying so doesn't make it so.

Let's now return to the absolute skeptics who claim that genuine knowledge doesn't exist. All we have, they say, are unjustified opinions (and one opinion is as valid or true as any other). Set aside the problem that their view undermines itself (for if their view is true, then it is nothing but one more unjustified opinion). Isn't it a matter of common sense that many beliefs *are* epistemically justified (while many are not)? Aren't we epistemically justified in believing that there are craters on the moon? That electrons have a negative charge? That basketballs are bigger than atoms? Hasn't it been proven that many diseases are caused by viruses and bacteria? Don't we *know* these things? Don't we know them because we have sufficient reason to believe that they are objectively true?

And aren't the following three beliefs epistemically *un*justified? Cancer is caused by witches. A secret civilization of green giants inhabits the center of the earth. The sun orbits the moon. Can we give up the traditional notions of objective truth and knowledge and still make sense of our world?

One last point bears repeating. If the claim that knowledge doesn't exist is true, then no beliefs are epistemically justified, including the claim that knowledge doesn't exist. But if the claim is unjustified, then why believe it? Does absolute skepticism refute itself? You decide.

Cultural Relativism and Knowledge

Some who reject the traditional definition of knowledge advocate in its place a culturally relative notion. Each culture, they claim, has its own "way of knowing," and no one way of knowing is better or worse than any other. All ways of knowing are equally valid. The supporting premise is the claim that there is no objective basis from which to compare one society's way of knowing with that of another. So, if a shaman in a traditional or premodern society claims that disease is caused by witches casting magic spells, his claim is true relative to his culture and counts as knowledge within his culture. If a scientist from a Western society claims that disease is caused by bacteria and viruses, his claim is true relative to his culture and counts as knowledge within his culture. Both "ways of knowing" are equally valid or true, says the cultural relativist about knowledge, for there is no objective basis for saying that one culture is right and the other is wrong on any matter.

I have known cultural relativists who claimed that shamans casting out witches are as valid as doctors trained in Western medical schools prescribing scientifically tested medicines. However, when they contracted a serious illness, they went to a Western-trained doctor working in a modern hospital equipped with sophisticated instruments and drugs tested in clinical trials.

Questions for Reflection and Discussion 8.1

1. What is epistemic justification?
2. Give an example of something we know and an example of something many people mistakenly think they know. Explain the difference in epistemological terms.

3. What is the difference between true belief and knowledge?
4. What is the difference between opinion and knowledge, according to the classical theory?
5. Can someone claim that all truth is subjective without contradicting himself or herself?
6. Can alethic relativism be defended without self-contradiction?
7. Can absolute skepticism be defended without self-contradiction?
8. Is it always better to know the truth than to remain in darkness?

HOW DOES JUSTIFICATION FIRST ARISE?

According to the classical theory, a true belief only qualifies as knowledge if it is sufficiently justified. But how does epistemic justification get started in the first place? What is the first premise? BonJour gives the mainstream answer in contemporary epistemology:

> Historically, most epistemologists have distinguished two main sources from which the epistemic justification of a belief might arise. It has seemed obvious to all but a very few that many beliefs are justified by appeal to one's sensory (and introspective) experience of the world. But it has seemed equally obvious to most that there are other beliefs, including many of the most important ones that we have, that are justified in a way that does not depend at all on such an appeal to experience, justified, as it is usually put, by reason or pure thought alone.[13]

Surely a great deal of what we know about the material world is justified at least in part on the basis of sensory experience, that is, on the basis of information we received through our physical senses (sight, taste, touch, smell, and hearing). For example, I know that Mount Rainier has snow on its peak. How do I know? What justifies my belief? At least part of the answer is that I saw the snow with my own eyes. For another example, I know that soap tastes bitter. How do I know? What justifies my belief? I've tasted soap.

If sense experience is required—at least in part—for the justification of an item of knowledge, then that item is called *a posteriori* knowledge

(Latin for "from the latter," or "relating to or derived by reasoning from observed facts"). Such knowledge is also called "*empirical* knowledge" (Latin *empiricus*, from the Greek *empiricos*, "experience"), or simply "*experiential* knowledge."[14] All our knowledge of the material world that is justified by natural science is justified a posteriori and qualifies as a posteriori, or empirical, knowledge.

Other beliefs, as BonJour notes, are justified on the basis of pure reasoning alone, without any reliance on experiential input from the physical senses. For example, we know that the decimal expansion of the square root of 2 goes on to infinity without ever repeating itself. How do we know this? The justification does not depend at all on what our five senses tell us about the material world, for it would take an infinite number of lifetimes to physically look at every number in the decimal expansion of the square root of 2 so as to justify the proposition by empirical observation. Fortunately, we don't need to look at *any* physical objects when we justify this mathematical truth. We know that the proposition is true (that the decimal expansion of the square root of 2 goes to infinity) through an inner process of mathematical reasoning alone—an intellectual process that occurs inside our minds, a train of pure thought that justifies the claim to knowledge without reliance on anything the senses might tell us about material objects.

If an item of knowledge can be justified on the basis of "reason or pure thought alone," without reliance on sense experience of the material world, then it is called *a priori* knowledge (Latin for "from the former," thus "formed or conceived beforehand"). This kind of knowledge is also called *ratiocinative* knowledge (Latin *ratio*, "reason"). All our knowledge of purely mathematical objects (in fields such as algebra, geometry, trigonometry, and calculus) is justified a priori and qualifies as a priori knowledge. This will make more sense after we look at examples.

Examples of *a posteriori* Knowledge

Nearly everyone knows that the moon has phases. But what justifies our belief in this case? The answer is obvious: we *observe* the moon's phases with our own eyes. The justification may involve reasoning, but sense experience is also required. The following are additional examples of knowledge justified on an a posteriori basis:

- The ocean contains salt.
- Ripe bananas are usually yellow.
- Lemons taste sour.
- The moon has craters.
- The earth is round.

So, if I were to claim that the moon has craters and someone were to ask me to justify my belief, I would reply, "I saw them through a pair of binoculars." Ask me how I know that the earth is round, and I will begin by pointing out that when ships disappear over the horizon, we see their masts disappear last. I might add that photos taken from space show that the earth is round. In each case, my knowledge is justified a posteriori.

Examples of *a priori* Knowledge

Think carefully about the following statement, labeled N: "N: Nothing in the universe is both purely red all over and purely green all over at the same time."

We know with certainty that N is true. But what justifies our knowledge in this case? How do we know? Our knowledge that N is true can't possibly be justified on the basis of particular sensory experiences of physical objects. Think about it. Wouldn't you have to travel around the entire universe looking carefully at each object, checking each thing to make sure it is not both purely red all over and purely green all over at the same time? You would have to keep a list, and your travels would take you not just to the other planets of our solar system but to the 400 billion stars of the Milky Way galaxy and eventually to the 100 billion other galaxies, each containing on average several hundred billion stars. Wouldn't it take more than a lifetime to visually check *every* colored object in the universe?

Our knowledge in this case is justified on the basis of reason alone, without reliance on sensory experience. To justify N, all we need to do is to think carefully (and rationally) about its meaning. Once we understand the meaning or content of the statement, we next see directly, with a kind of intellectual insight, that the proposition expressed must be true. This is a rational, rather than a physical, kind of seeing, because you can think about N with your eyes closed and your other physical senses deadened and still see, just by reasoning, that the proposition must be true.

It might be that we use our physical senses to learn the *meaning* of the English sentence expressing N. But our knowledge that N is *true* is justified on the basis of "reason or pure thought" alone.

If further examples are called for, consider the statement, or proposition, that the number 3 is greater than the number 2. What justifies this mathematical certainty? No information gained from the physical senses about objects in the material world could possibly prove it true. (The number 3 is not *physically* greater than the number 2.) Our knowledge in this case is justified on the basis of an interior act of reasoning alone, without reliance on sensory data.

Epistemologists commonly distinguish four kinds of a priori knowledge, that is, knowledge justified on an a priori basis: *mathematical, logical, moral,* and *conceptual.* The following are examples of mathematical truths justified a priori.

- There are an infinite number of positive integers.
- The rational number line is dense.
- Every square has four sides.
- Two angles equal to a third angle must be equal to each other.

To reinforce the point yet again, consider the second example. How could you ever prove empirically, using your senses alone, looking at physical objects, that the rational number line is dense (that a rational number exists between *any* two rational numbers to infinity)? Wouldn't it take more than a lifetime to physically observe every case? Yet, we know the truth in question with complete certainty. And isn't our certainty in this case eminently reasonable?[15] We know the proposition is true on the basis of a priori reasoning alone. No knowledge of atoms, molecules, mountains, and bears is needed.

Principles of logic are also justified a priori. For instance,

- If all As are Bs and all Bs are Cs, then necessarily all As are Cs, where A, B, and C are variables ranging over categories of things.

The realm of a priori knowledge is generally also thought to include abstract truths about morality. For example:

- If an act A is morally right in situation S, then A is morally right in any other morally similar situation.

- If it is morally wrong to treat one person P in a certain way in a certain situation, then it is morally wrong to treat any other person in that way in a similar situation.

The standard list of truths justified a priori also includes conceptual truths such as these:

- The whole is always greater than the part.
- All bachelors are unmarried.

Think about the last example, the proposition that all bachelors are unmarried. Is this justified through an empirical survey of all bachelors around the world? The epistemologist Dan O'Brien gives the standard answer in his field: "The answer is No. You do not have to ask your bachelor friends whether they are married; you are justified in believing they're not, simply by virtue of possessing the relevant concepts."[16]

The human faculty of a priori reasoning is amazing. Using reason alone, we discover vast realms of highly abstract and complex mathematical truths in fields such as algebra, geometry, trigonometry, calculus, and topology. Reason operating a priori also discovers vast domains of highly abstract truths in mathematical logic, including the many fascinating theorems of modal logic, tense logic (the logic of statements about time), deontic logic (the logic of obligation), and epistemic logic.

Our sense faculties are amazing too. Using our senses aided by our ability to reason we have discovered remarkable truths about the very small and the very large, the distant past and the distant future, in the highly theoretical fields of quantum and relativistic physics, chemistry, biology, geology, and astrophysics. We'll come back to the amazing capabilities of the human mind in chapter 9, when we ask, Can a naturalistic or purely materialistic account of the evolutionary process explain the surprising reach of human reason?

With the traditional accounts of *a priori* and *a posteriori* justification clarified, it's time to apply epistemology to real life.

Questions for Reflection and Discussion 8.2

1. List two examples of a posteriori knowledge. How would you justify each one if pressed to do so?

2. List two examples of a priori knowledge. How would you justify each one if pressed to do so?
3. This may require research. How do we know that the square root of 2 is irrational?
4. In each case, is the following proposition known a priori or a posteriori? Explain.
    a. The White House is white.
    b. The Rolling Stones performed in Moscow in 1998.
    c. $1 + 1 = 2$.
    d. All octogenarians are at least eighty years old.
    e. Octopuses are very intelligent.
    f. All triangles have three sides.
    g. Some people are one hundred years old.
    h. Soap tastes bitter.
    i. Unsweetened baking chocolate tastes awful.
    j. The decimal expansion of *pi* goes on forever and never repeats itself.

APPLICATION: CRITICALLY EVALUATE YOUR BELIEFS

A great deal of what we know about the world is known on the basis of testimony received from others. Beliefs supported by testimony can and should be evaluated rationally.[17]

Belief Supported by Testimony

Testimony may be defined as "purported information received from other people." Much of what we know about the world is based on testimony received from others. For example, I know that there is a scientific research station on the South Pole. However, I have never been there and have never seen it with my own eyes. I also know that protons weigh more than electrons, but I can't prove it and wouldn't know how to operate the complicated instruments in a physics lab.

Of course, the mere fact that a belief is based on testimony received from others does not by itself show that the belief is true. The person supplying the information may be lying, misinformed, or biased. Which raises the question: When should we trust testimony, and when should we doubt it? When does testimony give us knowledge, and when does it give us only opinion?

A good suggestion is that we go with ordinary common sense. It is common sense to accept someone's testimony as veridical (truthful) unless we have good reason to doubt it. This principle was first stated and defended by the Scottish philosopher Thomas Reid (1710–96), known as the "philosopher of common sense." Reid argued that when it comes to ordinary testimony, the default position is trust, and the default is only overridden when we have good reason to suspect someone's testimony is false. In defense of his principle, known as "the principle of testimony," Reid argued that in ordinary situations people have a natural "propensity to speak truth" and that lying "is doing violence to our nature."[18]

Something worth considering is the fact that we *do* follow Reid's principle in everyday life. Furthermore, if we did not follow it, we would know very little about the world around us (and probably could not even function).

However, it is also good to keep in mind that people are fallible, and therefore testimony is never completely certain. Here are some reasons we might have for doubting a person's testimony:

- The person has a record of lying.
- The person has a record of providing incorrect information.
- The person has a motive to be less than truthful.
- The person is known to have biases that may have distorted his perceptions.
- The person is known to have been mentally or physically impaired at the time.
- The testimony conflicts with previously established (prior) information.
- The testimony conflicts with the reliable testimony of others who were present.
- The best explanation of all the facts is that the person giving the testimony is lying or deluded.

When we are unsure of an item of testimony and want to test it, we can do the following:

- Check the person's reliability by looking at his or her past testimony.
- Try to corroborate the testimony with the testimony of others.

- Investigate the person's cognitive condition at the time: Were the person's faculties working properly? Is there any evidence the person's perception was impaired by bias, prejudice, wishful thinking, illness, drugs, and so forth?
- Investigate the person's motives.

Expert Testimony. Some of our testimony comes from ordinary people with no expertise in a subject (friends, associates, pundits on TV, etc.). Other testimony comes from experts, individuals who have a great deal of verified knowledge in a particular area. For example, someone with a PhD in chemistry from a reputable institution qualifies as an expert in chemistry; a person who has worked successfully as a journeyman plumber for many years qualifies as an expert in plumbing, and so on. Evaluating expert testimony calls for additional criteria. Before we turn to those, what exactly makes a person an expert in an area?

Someone's status as an expert is normally based on one or more of the following: (1) academic education or nonacademic training and experience in the subject; (2) professional accomplishments; (3) reputation among peers in the field; and (4) a history of reliable judgment. For example, Richard Feynman (1918–88) was widely considered an expert on quantum mechanics (a branch of physics that studies the motions of subatomic particles), and rightly so. On his graduate school entrance exam, he earned a perfect score in mathematics and physics, something no one had ever before accomplished. He earned a PhD in physics from Princeton University in 1942, taught at leading universities, and was awarded the Nobel Prize in Physics for his work in quantum electrodynamics. The theories he developed were confirmed on the basis of the precise predictions they yielded. In a worldwide poll of physicists in 1999, he was ranked one of the ten greatest physicists of all time. Feynman's opinion *on matters having to do with physics* carried great weight, and for good reason.[19]

However, since experts are fallible human beings, their testimony should not always be accepted without question. First, expert opinion carries more weight than the opinion of a nonexpert only when an expert is rendering a considered opinion *in his or her area of expertise*. A nuclear physicist's opinion on politics or religion, for example, does not qualify as expert opinion, any more than does a politician's opinion on nuclear physics. An expert is only an expert in his or her area of expertise.

Second, if an expert makes a claim, but many qualified experts disagree on the point at issue, that is grounds for doubt. In such a case, it may be reasonable to withhold judgment and investigate the matter before reaching a conclusion.

Third, if an expert is an "interested party" in a matter, that is, if the expert stands to personally gain if his or her testimony is believed, that calls his or her testimony into question. For example, imagine that an expert on cures for the common cold testifies in favor of a particular commercial cold remedy while owning stock in the company. This information suggests that the expert might not be objective. Further evidence is needed before taking his testimony at face value.

Fourth, experts are often invited to comment on issues that cannot be settled on a factual basis. For example, a famous detective is asked to speculate on the real identity of the infamous skyjacker D. B. Cooper. Economists and other social scientists are often asked to predict the future. However, their expertise does not extend to such matters and, even though their opinions may be more probable than those of the ordinary person, they abuse their power if they claim scientific authority for their prognostications.[20]

A final reason to doubt the testimony of an expert hardly needs saying. If the expert gives poor arguments or violates principles of critical thinking, that is grounds for doubt. Experts are human, and they can, like all of us, make mistakes.

Questions for Reflection and Discussion 8.3

1. When is testimony trustworthy? When is it not?
2. What, according to Thomas Reid, is the commonsense principle governing testimony received from ordinary people? Is Reid's principle of testimony reasonable?
3. How do we evaluate expert testimony?
4. How do we evaluate nonexpert testimony?
5. Choose a public expert on some subject, and critically evaluate his or her expertise.
6. State an item of information that you know on the basis of nonexpert testimony alone. Give an argument that supports your claim to know.
7. State an item of information that you know on the basis of expert testimony alone. Give an argument that supports your claim to know.

IT GETS COMPLICATED: THE GETTIER PARADOXES

Until 1963, philosophers writing on epistemology agreed with the Socratic account of knowledge. The standard view was that the *belief, truth*, and *justification* conditions are individually necessary and jointly sufficient for knowledge. In 1963, this consensus changed almost overnight when a relatively unknown philosopher named Edmund Gettier, teaching at Wayne State University in Michigan, published a three-page academic paper that immediately convinced the entire philosophical profession that the Socratic theory is partly right but incomplete.

In his paper, "Is Justified True Belief Knowledge?," Gettier constructed realistic situations in which (1) all three conditions are satisfied and yet (2) knowledge is not present. A situation like this, in which the three Socratic conditions are satisfied but knowledge is not present, is now called a "Gettier case" in his honor.

As a result of his work, most philosophers agree that although the three conditions may be individually necessary for knowledge, they are not jointly *sufficient*.[21] At the least, a fourth condition is needed before real knowledge is present. Although Gettier's paper was only three pages long, its concise argument revolutionized epistemology in the Western world. Hundreds of scholarly books and articles have discussed his paper, making Gettier's argument one of the most influential pieces of philosophy ever written. And the discussion is by no means over, once again illustrating that progress has been made in philosophy. Here is my brief summary of the debate.[22]

Gettier's Argument

Gettier's famous argument relied on two noncontroversial assumptions, both accepted by advocates of the traditional theory of knowledge. The first was the principle that epistemic justification is always preserved by logical entailment:

(1) Beliefs entailed by other justified beliefs are themselves justified.

A proposition or statement P *entails* a proposition Q when it is the case that if P is true, then Q *must* also be true. For example, the proposition that some cats are pets entails the proposition that some pets are cats. Here is an illustration of assumption (1). Suppose you are justified in believing that the mayor of Seattle is always a Democrat. Imagine you are also justified in believing that Smith is the current mayor of Seattle. Now, suppose you see that the first two beliefs together entail that the current mayor is a Democrat. You are then justified in believing that Smith is a Democrat.

Gettier's second stated assumption may be put this way:

(2) In some cases, one can be justified in believing a proposition even though the belief later turns out to have been false.

For example, imagine a court case in which the evidence overwhelmingly indicates Joe's guilt. Five eyewitnesses claim they saw him commit the crime, his fingerprints are all over the murder weapon, he confessed, and so forth. The jury is epistemically justified in believing that Joe committed the crime. But years later new evidence is discovered showing that someone else actually committed the murder.

Next, Gettier proposed the following thought experiment: Smith and Jones have applied for the same job. Smith has extremely strong evidence that

(a) Jones will get the job and that Jones has ten coins in his pocket.

Suppose Smith also sees that this entails the following proposition:

(b) The man who will get the job has ten coins in his pocket.

Seeing that (a) entails (b), Smith concludes (b). It seems clear that Smith believes (b) and is *justified* in believing (b).

Now imagine that the situation changes for reasons no one could have predicted, and Smith ends up getting the job. In addition, assume that Smith himself also has ten coins in his pocket, although he does not realize it. Thus, (b) is true, even though (a), the evidence it was based on, is false. It seems we now have a case in which

1. Smith believes (b).

2. Proposition (b) is true.

3. Smith has adequate justification for believing (b) is true.

It follows, on the Socratic account, that Smith genuinely knows (b). However, it seems clear that Smith does not genuinely know (b), for proposition (b) is true by virtue of the number of coins in Smith's pocket, while Smith does not know how many coins are in his own pocket and bases his belief in (b) on a count of the coins in Jones's pocket, whom he falsely believes to be the man who will get the job.[23]

Thus, Gettier concludes, there is something wrong with either his argument's two assumptions or with the Socratic theory of knowledge. But the assumptions seem undeniable. Therefore the Socratic theory needs amendment.

RESPONSES

A Socratic Reply

Gettier's case is not a counterexample to the traditional definition of knowledge. Smith believes that (b) is the case only because he believes (a). But (a) is false. Because (a) is false, Smith's belief that (b) is true is not epistemically justified for Smith. Furthermore, on the traditional account, if the evidence for (a) had been epistemically sufficient for believing it, (a) would not have turned out to be false. If Smith were to be informed of his error, he would admit that he was not justified in believing (a), and so was not justified in believing (b) on the basis of (a). Gettier has given us no reason to modify the traditional account of knowledge.

The No-Defeaters Reply

The Socratic theory can be fixed by adding the following clause as an additional necessary condition on knowledge: "No defeater for P exists."[24] What is a defeater? Suppose that S believes that proposition P is true. A defeater for S's belief would be a true proposition P* that S does not know but that would have ruled out S's justification for believing P, had S known it. More formally, P* is a defeater for P if P* is true, S does not know that P* is true, and if S had known that P* is true, S would not have been justified in believing P.

The philosopher Jim Slagle cites a helpful example. You are touring a factory and see red widgets emerging from a machine on a conveyor belt.

You form the belief, "Those widgets are red." But then someone with inside knowledge comes along and states that the widgets "are irradiated by a red light . . . to reveal potential flaws such as hairline cracks. Your reason for believing the widgets are red has been taken from you. The belief that the widgets are irradiated by a red light is a defeater for the belief that the widgets are red."[25]

Adding the suggested clause (no defeater for P exists) to the original three clauses (belief, truth, and justification) works in many cases. For example, going back to Gettier's example, suppose that (unbeknownst to Smith) his extremely strong evidence comes from a source that is unreliable. Knowing this would have undermined his justification for believing that Jones would get the job. In other words, Smith would have had a defeater for his belief (that the man who would get the job would have ten coins in his pocket). The presence of the defeater would explain why Smith does not have knowledge in the case.

However, critics have proposed counterexamples in the form of cases where the existence of a defeater would not undermine a claim to knowledge. Consider this case, suggested by Robert Martin:

> Stu believes (correctly and with excellent justification) that Pru is on her way and will arrive at his house in five minutes. By coincidence, the phone will ring at exactly the instant Pru will ring the doorbell after arriving, so Stu won't hear it. Had he believed the true proposition that he won't hear the doorbell in five minutes, his justification for his belief about Pru's arrival would have been undermined.[26]

Although the true proposition (that Stu won't hear the doorbell in five minutes) is a defeater for his belief, doesn't it seem intuitively obvious that Stu *does* know that Pru will arrive as predicted? If so, then the presence of a defeater does not rule out the presence of knowledge, and the no-defeater solution fails.

Other philosophers conclude that the classical theory cannot be fixed. They reject it and propose alternative accounts of knowledge and justification. *Externalism* and *naturalized epistemology* are two such schools of thought. The reader who wants to pursue the issues further should consult a textbook in epistemology.[27]

Gettier's paper caused epistemologists to probe the concept of knowledge more deeply and sparked a massive amount of research. The Gettier paradoxes are yet another example of the dialectical nature of philosophy, the information spillover that philosophy gives rise to, and the fact that advances in philosophy have been made.

Questions for Reflection and Discussion 8.4

1. What is a Gettier case?
2. Are there examples of knowledge that do not fit the Socratic account? Make your case.
3. Can the Socratic account be defended against the Gettier counter-examples?
4. If you believe that the classical analysis is on the wrong track, can you state an alternative? Does your theory agree with the way we ordinarily use the word *knowledge*?

NINE

C. S. Lewis and the Argument from Reason

NATURALISM AND SUPERNATURALISM

In his book *Miracles*, C. S. Lewis, tutor of English literature at Oxford University and probably the most famous Christian writer of the twentieth century, presented what would become one of the most talked-about epistemological arguments of recent times.[1] In the usual philosophical manner, Lewis began his argument with a definition. *Naturalism* is the view that

> the ultimate Fact, the thing you can't go behind, is a vast process in space and time which is going on of its own accord. Inside that total system every particular event (such as your sitting reading this book) happens because some other event has happened. . . . All the things and events are so completely interlocked that no one of them can claim the slightest independence from "the whole show." None of them exists "on its own" or "goes on of its own accord."[2]

211

The worldview Lewis has in mind here accepts modern science, including the theory of evolution, but denies all supernatural and religious claims. Broken down to its main components, then, naturalism is the view that

- Nature is all that exists, with nature understood as the whole system of space, time, matter, and energy recognized by science.
- Nature was not created by, and is not guided by, a supernatural intelligence or supreme being such as God or a higher power. The supernatural does not exist.
- At the most fundamental level, nature is not purposeful or goal-directed; that is, it is not guided by a higher power, it has no built-in goals, it is not intentionally aimed at anything.
- The laws of nature are therefore blind in the sense that they are not aimed at a goal, they were not created for a purpose, they do not act with a result in mind.

Lewis next defines the opposing view, supernaturalism, as the claim that "besides Nature, there exists something else." The "something else" Lewis had in mind would be an intelligent designer of nature, that is, God or a higher power who created the world on purpose.[3]

THE VALIDITY OF REASON

The next step is an assumption basic to Western epistemology since Socrates — the claim that human reasoning is generally a valid or trustworthy guide to truth or correspondence with reality:

All possible knowledge . . . depends on the validity of reasoning. If the feeling of certainty which we express by words like *must be* and *therefore* and *since* is a real perception of how things outside our own minds "really" must be, well and good. But if this certainty is merely a feeling in our own minds, and not a genuine insight into realities beyond them — if it merely represents the way our minds happen to work — then we can have no knowledge. Unless human reasoning is valid no science can be true.[4]

More fully, we have real knowledge only if human reasoning is generally valid, that is, only if it generally gives us justified true beliefs about objects existing outside our minds. If human reason is not generally valid, then knowledge does not really exist. Therefore,

> no account of our universe can be [known to be] true unless that account leaves it possible for our thinking to be a real insight [into a mind-independent reality]. A theory that explained everything else in the whole universe but which made it impossible to believe that our [reasoning is] valid, would be utterly out of court. For that theory would itself have been reached by [reasoning], and if [reasoning] is not valid, that theory, of course, would be itself utterly demolished. It would have destroyed its own credentials. It would be an argument which proved that no argument was sound—a proof that there are no proofs—which is nonsense. So, we must believe in the validity of rational thought.[5]

Common sense, science, and every academic subject rely on the assumption that human reason, when it is critically employed, generally gives us knowledge of the world.

THE PROBLEM FOR NATURALISM
AND THE ARGUMENT COMPLETED

Now, if naturalism is true, "the mind, like every other particular thing or event, is simply the product of the Total System . . . and nothing more."[6] But the total system (according to naturalism) is not rational. It is "blind" in the sense that it is not aimed at anything. It has no built-in goals, it is not directed by an intelligence, it has no purpose or end game. So, if naturalism is true, several significant results follow. First, our beliefs are physical events in our brains. Second, the physical events in our brains are ultimately caused by mindless, undirected forces of nature that originated billions of years ago. Furthermore, these forces are blind in the sense that they are not aimed at any goal. If so, then our beliefs can be fully explained as the product of blind, nonrational causes that have no purpose or goal.

But in everyday life, Lewis continues, when we discover that a belief can be fully explained as the product of a blind, nonrational process, we reject it. Lewis had in mind the following kind of example. Someone claims that snakes are crawling on his wall. We accept his claim until we learn that his belief was produced by alcohol-induced delirium tremens — a nonrational cause — rather than by logical reasoning applied to sensory evidence. Once we learn that his thoughts were produced by a nonrational process, we no longer believe his testimony. We would not say the man "knows" snakes are crawling on his wall; we would say only that he "believes" it. We would add that the man appears to be deluded.

Or a man in a nursing home claims that the staff members are all Russian secret agents. His claim loses its rational credentials when we are told that he has a brain disease, such as Alzheimer's, which is known to degrade reasoning and judgment. We would not say that the man "knows" that the staff are secret agents; we would say only that he "believes" that they are. Again, no one grants any credence to a belief that has been shown to have originated in a nonrational cause.[7] Thus, any "particular thought is valueless if it is the result of [nonrational] causes. Obviously, then, the whole process of human thought, what we call Reason, is equally valueless if it is the result of [nonrational] causes."[8]

It follows, Lewis argues, that if naturalism is true, "the finest piece of scientific reasoning is caused in just the same [nonrational] way as the thoughts a man has because a bit of bone is pressing on his brain."[9] Since no thought is valid if it can be fully explained as the result of nonrational causes, it follows that if naturalism is true, reason cannot be trusted to generally give us truth about the world. But if reason cannot be trusted, then no belief reached by reasoning is justified or valid. But *naturalism* is a belief reached by reasoning. Therefore, if naturalism is true, it logically follows that naturalism cannot be rationally believed. In other words, if naturalism is true, it is not reasonable to believe that naturalism is true. Naturalism thus "destroys its own credentials."[10]

In philosophy there is a technical word for a belief such as this. A belief B is said to be "self-refuting" if the following is true: If B is true, then C logically follows, and C is a sufficient reason to conclude that B is false. Thus, Lewis's iconoclastic conclusion: naturalism refutes itself. This, in summary form, is Lewis's famous argument against naturalism, known today as "the argument from reason." And of course, if naturalism is false, then supernaturalism is true.

THE EVOLUTIONARY OBJECTION

The obvious objection to Lewis's argument is based on modern evolutionary theory. Most students, when they hear a summary of Lewis's argument from reason, respond immediately with something like this: "But natural selection surely favored creatures who could reason correctly about their world; creatures lacking the ability to reason well died off long ago. That's why we have the ability to reason correctly and gain knowledge of the world."

Lewis was aware of this objection to his own argument; he thought it was so important that he actually stated it and responded to it in his book. (This is the mark of a good philosopher, that he considers and replies to arguments that could be raised against his own proposal.) Here is Lewis's own statement of what is surely the main objection to his argument from reason:

> An attempt to get out of the difficulty might be made along the following lines. Even if our thoughts are produced by nonrational causes, still it might happen by mere accident that some of them were true. . . . Now individuals whose thoughts happened in this accidental way to be truer than other people's would have an advantage in the struggle for existence. And if habits of thought can be inherited, natural selection would gradually eliminate or weed out the people who have the less useful types of thought. It might therefore have come about by now that the present type of human mind—the sort of thought that has survived—was tolerably reliable.[11]

By *reliable* Lewis means what contemporary epistemologists mean: a cognitive faculty is reliable if it generally or most of the time delivers knowledge (i.e., justified true beliefs). So, the objection Lewis is raising against his own argument is that unguided natural selection alone, acting blindly over long periods of time, can be expected to select for and produce creatures with rational faculties that generally deliver truth about the world. For reliable cognitive faculties would likely confer advantages in the struggle for survival and would therefore tend to spread within an unguided, or blind, process of natural selection. In this way, over a long period of time, with nature favoring the most reliable cognitive abilities, our present minds evolved.

Thus, the objection continues, there is no need to suppose that God designed or guides the evolutionary process. Rather, we can explain the validity of our reasoning in terms of undirected natural selection alone, without reference to a supernatural guiding intelligence. Call this reply to Lewis's argument—stated by Lewis himself—the "evolutionary reply."

LEWIS'S REPLY TO THE EVOLUTIONARY REPLY

This objection seems decisive at first glance. However, Lewis offered a thought-provoking reply. His first move, boiled down to essentials and with some fleshing out based on the current discussion, was to agree that the possession of cognitive faculties that are reliable to some degree would confer a reproductive advantage within an unguided process of natural selection. Creatures with extremely unreliable cognitive abilities would find it harder to survive, would tend to die off in larger numbers compared to those with more reliable faculties, and therefore would reproduce in smaller numbers. Thus, we should expect that an unguided, naturalistic process of evolution would "select for" beings with cognitive faculties that are reliable to some degree, and we should expect that such creatures would eventually arise—given a long enough period of time.

Lewis next takes the discussion deeper when he asks *which* cognitive abilities would be favored by a blind process of natural selection. Which abilities would increase genetic fitness (confer advantages in the struggle for survival)? The first answer that comes to mind: only those that help individuals survive. The deeper answer: only those cognitive abilities that enable a creature to know features of its *local* environment. At this point in Lewis's argument, I'll introduce two contemporary terms used by philosophers who discuss his argument today.

- *Elementary cognitive abilities* are those that allow creatures to know features of their local, or immediate, environment. These abilities have been described as the ability to attain local truths. Examples of local truths would include, "A large animal with big teeth is approaching," and "That fire is hot."
- *Higher cognitive abilities* are those that allow human beings to know highly abstract and theoretical truths in advanced mathematics (calculus, trigonometry, differential geometry, topology, and so forth),

theoretical physics (quantum electrodynamics, general and special relativity theory, and so forth), organic chemistry, mathematical logic, evolutionary biology, and the like. These abilities have been described as the capacity to reason to and grasp universal and abstract truths. For example, truths about the extremely large in relativistic physics and the extremely small in quantum theory, the remote past and the distant future in astrophysics, and the extremely abstract in calculus, differential geometry, modal logic, and topology. Truths, in short, that go far, far beyond the local environment to the material universe as a whole at its largest and smallest scales.

Back to Lewis's deeper answer. Clearly, the possession of the *elementary* cognitive abilities would be advantageous in the struggle for survival. Therefore, we can expect that an unguided process of natural selection would eventually produce beings with the elementary cognitive abilities that allow them to know features of their local environments.

However, it is just as clear that in the distant past, possession of the higher cognitive capacities would not be fitness enhancing at all, that is, would not confer any advantage in the struggle for survival.

If this is not obvious, consider that 100,000 years ago, when (according to naturalism) our cognitive abilities were slowly forming through a blind, unguided process of natural selection, the possession of some of the higher cognitive abilities in a latent or unused form—for these capacities would not be put to use for 100,000 years—would have made no difference at all with respect to reproduction and survival. Therefore, in prehistoric times, there would have been zero selective pressure for their presence in any human population. Put another way, the higher cognitive abilities and the advanced, highly theoretical and abstract truths at which they are aimed would be *invisible* to any unguided evolutionary process.

Indeed, it seems that the higher cognitive abilities would not merely have not been selected *for* by an undirected process of evolution, they would have been selected *against* because of the extra time and energy expenditure they would have cost their possessors, thus reducing their possessors' chances of survival.[12]

If the point is not clear, perhaps an argument given by the philosopher Peter van Inwagen in support of Lewis's argument will help. Consider, he writes, "the evolution of those cognitive capacities that make humanity so strikingly different from all other species: I mean the capacities that allow us to do fantastic things like theoretical physics or evolutionary biology or drawing in perspective or, for that matter, making a promise."[13] If these capacities evolved by a process of unguided natural selection, it follows that 100,000 years ago "there was some character, or set of characters, such that (a) possession of those characters conferred a reproductive advantage upon some population composed of our remote ancestors, and (b) the presence of those characters within the present human population constitutes the biological basis of the human capacity for theoretical physics and evolutionary biology."[14]

But do we have "any reason to think that there exists any set of characters having both these features?" The answer, van Inwagen argues, is clearly no:

> Couldn't we easily imagine a population whose members were as intelligent as we—if they were dispersed among us, we should hear them commended for their "intelligence" with about the same frequency as we should hear the members of any randomly chosen group of our fellows commended—but who were . . . lacking in [the cognitive capacities that allow us to engage in highly theoretical and abstract thought such as relativistic physics, differential geometry, genetics, and evolutionary biology]. Couldn't such a population develop quite an impressive civilization—as impressive, say, as classical Chinese civilization or the civilization of ancient Egypt? The point raised by this question would seem to apply a fortiori to the reproductive success of such a population in a "state of nature." Why should a population with the gene frequencies I have imagined fare any worse in the forests or on the savannas than a population in which the genes that, in the right combination, yield the capacity for [highly theoretical and extreme abstract thought] are relatively numerous? . . . I once heard Noam Chomsky say that our ability to do physical science depends on a very specific set of cognitive capacities, and that, quite possibly, the reason that there are no real social sciences may be that we just happen to lack a certain equally specific set of cognitive capacities. He went on to speculate that we might one day discover among the stars a species as good at social science as we are at physical science and as bad at physical science as we are at social science. He did not raise the question why natural selection would bother to confer either of these highly specific sets of capacities on a species.[15]

Since naturalists believe that unguided natural selection is "the sole engine of evolution," they must believe in the existence of the "special" set of characters that at one time in the distant past "conferred a reproductive advantage on some population of our remote ancestors and that also underlies our ability to do science." But no scientific data indicates the existence of this special set of characteristics. So argues van Inwagen.

The philosopher Steven M. Duncan suggests another way to think of the matter:

Whether we are Aristotelians, Platonists, Newtonians, or relativity theorists, our highly abstract theoretical beliefs have no impact on our ability to pass on our genes. Similarly, Christians, Buddhists, Muslims, and Hindus are all able to survive and reproduce regardless of their differing religious beliefs. Clearly the highly abstract beliefs we hold have little to no impact on our basic survival or our ability to pass on our genes. From an evolutionary point of view, our theoretical beliefs (even our belief in evolution itself) are superfluous and contribute nothing directly to our survival, either as individuals or as a species. They appear to have another origin altogether.[16]

The philosopher Jim Slagle suggests yet another way to look at Lewis's point. He notes that false beliefs about one's *local* environment could have a direct and harmful effect on an organism's ability to survive and reproduce; however, false highly theoretical and abstract beliefs about such matters as integral calculus and quantum electrodynamics would have no effect at all. Slagle writes, "If a hominid incorrectly believed that an approaching tiger was a nice, warm cinnamon roll, this would presumably impact its ability to survive." If the same hominid held incorrect beliefs about protons or quarks, its survival would not be threatened at all.[17]

It follows that a blind process of natural selection would not select for the higher cognitive capacities. The probability that a completely unguided evolutionary process accidentally produces creatures with those abilities, given their complexity, is therefore extremely close to zero. Indeed, that probability is likely less than the probability that a super-duper arrow shot at random from earth with no aim hits a target the size of a dime on the other side of the universe.

ANOTHER OBJECTION AND A REPLY

Creatures possessing only the elementary cognitive abilities will learn many things about their local environment. Once they know enough, they will extend their local reasoning to the rest of the universe and thereby discover everything said to be known by the higher abilities. For instance, once they see that dropped objects fall toward the center of the earth, they will eventually extrapolate to the universal law of gravity and in time to the inverse square mathematical equation describing the universal gravitational force. Therefore, so this objection goes, contrary to Lewis's argument, we *can* expect the higher abilities to evolve in the course of a blind, unguided process of natural selection—they will develop gradually as an extension of the elementary cognitive abilities.

There are serious problems with this proposal. The first was raised by the philosopher William Talbott. Any reasoning from the local to the universal and the highly abstract would require the use of nonlocal reasoning.[18] For there is no *local* reason to believe that what is true locally will also be true universally. Rather, any reason to believe that what is true locally is true universally will be a *universal* reason. Therefore, on a naturalistic basis alone, we cannot expect that creatures possessing only elementary cognitive abilities related to local knowledge would discover universal and highly abstract truths.

Furthermore, prehistoric creatures possessing only the elementary cognitive abilities would not have the inclination to extrapolate correctly to universal mathematical equations and highly abstract theorems. Indeed, they would not understand such matters in the first place.

The next problem with the proposal takes us back to the idea, crucial to science, that the universe is intelligible. We cannot successfully reason from purely local knowledge to universal knowledge—such as the claim that the force of gravity pervades the entire universe—unless we already suppose that the universe is intelligible. But the claim that the universe is intelligible goes far beyond what can be justified on the basis of local knowledge using local reasoning.

Furthermore, the belief that the universe is intelligible counts heavily against naturalism, for as we saw in chapter 4, the intelligibility thesis only makes sense on the hypothesis that the universe is the product of a superintending mind, and naturalism denies the existence of anything supernatural.

What follows? First, perhaps naturalism combined with modern evolutionary theory can explain the existence of our elementary cognitive abilities; it clearly cannot explain why we have the higher abilities that we use in mathematics, theoretical physics, evolutionary biology, genetics, organic chemistry, mathematical logic, and such. Naturalists can justify local knowledge; they cannot justify universal and abstract knowledge.

Second, naturalists who believe that their cognitive capacities are the product of a blind evolutionary process and who understand Lewis's argument have a reason to trust their cognitive abilities with respect to local knowledge. However, they have no reason to trust their abilities with respect to highly theoretical and abstract truth claims in fields such as higher math, theoretical physics, and evolutionary biology. Indeed, they have a strong reason to distrust their abilities with respect to highly theoretical claims.

Consider this analogy. A collector buys a Beatles album said to be signed by all four Beatles. He is confident it is authentic because he bought it from a reputable dealer. The next day he learns that the dealer is known to be selling fakes. The dealer has no intention of providing authentic items. The collector now has a good reason to doubt his belief that the signatures are authentic.

Recall that a belief B is self-refuting if the following is true. If B is true, then C logically follows, and C is a sufficient reason to conclude that B is false. Naturalism and naturalistic evolutionary theory are highly theoretical, highly abstract belief systems full of universal claims. But if naturalism is true, we have a strong reason to distrust our abilities with respect to highly theoretical claims.

It follows that naturalists who understand the argument from reason logically ought to reject both naturalism and naturalistic evolutionary theory. Naturalism, in short, is self-refuting. Supernaturalists, of course, are under no logical obligation to reject the theory of evolution *if it is stripped of its naturalistic, nonscientific assumptions.*

Here are three ways to distill and summarize Lewis's reasoning. The first argument concludes that naturalism is self-refuting:

1. If naturalism is true, the probability is very close to zero that the blind process of natural selection conferred on us the higher cognitive abilities needed to attain universal, abstract knowledge, including

knowledge of highly theoretical truths about the very large and the very small, the remote past and the distant future, and the highly abstract.

2. Therefore, if naturalism is true, it is not reasonable to believe any highly theoretical or abstract truth claims.

3. But naturalism itself is a highly theoretical and abstract truth claim.

4. Therefore, if naturalism is true, it is not reasonable to believe that naturalism is true.

5. Naturalism is therefore a self-refuting belief.

6. It is not reasonable to accept a belief that is self-refuting.

7. Therefore, it is not reasonable to believe that naturalism is true.

8. If naturalism is false, then supernaturalism is true.

9. Therefore, it is reasonable to believe that supernaturalism is true.

The second argument takes the form of an inference to the best explanation.

1. Human beings possess the higher cognitive capacities, namely, those they employ in the upper reaches of mathematics (in differential geometry, calculus, and topology, for instance), theoretical physics (general and special relativity theory and quantum electrodynamics, etc.), and mathematical logic. (This is the data to be explained.)

2. Consider the two great worldviews competing for our allegiance today: naturalism and theism.

A. According to naturalism, we are the product of an unguided, blind, naturalistic evolutionary process that had no goal and that did not intend to create us.

B. According to theism, the process that brought us into existence was designed and guided by a higher power for the purpose of creating creatures with higher cognitive capacities.

3. The data is astronomically improbable on the naturalistic hypothesis.

4. The data is highly probable on the theistic hypothesis.

5. The theistic hypothesis is therefore the best explanation of the data.

6. Therefore, of the two great worldviews competing for our allegiance today, theism is the most reasonable view.

Here is the third:

1. If naturalism is true, the probability is close to zero that we possess the higher cognitive abilities.

2. But we do have these cognitive abilities.

3. Therefore, naturalism is almost certainly false.

4. Therefore, the opposite, supernaturalism, is almost certainly true.

Can we make sense of our present cognitive abilities on a purely naturalistic worldview? You decide.[19]

RADICAL IMPLICATIONS

In *Where the Conflict Really Lies: Science, Religion, and Naturalism*, the philosopher Alvin Plantinga updates and defends Lewis's argument from reason using the methods of contemporary confirmation theory, philosophy of mind, and epistemology.[20] Plantinga's updated version of Lewis's argument from reason is known as the "evolutionary argument against naturalism." After defending his argument against objections, Plantinga makes some interesting observations. It is fashionable, he says, at least in many intellectual circles, to say that science and religion are incompatible. One can be scientific or religious, but one cannot consistently be both, for science conflicts with belief in God. Based on some such reasoning, many assume that naturalism and science logically go together whereas theism fits only a prescientific outlook.

However, Plantinga continues, if the evolutionary argument against naturalism is sound, the truth is the reverse. Naturalism and contemporary evolutionary theory with its naturalistic assumptions are at "serious odds," for the conjunction of naturalism and current, naturalistic evolutionary theory is self-defeating. However, there is no similar logical conflict with the conjunction of *theism* and current evolutionary theory minus its naturalistic assumptions. These two views are logically compatible, for a theist might, without any logical inconsistency, believe that a guided evolutionary process was God's way of bringing about rational creatures capable of knowing and loving him. Hence, Plantinga's conclusion at the end of his defense of the argument from reason: "There is superficial conflict but deep concord between science and theistic belief, but superficial concord and deep conflict between science and naturalism."[21]

One of the greatest honors that can be paid to a philosopher is to have other serious thinkers take up your arguments and develop them to further depths. In recent years, a number of other notable philosophers have defended and deepened in one way or another Lewis's argument from reason, including Thomas Nagel (New York University), Richard Taylor (University of Rochester), and Peter van Inwagen (University of Notre Dame).[22]

REFLECTIONS ON THE ARGUMENT FROM REASON

If Lewis's argument from reason is sound, naturalism is self-refuting. Naturalism can be held as an item of sheer blind faith; it cannot rationally be believed. Someone inclined toward naturalism might reply, "All Lewis's argument shows is that naturalism cannot rationally be believed. Naturalism might be true nonetheless, for to show that a view is irrational does not show that it is false." In response to this thought, Slagle asks: "Yet how could any proposition that would be irrational to believe if it were true *be* true? . . . how could something be true when it requires every single person on every possible occasion to not believe it?"[23]

In philosophy today, most atheists call themselves "naturalists." They assume that atheism and science fit together logically. If you believe in science, they say, then you ought to be an atheist. Theism, they claim, is incompatible with a modern scientific worldview. Now that we understand atoms, molecules, and quarks, they claim, it is illogical to believe in God.

But if Lewis's argument from reason is cogent, these atheists have everything backward. Atheism and science do *not* fit together logically. Science only makes sense as part of a *theistic* worldview. If you are an atheist, and you understand the argument from reason, then you have a sufficient reason to *reject* science—along with all other general, theoretical beliefs you hold about the universe. But then you also have a solid reason to reject atheism (and naturalism), for both are general, theoretical beliefs about the universe. On the other hand, if Lewis's argument is cogent, it follows that anyone who accepts modern science and understands the argument from reason has a compelling reason to accept theism.

Lewis's *Miracles*, published in 1947, is one of the most significant books of the twentieth century. For in this, perhaps his deepest philosophical work, Lewis highlighted what many see as *the* definitive intellectual conflict of our time, namely, the debate between naturalism and theism. The argument from reason is one more intriguing argument in favor of theism. Of the two worldviews in conflict today, theism and atheism, which do *you* think is the most reasonable?

Questions for Reflection and Discussion 9.1

1. Explain in your own words the distinction between the elementary and the higher cognitive abilities.
2. Why believe that a naturalistic, unguided process of evolution would select for the elementary cognitive abilities but would not select for the higher abilities?
3. Explain and evaluate an objection to Lewis's argument.
4. What do philosophers mean when they claim that a belief is self-refuting?
5. Does Lewis's argument show that naturalism refutes itself? Offer the most intelligent and strongest reasons you can for your position.

Philosophy of the Human Person

TEN

The Mind-Body Problem

ARE YOU YOUR BRAIN?

Sometimes we refer to our brains; other times we refer to our minds. BJ the Chicago Kid titled his second album *In My Mind*. But Screeching Weasel titled its third studio album *My Brain Hurts*. Are the mind and the brain two different things? Or are they one and the same? To put the question another way: Are thoughts, sensations, mental images, and such nothing more than physical events or processes of the physical brain? Are they just neurons (brain cells) firing or something physical like that? Or is the mind an immaterial, nonphysical entity distinct from the brain but interacting in some way with it? Or are mental states nonphysical properties arising from the physical brain analogous to smoke rising from fire? In philosophy, these and related questions make up the mind-body problem.

Introducing Dualism

Since ancient times, the traditional, most common view around the world has been that the mind—the part of us that is conscious, thinks, makes choices, and bears moral responsibility—is a single immaterial entity that cannot be physically seen, touched, or otherwise directly detected by instruments. On this view, the mind—often called the "soul," "spirit," or "self"—is not the brain or any part of the physical body. However, since mind and body obviously interact, the traditional view has long been that the mind or soul can affect the body and the body can affect the mind. More specifically, the mind can cause changes in the physical body, and the body can cause changes in the mind.

Most religions of the world teach the traditional view just described, along with the claim that the soul lives on in a higher, immaterial realm or heaven after the death of the physical body. According to the common view, it is the soul that is judged by God after bodily death, not the physical body. As the basis of moral responsibility, the soul is the true self—the root of one's identity as a person. When we say "I"—as in "I did it"—we are referring to our soul rather than our brain or physical body.

Although belief in an immaterial soul and in life after bodily death has been declining over the past century, polls show that the majority of people today still accept both. A 2014 CBS News poll found that 66 percent of Americans believe in heaven and hell. Surprisingly, a 2013 Pew poll found that 27 percent of agnostics and 13 percent of atheists believe in an afterlife.[1]

In the field of philosophy of mind, theories claiming that mind and body, or mind and brain, are two distinct substances are called "dualistic theories" of the mind-body relation. The traditional view is also called "substance dualism." Before we proceed, the term *substance* requires a short explanation.

Philosophers use the term *substance* in a technical way to mean "an entity that can exist on its own." Substances are usually contrasted with properties (attributes, characteristics) *of* substances. An individual Red Delicious apple can sit on the kitchen counter on its own. That makes it a substance. However, its color—redness—cannot sit on a counter by itself. It would make no sense to say, "Redness is sitting on the counter all by itself." The redness of an apple is a property of an apple. So, an apple, being a substance, can exist on its own, even after its redness has faded away. Its redness, being a property, cannot exist on its own, without the apple. The redness only exists as a property of the apple.

Not all dualists accept substance dualism. Aristotle formulated an alternative dualistic theory known as *hylomorphism*. On his account, the human mind, rather than being a separate substance, is the active yet nonphysical "form" or organizational structure of a living human body. A human being is a compound of form and matter, and both are essential: the form without the bodily matter is not a complete person. We'll look at this view in more detail shortly.

A third and less common dualistic theory of mind and body is called "property dualism." On this view, the mind is not a separately existing substance; rather, mental states are nonphysical properties arising from the physical brain somewhat like smoke rising from a fire. The dualism here is a dualism of properties rather than of substances.[2]

Introducing Materialism

Opposing all dualistic theories of the mind is the view that nothing but matter exists, with *matter* defined as that which physics in principle recognizes— atoms, subatomic particles, molecules, quanta of energy, forces, fields, and everything composed of such things. It is common these days to call this view "naturalism," but in the philosophy of mind, this view is more commonly called "materialism" (it is also sometimes called "physicalism"). Some materialists put their claim this way: nothing exists outside the system of nature recognized by physical science. Still others put it this way: nothing but physical objects and processes exist.

Whether you call the view materialism, naturalism, or physicalism, the essential claim is that nothing supernatural exists. Thus, there is no such being as God. Heaven, immaterial souls, spirits, angels, and such things do not exist. On the materialist view, the mind is nothing more than the physical brain or (as some materialists put it) the functioning of the brain, or (as still others claim) observable behavior caused by the brain.

Many advocates of materialism today identify the self with the brain. As they see it, when we say "I," we are referring directly to our physical brains. When we say, "I did it," we are in effect saying, "My brain did it." (But notice that the very word *My* in the sentence "My brain did it" implies that the self is not the brain but rather is something distinct from the brain that "owns" the brain, which reflects a dualist view of the self.)

Our discussion will begin with mind-body dualism. Socrates, as recorded by Plato in his dialogues, gave the first systematic and influential philosophical arguments for substance dualism and for the belief that the soul lives on after the death of the body in a higher realm or heaven. But the big arguments under discussion today in universities across the world originated in Europe during the early modern period (i.e., the sixteenth and seventeenth centuries). The first historically significant modern argument for a dualistic theory of the human person was given by the French philosopher René Descartes (1596–1650), the founder of modern philosophy, who was also one of the founders of modern science and one of the greatest mathematicians of all times. In addition to his contributions to physics and the early scientific method, he invented analytic geometry, which is why the axes on those graphs in math class are called the "Cartesian coordinate system."[3]

DESCARTES'S DIVISIBILITY ARGUMENT

In his *Meditations on First Philosophy* (1641), subtitled *In Which Is Proved the Existence of God and the Immortality of the Soul,* Descartes observes that

> there is a great difference between a mind and a body, because the body, by its very nature, is something divisible, whereas the mind is plainly indivisible. For in truth, when I consider the mind, that is, when I consider myself in so far only as I am a thinking thing, I can distinguish in myself no parts, but I very clearly discern that I am somewhat absolutely one and entire; and although the whole mind seems to be united to the whole body, yet, when a foot, an arm, or any other part is cut off, I am conscious that nothing has been taken from my mind; nor can the faculties of willing, perceiving, conceiving, etc., properly be called its parts, for it is the same mind that is exercised in willing, in perceiving, and in conceiving, etc. But quite the opposite holds in corporeal or extended things; for I cannot imagine any one of them which I cannot easily sunder in thought. This would be sufficient to teach me that the mind, or soul, of man is entirely different from the body, if I had not already been apprised of it on other grounds.[4]

This famous line of reasoning, known today as "Descartes's divisibility argument," makes more sense once it has been fleshed out in contemporary terms. The following is my interpretation:

1. The human mind has a property (an attribute or characteristic) that the human brain—and any other physical or material object—lacks.[5]

2. Necessarily, for any x and for any y, if x has a property that y lacks, then x and y are not one and the same entity; rather, they must be two distinct entities.

3. Therefore, the human mind and the human brain are not one and the same entity; rather, they must be two distinct entities.

4. It also follows that the human mind is not identical to any physical or material part of the brain, the body, or the material world.

5. Therefore, mind-body dualism is *certainly* true.

The presence of the word *certainly* indicates that Descartes's argument is deductive. His claim is therefore that if the premises are true, the conclusion must be true. In addition, the argument is clearly valid. That is, its conclusion must be true if all its premises are true. The only way to attack Descartes's argument, then, is to give an argument against one of its premises. But first we'll see how each premise can be supported by a subargument.

Argument for Premise 1

In what follows, I am assuming that by "part" Descartes means a "stand-alone" part—a part of a whole that can be detached so as to stand apart from the whole.

1a. Every macroscopic part of the human body—including every part of the human brain—is divisible into stand-alone parts.

1b. The human mind is not divisible into stand-alone parts.

1c. Therefore, premise 1 is true.

Argument for Premise 2

2a. Necessarily, for any x and for any y, if x and y are numerically identical (are one and the same entity), then every property of x is a property of y, and every property of y is a property of x.

2b. Therefore, premise 2 is true.

Argument for Premise 1a

This premise is not controversial. Each cell in the brain, like every cell in the rest of the body, can be surgically removed and placed on a microscope slide to be viewed at high magnification. The same can be said for each subcellular part of the brain and each subcellular part of the rest of the body.

Argument for Premise 1b

The ordinary parts of the mind—the parts we know directly within our consciousness—thoughts, beliefs, hopes, images, ideas, wishes, sensations, and so forth—have never been surgically removed from the mind and placed on a lab bench or microscope slide to be viewed apart from the mind. No scientist has ever claimed to have removed a belief (for instance, a belief that 1 + 1 = 2) from a patient's mind and placed it on a microscope slide. No scientist has ever claimed to have removed a patient's hope (for instance, a hope that tomorrow will be sunny) from the patient's mind and placed it in a test tube. Indeed, the very idea of such a thing happening is conceptually incoherent. Therefore, conscious mental states cannot possibly be physically removed from the mind, mounted, and studied using a microscope. The mind's parts are not stand-alone parts.

Before we assess this argument, the term *numerical identity* needs to be clarified and the second premise needs an explanation. As many people know, Bob Dylan (born in Duluth, Minnesota, on May 24, 1941) and Robert Zimmerman (born in Duluth, Minnesota, on May 24, 1941) are one and the same person; they are not two different people. In logic, x and y are numerically (or quantitatively) identical if they are one and the same entity and not two different entities. Bob Dylan and Robert Zimmerman are thus numerically identical, for they are one and the same entity.

Contrasts are always important when learning an abstract concept. Be careful not to confuse numerical identity with *qualitative* identity. Two things x and y are qualitatively identical if they have exactly the same properties, or qualities. Two separate whiteboard dry-erase markers that look exactly alike (same color, same shape, same brand, etc.) are qualitatively identical, but they are not *numerically* identical (because they are two distinct markers, not one and the same marker).

Now to premise 2. This premise is a theorem of the branch of logic called "quantificational logic with identity." An application will help make the premise clear. Suppose that the police claim that Joe Doakes robbed the local bank, and they offer video surveillance footage to prove it. Now suppose that upon further investigation, the police determine that the robber in the video is six feet tall, but Joe Doakes is only five feet tall. In this case, Doakes has a property or attribute that the robber lacks, namely, the property of being five feet tall. Common sense says that if the robber has an attribute (being six feet tall) that Joe Doakes lacks (he is only five feet tall), the robber and Joe Doakes must be two different people, not one and the same person. Despite its technical appearance, premise 2 is simply a formal logical expression of a commonsense idea employed in everyday life.

The supporting premise 2a is an axiom of logic known as "Leibniz's law" (it is also known as the "principle of the indiscernibility of identicals"). The name sounds forbidding, but the principle is actually common sense. In plain terms, Leibniz's law states that if x and y are numerically identical (are one and the same thing), then any property possessed by x is also possessed by y, and vice versa. The law sounds self-evident, doesn't it? For a fictional example, since Clark Kent and Superman are numerically identical (one and the same person), then any property possessed by one is possessed by the other. So, if Clark Kent is standing, then Superman is standing, if Clark Kent has black hair, then Superman has black hair, and so forth. It can be proved using modern symbolic logic that premise 2 is logically implied by Leibniz's law.[6] The second premise is on very solid logical ground. Descartes's argument is complete.

Objections from Cognitive Scientists

Some cognitive scientists challenge the supporting premise 1b—the claim that the mind cannot be divided into stand-alone parts. Their argument goes like this:

1. The mind contains ideas, memories, thoughts, sensations, and so forth.

2. Each of these can be thought of or imagined (and then studied) in some sense apart from the mind itself.

3. Therefore, the mind, too, contains stand-alone parts, and 1b is false.

4. But if 1b is false, then premise 1 lacks support.

5. Therefore, Descartes's first premise lacks support, and his argument fails.

This line of reasoning sounds promising until it is examined. It is true that the parts of the mind cited — thoughts, ideas, memories, feelings, hopes, and the like — can be thought of and studied analytically. However, it remains the case that thoughts, hopes, memories, and such cannot be surgically removed from a mind and physically placed on microscope slides to be viewed outside that mind. Your memory of last Christmas cannot be surgically removed from your mind and placed in a test tube. The very idea of a hope or a belief separated from a mind and sitting all by itself on a lab bench or mounted on a microscope slide is conceptually incoherent. The reason is intriguing. *It makes no sense at all to imagine an unowned thought standing completely apart from a mind currently thinking it.* A thought that is not part of a mind (i.e., that is not being thought by a mind, sitting alone by itself on a table) makes no sense at all.

So, if the mind has parts, the *way* in which it has parts is radically different from the way in which the brain has parts, in which case it still follows that the mind has properties the brain lacks and mind and brain must be two distinct entities. It also follows that the mind is not numerically identical to any other part of the body or to any material, natural, or physical object.

Descartes's central claim — that the mind is such that cannot be divided into stand-alone parts — has also been challenged by scientists who put forward dissociative identity disorder (multiple personality disorder) and split-brain syndrome as counterexamples. They argue that in these cases, the mind appears to split into separate parts that can be studied individually. Does this imply that 1b is false? Let's examine.

Split-brain syndrome occurs when the *corpus callosum* (a bundle of nerve fibers connecting the two hemispheres of a person's brain) is damaged or severed and the individual experiences what seem to be two separate streams of consciousness, each wholly or partly unaware of the other. In a case of dissociative identity disorder, the mind appears to divide into two or more separate personalities, or streams of consciousness, each wholly or partly unaware of the other. According to these critics, both disorders are cases in which the mind breaks down into stand-alone parts—contrary to Descartes's claim. Their argument goes about like this:

1. In cases of dissociative identity disorder, the mind appears to divide into two or more separate personalities, each wholly or partly unaware of the other.

2. In cases of split-brain syndrome, the mind appears to divide into two separate streams of consciousness.

3. Both disorders are therefore cases where the mind breaks down into stand-alone parts.

4. If the mind can break down into stand-alone parts, then Descartes's premise 1b is false.

5. Therefore, Descartes's premise 1b is false.

Not so fast, reply Descartes's defenders. In the split-brain cases, the two streams of consciousness cannot be physically removed, separated, stained, and placed on different microscope slides; nor can they be mounted side by side on a lab bench. Indeed, it makes no sense to think of a stream of consciousness physically sitting on a table like a beaker full of chemicals. If there are two separate streams of consciousness within one mind, they cannot physically stand alone in isolation from the mind they belong to. Likewise, for cases of multiple personality disorder: the different personalities cannot be physically removed from the mind they belong to and placed side by side in separate test tubes on a lab bench for close viewing. The very idea of a personality, or even a part of a personality, sitting on a table *apart from a mind* makes no sense at all.

It follows, again, that the way in which the mind has parts is radically different from the way in which a material object such as the brain has parts. Therefore, the mind has properties the brain lacks. But if so, it validly follows that mind-body dualism must be true.

Princess Elisabeth's Famous Question

Shortly after Descartes's *Meditations* was published, he received a letter from an avocational philosopher who was also a member of the royalty. "Tell me please," wrote Princess Elisabeth of Bohemia (1618–80), "how the soul of a human being (it being only a thinking substance) can [move] the bodily spirits and so bring about voluntary actions." In other words, how can mind and body interact if they are as radically different as Descartes claims? How can an immaterial soul possessing no solidity, shape, or weight have an effect on a solid physical object such as the brain? In philosophy of mind, this is called "the interaction problem."

Here is one reply a dualist might give. If you are looking for a scientific explanation, you will be disappointed, for scientific explanations, by their very nature, refer only to material things, and the mind (on the assumption that dualism is true) is immaterial. Thus, no scientific explanation of mind-body interaction is even possible if dualism is true. However, the fact that dualism offers no *scientific* explanation of mind-body interaction does not prove that dualism is false. For why should we suppose that the only kinds of interaction are those that can be explained scientifically? If dualism is true, there are forms of interaction that cannot be explained scientifically, with mind-body interaction being one such form. Thus, if mind-body dualism is true, the explanation of mind-body interaction will be philosophical in nature—not scientific.

Therefore, it does not follow, from the fact that we have no scientific explanation of mind-body interaction, that dualism is false. Put another way, the fact that dualism offers no *scientific* explanation of mind-body interaction does not prove that dualism is false.

To those who say that they will only consider scientific explanations, the dualist has this reply. As we saw in chapter 1, there cannot be a scientific argument for the claim that the only legitimate explanations are scientific. So, the claim (that the only explanations worth considering are scientific explanations) is not itself supported by science. Furthermore, counterexamples are everywhere. Surely beauty exists. Yet the beauty of a musical composition, a work of architecture, a statue, or a painting cannot be detected and measured with scientific instruments. Beauty also has no purely scientific explanation.

For another example, surely each human being possesses absolute value. But this value cannot be measured or explained scientifically. Absolute value does not have a symbol in the *Handbook of Physics and Chemistry*. (We'll examine the notion of absolute value in chapters 12 and 13.)

Dualists in the tradition of Descartes have offered philosophical analyses of mind-body interaction; however, an examination of these theories would take us far beyond the introductory level of this book. Edward Feser offers this thought on the interaction problem raised by Princess Elisabeth:

> Dualism is in this respect really no worse off than those most fundamental theories of modern physics: relativity and quantum mechanics. Notoriously, there are respects in which these theories seem to be in conflict, and yet the evidence for each is very powerful. There are various ways of trying to reconcile them, but as yet no consensus as to which, if any, is the right one. It would be silly to insist that physicists must reject these theories, or at least one of them, until some generally accepted solution to the problem of reconciling them has been worked out. . . . Similarly, it is unreasonable to expect the dualist to give up dualism simply because the interaction problem exists, when there are arguments in favor of dualism that are at least as powerful and worthy of consideration as any others in philosophy.[7]

FOUR MORE ASPECTS OF CONSCIOUSNESS THAT DEFY MATERIALIST EXPLANATION

Today, renowned experts and researchers in the philosophy of mind, including Thomas Nagel, David Chalmers, John Foster, and Frank Jackson—all advocates of dualism in one form or another—are discussing four aspects of consciousness that they claim cannot be explained in materialistic terms: *qualia, intentionality, subjectivity,* and *privacy.* We'll briefly examine four of their arguments.

Qualia

Close your eyes and imagine a stop sign. What color is the experienced image? If you imagined an ordinary stop sign, the image in your mind is experienced as red (and white). You are aware of its color directly, from inside your consciousness. Philosophers use the term *qualia* (singular: *quale*) for experiential mental states such as the experienced color of a sunset, the taste of chocolate, the smell of a rose, the sound of a bell, and the feel of velvet.

Now, as you experience this red image in your mind—this quale—certain physical things are occurring in your brain at the same time. For instance, brain scientists say that when we experience the color red, certain electrical activity occurs among the cells in a particular part of the brain. However, if a brain surgeon were to open your brain at the moment you are experiencing the red image, she would *not* see a red spot shaped like a stop sign physically in, or on, some part of your brain like a physical image on a movie screen. Your brain is normally gray. Nothing in your brain turns from gray to red when you form and experience a red image in your mind. It follows, by the theorem of logic stating that if x has a property that y does not have, then x and y are two different entities, that the quale—the red image you directly experience inside your consciousness—is not numerically identical to any physical part of your brain. The *quale* is a part of your mind but not a part of your brain. Therefore, your mind has a property that your brain lacks. It follows that mind-body dualism is true. Thus:

The Qualia Argument

1. Some mental states have a qualitative content.

2. No brain states possess a qualitative content.

3. If x has a property not possessed by y, then x and y are not numerically identical.

4. Therefore, the mind is not the brain.

5. If so, then mind-body dualism is true, and materialism is false.

6. Therefore, mind-body dualism is true, and materialism is false.

Intentionality

Some kinds of mental states possess a property that philosophers of mind call "intentionality." (This property is also called "aboutness.") This is a difficult notion to understand. A mental state is intentional if it is *about* something. That which an intentional mental state is *about* is called that state's "intentional object." For instance, my belief that Sir Paul McCartney plays bass guitar is *about* Paul McCartney, and Sir Paul is the intentional object of my belief. My hope that tomorrow will be sunny is *about* tomorrow's weather.

The aboutness of thought is a directly experienced mental property that is hard to deny. Unless at least some of our mental states possess intentionality or aboutness, thinking about anything outside our minds would be impossible. However odd intentionality may seem when we think about it in the abstract, it is an undeniable feature of our mental lives.

A word of caution is called for here. The word *intentional* in philosophy of mind has nothing to do with "intending" to do something or with having a purpose. The intentionality of the mental is merely the property of being *about* something.

The problem for materialists is that, for a number of reasons, it seems certain that intentionality, or aboutness, cannot possibly be a property possessed by a purely material, or physical, object. Why?

First, the aboutness of a thought is not a property recognized within current physics. (Aboutness does not appear in any of the physics manuals listing measured physical properties.) Furthermore, the latest science indicates that the physical nature of any material object will one day be fully explained in terms of standard physical properties without mentioning intentionality at all or anything remotely like it. An atom, or clump of atoms, or a quantum of energy, considered merely as a physical object, isn't *about* anything; it just *is*.

The question dualists put to materialists is therefore, How can an atom, or a neuron, or a chemical in someone's brain, or a clump of nerve fibers in a person's frontal lobe, be *about* Paul McCartney? Or about tomorrow? Which physical properties would make a bundle of neurons a belief about McCartney rather than about Sir Ringo Starr? About tomorrow rather than about next week? No one in neuroscience has the slightest idea. No one in neuroscience has ever successfully explained how intentionality can be reduced to (explained solely in terms of) neurons, electrochemical brain signals, molecules, chemicals, or any other purely physical objects. Laurence BonJour writes: "There is no reason at all to think that the internal structure of my physical and neurophysiological states could somehow by itself determine that I am thinking about the weather rather than about the Middle East or the stock market."[8]

The Intentionality Argument

1. Some mental states possess intentionality, but nothing in the physical brain or body possesses intentionality.

2. If *x* has a property not possessed by *y*, then *x* and *y* are not numerically identical.

3. Therefore, the mind is not the brain or any part of the brain or body.

4. If so, then mind-body dualism is true, and materialism is false.

5. Therefore, mind-body dualism is certainly true, and materialism is false.

Argument for Premise 1

1a. Many kinds of mental states are intentional — they are about something.

1b. No physical states are intentional.

1c. Therefore, premise 1 is true.

Materialists agree that science has not yet explained intentionality. However, they hope that scientists will someday succeed and we will then see that the supporting premise 1b is false. BonJour replies:

> Here we have a piece of materialist doctrine that again has a status very similar to that of a claim of theology. It is obvious that no one has even the beginnings of an idea of how to actually carry out an investigation that would yield a result of this kind — that the only reason for thinking that this could be done is the overriding assumption, for which we have found no cogent basis, that materialism must be true.[9]

Subjectivity

In recent years, Nagel, Jackson, and other prominent philosophers specializing in the study of consciousness have put forward a new argument for dualism. Their case begins with the claim that mental states have a directly experienced, subjective quality that cannot be fully expressed quantitatively, that is, objectively in the language of any of the physical sciences. In the case of any conscious mental state, they argue, *there is something it is like* to be in that state. For instance, there is something it is like to feel nostalgic, to taste chocolate, to remember last summer fondly, to hope for snow, to be in love. In each case, this "something it is like" is an experienced aspect of a quale. And this "something it is like" cannot be defined mathematically. Nor can it be characterized within the language of any of the physical sciences. Nagel calls this subjective aspect of consciousness the "what it is like" quality of the mental.

Nor can this subjective quality of consciousness possibly be reduced to (explained without remainder in terms of) particles of matter and quanta of energy moving in space and time under the governance of the laws of physics and chemistry alone. This is indicated by the failure of all materialist attempts to reduce conscious experience to purely physical events and objects. It follows, these dualists argue, that subjective consciousness and the physical brain are not one and the same thing. It also follows that the mind is not identical to any physical object.

Nagel argues that the reason why science has not, and never will, explain the subjective nature of consciousness is that science, by its very nature, explains everything from an objective, or third-person, public perspective. But the subjectivity of consciousness can only be understood from within a first-person perspective.

How can a physical pile of atoms or a quark or an electromagnetic field have a subjective, qualitative awareness? How can there possibly be "something it is like" to be a proton, an atom, a sugar molecule, or a potassium ion? Scientists haven't the foggiest idea. The subjective aspect of consciousness clearly appears to be yet another mental property that cannot be reduced to matter in motion governed by the laws of physics and chemistry as they apply to the brain. More formally:

The Subjectivity Argument

1. Conscious mental states have a subjective aspect.

2. No atom, clump of atoms, material object, or physical part of the body has this subjective aspect.

3. If x has a property not possessed by y, then x and y are not quantitatively identical.

4. Therefore, the mind is not the brain or any part of the body.

5. If so, then mind-body dualism is certainly true, and materialism is false.

6. Therefore, mind-body dualism is true, and materialism is false.

Privacy

It is common sense that our mental states are private, but our brain states are publicly observable. I am the only one who has immediate access to my thoughts, feelings, sensations, and other mental states, and you are the only one who has immediate access to your thoughts and other mental states. More specifically, others can ask me what I am thinking but only I can literally have my thoughts. And only you can have your thoughts. If I take a bite of a Hershey bar, I taste chocolate. No one else can have or experience my taste of chocolate, although they can take a bite of my candy bar and experience their own taste of chocolate. Some philosophers sum up the point this way: each of us has private, or privileged, access to the directly experienced contents of our mind. Brain scientists can ask us what we are thinking about, but they must take our word for it; they cannot literally experience our thoughts and sensations.

However, each physical part of the brain can be publicly examined in a lab by a team of scientists. Every physical aspect of the brain can be observed and fully described publicly, in the third person—in the languages of science and mathematics—without using the word "I."

Now, if the mind is private, in the sense defined, and the brain is public, in the sense defined, then the mind and the brain have differing properties. It follows again that the mind and the brain must be two distinct substances, and dualism in one form or another is true.

The Privacy Argument

1. The brain is publicly accessible.

2. The mind is not publicly accessible.

3. If x has a property not possessed by y, then x and y are not quantitatively identical.

4. Therefore, the mind is not the brain.

5. If so, then mind-body dualism is true.

6. Therefore, mind-body dualism is certainly true, and materialism is false.

The arguments for dualism considered here remain standing despite numerous attempts to knock them down. No scientific experiment, or series of experiments, has ever proved that dualism is false and that materialism regarding the mind is true.[10]

After we take a closer look at dualism, we'll consider the two most recent attempts to explain consciousness materialistically, that is, in terms of matter in motion governed by the laws of physics and chemistry alone, without reference to anything immaterial, such as a soul or immaterial mind. Although each theory failed to explain consciousness, the way each failed teaches us about the nature of the mind. The first of these theories emerged during the 1960s. In philosophy it is called "the identity theory."

GOING DEEPER. VARIETIES OF DUALISM

An Aristotelian Theory

Aristotle argued that every material substance is a hybrid being composed of matter and form. We saw that his theory is called *hylomorphism* (Greek *hyle*, "matter," and *morphe*, "form"). The form is the organizational structure; the matter is the underlying stuff structured by the form. For example, a penny is round, and it is composed of copper. Its roundness is part of its form; its copper is the matter structured by the form. The "substantial form" of a material object is the organizational structure that makes it the kind of substance it is. So, forms are abstract and immaterial, not to be identified with any particular bit of matter. Now, although forms exist "in" substances and not outside them or above them, they are active entities, for they impart powers to the underlying matter. A material substance is thus not just a collection of atoms of matter, it is a combination of matter and form. The human soul, Aristotle argued, is the form and the material body is the matter of a living human being.

Aristotle's dualism has significant implications. Descartes argued that the human soul is a complete person on its own, but on Aristotle's view, a soul without a body to structure is not a complete person. The soul, as an active but nonphysical form, can continue to exist apart from the physical body after earthly death. But lacking a body to animate, the soul exists in an incomplete and "unnatural" state, for it is the nature of the soul to be related to and animate a body. Substance dualists such as Descartes who argue for life after death do not see bodily death as the death of a person, for they identify the person with the immaterial soul and argue that the soul lives on in a higher realm after the death of the body. On the hylomorphic account, bodily death *is* the death of the person, even though the soul can live on in a diminished and incomplete state after earthly death. On this view, body and soul are both essential for full personhood. In the next life, the whole person begins to exist again only when God joins a resurrected body—related in some way to the person's earthly body—to the person's soul.

Although numerous Christian philosophers have defended Descartes's view of the mind, the traditional Christian view is not substance dualism. Rather, it is the hylomorphic view going back to Aristotle and defended by philosophers such as Robert P. George: our souls continue to exist after bodily death, but the full person returns to life only after the soul is joined to a resurrected body.[11]

Property Dualism

According to property dualism, the mind is not a substance. However, the mind is not simply the physical brain. Rather, on this view the mind is a system of immaterial properties (attributes, characteristics) that arise from the brain. These properties are nonphysical in the sense that they cannot be reduced to (explained fully in terms of) the physical properties of the brain. Being nonphysical, they arise from the brain without being logically entailed by the physical properties of the brain. Some advocates of property dualism use the following analogy: mental properties arise from the brain somewhat the way smoke rises from a chimney. On this idea, known as *epiphenomenalism*, the mind is the caused result of physical brain activity but does not itself act back on the brain and cause brain activity. (Similarly, smoke is caused by a fire but does not causally affect the fire that caused it.)

As you might have expected, property dualism faces many of the questions faced by substance dualism, including these: What is the nature of the relation between the mental and the physical? How can nonphysical properties arise from a physical object composed of nothing but atoms and molecules?

Another problem has to do with the unity of the mental. Each of my thoughts and sensations is *my* thought or sensation. Likewise, each of your thoughts and sensations is thought or felt by *you*. If property dualism is true and the mind is a cloud of millions of immaterial properties arising from the brain like smoke rising from fire, what could possibly be the underlying self that possesses mental properties? Put another way, what makes a person's mental properties the properties of one and the same person? And for that matter, what is the self that acts? That possesses free will? That bears moral responsibility? That experiences things? If property dualism is true, it seems to follow that these questions have no answers. Indeed, it seems to follow that the self doesn't exist.

Let's think about this further. When we say the word "I" (as in "I did it"), what are we referring to? The "I" or self can't simply be one nonphysical property among millions, for properties are aspects or qualities of an underlying substance and as such don't act or bear moral responsibility, yet a self acts and bears moral responsibility. But the self can't possibly be the brain, for as Edward Feser notes, "You can't break down an *I* into two or more *I*'s the way you can break down a . . . physical thing [such as the brain] into two or more . . . physical things."[12] The self therefore has properties that the brain lacks. Again, it is hard to see how there is any acting self if property dualism is true.

Questions for Reflection and Discussion 10.1

1.   State the mind-body problem in your own words.
2.   Compare and contrast materialism and dualism.
3.   Explain two varieties of dualism.
4.   Evaluate Descartes's argument for mind-body dualism. Offer the most intelligent and strongest reasons you can for your position.
5.   Explain the causal interaction objection. How might a dualist reply?
6.   Explain an aspect of consciousness that dualists claim defies materialist explanation.

THE MATERIALIST ATTEMPT TO EXPLAIN CONSCIOUSNESS BASED ON BRAIN SCIENCE ALONE

During the 1960s, a philosophical theory emerged that, it was claimed, explains consciousness in purely material terms consistent with the latest results of brain science. According to the *mind-brain identity theory* (the "identity theory" for short), thoughts, sensations, beliefs, and the like are nothing more than physical events, states, and processes of the brain. (From here on, *mental events* will be shorthand for "mental events, states, and processes," and *brain events* will abbreviate "brain events, states, and processes.") The mind, in other words, is numerically identical with the physical brain.[13]

Keep in mind, as we discuss this theory, the precise logical meaning of *numerically identical*. To claim that the mind and the brain are numerically identical is to claim that they are one and the same thing, not two different things. Again, Bob Dylan is numerically identical to Robert Zimmerman—they are one and the same person. Ringo Starr is numerically identical to Richard Starkey—they are one and the same drummer. Of course, if the mind and the brain are numerically identical, then any property of the mind is a property of the brain, and any property of the brain is a property of the mind—that follows from the theorem of logic we examined earlier in this chapter.

Two major arguments for the identity theory were given: one based on neuroscience, a second based on Ockham's razor. The argument from neuroscience relies on laboratory studies that reveal timed correlations between observed brain events and reported mental events.[14]

The Argument from Neuroscience

1. Brain scientists have discovered correlations between reported mental events and observed brain events. For instance, every time a patient reports feeling a pain in the arm, neurons x, y, and z light up at the same moment at a certain spot in the brain; every time a patient reports seeing red, neurons a, b, and c activate at the same moment at a certain spot in the brain, and so forth.

2. In addition, when one specific part of the brain is damaged, a specific mental function is lost.

3. If reported mental events can be correlated with observed brain events occurring at the same time and if the loss of a mental function can be correlated with the loss of a brain function, then it follows that each mental event is (numerically) identical to a brain event, and the mind simply is the brain.

4. Therefore, the mind-brain identity theory must be true (and dualism is false).

This argument may seem compelling at first glance, but it has severe problems. To begin with, premise 3 is false. Here is why. First, correlation is not the same as, and does not prove, numerical identity. The mere fact that A and B occur at the same time within a complex system does not prove that A and B are one and the same thing.

Second, the two sides of the correlation—reported mental events and observed brain events—have numerous radically different properties, as we have seen. But if the two sides of a correlation have radically different properties, then the correlation most certainly does not establish numerical identity.

In short, brain studies that correlate reported mental states and observed brain states happening at the same time do not rule out the possibility that the mental state and the physical state are separate and distinct entities occurring within a bigger system. These brain studies, in other words, are consistent with the truth of dualism.

The third reason the laboratory correlations do not disprove dualism or prove the identity theory is that mind-body dualism actually *predicts* the same experimental result, namely, the correlations between mental states and brain states discovered in the lab. The point is so important and so often overlooked that some elaboration is called for.

Mind-body dualism claims that the brain and the mind—though distinct—causally interact: minds cause changes in brains, and brains cause changes in minds. Therefore, if mind-body dualism is true, we should logically expect that an observable brain event will occur each time a reported mental event occurs, and vice versa. Thus, if dualism is true, a reported mental event—such as experiencing the taste of chocolate while eating a candy bar—will always be found to be correlated with a predictable set of physical events occurring at a certain spot on the brain at the same time. If this sounds wrong, consider that on the dualist view, the brain is the cause-and-effect interface between the immaterial soul and the physical world. Mind and brain, according to dualism, are constantly interacting, each causing changes in the other.

The upshot is that the correlations between reported mental events and observed brain events discovered in the lab are expected if materialism is true, and they are also expected if dualism is true. If the correlations are predicted equally by both theories, then they neither prove nor disprove either theory. This popular argument for materialism fails. The next argument is a slight improvement.

The Ockham's Razor Argument

The philosopher J. J. C. Smart, one of the most prominent defenders of the identity theory during the 1960s, wrote, "Why do I wish to resist [dualism] [and accept the identity theory]? Mainly because of Ockham's razor."[15] His argument goes like this:

> 1. Both dualism and the mind-brain identity theory explain exactly the same data.
>
> 2. But the identity theory is simpler than dualism.
>
> 3. Ockham's razor recommends adopting the simpler of two theories when both theories explain the same data.
>
> 4. Therefore, the identity theory is probably true.

Smart doesn't give an argument for premise 1; he simply assumes it. We'll see in a moment why this is problematic. Here is his subargument for premise 2:

> 2a. The identity theory explains consciousness in terms of one ultimate kind of substance (matter), while dualism posits two radically different kinds of substances (an immaterial mind and a physical brain).
>
> 2b. Therefore, premise 2 is true.

Smart is right: the identity theory is theoretically simpler than dualism, in the sense that it posits only one kind of substance—matter—while dualism posits two radically different kinds of substances (mind and matter).

However, dualists have a response. They point out that their theory explains many aspects of consciousness that the identity theory cannot explain, including qualia, intentionality, subjectivity, and the privacy of the mental. (We have already examined the arguments for this claim.) If the dualists are right and their theory explains more data than the identity theory explains, then premise 1 is false. But if so, then Ockham's razor does not favor the identity theory, for Ockham's razor only points to the simpler of two theories when both theories explain the very same data. The reader can draw his or her own conclusion.

ARGUMENTS THAT SANK THE IDENTITY THEORY

Recall the qualia, intentionality, privacy, and subjectivity arguments for dualism. If any of these arguments is sound, the identity theory is false. Therefore, each argument can be reconfigured as an argument against the identity theory by changing one premise.

The Qualia Argument against the Identity Theory

1. Experienced qualia have properties that brain states lack.

2. If x has a property that y lacks, then x is not numerically identical with y.

3. Therefore, a quale is not identical with any physical state of our brain.

4. If the identity theory is true, a quale is identical with a brain state.

5. Therefore, the identity theory is certainly false.

The Intentionality Argument against the Identity Theory

1. Mental states are intentional, but no brain state is intentional.

2. If x has a property not possessed by y, then x and y are not numerically identical.

3. Therefore, the mind is not the brain.

4. If the identity theory is true, the mind is identical to the brain.

5. Therefore, the identity theory is certainly false.

The Subjectivity Argument against the Identity Theory

1. Mental states have a directly experienced subjective, or qualitative, aspect.

2. No atom or clump of atoms or any part of the brain has a subjective, or qualitative, aspect.

3. If *x* has a property not possessed by *y*, then *x* and *y* are not quantitatively identical.

4. Therefore, the mind is not the brain.

5. If the identity theory is true, the mind is nothing but the brain.

6. Therefore, the identity theory is surely false.

The Privacy Argument against the Identity Theory

1. The brain (like every material object and physical part of the body) is publicly accessible.

2. The mind is private—it is not publicly accessible.

3. If *x* has a property not possessed by *y*, then *x* and *y* are not quantitatively identical.

4. Therefore, the mind is not the brain or any part of the body.

5. If the identity theory is true, then the mind is identical to the brain.

6. Therefore, the identity theory is false.

Downfall

Although the identity theory was popular in philosophy during the 1960s and 1970s, it fell out of favor and has now been abandoned by most academic philosophers of mind, for reasons we've examined. The next big theory of the mind, the one currently favored by many, if not most, materialists, likens mental states to the programmed states of a digital computer. What makes something a mind is not the material it is made of nor the way it is structured. What makes something a mind is simply the way it *functions.* A mind is not a substance; it is a function. According to the next theory, sometimes called "functionalism," if a machine such as a computer behaves, or functions, the way a conscious being behaves, it *is* conscious, and it has a mind.

Questions for Reflection and Discussion 10.2

1. In your own words, what does the identity theory claim?
2. Explain and evaluate one of the arguments for the identity theory.
3. Explain and evaluate one of the arguments against the identity theory.
4. Do correlation studies prove that the mind is the brain? Argue for your answer.
5. Why have most materialists rejected the identity theory?
6. At this point in the discussion, are you a dualist or a materialist? Support your view with a philosophical argument. Offer the most intelligent and strongest reasons you can for your position.

THE MATERIALIST ATTEMPT TO EXPLAIN CONSCIOUSNESS IN ACCORD WITH COMPUTER SCIENCE

The initial idea underlying the latest materialism-friendly theory of the mind—a theory logically consistent with materialism—can be introduced with a question. What is a clock? Clearly, the concept of a clock cannot be defined in terms of the materials out of which a clock is constructed, for some clocks are made of metal, others of wood, or plastic; some are even made of paper. The concept of a clock also cannot be defined in terms of how a clock is structured. Some contain gears and springs, wheels, cogs, hands, and numbers; others do not. (Digital clocks have circuits but neither cogs nor gears; water clocks have basins and tubes, and so forth.)

Clearly, the only thing all clocks have in common is the way they *function*. No matter what they are made of or how they are structured, clocks are devices that tell time. So, a clock cannot be defined in terms of any one type of physical substance (wood or metal) or physical organization (gears or silicon chips); it can be defined only in terms of the way it functions, that is, the way it *behaves*. The clock function is therefore an abstraction.

Now think about the embodiment of the clock function. Like a computer program, the clock function is typically "realized within," or "run on," a physical medium or platform. If a clock is constructed of metal and glass with gears and springs, its function is realized within the medium of metal, glass, gears, and springs. If a clock is constructed of wooden parts, its function is being run on a wooden platform, and so on. The clock function is thus "multiply realizable"—it can be realized or run on many different material substances or platforms.

Functionalism's big idea—put somewhat crudely—is that the mind is not any particular substance, nor is it a particular organization of stuff. It is simply a function. Like a clock, the conscious mind cannot be defined in terms of the material out of which it is composed or the way that material is put together; it can be defined only in terms of its function. The mind is simply an abstract function running on an underlying platform.[16]

Big consequences follow. If the mind, like a clock, is nothing more than an abstract function, then the mind function can be realized on many different kinds of media, or platforms. Thought of in this way, there is no reason why the "consciousness function" can't be realized on, or run on, a purely physical platform such as a digital computer or a chip inside a robot. Thus, if a computer functions the way a conscious mind functions, the computer *is* a conscious mind. If a computerized robot behaves the way a conscious person behaves, the robot *is* conscious. In the computer's case, the mind function is being run on a silicon chip. In the human case, functionalists who are materialists claim that the mind function is realized on the medium of a physical brain. This gives us the following functionalist argument:

1. To be conscious is nothing more than to function or behave like a conscious being functions or behaves.

2. Consciousness is therefore a function that can be realized or run on many different platforms or media.

3. Therefore, if a machine functions or behaves the way a conscious being functions or behaves, then it *is* conscious, no matter what it is composed of and no matter how it is structured.

4. Many computers function as if they are conscious and thinking.

5. Therefore, many computers are conscious and possess conscious minds.

The functionalist idea can also be applied to specific mental states. On the functionalist view, a mental state such as a belief or a wish is constituted solely by its functional role within a larger system of functions. So, if a computer functions the way a human being functions when the person believes in Santa, then the computer is conscious and actually *believes in Santa*. The computer is not simply behaving as if it believes in Santa, it actually does believe in Santa. If a computer functions the way a person functions when he or she is in love, then the computer is conscious and actually is in love. The computer is not just simulating loving behavior, it really is in love. If a computer functions the way a person functions when the person has an itch, the computer actually *feels* an itch.

The following will sound surprising at first: functionalism is logically consistent with both mind-body dualism and materialism. Functionalists who are mind-body dualists say that in the human case the mind function is being run on an immaterial platform (the soul or immaterial mind). Functionalists who are materialists may claim that the mind function is realized on the medium or platform of a physical brain. Most advocates of functionalism, however, are materialists.

Functionalism is attractive to modern materialists for two reasons. First, it is logically consistent with materialism, even though it does not imply materialism. Second, functionalism holds out hope that consciousness will someday be fully explained in scientific or materialistic terms alone, thus eliminating any need to believe in an immaterial mind or soul. An intriguing theory. But is it true?

One of the first mechanical models of the mind appeared in 1748 in *Man a Machine*, a book by the French philosopher Julien Offray de La Mettrie. La Mettrie, a materialist, was fascinated by the hydraulic robots he had seen in some of the French gardens.[17] As water flowed through the robot's body, it simulated simple human behavior. He argued that we are all just complicated versions of these simple water-powered machines and our mental activity is no more than a mechanical process. La Mettrie's ideas anticipated modern functionalism.

MAJOR PROBLEMS FOR FUNCTIONALISM

Searle's Chinese Room

In a famous article, "Minds, Brains, Programs," in the journal *Brain and Behavioral Science*, John Searle, professor of philosophy at the University of California at Berkeley, proposed a thought experiment that he claimed shows vividly that functionalism is false.[18] Imagine that someone who does not understand Chinese is placed in a windowless room with one door. Inside the room is a large pile of instructions written in English, which the person understands. Each instruction states that when a piece of paper with a symbol of such and such a physical shape is passed into the room through a thin slot in the door, a piece of paper with a symbol of such and such shape is to be passed back. The instructions are phrased solely in terms of the physical shapes of the symbols, described in English, not in terms of the meanings of the symbols. Unbeknownst to the person inside the room, the shapes are Chinese characters.

With everything set to go, pieces of paper containing Chinese characters are passed into the room through the slit in the door, and the person returns pieces of paper containing other Chinese characters, following the instruction book written in English. To an observer outside the room who speaks Chinese, the flow of characters in and out of the room is indistinguishable from what it would be if the person inside the room understood Chinese. The flow of characters *exactly* simulates an intelligible conversation in Chinese.

From the outside, then, the behavior of the person in the room is indistinguishable from that of a Chinese speaker. The room functions as if it understands Chinese. Therefore, if functionalism is true, the person inside the room *understands Chinese*. However, the person inside the room (by hypothesis) does not speak a word of the language. It follows that functionalism is false. It also follows that there is more to consciousness than merely following a program that makes one function in a certain way. Thus:

1. If functionalism is true, the person in the Chinese room understands Chinese.

2. But the person in the room does not understand Chinese.

3. Therefore, functionalism is false.

In Searle's analogy, the room as a whole corresponds to a computer, the person inside the room corresponds to the central processing unit (CPU) of the computer, and the pile of instructions written in English corresponds to the computer's program (software).

Searle's thought experiment raises an important question. What is the difference between a conscious mind processing information and a computer that is behaving *like* a conscious mind that is processing information? Both process symbols: computers take in electrical impulses and output electrical impulses; minds process words and other kinds of linguistic symbols and output words and other kinds of linguistic symbols.

The difference, Searle argues, is that a real mind processes symbols by reference to what they mean, which it accomplishes by knowing what they are *about*. The symbols processed by a real mind thus mean something to the mind. Although a computer also processes symbols, the items it crunches (electrical impulses) mean nothing to it, for it manipulates them in terms of their physical properties alone, not by reference to their meanings or what they are about.

To elaborate, the symbols being processed by a digital computer are streams of electrons flowing through logic circuits. They are processed *as electrical impulses*, not as bits of meaning. Put another way, the electrical pulses processed by a computer are not processed as symbols standing intentionally for something. To the computer, the electrons passing through its circuits are not about anything at all and mean nothing at all.

A human chess player, for example, actually plays chess—he or she thinks, reasons, and calculates, with an end in mind, namely, to win a game. A "chess-playing computer" does nothing of the sort; it simply crunches electrical impulses according to a program, without any idea what it is doing.

If Searle is right, then, no digital computer will ever be a conscious mind, no matter how closely it mimics conscious behavior, because (again) all computers ever do is process meaningless electrical impulses on the basis of the physical properties of those signals, with no reference to any meanings or intentional objects, but real minds process symbols by reference to what they mean and are about.[19]

Scientists in the field of artificial intelligence (AI) attempt to create machines that mimic intelligent behavior. Philosophers distinguish two schools of thought within the field. Advocates of "strong AI" believe that if a computer behaves as if it is conscious, then it really is conscious. In contrast, advocates of "weak AI" make a more modest claim: computers are not conscious minds; they merely behave *as if* they are conscious. Searle's argument is an attack on strong AI; it is not directed at weak AI.

Block's Gigantic Mind

Ned Block, professor of philosophy at MIT, proposed another famous counterexample to functionalism, which I will simplify and condense with help from the imaginary idea of Santa Claus.[20] According to functionalism, if a system behaves, or functions, exactly the way someone who believes in Santa Claus behaves, then the system (no matter what it is made of) is conscious and actually believes in Santa. With this in mind, Block asks us to imagine a software program that causes any system running it to behave exactly like someone who believes in Santa Claus behaves. Call this the "belief in Santa program." If functionalism is true, it is theoretically possible to write such a program. The pattern of inputs and outputs of any platform running this program will exactly match the behavioral input-output pattern of a human believer in Santa. According to functionalism, any system running this program actually is a conscious mind that believes in Santa.

The next step requires a short explanation. Basic computer circuits have only two positions: open and closed. Any computer program, no matter how complex, can be represented by a long string of 1's and 0's specifying in order the openings and closings for the circuits of the computer running the program. A computer chip consists of millions of tiny circuits (called "logic gates") that open and close corresponding to the (millions of) 1's and 0's specified by a computer program.

Now suppose that one billion people have been choreographed to stand and sit in a sequence that exactly mimics, in the right order, the 1's and 0's of a belief in Santa program. In other words, these people have been choreographed to behave in a way that functionally imitates the opening and closing of the logic gates of a computer running a belief in Santa program. This is in theory possible. Standing might correspond to 1, sitting to 0.

This group of one billion people would then constitute a platform realizing the belief in Santa program.

If functionalism is true, *this group of people constitutes a giant mind that is conscious and that actually believes in Santa—even if no individual in the group actually believes in Santa.*

Is it reasonable to believe that if one billion people were to behave in this way, a giant mind that believes in Santa would suddenly come into existence? This implication of functionalism, Block argues, is simply absurd. But if a theory has an absurd consequence, that is a good reason to reject the theory. Thus:

1. If functionalism is true, then a giant conscious mind that believes in Santa Claus suddenly comes into existence when one billion people stand up and sit down so as to realize, or run, a belief in Santa program.

2. It is absurd to suppose that a giant mind could come into existence in this way.

3. Therefore, functionalism is clearly false.

Chalmers's Zombies

The Australian philosopher David Chalmers, a leading figure in the philosophy of mind today, proposed an influential argument against functionalism based on the philosophical concept of a zombie. In philosophy, a *zombie* is defined as "a being who functions exactly like a conscious person functions but who nevertheless has no conscious internal mental states whatsoever." Zombies, he argues, are conceivable without self-contradiction. But if they are conceivable without self-contradiction, then they are logically possible. (A standard principle of modern logic and mathematics is the idea that if something is conceivable without self-contradiction, then that is a strong reason to believe it is logically possible.) However, if functionalism is true, zombies are not logically possible, for according to functionalism, if something functions exactly like a conscious being functions, it *necessarily* is conscious. For (again) according to functionalism, there is nothing more to being conscious than functioning *as if* you are conscious. So, according to functionalism, it is impossible that something is not conscious and yet functions exactly like it is conscious. In other words, if functionalism is true, zombies are logically impossible. The argument follows:

1. Let a *zombie* be defined as "a being who functions exactly like a conscious person functions but who nevertheless has no conscious mental states whatsoever."

2. It is logically possible that a being that has no conscious mental states nevertheless functions exactly like a conscious being functions.

3. Zombies are therefore logically possible.

4. If functionalism is true, zombies are not logically possible.

5. Therefore, functionalism is false.[21]

Applied to neuroscience, Chalmers's zombie argument raises a difficult question: Why is the purely physical, neurological functioning of a living human brain accompanied by a subjective inner life consisting of private conscious experiences, vivid color sensations, thoughts about intentional objects, and so forth, rather than by no consciousness at all? As Chalmers puts it, why doesn't all the neurological functioning inside the brain go on in the dark, so to speak, without any attendant conscious mental states? Put yet another way, Why is neurological functioning accompanied by a stream of consciousness consisting of experienced smells, tastes, colors, sounds, vivid images — in short, an "inner movie"? Chalmers calls these questions the "hard problem of consciousness."[22] Neuroscientists have no scientifically confirmed answers. Yet, writes Chalmers, "it seems to me that we are surer of the existence of conscious experience than we are of anything else in the world."[23]

Dualism, of course, supplies the beginning of an answer. The neural functioning of a living human brain is accompanied by conscious states because a human being is an immaterial mind, or soul, interacting with the physical brain, and the soul brings the conscious, subjective side of life to the equation. Zombies would lack conscious mental states because they would lack souls.

Chalmers on the Hard Problem of Consciousness

Watch Chalmers's TED Talk, "How Do You Explain Consciousness?," July 14, 2014, https://www.youtube.com/watch?v=uhRhtFFhNzQ.

DOES FUNCTIONALISM EXPLAIN CONSCIOUSNESS?

The arguments we've just examined indicate that there is more to consciousness than merely functioning, or behaving, the way a conscious being behaves. Critics of functionalism, such as Nagel, Searle, Block, and Chalmers, argue that functionalists, by focusing solely on outward behavior, miss what goes on *inside* our stream of consciousness. Specifically, they overlook the private, subjective life-process experienced only from the inside. Functionalism, in other words, ignores (and can't explain) the subjective nature of thought, the part we experience privately.

Nagel puts the idea this way. A conscious being has an inner mental life. If a being has an inner mental life, there's *something it is like to be that individual.* And this inner life is not simply an outward pattern of behavior because it can exist without any attendant behavior.[24] Since this inner life is nonpublic and subjective, it cannot be "functionalized" (explained solely in external, functional terms).

If consciousness is subjective, internal, and private in this way, while functioning is entirely public, then the mind is not simply a function that can be run on a platform, material or immaterial.

Each of us knows by personal experience that qualia are real. We know by direct experience that our minds have the private, subjective, and nonfunctional aspects described by the critics of functionalism. We know our thoughts are intentional and not merely functional. We verify these facts every time we directly experience our own consciousness from the inside. Functionalism stands in conflict with our common human experience.

SUMMING UP

During the twentieth century, many philosophers rejected dualism, assumed without any proof—scientific or philosophical—that materialism is true, and attempted to explain the mind in terms consistent with materialism. They tried to explain consciousness based on brain science. After that research program failed, they tried to explain consciousness in terms consistent with computer science. However, none of the major materialist attempts to explain the mind in material terms alone succeeded. In particular, no materialist theory of the mind successfully explained

- the directly experienced, subjective, internal mental states called *qualia*;
- the intentionality or aboutness of our conscious mental states;
- the subjectivity of the mental;
- the privacy of the mental;
- why the person in the Chinese room does not understand Chinese;
- why the group of one billion people realizing the 1's and 0's of a belief in Santa program does not constitute a giant mind that believes in Santa;
- why humans experience consciousness but zombies would not.

After 2,500 years of the rational investigation of the system of nature and the nature of matter and nearly 500 years of modern science, scientists still have no good answer at all to questions such as these:

1. How can any purely material object have qualitative content?
2. How can any purely material object possess subjectivity?
3. How can any purely material object possess private mental states?
4. How can any purely material object intentionally follow the objective laws of logic?
5. How can any purely material object have a subjective point of view?
6. How can any purely material object possess consciousness?

And a question that will arise in chapter 11:

7. How can a purely material object whose operations are completely governed by the laws of physics and chemistry have free will and bear moral responsibility?

If materialism cannot account for the nature of consciousness, perhaps mind-body dualism — the common view held by most human beings and most religions of the world throughout history — deserves a second look. Perhaps the only barrier to taking dualism seriously is a materialist bias that blocks some people from thinking outside the scientific box. If dualism is true, there is more to consciousness than meets the scientific eye.[25]

Questions for Reflection and Discussion 10.3

1. In your own words, explain functionalism's basic claim.
2. Does Searle's Chinese room actually understand Chinese? Does anything within the room understand Chinese? What follows?
3. Critically evaluate Ned Block's thought experiment. Does a giant mind come into existence? Does his argument raise troubles for functionalism?
4. Is functionalism an adequate theory of consciousness? Offer the most intelligent and strongest reasons you can for your position.
5. Are you a materialist or a dualist with respect to the mind? What is the basis for your answer? Offer the most intelligent and strongest reasons you can for your position.

APPENDIX:
FROM SUBSTANCE DUALISM TO THEISM

Anyone who accepts substance dualism faces the following question: What creates an immaterial soul and unites it to a physical body the moment a new human being comes into existence? If substance dualism is true and if our modern understanding of science is correct, the answer cannot be a purely material process or agent. Since the laws of science refer only to material objects, science will be no help here.

Theism offers at least the start of an explanation. On a theistic worldview, God, as the creator of the material universe, is an immaterial mind or spirit who creates each immaterial soul and unites it to a physical body each time a new human being comes into existence. As the designer of the universe, God is not only the author of the laws of physics but of the laws that govern the interactions of mind and matter, body and soul. This is the start of an explanation, but the explanation is philosophical.

The union of mind and body is thus one more area where theism helps us make sense of a phenomenon that would otherwise be unexplained. Many dualists are theists as the result of a best explanation argument that runs something like this:

A Dualistic Argument for God's Existence

1. Substance dualism is true.

2. Some agent or process creates an immaterial soul and unites it to a physical body each time a new human being comes into existence. (This is the data to be explained.)

3. This agent or process cannot possibly be a purely material agent or process.

4. Therefore, an immaterial agent or process creates a soul and unites it to a body when a new human being comes into existence.

5. God is the most plausible candidate for this role.

6. Therefore, theism is the best explanation of the data.

7. It is therefore reasonable to believe that God or a supreme being exists.

Argument for Premise 3

If substance dualism is true, and if our modern understanding of science is correct, the agent or process that unites body and soul cannot be a purely material being or process, for material processes are (1) mindless, (2) they are completely governed by the laws of physics and chemistry, and (3) no law of physics or chemistry relates mind and body.

Theism and substance dualism are related in many complex ways. The previous argument was an inference to the best explanation; the following is a deductive argument from substance dualism to theism. Premise 1 reflects the fact that theism and materialism are the two great worldviews competing for our allegiance today.

1. Either (a) materialism is true and the first cause of all things is mindless matter in motion, or (b) theism is true and a supreme immaterial being is the first cause of all things.

2. Substance dualism is true.

3. If substance dualism is true, a mind cannot be produced by a mindless, purely material agent or process.

4. Therefore, a mind cannot be produced by a mindless, purely material agent or process.

5. Minds exist.

6. If materialism is true and the first cause of all things is pure, mindless matter, then minds do not exist.

7. Therefore, materialism is false.

8. Therefore, theism is true.[26]

The German philosopher Martin Heidegger (1889–1976) observed that each philosophical position is logically linked to other philosophical positions so that the view we adopt on one issue influences the views we hold on other issues. All philosophical topics, he suggested, are logically interrelated. Does mind-body dualism make the most sense within a theistic framework? Does mind-body dualism logically point to theism? If you believe that dualism is true, should you also believe that God exists? In short, is substance dualism evidence for God's existence? You decide.

ELEVEN

Do We Have Free Will?

THE PSYCHOLOGY STUDENT

In his thought-provoking book, *The Strangeness of the Ordinary: Problems and Issues in Contemporary Metaphysics*, the philosopher Robert Coburn (1931–2018) asks us to imagine the following scenario. A group of scientists have discovered a way to send radio signals to an experimental subject's brain and activate individual brain cells.[1] They also know which kinds of actions are caused by which groups of cells. So, they know that if they send signal X into a certain region in the brain, the subject will automatically stand up, if they send signal Y, he will eat a hamburger, and so forth. By targeting specific brain cells, they can manipulate a test subject as if he were a puppet on a string.[2]

Coburn next asks us to imagine that an undergrad in psychology volunteers to be the first test subject. Everything the volunteer will do during the next month will be caused remotely by these scientists from their laboratory.

So, with the consent forms signed and the electrodes in place, the experiment begins. On the first day, the scientists send signals into the student's brain that cause him to watch reruns of the 1950s TV series *Gunsmoke*. On the second day, they cause him to order takeout online, and so forth.[3] At any moment during the month, there is only one thing the test subject can do—that which the scientists in their lab cause him to do at the moment. The subject cannot do anything but exactly what he is caused to do by the radio signals the scientists sent.

Coburn's thought experiment raises many questions relating to free will. Was the student acting of his own free will during the experiment? Would we hold him morally responsible for his actions during the test month? Would we blame *him* if the scientists caused him to rob a bank? Would we give him credit if they made him rescue someone drowning in a lake? These questions are asked within the context of our ordinary, everyday moral thinking.

Surely, we would not hold the student accountable if the scientists caused him to rob a bank or steal a car. Nor would we praise him if the scientists caused him to save a life. And the reason we would not is that at each moment during the experiment, the student couldn't do anything other than exactly what they caused him to do.

The general principle we apply here is this. If a person does something and the person could not possibly have done anything else at the moment, given the causes at work just prior to the moment of action, then the person is not acting of his or her own free will, the person is not morally responsible, and the person deserves neither praise nor blame.

Next, Coburn brings in our ordinary concept of causation. In everyday life, we assume that every event has a cause. If your car's engine dies, you naturally suppose that something caused it to die. If you get sick, you assume that something caused your illness. But we also assume that human actions have causes. If someone does something odd, we say, "I wonder what caused him to do that?" Sometimes we say to ourselves, "What made me to do such a thing?" or "What got into me?"

Coburn now brings up a great question. Does it make any difference, with respect to free will, praise, blame, and moral responsibility, whether (1) our actions are caused by scientists in a remote lab sending signals into our brains, or (2) our actions are caused by our social environment, our genes, the wiring in our brains, and the sum total of all previous causes at work in the universe just before we acted? Aren't we unfree in either case? But doesn't everything have a cause? If so, how is it even *possible* that we have free will and bear moral responsibility for our actions?[4]

DEFINITIONS BEFORE WE PROCEED

Our discussion so far has brought to the surface several key concepts. Each needs to be sharpened before we proceed, or things will get murky, and lines of reasoning will fray.

Moral Responsibility

Suppose that Pat is admiring a painting at an art museum when someone rushes up behind her and without warning violently pushes her into the painting. Would we blame her for the damage? Would we hold her morally responsible? Or would we blame the person who pushed her? Surely, we would not blame the victim here. And the reason we would not is obvious: once she was violently pushed from behind without warning, she could not have done otherwise (than fall into the painting). Two principles are at work in this case: the first is known in philosophy as the "principle of alternate possibilities"; the second we'll call the "praise and blame principle."[5] Both reflect our moral common sense:

> The Principle of Alternate Possibilities: If a person on a particular occasion performs an action and the person at the moment could not have done otherwise, then the person is not morally responsible for performing the action.

This is logically equivalent to the following:

> If a person on a particular occasion is morally responsible for performing an action, then the person could have done otherwise at the time.

Next:

> The Praise and Blame Principle: If a person is not morally responsible for performing an action, then that person deserves neither praise nor blame for the action.

These ideas lead us to think about the meaning of *free will*. This is a difficult concept.

Toward an Account of Free Will

Suppose that a person who suffers from epilepsy has a seizure and uncontrollably falls to the ground. We would not ordinarily say that the person fell of his or her own free will. And the reason we would not is surely that once the seizure occurred, that person could not have done anything else but fall. This suggests the following:

> If a person at a particular moment does something and the person could not possibly have done otherwise at that moment, given all the prior causes and conditions that led up to the moment, then the individual was not acting of his or her own free will.

This is logically equivalent to the following:

> If a person at a particular moment does something of his or her own free will, then that individual *could have* done otherwise, given the very same antecedent causes and conditions leading up to the moment.

An important consequence follows. If a person performs an action at a time *t* and that person could have done otherwise at *t*, *given the very same antecedent causes and conditions*, then at time *t* the person had the power to do what he did, call it "action A," and at the same time and with *the same antecedent causes and conditions*, the person also had the power to do something else instead, call it "action B." These thoughts suggest a tentative account of free will:

> A person P has free will at a moment in time *t* if, and only if, at time *t*, P has it within his or her power to do one thing, action A, and at the same time and given the same antecedent causes and conditions, P also has it within his or her power to do something else instead, action B.

For example, suppose that someone orders a salad in a restaurant. We would ordinarily say that the person "freely" ordered the salad if we believe that (1) at the moment the person placed his order, he had it within his power to order the salad, and (2) at the same moment the person also had the power to order something else instead, or nothing at all. Some philosophers express the same idea when they define *free will* concisely as "the ability to have done otherwise." On the basis of a similar idea, the philosopher Robert Kane describes free will as the possession of "dual power."

Let's incorporate these thoughts into our account by saying that a person has free will if, on at least some occasions, the person possesses two powers at the same time: the power or ability to perform one action, A, and the power or ability to perform an alternative action, B. If you have dual power, then on some occasions, you do one thing, but at the same time, given the same past causes, you could have done something else instead. Put differently, you act of your own free will if you do something while at the same time possessing the (unactualized) power to have done something else instead, given the same antecedent circumstances and past events. This is an analysis of the common account of free will.

We are often urged to take ownership of our actions, and we often say things like, "That was my bad," "It's up to you," and "You own that one." The common account of free will just sketched helps explain the sense in which our free actions are truly our own, the sense in which our actions are up to us in the final analysis. For on this account, we are the ultimate cause of our free actions. Whether we have free will or not, this would seem to be the kind of freedom required by our ordinary notions of free will, praise, blame, and moral responsibility.

Cause and Effect

What do we ordinarily mean when we say that A "caused" B? We normally mean that the occurrence of A was a *sufficient condition* for the occurrence of B. If A is a sufficient condition for some event B, then once A happens, or obtains, B must happen, in the same sense that a normal cube of sugar must melt once it is dropped into a cup of boiling water, or an ordinary wine glass must shatter if it is dropped from twenty feet above onto a concrete surface.[6] If B must occur once A has occurred, then nothing else but B can occur (once A has occurred). Put still another way, if A is sufficient for B, then once A occurs, B is inevitable.

The point is so important it must be reinforced with a visual image. Imagine a row of dominoes lined up so that when the first one falls, it will knock over the second one, and so on down the line. Once the first domino is pushed, it is only a matter of time before the last domino inevitably falls. Similarly, if A causes B and B causes C and so on to Z, then once A happens, Z must eventually occur; Z is inevitable.

Determinism

One final building block idea remains to be explained. *Universal determinism* is the view that every event in the universe, including the occurrence of every human action, has a sufficient cause (hereafter "cause" for short), which in turn has a cause, and so forth back and back as far as cause and effect go. If universal determinism is true (hereafter simply "determinism"), then we live in a "deterministic universe"—a universe in which every event is causally determined by a previous event. As we've seen, cosmologists have already traced an unbroken chain of physical causes and effects back 14 billion years to the big bang. Thus, according to determinism informed by modern science, every event that occurs today—including every human action—can be traced back, through a deterministic chain of causes and effects, 14 billion years to the big bang. If we live in a deterministic universe, then the event consisting of you reading this sentence at exactly this moment was already set to occur 14 billion years ago. Indeed, if determinism is true, every event in your life was already set to occur billions of years before you were born.

Now, with these fundamental concepts sharpened, we are ready for the big arguments. In modern philosophy, there are four major positions on the question of free will, standardly named *hard determinism*, *soft determinism* (also called "compatibilism"), *simple indeterminism*, and *agent causation*. Just about every theory of free will under discussion today is a variation on, or is derived from, one of these four major viewpoints.

Questions for Reflection and Discussion 11.1

1. In Coburn's thought experiment, is the experimental subject acting of his own free will?
2. Is the subject morally responsible for his actions?
3. Does the subject ever deserve praise or blame during the experiment?
4. According to the common account, when are we morally responsible for our actions?
5. On the common account, when do we deserve praise or blame for our actions?
6. According to the common notion, what is a free action?
7. What is dual power alleged to be?

8. Does it matter whether we have free will? What difference does it make?

9. At this point in the discussion, do you believe we have free will? Why or why not?

HARD DETERMINISM

Consider the following argument:

1. Determinism is true, that is, every event, including the occurrence of every human action, has a determining or sufficient cause, which has a cause, and so forth back and back billions of years, as far back as cause and effect go.

2. If A caused B, then once A happened, B had to happen in the sense that nothing but B could happen next. Put another way, once A happened, B became inevitable.

3. It follows that at any moment in time, when a person performs an action, that person could not have done otherwise at the moment.

4. If at a moment in time, a person could not have done otherwise, then at that moment, the person was not acting of his or her own free will. (This is the common account of free will.)

5. If a person could not have done otherwise in a situation, then that person is not morally responsible for what he or she has done. (This is the principle of alternate possibilities.)

6. If a person is not morally responsible for his or her action, then he or she deserves neither praise nor blame. (This is the praise and blame principle.)

7. If no one deserves praise or blame, then no one deserves reward or punishment.

8. Therefore, necessarily, no one has free will, no one is ever morally responsible for his or her actions, and no one ever deserves praise or blame, reward or punishment.

If you accept the premises and conclusion of this deductive argument, your philosophical position is called *hard determinism*, and you are a *hard determinist* (an advocate of hard determinism). Notice that hard determinists accept the common definitions of *free will* and *moral responsibility* — they simply claim that these definitions do not apply to anyone. In other words, they believe that *free will* and *moral responsibility*, even though they can be defined, are illusions.

The eight-step argument for hard determinism just stated is deductively valid (if its premises are true, its conclusion *must* be true). The only question is therefore, is it sound? (In addition to being valid, are its premises true?)

Incompatibilism

If you read books on hard determinism, you'll notice that hard determinists are sometimes called "incompatibilists." *Incompatibilism* in this context is the view that freedom and determinism are logically incompatible. What does this mean? Two statements P and Q are logically incompatible if it is impossible that both are true. Incompatibilism with respect to free will and determinism is therefore the claim that it is impossible that (1) determinism is true, and at the same time (2) we have free will. Here is an argument for incompatibilism:

1. If at a moment in time a person performs an action and at that moment the person could not have done otherwise, then the person was not acting of his or her own free will.

2. If at a moment in time a person performs an action and at that moment the person *could* have done otherwise, then the person *was* acting of his or her own free will.

3. If determinism is true, then at each moment in time, no one could have done otherwise.

4. Thus, if determinism is true, no one has free will, and if we sometimes act of our own free will, then determinism is false.

5. Therefore, the doctrines of freedom and determinism are logically incompatible — they cannot both be true.

Hard determinists endorse incompatibilism, for they believe that we cannot be both free and determined. With incompatibilism defined, a shorter argument for hard determinism can be given.

1. Determinism is true.

2. Incompatibilism is true.

3. Therefore, necessarily, no one has free will.

This argument, like the longer argument for hard determinism, is valid. But are its premises true?

Hard Determinism's Early Boosters

Baron Paul-Henri d'Holbach (1723–89), a famous eighteenth-century German intellectual, gave hard determinism one of its first modern expressions. On the assumption that the principle of universal determinism is true, Holbach argues:

> In whatever manner man is considered, he is connected to universal nature, and submitted to the necessary and immutable laws that she imposes on all the beings she contains. . . . Man's life is a line that nature commands him to outline upon the surface of the earth, without his ever being able to swerve from it, even for an instant. He is born without his own consent; his organization does in nowise depend upon himself; his ideas come to him involuntarily; his habits are in the power of those who cause him to contract them; he is unceasingly modified by causes, whether visible or concealed, over which he has no control, which necessarily regulate his mode of existence, give the hue to his way of thinking, and determine his manner of acting. He is good or bad . . . without his will counting for anything in these various states.[7]

From this he concluded that free will and moral responsibility do not exist.

At about the same time, the French mathematical physicist Pierre-Simon Laplace (1749–1827) illustrated the idea of hard determinism with a colorful example. In *The System of the World*, Laplace used calculus and Newton's mathematics to calculate the future paths of the planets with precision. After this accomplishment, he assumed that his calculations apply to everything in the entire universe, including each human action. Human actions, he concluded, are as predictable as the motions of the planets. Thus, if a superintelligence were to know all the laws of physics and the position and momentum of every particle of matter in the universe, including every particle of matter composing every human body, it could predict every future event, including every future human action. Laplace writes:

> Given for one instant an intelligence which could comprehend all the forces by which nature is animated and the respective situations of the beings who compose it — an intelligence sufficiently vast to submit these data to analysis — it would embrace in the same formula the movements of the greatest bodies of the universe and those of the lightest atom; for it, nothing would be uncertain and the future, as the past, would be present to its eyes.[8]

Claims like these, coming from respected scholars and scientists, convinced many people during the eighteenth and nineteenth centuries that hard determinism is true and thus that free will and moral responsibility are illusions. There was just one problem. Holbach never gave an argument for his key claim, that everything, including each human action, is determined. He simply assumed that determinism is true.

Likewise, Laplace gave no argument for his key claim, that everything in the universe is determined, including every human action. He simply assumed this without any scientific proof at all. The principle of determinism had not been proved by the science of his day, and it has not been proved to this day. Indeed, we now know that it cannot be proved by science alone, for it is a metaphysical, rather than a scientific, claim.

Both men also assumed without argument that human actions are natural events caused in the same way everything else is caused — by physical sequences of cause and effect. This, too, had not been proved by the science of their day and it has not been proved by science to this day, as we saw in chapter 10. Despite their scientific pretensions, then, Holbach and Laplace offered no scientific proof for their deterministic and materialist claims and by extension their thesis that free will and moral responsibility are illusions. There is a word for this kind of thinking: it is called "dogmatism." It can also be called "sophistry."

TWO PHILOSOPHICAL ARGUMENTS
AGAINST HARD DETERMINISM

Van Inwagen's Deliberation Argument

To this day science has not proved that hard determinism is true. However, there are philosophical arguments that claim to show that it is false. Peter van Inwagen offers one in the form of a thought experiment that I will summarize.[9] Imagine that you are seated in a windowless room with no exits other than two solid steel doors in front of you. You are told that one of the two doors is welded shut, but you do not know which of the two this is. Given these details, try to imagine deliberating over which door to *exit by*.

Van Inwagen argues that, although it would make sense to deliberate about which of the two doors to *try* to exit by, that is, which door handle to *try* to turn, it would not make sense to deliberate about which door to *exit by*. Why? I am paraphrasing his answer:

> You cannot rationally deliberate over whether to take one course of action (call it "A") or an alternative, incompatible course of action B unless you believe at some level that at the moment of choice you have it within your power to do A, and at the same time you also have it within your power to do B. If you know that of two incompatible courses of action A and B, one of the two is impossible and the other is possible, then it makes no sense to deliberate ahead of time over which of the two courses of action to actually take. If you do not know which is possible and which is impossible, you might deliberate over which course of action to attempt, but not over which course of action to take.[10]

Now imagine a different setup. This time you know that both steel doors are unlocked. If you turn the knob on the first door, it will open. If you turn the knob on the second door, it will open. You know that each course of action is possible. In this case, it does make sense to imagine deliberating ahead of time over which door to exit by.

Van Inwagen argues that this thought experiment uncovers an important logical truth about human action, namely, that you cannot rationally deliberate about whether to do A or to do B unless you believe at some level that both courses of action are open to you, that is, are possible at the moment. In other words, unless you believe that you can do A *and* you can do B. Recalling the commonsense "dual power" account of free will, it follows that you cannot rationally deliberate unless you at least *believe* that you have free will.

Next, van Inwagen observes, human behavior can manifest an unstated and even an unacknowledged belief. If Joe acts frightened and runs away every time a dog approaches, his behavior expresses a belief that dogs are dangerous, even if he has never stated or admitted it. Likewise, on the basis of the principle uncovered in the thought experiment, when a person sincerely deliberates over whether to do A or B, that person's behavior manifests a belief in free will, even if the person says that he does not believe in free will and even if that person has never thought about the issue.

But each of us deliberates. Two things follow. First, at some level, everyone *believes* in free will. Second, every time the hard determinist deliberates, her own behavior expresses a belief in free will that contradicts her professed belief in hard determinism. Thus, if you endorse hard determinism, you contradict yourself every time you make a deliberate choice.[11] Hard determinism is thus a philosophical doctrine that cannot consistently be *lived*.

To a hard determinist, then, we might argue, "Since deliberation is a necessary part of life and since deliberation presupposes a belief in free will, you cannot live and be logically consistent and at the same time assert hard determinism. But you can assert free will and live without any inconsistency. Reason therefore calls on you to give up hard determinism, since that is the only one of the two options that can be dropped without self-contradiction."

If this reasoning is cogent, the hard determinist's life is absurd in the sense that it contains a logical conflict between belief and action, pretension and reality. To accept hard determinism and deny free will, van Inwagen concludes, is to condemn yourself to a life of constant self-contradiction, for (again) the hard determinist contradicts himself every time he deliberates.[12]

Of course, a hard determinist can bite the bullet and reply, "This doesn't show that hard determinism is false; all it shows is that one cannot actively live and at the same time consistently profess hard determinism. I'd rather be a walking self-contradiction than believe in free will." The hard determinist can indeed speak those words. However, it is hard to believe that a philosophical theory that cannot be consistently lived is true.[13]

The Moral Responsibility Argument

Van Inwagen believes that the following argument is an even stronger reason to reject hard determinism and admit the existence of free will: "Without free will, we would never be morally responsible for anything, and we are sometimes morally responsible."[14]

More formally and with some unstated premises filled in:

1. Free will is a necessary condition of moral responsibility.

2. It is rationally undeniable that we are at least sometimes morally responsible for our actions.

3. Therefore, human beings at least sometimes exercise free will.

4. If we have free will, then hard determinism is false.

5. Therefore, hard determinism is certainly false.

We've already seen the reasons for premise 1. In support of premise 2, van Inwagen writes:

> If we examine our convictions honestly and seriously and carefully, we shall discover that we cannot believe that this assent [to the thesis that moral responsibility exists] is merely something forced on us by our nature and the nature of human social life. We shall discover that we cannot but view our belief in moral responsibility as a justified belief, a belief that is simply not open to reasonable doubt. I myself would go further: in my view, the proposition that often we are morally responsible for what we have done is something that we all know to be true.[15]

Some philosophers deny the existence of moral responsibility. In other words, they deny premise 2 (above). No one, they say, is ever responsible for anything he or she does. Of course, to remain consistent, these philosophers must cease holding people morally responsible for anything they do. In other words, they must stop criticizing others (and *themselves*) on moral grounds. Van Inwagen believes that, although the denial of moral responsibility may be theoretically possible, it is not practically possible:

I have listened to philosophers who deny the existence of moral responsibility. I cannot take them seriously. I know a philosopher who has written a paper in which he denies the reality of moral responsibility. And yet this same philosopher, when certain of his books were stolen, said, "That was a shoddy thing to do!" But no one can consistently say that a certain act was a shoddy thing to do and say that its agent was not morally responsible when he performed it: those who are not morally responsible for what they do may perhaps deserve our pity, they certainly do not deserve our censure.[16]

Is the denial of moral responsibility a real option? Can we engage in Socratic critical thinking and improve our own lives on the basis of rational standards while at the same time sincerely denying the existence of moral responsibility? Can we live a Socratic life without believing that we have free will and without attributing moral responsibility to ourselves and to others? Socrates would answer no. His account of critical thinking presupposes both free will and moral responsibility. For critical thinking means freely evaluating our beliefs, values, and actions on the basis of independent, rational standards and then freely choosing to change when we believe we are in error. People can't practice critical thinking seriously unless they believe that they have the power within to change and that they must accept responsibility for their actions.

For that matter, can a child be properly raised to become a responsible adult without at some point being taught to accept responsibility for his or her actions? But how can anyone be taught to accept responsibility without at least sometimes being held responsible? More than 2,000 years ago, Aristotle observed that we learn to accept responsibility by being held responsible. (We'll examine Aristotle's theory in chapter 12.) His argument has stood the test of time. Is the denial of moral responsibility a practical option that anyone can live with? You decide.[17]

Questions for Reflection and Discussion 11.2

1. In your own words, what does the hard determinist claim?
2. Explain one of the arguments presented for hard determinism.
3. Explain one of the arguments presented against hard determinism.
4. Can hard determinism be sincerely lived?

5. What would a society of hard determinists be like?
6. If you don't accept hard determinism, how would accepting it change your view of yourself and your fellow human beings?
7. Does it matter whether we have free will? What difference does it make?
8. What would society be like if no one believed in moral responsibility?

SOFT DETERMINISM

We turn now to the second of the four major positions on free will. Soft determinism (also called "compatibilism") was conceived by philosophers who found themselves stuck between a rock and a hard place. They accepted determinism even though the doctrine has never been proved. Thus, they believed that every event, including each human action, is fully determined by the laws of nature and the sum total of all past causes and effects tracing back billions of years to the big bang. So, to make it vivid, they would say that when you started reading this paragraph a moment ago, the ultimate cause was an event that occurred billions of years before you were born. Once that event occurred, it became inevitable that billions of years later you would read this paragraph at exactly this time.

However, although they accepted determinism, they did not want to give up their commonsense belief in free will and moral responsibility. What do you do if you believe in both determinism *and* free will? The answer is, you try to reconcile freedom and determinism. In other words, you try to explain, without any inconsistency, how we might be free and yet at the same time fully determined. And how do you do that? One way is to develop a new definition of *free will*—one that is logically consistent with determinism. We'll approach their proposal in steps, beginning with their revised definition of free will.

Their suggestion was this: let's simply redefine *free will* as "doing what you want to do." More formally, "A person is acting of his own free will at a moment in time if he is doing what he wants to do." Now, if we think of free will this way, instead of in the traditional way as the ability to have done otherwise, in other words, as the possession of dual power, then it *is* possible we are both free and determined at the same time. Here's why. It is logically possible that a person P is doing what he *wants* to do (and thus is acting freely, according to the soft determinist's redefinition of *free*) while at the same time everything that happens in the universe, including the oc-currence of each of his wants (and hence each of his actions) was fully de-termined by events billions of years before (and thus he could *not* have done otherwise at the moment).

The claim that a person is acting of his own free will as long as he is doing what he wants to do is called a "soft determinist" account of free will; it is also called a "compatibilist" theory of free will.

Let's put this important point another way before we move on. If free will is nothing more than doing what we want to do, then it is possible we are free and determined at the same time, for it is possible someone is doing what he wants to do while at the same time his wants (along with everything else) were fully determined to occur before he was born so that he could not have *wanted* to do anything else at the moment and could not have done anything else at the time. With *free will* redefined so that it is compatible with determinism, we get the following argument.

An Argument for Soft Determinism

Let "soft determinism" (or "compatibilism") be defined as the thesis that (1) universal determinism is true; (2) you are acting of your own free will at a moment if you are doing what you want to do; (3) freedom and deter-minism are compatible; and (4) people sometimes act of their own free will and at least sometimes are morally responsible for what they do. Here is one way to argue for the view.

1. Let's define *free will* in a new way. A person is acting of his own free will at a moment if and only if he is doing what he wants to do.

2. Observation reveals that people sometimes do what they want to do.

3. So, people sometimes act of their own free will.

4. Let's agree with common sense that if someone performs an action of his own free will, he is morally responsible for his action.

5. So, people are sometimes morally responsible for what they do.

6. The principle of determinism is true.

7. Therefore, at any moment, no one could have done otherwise.

8. A person can be doing what he wants to do, even though all his wants and thus all his actions were fully determined to occur billions of years before he was born, and he cannot do otherwise.

9. Thus, freedom and determinism are logically compatible.

10. We are therefore free and yet fully determined at the same time.

11. Therefore, soft determinism is certainly true.

On this view, each of your wants and each of your actions were already set to occur billions of years before you were born. Every aspect of your life was inevitable long before you came into the world, like the events in a rigidly directed play; yet you have free will.

THE PROBLEM WITH SOFT DETERMINISM

The current conversation focuses on the soft determinist redefinition of *free will*. Critics ask, "Is 'doing what you want to do' what we normally mean by *free will*? Does it apply in the right cases? Is it genuine freedom?" As Socrates would say, let's examine. The soft determinist definition certainly matches *some* uses of the word *free*. For instance, if Joe has been forcefully placed in the back of a police car but does not want to be there, he clearly is not there through his own free will. For another example, no slave in his right mind wants to be someone's tool. So, a slave is not doing what he wants to do and clearly is not free. A person knocked over by a gust of wind probably did not want to fall over and so did not fall willingly. The compatibilist definition of *free will* seems appropriate in these test cases.

Furthermore, the soft determinist is logically correct in claiming that if we define *free will* in the compatibilist way, then free will *is* indeed compatible with determinism, and it is logically possible that we are free and yet determined at the same time. So far so good. But there are problems.

How can "doing what you want to do" be real freedom *if your wants (and therefore your actions) were themselves fully determined to occur billions of years before you were born?* How can acting inevitably on wants that were already determined before you were born be real free will? Recall that if determinism is true (as the soft determinist believes), then at the time of the big bang, each of your wants was already scheduled to occur, so that at each moment in your life, you could not have had any other want and could not have done anything else.

If free will is simply doing what you want to do and if each of your wants was the inevitable product of events that occurred billions of years ago, and if you could never have done otherwise, then how can your actions really be up to *you*? How can your actions really be *yours*? Keep in mind that on the soft determinist view, *free* does not mean "undetermined." Nor does it imply "could have done otherwise." The soft determinist rejects the claim that if you have free will, then at some times in your life, you could have done otherwise.

On the basis of thoughts like these, critics of soft determinism argue that soft determinist freedom is not genuine freedom; it is not what we ordinarily mean by *free will*.[18] These are some of the thoughts behind the formidable *consequence argument* first given by van Inwagen. Here is my summary:

1. If determinism is true, then our actions are the inevitable consequence of the laws of nature and events that occurred billions of years before we were born.

2. But it is not up to us what went on before we were born, nor is it up to us what the laws of nature are.

3. If P and Q are not up to us, then the necessary consequences of P and Q are not up to us.

4. Therefore, the necessary consequences of the laws of nature and events in the remote past are not up to us.

5. Therefore, our own actions are not up to us.

6. If our actions are not up to us, then we do not have real free will.

7. Therefore, if determinism is true, then we do not have real free will.

8. Therefore, freedom and determinism are not compatible.

9. If soft determinism is true, then freedom and determinism are compatible.

10. Therefore, soft determinism is certainly false.[19]

The soft determinist claims to offer us an account of *free will* compatible with determinism. But the arguments we've examined suggest that the soft determinist's notion of freedom is bogus. Can the soft determinist account be defended? Or is compatibilism in conflict with reason and common sense? You be the judge.

Questions for Reflection and Discussion 11.3

1. Compare and contrast soft determinism and hard determinism.
2. Is freedom doing what you want to do? How can "doing what you want to do" be real freedom if your wants were already determined at the time of the big bang?
3. Explain one of the arguments presented here for soft determinism.
4. Explain one of the arguments presented here against soft determinism.
5. Is soft determinism true? Offer the most intelligent and strongest reasons you can for your position.

SIMPLE INDETERMINISM

The third major position on free will requires a shift in perspective. We've been examining free will against the backdrop of determinism. Time to switch perspectives and bring indeterminism into the picture. The prefix *in* means "not" or "it is false that." Thus, *in*determinism is the claim that determinism is false. Since determinism asserts that all events are caused, indeterminism is the claim that not all events are caused. If indeterminism is true, it is still possible that *some* events have causes. However, if indeterminism is true, at least some events do not have causes.

Philosophers since ancient times have wondered: Does indeterminism hold the solution to the problem of free will? Could a free action simply be an uncaused and therefore undetermined event? This idea was first proposed by Epicurus (341–270 BC), the Greek philosopher who founded an influential school of ethics (Epicurean hedonism), which we'll examine in chapter 12 when we think critically about morality.

Epicurus was a materialist and an atomist. As a materialist, he believed that matter is all that exists. Recall (from chapter 4) that atomism was a school of Greek philosophy which claimed that every macroscopic chunk of matter breaks down into tiny bits of matter too small to be seen, which the founder of atomism had named "atoms" (Greek for "uncuttables"). Most of the atomists were determinists and materialists. The cosmos, they argued, formed when primeval atoms sailing through empty space along predetermined paths converged to form the universe. Epicurus accepted the core atomist beliefs, but he also believed in free will. This conflict led him to question his belief in determinism. We'll approach the rest of his idea in stages.

The initial puzzle was this. How can we have free will if we are composed of nothing but atoms moving through space in predetermined paths? This thought led to his famous hypothesis, known as "the swerve." Epicurus proposed that the motion of each atom is normally predetermined and inevitable; however, occasionally an atom inside a human being randomly swerves from its predetermined path, spontaneously, for no reason at all and due to no cause at all, and an action occurs. Perhaps, Epicurus thought, *that* is free will.

Epicurus's theory was the first indeterminist account of free will. So, on this view, a person acts freely when the person's body simply moves in an uncaused way, due to an undetermined, random atomic swerve within his brain or body. This account of free will is usually called "simple indeterminism."[20]

An interesting theory of free will, but is it true? Critics have identified severe problems. An uncaused, random atomic swerve occurring inside your brain or body would be something that happened to you; it would not be something you caused. Put another way, it would not be something you *did*. Thus, it would not be something you had control over. But if you had no control over it, then it would not be something you are responsible for. It seems to follow that if an action is the product of a random atomic swerve, it is no freer than an action that was fully determined. For this reason, virtually all philosophers today reject simple indeterminism.

This conclusion can be reinforced if we return to the psychology experiment with which we began this chapter. Suppose that after the psychology student commits some rotten deed, we trace the cause of his behavior back not to the scientists in the remote lab but to an uncaused, random atomic swerve that occurred in his brain. It is hard to see how his action in this case was under his control, isn't it? For an atomic swerve occurring in his brain would be something that happened to him—it would not be something he did. It is therefore hard to see how he ever could have done otherwise. It is also hard to see how his action was "up to him." In short, it is hard to see how *that* would be an act of free will—an action for which he was morally responsible. And we're back to where we started.

WILLIAM JAMES'S DILEMMA ARGUMENT

Before we move to the fourth major position on free will, a famous argument once given by the philosopher and psychologist William James (1842–1910) will help us put all we've considered so far in this chapter into perspective. Reasoning similar to what we've been conducting led James to formulate an influential but depressing argument known as the "dilemma of determinism."

1. If determinism is true, free will and moral responsibility do not exist.

2. If indeterminism is true, free will and moral responsibility do not exist.

3. Either determinism or indeterminism is true.

4. Therefore, free will and moral responsibility most assuredly do not exist.

At this point in our discussion, the outlook for free will looks dim. We've examined powerful arguments for the truth of premise 1 of James's dilemma argument. Premise 3 is necessarily true. However, is premise 2 true? Is free will really incompatible with *in*determinism? The swerve theory, which is indeterministic, doesn't account for free will. Free will can't be just a random atomic swerve. But is the Epicurean swerve the only possible indeterminist theory of freedom? Or is there another indeterminist way to understand free will? Is there an indeterminist account that makes sense of free will while avoiding uncaused randomness? Is it possible that a free action is neither determined nor random? In short, is there a logical space within indeterminism that allows for free will? Perhaps.

AGENT CAUSATION — A MODERN INDETERMINIST THEORY OF FREE WILL

We've now reached the fourth major viewpoint on free will, known as "agent causation theory."[21] The core idea can be summarized with seven theses:

1. Determinism is false and indeterminism is true.
2. Thus, hard determinism is false.
3. Incompatibilism is true (freedom and determinism are incompatible), thus, soft determinism is false.
4. A free action is not an uncaused random event or atomic swerve, thus, simple indeterminism is false.
5. Freedom and indeterminism are logically compatible.
6. People sometimes act of their own free will and are sometimes morally responsible for their actions.
7. The most reasonable account of free will is this: a free action is caused not by prior events and causes but by the person (the "agent") performing the action.

Thus, in acting freely, a person causes his or her action without being caused to cause the action by preexisting conditions and causes. Because it rejects determinism, agent causation theory is an indeterminist account of freedom.

Can any sense be made of this combination of seven claims? How can an action be neither determined nor random? How can a person cause an action to occur without being caused by prior events to cause it? For answers, we turn to the explanation proposed by Roderick Chisholm, who was a professor of philosophy at Brown University and one of the twentieth century's leading epistemologists. Chisholm gave the theory of agent causation its first systematic and detailed exposition and deep defense in a now-famous lecture delivered at the University of Kansas in 1964. He explained and defended his theory again in *Person and Object: A Metaphysical Study.*[22]

First, Chisholm accepts the common definitions of *free will* and *moral responsibility* presented at the start of this chapter. He also holds that free will and determinism are incompatible and that freedom and randomness are incompatible. Chisholm's former student Richard Taylor, who became a leading philosopher in his own right, summarizes the rest of Chisholm's account of agent causation:

> The only conception of action that accords with our data [our strong sense that sometimes what we do is up to us] is one according to which people—and perhaps some other things too—are sometimes, but of course not always, *self-determining beings*; that is, beings that are sometimes the causes of their own behavior. In the case of an action that is free, it must not only be such that it is caused by the agent who performs it, but also such that no antecedent conditions were sufficient for his performing just that action. In the case of an action that is both free and rational, it must be that the agent who performed it did so for some reason, but this reason cannot have been the cause of it. Now this conception fits what people take themselves to be, namely, beings who act, or who are agents, rather than beings that are merely acted upon, and whose behavior is simply the causal consequence of conditions that they have not wrought. When I believe that I have done something, I believe it is I who caused it to be done, I who made something happen, and not something within me, such as one of my own subjective states, which is not identical with myself. If I believe that something not identical with myself was the cause of my behavior, some event wholly external to myself, for example, or even one internal to myself, for instance, a nerve impulse, volition, or whatnot, then I cannot regard that behavior as an act of mine, unless I further believe that I was the cause of that external or internal event.[23] (my emphasis)

The theory of agent causation is not only an account of free will, it is also the beginning of an analysis of how free will works. However, the theory has puzzling implications. Taylor writes:

> Now this conception of activity, and of an agent who is the cause of it, involves two rather strange metaphysical notions that are not applied elsewhere in nature. The first is that of a self or person—for example, a man—who is not merely a collection of things or events but a self-moving being. For on this view, it is a person, and not merely some part of him or something within him, that is the cause of his

own activity. . . . Second, this conception of activity involves an extraordinary conception of causality according to which an agent, which is a substance and not an event, can nevertheless be the cause of an event. Indeed, if he is a free agent then he can, on this conception, cause an event to occur—namely, some act of his own—without anything else causing him to do so.[24]

To elaborate, in a case of event causation, one event E is caused by one or more previous events that were together sufficient for E to occur, given the laws of nature. When a rock smashes a window, for example, the standard analysis is that the *event* of the rock hitting the window was a sufficient condition for the *event* of the window breaking, as determined by the laws of physics.

But persons are not events. Events are not conscious, persons are. If it exists, agent causation—the power exercised by persons (agents) when they act freely—is a radically different kind of causation than event causation. In an act of free will, a person rather than an event causes something to happen. Moreover, if the person's action really is free, the sum total of all previous events did not cause the person to act in that particular way at that moment.

So, if Chisholm's theory is true, the universe contains at least two radically different kinds of causation: event causation and agent causation. An event cause is never more than a physical link in a rigid chain of causes going back to the big bang. An agent cause is a person making a free choice that is not a mere link in a deterministic causal chain going back billions of years.

One qualification is in order. Chisholm's theory is not meant to supplant the common notion of free will; it is an *analysis* of the common notion, offered to show how free will is theoretically possible and to suggest in general terms how it might work. Like most arguments for large-scale philosophical theories, the supporting argument is inductive and can be cast in the form of an inference to the best explanation.[25]

A Best Explanation Argument for Agent Causation Theory

1. The existence of free will and moral responsibility are as certain as anything can be. (Free will and moral responsibility thus constitute the data to be explained.)

2. Hard determinism fails to make sense of free will and moral responsibility.

3. Soft determinism fails to make sense of free will and moral responsibility.

4. Simple indeterminism does not explain free will, nor does it allow for moral responsibility.

5. Agent causation theory makes rational sense of free will and moral responsibility.

6. No other explanation that is equally or more plausible is available.

7. Therefore, agent causation theory is the best available explanation of the data.

8. Therefore, it is reasonable to accept the theory of agent causation.

We've already examined the arguments for the premises of this argument. Does agent causation theory make the best overall sense of free will? You be the judge. [26]

Is *Any* Argument against Free Will Inherently Self-Contradictory?

When the philosopher Richard Purtill (1931–2016) was a young man serving in the U.S. Army during the early 1950s, he was stationed in London. One day Purtill walked out of a bookstore and stopped to listen to a man preaching from a soapbox on the street corner. The man, a member of the Catholic Evidence Guild, was giving logical arguments in favor of Roman Catholicism. Suddenly, someone from the crowd began arguing with the speaker. The man from the crowd was a believer in determinism, and he was criticizing the Catholic belief in free will. After the debate, Purtill asked the Catholic speaker, "Why didn't you refute what he was saying by telling him that if determinism were true, he was determined by causes beyond his control to believe in determinism and you were determined by causes beyond your control not to believe in it, so there would be no use arguing? Since the man did seem to think there was some use in arguing, this in itself might be an argument against determinism."[27]

Someone once observed that the more a determinist argues for his view, the more it looks as if he thinks his opponent is free to change his mind.

In *Free Choice: A Self-Referential Argument*, Joseph Boyle Jr., Germain Grisez, and Olaf Tollefsen argue that the person who tries to convince us by rational argument that no one has free will actually contradicts himself, although he may not realize it. Here is my summary of their reasoning:

> Suppose person A argues that no one can make a free choice. Free will, he argues, does not exist. A is claiming that his position is more reasonable than the position of those who believe in free will. He is also claiming implicitly that reasonable people ought to agree (that no one can make a free choice.) Thus, although he may not realize it, A's act of arguing that free will doesn't exist presupposes the existence of free will. For his act of arguing for his claim presupposes a normative rule of reason calling on people interested in the issue to choose the most reasonable of two coherent possibilities. This, in turn, presupposes that persons have the power to choose the most reasonable option and at the same time the power to reject it. Thus, by arguing rationally against free will, person A implicitly assumes that people have the power to choose freely.[28]

Is it self-contradictory to reason with others and try to convince them that free will is an illusion? If the denial of free will cannot be argued for without self-contradiction, how can the denial of free will be a reasonable position? What do you think?

COMMON MISUNDERSTANDINGS OF
AGENT CAUSATION THEORY

The Miracle Objection

This is an argument against agent causation theory. According to the theory, an act of free will occurs when a person intentionally causes an action *without being caused to do so by the sum total of all prior events or conditions.* The ultimate fact is simply that the person causes his action. Period. But exactly how does a person cause something without being caused to do so? The agent's causing of an action, as Chisholm's theory describes it, has no sufficient cause at all. But if it has no sufficient cause, then it has no explanation. For we normally explain things by reference to their causes. Agent causation theory thus implies that a human action emerges out of a void, out of nowhere, with no explanation at all. An act of free will, if the theory is true, is therefore an unexplainable miracle, an impenetrable mystery. But it is irrational to believe in miracles, mysteries, and unexplainable things. Therefore, it is not reasonable to accept agent causation theory as an explanation of free will. So goes the "miracle" objection.

In reply, defenders of the theory deny the charge. They point out that we can accept agent causation theory and also rationally explain acts of free will. In fact, we naturally explain the free choices of others and ourselves in the course of everyday life. How? We explain human action in terms of the agent's beliefs, reasons, desires, and goals. We do so when we say things such as, "Josh went to the store because he wanted to buy some eggs, and knew the store had eggs." "She took the job because she believed that it was the best option available at the time and wanted to work."

Of course, if beliefs, desires, reasons, and so forth are sufficient causes, then our actions are determined, and we do not have free will. But they are not sufficient causes; they are forward-looking states of mind. Thus, we can accept the theory of agent causation and also explain free actions in a commonsense way, but the explanations (in terms of beliefs, desires, reasons, and so forth) will not refer to sufficient causes.

So, reflection on our ordinary explanations of human action shows that we often make perfectly good sense of our own free actions and the free choices of others, by reference to beliefs, reasons, desires, and goals, without supposing that our actions are predetermined or have sufficient causes. And these ordinary explanations are consistent with agent causation theory.

The defender of Chisholm's theory can also add that agent causation theory makes sense of another facet of our experience: it explains why we normally do not answer "why" questions about our free choices (such as "Why did you say that?") by referring to brain events and other physiological antecedents. Free actions are standardly explained in terms of the person's beliefs, desires, and reasons for acting, not in terms of the person's physical brain states.

The Randomness Objection

According to agent causation theory, an agent's causing of an action has no cause. How, then, does the theory differ from Epicurus's theory of the swerve? It is hard to see any difference. But Epicurus's random swerve theory is obviously inadequate—freedom is not simply uncaused randomness. Therefore, agent causation theory is no advance on the Epicurean swerve.

In reply, defenders of agent causation theory argue that if our free actions are explained in terms of our beliefs, reasons, desires, and so on, then they are intentional and rational. But if they are intentional and rational, then they are not random swerves at all.

The Hopeful Scientist Objection

The power of agent causation, if it exists, is a kind of causation that cannot be explained by physical science, for physical science restricts itself to event causes, each of which is a link in the universal chain of event causation stretching back to the big bang. Thus, if we adopt agent causation theory, we must give up hope that free will is ever going to be fully explained by science. However, so the argument continues, if a theory implies that some phenomenon cannot be explained by science, then that theory should be rejected, for nothing is beyond the reach of science—science will eventually explain everything. Therefore, agent causation theory, being nonscientific, should be rejected.

But why should we suppose that nothing is beyond the reach of science? No *scientific* proof has ever been given for the claim. Furthermore, in this book, we've examined many things that cannot, even in principle, be explained by science alone.

And why should we expect that science alone will one day fully explain free will? Science explains phenomena solely in terms of rigid chains of event causes going back in time, with each event governed by the laws of physics, chemistry, and so forth. If science ever succeeds in explaining the operation of the human will as the predetermined result of causes stretching back billions of years, it will not have explained free will—it will have explained free will away. For it will have explained each human action as a fully determined cog in the universal machine, and a cog in a machine does not turn of its own *free* will.

If agent causation is the correct account of free will, then free will, if it exists, is a part of us that will remain, in the final analysis, beyond the reach of scientific explanation. In that sense, an act of free will is a miracle, and a mystery as well.

Agent causation theory has another suggestive implication. Free will, if it exists, must stem from a part of us that was not preprogrammed by the laws of physics before we were born. A part of us that is not merely a cog or a gear in the universal machine. We'll consider this thought in the next section.

GOD, DUALISM, AND FREE WILL

Recall that in his Second Way (to argue for the existence of God), Thomas Aquinas called God, or the supreme being, the "First Cause." God, he argued, is the first cause in the sense that God caused the universe without being caused to do so by prior causes. (If God is truly the first cause, then no cause is prior to God.) In the First Way, Aquinas called God the "Unmoved Mover" since God imparts motion to the universe without being moved by prior causes. Reasoning by analogy, if agent causation theory is the correct account of free will, then a person is also a first cause every time he or she acts freely, albeit on a scale much smaller than God's. As the cause of our own free actions, we are miniature "first causes," or "unmoved movers." Chisholm writes: "If we are responsible, and if what I have been trying to say is true, then we have a prerogative which some would attribute only to God: each of us, when we act, is a prime mover unmoved. In doing what we do, we cause certain events to happen, and nothing more — or no one — causes us to cause those events to happen."[29]

Chisholm's thought brings us back to the philosophy of mind, which we examined in chapter 10. Free will, on his theory, is the power to intentionally cause something without being caused to do so by antecedent causes and external circumstances that trace back in a deterministic chain to the big bang. Call this "the power to *originate*." If agent causation theory is correct, each of us has the power to originate action.[30] The question arises: Where could this power reside? What part of us could possibly have such a power? Could this power to originate be lodged in the physical brain? Could free will simply be a physical function of the brain, a lobe of the brain, or a neuron in the brain?

The answer clearly seems to be no, for the brain is a purely material object composed of nothing but mindless particles of matter and quanta of energy, and mindless particles of matter and units of energy do not originate anything by themselves. A particle of matter only changes its position or momentum if it is acted on by an external force.

It follows that no purely material entity, such as the brain or a part of the brain, could hold the power to freely originate an action. Put another way, no purely material object, such as the brain—or a cell in the brain or a lobe of the brain—could be a first cause or "unmoved mover" in the sense required for free will. Thus, if agent causation theory is the correct account of free will, neither the brain nor any physical part of it, nor the body, is the source of our power to originate action. The power of free will must therefore be lodged somewhere else.[31]

Different philosophers conclude different things from these thoughts. Some are so certain that we are purely material beings and that the brain is simply a predetermined machine that they give up their belief in free will. These materialists conclude that we are complex robots programmed ultimately by the laws of physics and chemistry and by events that occurred long before we were born. Free will and moral responsibility, they assert, are illusions.

However, others are so certain that we have free will and bear moral responsibility for our choices that they give up their belief in materialism and conclude that the power of free will must reside in an immaterial part of us.

If the power of free will stems from an immaterial part of us, what part can this be? Mind-body dualism, which we examined in chapter 10, offers an answer. An immaterial soul with a rational will would seem to be just the kind of immaterial entity that could, in theory, possess the power to originate a free action. For the soul's operation, unlike the operation of a material, mechanical object such as the brain, would not be governed by the laws of physics and prior events, for according to science, the laws of physics govern only matter, packets of physical energy, and such. Nor would the operation of a rational immaterial soul be random, for it would be acting for reasons, at least when at its best. These thoughts suggest an argument from free will to dualism.

From Free Will to Dualism

1. Agent causation theory makes the best sense of free will.

2. So, free will is best understood as the power to cause an action without being caused to do so by antecedent events and external circumstances that trace back in a deterministic chain of causes to the big bang.

3. Each human being possesses free will.

4. The power of free will cannot be lodged in any material object, for free will is the power to originate an action, and no material object has such a power.

5. The power of free will must therefore reside in an immaterial part of us.

6. The body, including the brain, is a purely physical or material object.

7. The power of free will thus does not reside in the body or the brain.

8. Dualism offers a reasonable solution: each of us is an immaterial soul interacting with a physical body, and free will originates in the immaterial soul.

9. Materialism offers no solution.

10. The best explanation is therefore that the power of free will resides in the soul.

11. It is reasonable to accept the existence of entities implied by our best explanations.

12. Therefore, it is reasonable to believe that each of us has an immaterial soul and that dualism is true.

Recall Heidegger's observation (in chapter 10) that your position on one philosophical issue influences your position on other issues in such a way that all philosophical topics are logically interrelated. If we have free will, does it logically follow that mind-body dualism is true? Does agent causation theory make the most sense within a dualist explanatory framework? Is free will a supernatural power possessed not by the brain but by the mind, or soul? Is there a better explanation?

In chapter 10, we examined an argument for God's existence based on mind-body dualism. The argument there (reduced to a skeletal form) was that (1) mind-body dualism is true; (2) if mind-body dualism is true, then God exists; therefore (3) God exists. If free will makes the most sense within a dualist framework and if dualism makes the most sense within a theistic framework, then the question arises: Does free will ultimately make the most sense within a *theistic* philosophical framework? In other words, is free will further evidence for the existence of God or a supreme being? If we have free will, does it logically follow that God exists? You decide.

CONCLUDING REFLECTIONS

Our system of law and our court system are based on the assumption that human beings at least sometimes exercise free will and make choices for which they are morally responsible. Indeed, all our basic social institutions are predicated on the assumptions of free will and moral responsibility. It is hard to imagine a functioning society that does not affirm free will and moral responsibility in its laws and institutions.

It is also hard to imagine raising children without treating them as if they have free will and as if they are at least sometimes responsible for their choices. Aristotle argued wisely that the only way we learn to be responsible is by being held responsible for our actions.

Furthermore, as we've seen, Socratic critical thinking presupposes the existence of free will and moral responsibility. For critical thinking requires that we freely evaluate our beliefs and values on the basis of rational, realistic criteria and then freely accept responsibility and make changes when improvement is called for. Socrates's efforts were in vain if no one has the power to freely examine his or her life and change.

If agent causation theory is true, free will and moral responsibility reflect our power to originate, our power to introduce a new series of causes into the world, causes that were not already programmed into the world billions of years before. The theory of agent causation explains the deep sense in which rocks and other purely material things are *passive* members of the universe, while persons are *active* and creative participants. If we have free will, we contribute something new to the universe each time we make a choice.

Does agent causation theory lay the groundwork for a plausible account of free will? Does it help us see how our actions are at least sometimes truly our own? Does it explain how it can be that our actions are really up to us? Does it allow us to see ourselves as beings who are the authors of our lives and not just puppets on strings pulled by the irresistible forces of the cosmos? Which of the major accounts of free will surveyed in this chapter makes the most sense of your personal and intimate feeling — experienced every time you act — that you are free and morally responsible for your choices? We've examined many arguments. You be the judge.

Questions for Reflection and Discussion 11.4

1. In your own words, explain Epicurus's theory of the swerve. What is the philosophical problem with his theory?
2. In your own words, what does the agent causation theorist claim?
3. Compare and contrast two of the four theories of free will.
4. Explain an argument for agent causation theory.
5. Explain an argument against agent causation theory.
6. Is it unscientific to believe in free will?
7. In your own words, explain the claim made by Chisholm that there is something God-like, or divine, about having free will.
8. Is agent causation theory logically linked to mind-body dualism?
9. Is agent causation theory logically linked to theism?
10. Which of the four views we examined makes the most sense of our experiences? Offer the most intelligent and strongest reasons you can for your position.

Philosophical Ethics

Can We Reason about Morality?

COME NOW, AND LET US REASON TOGETHER

Dr. Martin Luther King Jr. observed that if a man-made law conflicts with morality, it is unjust and should be repealed because morality, not man-made law, is our highest standard of conduct. Similarly, if a business owner could increase his profits by putting false labels on his products, he should not do so, even if he could get away with it, because it would be immoral. Morality takes precedence over deceptive business practices — no matter how profitable they might be. Morality also takes precedence over unexamined self-interest. A criminal may want to snatch a purse from an old lady walking with a cane and may need the money, but he should not do so because it would be morally wrong.[1] Surely these are eminently reasonable observations.

These thoughts remind us that morality is the ultimate criterion of good and bad, right and wrong, that we ought to live by, all things considered. Morality is ultimate in the sense that the obligations it imposes on us take precedence over all nonmoral considerations, including laws passed by legislatures, the profit and loss calculations of businesses, social customs, instincts, and unexamined impulses of ego, desire, prejudice, self-interest, and cognitive bias.

The principles or "laws" of morality have other important properties. First, they are prescriptive rather than descriptive. That is, they prescribe how we ought to act; they do not describe how we do in fact act. Put another way, moral principles are not empirical generalizations about the way people actually behave, and they are not statements about the way people have behaved in the past or will behave in the future. Rather, they are norms or standards that we ought to follow, whether we want to follow them or do, in fact, follow them. If someday it should come about that most people hate each other, that descriptive fact would not make it moral to hate. Hatred would still be morally wrong. If someday it should happen that every government in the world practices genocide, that descriptive fact would not make genocide morally right—genocide would still be morally wrong. For (again) morality is not empirical generalizations about the way we actually behave, it is a standard prescribing how we *ought* to behave, all things considered.

Ethics, also called "moral philosophy," is the philosophical study of the nature and principles of morality. Among the questions examined in this branch of philosophy are these: What exactly are the true, or correct, principles of morality? How do we tell the difference between right and wrong, and good and bad? What is morality rooted in or based on? Where does it come from?

Some people believe that on moral matters, nothing is certain; everything is gray. But this is not true: people all around the world generally agree on many basic moral principles. In *The Abolition of Man*, C. S. Lewis assembles a collection of universally accepted moral values—principles broadly accepted East and West—which he names the *Tao* (the "Way"). Lewis's list includes laws of beneficence, honesty, good faith, truth-telling, duties to parents, children, elders, and posterity, mercy, and magnanimity. These values, he argues, are so fundamental to our moral consciousness that even the values of those who attack it are derived from it:

> This thing which I have called for convenience the Tao, and which others may call Natural Law or Traditional Morality or the First Principles of Practical Reason or the First Platitudes, is not one among a

series of possible systems of value. It is the source of all value judge-
ments. If it is rejected, all value is rejected. The effort to refute it and
raise a new system of value in its place is self-contradictory. . . . What
purport to be new systems of value . . . all consist of fragments from
the Tao itself, arbitrarily wrenched from their context in the whole and
then swollen to madness in their isolation.[2]

"This," Lewis argues, "is what Confucius meant when he said, 'With those
who follow a different Way it is difficult to take counsel.'"[3]

Reasonable people all over the world today agree that genocide, slavery, kidnapping, violent assault, stealing, lying, sex trafficking, and dicta-
torship are morally wrong. We agree that we ought to treat ourselves and
all others with a certain degree of respect and care. Most of us agree on the
absolute value of an individual human life. When we are at our best, we
agree that human relations and transactions ought to be consensual and
peaceful rather than forced, violent, or coerced. And don't we all agree now
that government should be accountable to the people?

It is true that other moral issues are still being debated. For example, is
capital punishment morally right? Is abortion the morally wrong taking of
an innocent human life? Or is it morally permissible? Should the wealthy
pay more in taxes? But the fact that we have not reached universal agreement on some issues does not mean that everything is gray. In moral philosophy, we seek rational principles that can help us make principled moral
decisions in real time.

Socrates was the first philosopher in recorded history to teach moral
philosophy as a systematic academic discipline based on independent
critical thinking. He believed that we can find sensible answers to moral
questions if we will reason together calmly, rationally, honestly, and respectfully. Scholars in the field of moral philosophy agree with Socrates.
In moral philosophy, as in the wider field of philosophy, reason is our
common currency.

So, let's reason together about some of the most fundamental ethical
matters of all, beginning with the vitally important concepts of moral good
and bad. Thinking philosophically about good and bad can help you attain
a higher degree of moral clarity. After examining these concepts, we'll turn
to the equally important concepts of moral right and wrong.

WHAT IN LIFE IS MORALLY GOOD?

Philosophers distinguish two kinds of goodness. Something is instrumentally, or extrinsically, good if it is good only insofar as it can be used to attain something else that is itself good. In common terms, an instrumental good is good only as a means to an end. It derives its goodness from the purpose it serves. A hammer, for example, is instrumentally good—valued not for its own sake but for the good it helps us attain (building something). In other words, we value it only as a tool. In contrast, something is intrinsically good if it is good in itself, apart from any use to which it may be put or any good that it leads to. It is good completely on its own.

Now, many things in life possess only instrumental goodness or value. A dollar bill is usually valuable only because we can use it to buy something we value. Lacking intrinsic value, it is valuable only as a means to an end. Other examples are easy to think of: a trip to the dentist, a vitamin pill, a credit card, a ride on the bus.

So, many things in life are valued only for what they help us attain. And in most cases, what they help us attain is itself valued only for something further *it* helps us attain, and so forth. Is anything intrinsically good in a moral sense?

EGOISTIC HEDONISM:
THE FIRST THEORY OF THE GOOD LIFE

One answer has seemed obvious to many people throughout history. Pleasure, they answer, is the only thing in life that is intrinsically good in a moral sense. Everything else is morally good only insofar as it produces or helps us attain pleasure or avoid pain. If something does not give us at least some pleasure, or help us attain pleasure, it has no worth at all. Pleasure is thus the one intrinsic good that imparts moral goodness to everything else.

In philosophy this theory is known as "hedonism" (Greek *hedone*, "pleasure"). The hedonist philosophy has been stated in many different forms; the simplest is called *egoistic hedonism* (Latin *ego*, "I," or "self"). You are living the morally best life possible, says the advocate of egoistic hedonism, if your life is filled with as much net pleasure as possible, with *net pleasure* defined as "the total quantity of pleasure left after the total quantity of pain has been subtracted." In everything you do, your own net plea-sure (hereafter simply *pleasure*) is the bottom line, the only consideration that finally matters. On this view, the more pleasure you have, the better your life is.

Egoistic hedonism is one of the oldest ethical theories ever proposed. We know from Plato's dialogues that it was taught by some of the Soph-ists during the fifth century BC. As we saw in chapter 8, the Sophists were professional teachers who traveled from one Greek city-state to an-other, offering private instruction for a fee in subjects ranging from ath-letics, law, and poetry to speech communication and rhetoric (the art of persuasive speech). Their services were in great demand because the Greeks were conducting the world's first experiment in democratic gov-ernment at the time, and democracy requires an educated citizenry with activists and public speakers trained in rhetoric and other communica-tion skills. The Sophists claimed to meet the needs of the fledgling Greek democracy.

Some people today certainly act as if they believe that their own per-sonal pleasure is the only thing that ultimately matters in life. If something doesn't promise them pleasure, they abandon it. They spend a great deal of money and time pursuing drugs, sex, thrills, and other things that bring pleasure. Egoistic hedonism has always attracted converts. If you adopt egoistic hedonism as your theory of the morally good life, then you should evaluate everything on the basis of only one consideration: Does it, or will it, give me enough pleasure?

SOCRATES CHALLENGES THE HEDONISTS

Socrates entered the public square to counter the Sophists and their he-donistic theory of the good life. The historic debate that followed covered many of the most important issues in ethics, including questions we're still discussing today. Plato re-created the discussions between Socrates and the hedonists in a number of his dialogues, including the *Gorgias* and the *Republic*.

Several Socratic arguments can be distilled from the discussions as Plato recorded them. First, pleasure in itself is not intrinsically good in a moral sense, for clearly not all pleasures are morally good. For example, pleasure gained by harming others is morally bad, isn't it? So, if some pleasures are not morally good, then there must be a standard of moral goodness above that of pleasure, an objective standard by which pleasures can be judged. If so, then pleasure in itself is not intrinsically good in a moral sense.

A second and deeper Socratic argument against hedonism began with his observations on the nature of the soul. We discussed Socrates's account of the soul in chapter 2. We know, he argued, that our soul, or inner self, contains three distinct parts: reason, emotion, and bodily desire. The proof that these parts are distinct is that they can oppose each other: emotion can oppose reason (and vice versa), desire can oppose reason (and vice versa), and emotion can oppose desire (and vice versa).

Next, life experience teaches that when our raw, unexamined emotions overrule our reason, the result is usually something we later realize, using our best reasoning, was harmful. In such cases, we look back and wish we had followed the prompts of sound reasoning rather than uncontrolled emotion. Road rage is a contemporary example.

Similarly, experience teaches that when our unexamined bodily desires overcome our reason, the result is usually something we later realize, again using our best reasoning, was unhealthy. In such cases, we look back and wish we had followed critical reason rather than unexamined bodily desire. Overeating and drinking too much are examples.

Life experience teaches, in short, that we live better when our soul is ruled by sound reasoning—educated reason following realistic principles of critical thinking—than when it is ruled by unexamined emotions or raw bodily desires.

At this point in the exposition of Socrates's theory, some students point out that reason can also lead us astray. For our reasoning can be biased, it can be errant, it sometimes operates on half-truths, prejudice, and so forth. People can also use their reasoning dishonestly to justify bad things, to figure out how to rob banks, to calculate the best way to steal without getting caught, and so on. So why, they ask, does the faculty of reason deserve an exalted status?

Socrates agreed that our own personal reasoning can sometimes take an illogical path and lead us to a fallacious conclusion. It can be biased. It can also be used to rationalize bad actions. He was keenly aware of the many ways people misuse their faculty of reason. After all, his life mission, as we saw in chapter 2, was to help people reason more realistically. This leads to his reply.

By *reason* Socrates meant "trained and educated reasoning." When we are young and immature, our reasoning is not functioning at its best. When we are heated by emotion or inflamed by bodily desire, our reason does not always function well. Reason needs to be trained in the objective and realistic methods of critical thinking. It also needs to be educated in the nature of true goodness. But once educated and functioning well, in accord with objective and realistic criteria, reason is capable of realistic self-criticism on the basis of objective standards.

The next step in Socrates's theory of moral goodness is his argument for God's existence, which we examined in chapter 4. On the basis of the design argument, Socrates argued that we live in a purpose-filled world, a rational world in which everything has a unique role to play in the overall scheme of things designed and overseen by God. It follows that the human soul—like everything else within the universe—was designed to function in a certain way and has a role to play.

Experience indicates that when educated, trained reason rules and balances the soul, the soul functions smoothly like a well-built machine in prime condition. Given that we live in a purpose-filled world, and given that each thing has a role to play in the overall scheme of things, it follows that the soul functions properly, as it was meant to function, when educated reason governs and balances the emotions and desires while directing the soul toward true goodness.

Life experience shows that when the soul functions as it was meant to, it attains an internal harmony that is experienced as a state of well-being distinct from irrational pleasure. Socrates called this state of well-being *eudaimonia* (Greek, lit. "good indwelling spirit"). Although *eudaimonia* (or the English spelling, "eudaemonia") is sometimes translated "happiness," its meaning is closer to "well-being" or even "flourishing." Socrates argued that the intrinsic value of having a smoothly functioning soul surpasses anything else in life, including the alleged goods of sensuous pleasure, money, fame, power, and glory. Since he believed in (and argued for) life after death, he also argued that the attainment of an even higher degree of flourishing awaits us in the next life.

So, why reject egoistic hedonism? Socrates had an answer. Those who have experienced both hedonistic pleasure and the goodness of *eudaemonia* know that the latter is superior. The hedonistic pleasure gained through irrational pursuits is not worth the opportunity cost (the loss of real well-being, or flourishing).

Socrates added a startling claim to his theory when he argued that the state of *eudaemonia* cannot be ruined or diminished by any external circumstances. True well-being once attained cannot be lost because it is an internal, spiritual state that exists above the flux of ever-changing circumstances. Even the good person who has been wrongly imprisoned does not lose the internal wellness, or flourishing, flowing from within his harmonious soul. Pleasures can lose their allure. Wealth can be taken away. Power can be lost. Nothing can take away the spiritual goodness flowing from within the well-balanced soul. This is what Socrates meant when he claimed that the just (moral) person cannot be harmed. We find a similar idea in classical Chinese and Indian philosophy, and in Judaism, Islam, and Christianity.

As I mentioned in chapter 2, many people have improved their lives after learning that their soul has three parts—reason, emotion, and desire—and that they have the power within themselves to achieve a rational balance and a more harmonious, reasonable, and fulfilling life—regardless of circumstances.

On a personal note. I have known people who completely changed their lives for the better by intentionally choosing to cut out an unhealthy behavior that was wrecking their lives. In each case, their reason played a large role in their recovery. But in most cases, prayer and grace played a role too. Christianity along with other religious traditions (including those of the ancient Greeks) teaches that (to use a personal example) just as a grandpa helps his little grandson reach up to a higher shelf in the kitchen, God responds to prayer and may help an individual reach a higher place in life. In many cases today, people make a radical change with help from groups such as Alcoholics Anonymous (AA). It is worth noting that individuals in AA are encouraged to acknowledge God's existence and to call on a higher power for help. One-on-one professional counseling can also be an effective way to end an unhealthy lifestyle and reach a higher level of functioning and balance. Reason often points the way when our lives spin out of control, but we almost always need outside help if we are going to make a permanent change.

MODERN CONSIDERATIONS

Imagine an attorney who has figured out how to steal funds from his clients without being detected. He steals a lot of money, which he uses to maximize the quantity of pleasure in his life. He doesn't care how his actions affect others—pleasure is all that matters. According to egoistic hedonism, he is living a morally good life.

Consider this case calmly and rationally. Isn't it clearly, distinctly, and indubitably wrong to live this way? Isn't it just clearly wrong to use others merely to gain pleasure for yourself? Isn't it most certainly morally wrong to treat others as if they are mere tools put on earth for our own satisfaction? Couldn't he do better than this? I realize these are rhetorical questions. I ask them because I want you, the reader, to think for yourself. Critical thinkers can come up with other test cases on their own.

The problem here is that egoistic hedonism does not require that people take into account the intrinsic value of *other* people. Would you want to be in a relationship with someone who cared only about his or her own pleasure? Is egoistic hedonism an adequate theory of goodness? Or does it justify actions that are clearly, distinctly, and rationally just plain morally wrong? Virtually all ethicists agree: hedonism, in its egoistic form, is a selfish and inhumane theory. It is also antisocial.

Egoistic hedonism is questionable for another set of reasons. Aren't there other things in life apart from pleasure that are intrinsically valuable? Autonomy, for instance—the power to chart your own path through life on the basis of careful reasoning? Isn't autonomy valuable even when the going is hard, even when it does *not* bring pleasure? How about love, friendship, political freedom, and community? Aren't these also intrinsically valuable? Aren't they good, even when they do not translate into quantities of net pleasure? Even when they require hard work, overcoming challenges, and suffering?

Who can rationally deny, for example, that love is intrinsically valuable apart from all considerations of pleasure? Isn't this about as clear and distinct and reasonable as anything can be? None of these goods (autonomy, friendship, love, community, etc.) is good only insofar as it leads to pleasure. If so, then there must be more to the good life than the mere experience of pleasure.

Did you notice what we've been doing? We've been reasoning about morality. We evaluated two ethical theories using reason—our common currency. This is what ethics, the philosophical examination of moral questions, is all about.

Questions for Reflection and Discussion 12.1

1. Explain Socrates's disagreement with the Sophists.
2. In your own words, explain Socrates's theory of goodness, and evaluate it philosophically.
3. Have you noticed that wealth, power, and fame do not always bring pleasure? Have you observed people who are either wealthy, powerful, or famous living wretched, miserable lives? Socrates makes the point that each of these things, being merely instrumentally valuable, only benefits us if we use it properly, that is, in a manner which helps us pursue the truly good. Comment philosophically.

VIRTUE ETHICS:
ARISTOTLE'S THEORY OF THE GOOD LIFE

Aristotle (384–322 BC) rejected egoistic hedonism. However, he also sought a theory of the good life that would be more definite and down-to-earth than that proposed by Socrates and later defended by Plato. He presented his theory in a book that would become one of the most influential works of ethical theory ever published: the *Nicomachean Ethics* (named after his son). More than 2,000 years after it first appeared, his theory remains one of the three or four major accounts of morality still under extended discussion.

The *Nicomachean Ethics* is profound and rigorous. Hundreds of scholarly books have been written about it. Hundreds more have built upon its ideas. It is impossible to do Aristotle's theory justice in a short introduction. All we'll do is scratch the surface of his magnificent book, the first systematic presentation of the school of ethical thought known today as "virtue ethics."[4]

Aristotle argues, on the basis of a systematic examination of nature, that each kind of living thing has a characteristic *ergon* (function or characteristic mode of operation) flowing from within its internal nature. To perform that function well is its *telos* (purpose) in life. As Socrates and Plato had argued before him, Aristotle argues that we live in a purpose-filled universe designed to operate according to a rational scheme by God.

Next, the characteristic function of a particular kind of creature is the activity that is unique to that kind of creature. This leads Aristotle to ask an amazing question: What is the unique function of a human being? By this he means, What is the function of a human being *qua human being*—not qua father, mother, doctor, or farmer—just *as a human being*? A carpenter builds things, mothers and fathers raise children, artists create beauty, barbers cut hair, and so forth. Their functions distinguish them from other human beings. But what is the unique activity that distinguishes humans from other kinds of living creatures? Aristotle writes:

> Should we not assume that just as the eye, the hand, the foot, and in general each part of the body clearly has its own proper function, so man too has some function over and above the functions of his parts? What can this function possibly be? Simply living? He shares that even with plants, but we are now looking for something peculiar to man. Accordingly, the life of nutrition and growth must be excluded. Next in line there is a life of sense perception. But this, too, man has in common with the horse, the ox, and every animal. There remains then an active life of the rational element. . . . The proper function of man, then, consists in an activity of the soul in conformity with a rational principle or, at least, not without it.[5]

By an *activity of the soul in conformity with a rational principle* Aristotle means what we mean today by critical thinking. Reasoning on the basis of critical standards is therefore the unique human function, the characteristic activity that flows from human nature and distinguishes humans from other kinds of creatures. Aristotle has a point here: nonhuman animals of various kinds reason to some degree, but no other kind of animal reasons at the human level. No other species writes books, studies mathematics, maps the world, builds factories, composes poetry, and draws in perspective.

Function and Goodness

Aristotle next connects function and goodness. Observation of the many ways in which we use the word *good* reveals that the word is not univocal— it does not have one fixed meaning. Rather, its meaning is relative to the kind of thing being evaluated. In general, a good thing is something that performs its *ergon* well. A good knife is one that cuts well, a good lamp is one that lights well, and so forth. Furthermore, an entity performs its unique function well when it operates in accordance with its nature, its design plan. Notice that the design plan of a lamp is built into the device by its designer and maker.

The Virtues

This leads Aristotle to the notion of moral virtue. In each general kind of human activity, when reason is employed realistically and critically, it directs our action to a mean between two extremes. One extreme involves a deficiency of something good, the other an excess. The *mean* is the rational balance or midpoint recommended by critical reasoning.

For example, in battle, courage is the mean between the extremes of cowardice (the deficiency) and foolhardiness (the excess). The foolhardy soldier charges into battle recklessly, without thinking, and wastes his life. At the other extreme, the coward hides or runs away when he should stand and fight. The soldier with courage strikes the rational balance—his actions are neither foolhardy nor cowardly. Courage is the mean recommended by critical thinking. Of course, the mean in this case needs to be defined and clarified—that is also a task for critical reasoning. Soldiers in basic training learn about this rational mean.

For another example, generosity (proper giving of money) is the mean between the extremes of stinginess (giving too little) and extravagance (giving too much). The generous person takes the middle path recommended by reason and helps someone in need without giving too much (which spoils) or doing too little (which neglects). And how do we find the mean? We find it by reasoning carefully in everyday life-situations.

Next, Aristotle introduces the idea of a *character trait*, which he defines as "a deliberately cultivated habit or disposition to behave in a certain way." Consider the character trait of being honest. If honesty is one of your character traits, you have a habit of being honest. Being honest is just the kind of person you are; it's just what you do. People who know you expect honest behavior from you. In this case, you have a disposition, or tendency, to be honest.

Aristotle adds psychological depth when he observes that a character trait involves more than habitual outward behavior; it also includes an inner motive. The honest person is honest because she values integrity and truth, both good things and both aspects of honesty. And she sincerely wants to be honest—that is the kind of person she truly wants to be.

Aristotle's idea of moral virtue can now be defined. A *moral virtue* is a character trait that is (1) aimed at the rational mean between two extremes and (2) required for living a morally good life, which is a life guided by the best reasoning possible. A fully virtuous person habitually aims at the mean between the extremes in every area of life, guided every step of the way by careful critical thinking. This explains Aristotle's definition of moral *virtue* as "a habit, or disposition, of the soul to seek the rational mean in the pursuit of the good."

Aristotle's theory has room for moral principles, but true moral principles of right and wrong—such as "Tell the truth" and "It is wrong to steal"—are grounded in the virtues. For the ultimate purpose of moral rules, on Aristotle's view, is to point us in the direction of virtuous action. Aristotle's theory is known as "virtue ethics" because it holds that the cultivation of virtuous character is the fundamental ethical requirement and the goal of the moral life.

Is Virtue Innate?

Aristotle made wise observations on the moral life that are still meaningful in the twenty-first century. For instance, he observed that we are not born virtuous. We do not begin life with virtuous characters fully formed and aimed at the rational mean. Virtue must be learned and then cultivated over time. Virtue is therefore a learned skill, like playing the flute or driving a chariot.

And how do we learn to be virtuous? We learn by imitating moral role models, also called "moral exemplars." Just as Magic Johnson in his heyday was an exemplar in professional basketball for younger and less experienced players, a moral exemplar is someone skilled in the practice of moral virtue who serves as an inspiring example to others. Serving as a moral role model is one of the great responsibilities of being an adult.

Aristotle's observations on role models agree with common sense. From an early age we are imitators. Little toddlers instinctively imitate their parents and other adults. This is how we first learn. Which leads to a wise bit of Aristotelian advice. Children raised in a loving environment will learn to be loving. Likewise, children raised in an honest environment will learn to be honest. But children raised in an abusive and violent environment will learn to be abusive and violent. If you have children, think about the environment you are creating for them and the behaviors you are modeling. Ask yourself, What kind of person do I want to help them become? This might help *you* grow morally as well.[6]

The Role of Emotions in the Moral Life

To many, Aristotle's theory sounds excessively rationalistic. It sounds as if the moral life is all cold, hard reasoning. However, in recent years, virtue ethics theorists in the Aristotelian tradition have moved away from an extremely rationalistic interpretation and now argue that the emotions, including the empathic understanding of others, play a role in the cultivation of moral virtue.

The philosopher Martha Nussbaum, for example, argues that the emotions have a cognitive dimension: they work alongside reason in pointing us to morally good behavior. This seems right. Mature emotional awareness of others can make us cognizant of morally relevant features of a situation that abstract reasoning alone may have missed. For instance, an emotionally sensitive and compassionate person might see that his words are hurting someone and will stop; a less sensitive and coldly rational person might not get it. An emotionally aware person might see that someone needs help; others miss the signs entirely. The compassionate person might see things the selfish person misses. The consensus today is that healthy emotions are an integral part of the moral life; reason cannot do the job alone.

However, a critical thinker must keep in mind that unexamined emotions and feelings can also lead us astray. For raw emotions can sometimes be the product of a morally inadequate education, biased cultural conditioning, brainwashing, prejudice, bigotry, pride, misinformation, and other questionable factors. For this reason, we must critically examine our emotional reactions on the basis of the best reasoning possible so that our emotions work with reason, not against it, to help us live the best life possible, a life of virtue.

Intellectual and Moral Virtues Distinguished

Aristotle began his search for the human good by seeking to identify the activity that is unique to humans. He found it, as we have seen, in the human faculty of critical reasoning. However, he did not hold that human flourishing consists solely in abstract reasoning, such as a scholar lost in thought and buried in books. Human well-being also includes doing the right thing:

It is well said, then, that it is by doing just acts that someone becomes just, and by doing temperate acts that they become temperate. Without doing these, no one would have any chance of becoming good. But most people do not perform these actions but take refuge in theory, thinking that they are being philosophers and will become good in this way. They behave a bit like patients who listen carefully to their doctors, but do none of the things they were told to do. As the latter will not be made well in body by such a method of treatment, the former will not be made well in soul by such an approach to philosophy.[7]

Thus, the study of philosophical ethics "is not aimed at theoretical knowledge. We are not conducting our inquiry in order to know the definition of virtue, but in order to become good, otherwise it would not benefit us at all. So we must think about what concerns actions and how we ought to perform them."[8]

Consequently, Aristotle distinguished intellectual virtues (character traits of the mind that lead to excellence in the pursuit of truth) from moral virtues (character traits that lead to morally good action). Both kinds of virtue are required for a morally good human life.

The intellectual virtues include mental habits that lead to scientific truth and *phronesis* (practical wisdom) — the ability to discover the right thing to do in real-life situations. This virtue is also called "prudence." Modern ethicists in the Aristotelian tradition add the following to the list of intellectual virtues: open-mindedness, fair-mindedness, the love of truth, perseverance in the pursuit of truth, curiosity, intellectual humility, and the ability to listen well.

The traditional moral virtues include courage, temperance, charity, truthfulness, civility, citizenship, and friendship. Reflection on Aristotle's distinction between intellectual and moral virtues suggests an important corollary: being intellectual does not by itself make a person morally better than someone who is not intellectually inclined. Being college-educated does not make a person morally superior to someone who lacks a college degree. Aristotle doesn't address the issue, but his theory of ethics rules out the vice of intellectual conceit.

Becoming Real

Aristotle introduces an important idea when he brings into moral theory his metaphysical distinction between actuality and potentiality. He argues that when we are born, the moral virtues exist in our human nature only as unrealized potentials to behave in certain moral ways (to be compassionate, loving, kind, honest, friendly, courageous, etc.). Like all potentials, they must be actualized before they become real in our lives. When a potential is made actual, we say that the person has "realized" or "actualized" his potential. The moral life, as Aristotle sees it, is one of actualizing, or realizing, the moral potentials within our human nature. From an Aristotelian point of view, the moral life is a process of becoming more real.

Eudaemonia

One final idea and you will have a well-rounded view of virtue ethics. When we actualize our human potential, Aristotle argues, a state of eudaemonia results. Aristotle calls this the "good life for a human being." So, what does morality require? Aristotle's answer is, use your faculty of reason to actualize your human potential and attain eudaemonia. In short, get real!

God, Morality, and the Blessed Life

Aristotle observes that human beings have functions in common with plants (such as reproduction) and with animals (such as perception). However, he notes, we differ from both in having rational minds capable of abstracting from material concerns to contemplate God, eternity, and divine matters.[9] The contemplation of the divine is the highest and most noble aspect of the human function, for in "contemplating what is eternal and divine, our minds become god-like, or divine."[10] And spiritual thought is not wasted energy: "The contemplation of the divine helps with moral action just as sight helps with motion."[11] When contemplation of the divine becomes an important part of our lives, our lives are "blessed" and also happy. Aristotle refers to God and divine matters numerous times throughout his writings on ethics. For Aristotle, God and morality are closely intertwined.

Christian Ethics

Philosophers have noted similarities between Aristotle's virtue ethics and Christian ethics as developed in the New Testament. Christ is presented as the Son of God, the Messiah, and the sacrificial lamb. He is also presented as a moral exemplar, and Christians are called to imitate him. And what does Jesus model? Virtues. Specifically, the character traits of love, humility, charity, compassion, mercy, honesty, courage of conviction, forgiveness, purity of heart, peace, and obedience to God, among others. Although Jesus was certainly not teaching Aristotle's philosophy of ethics, the Sermon on the Mount (Matthew 5–7) is a discourse on virtue ethics.

Jesus also stated moral principles, but the ultimate purpose of each principle or command was to promote virtuous character and conduct. For instance:

- In everything, do to others as you would have them do to you (Matthew 7:12).[12]
- Love your enemies and pray for those who persecute you (Matthew 6:46).
- You shall love the Lord your God with all your heart, and with all your soul, and with all your mind. This is the greatest and first commandment. And a second is like it. You shall love your neighbor as yourself (Matthew 22:37–39).

Jesus often taught the virtues in the form of stories or parables. When a lawyer asked him, "And who is my neighbor?" he replied with the story of the Good Samaritan:

A man was going down from Jerusalem to Jericho, and fell into the hands of robbers, who stripped him of his clothes, beat him, and went away, leaving him half dead. Now by chance a priest was going down that road, and when he saw him, he passed by on the other side. So likewise a Levite, when he came to the place and saw him, passed by on the other side. But a Samaritan while traveling came near him; and when he saw him he was moved with pity. He went to him and bandaged his wounds, having poured oil and wine on them. Then he put him on his own animal, brought him to an inn, and took care of him. The next day he took out two denarii, gave them to the innkeeper, and said, "Take care of him, and when I come back I will repay you whatever more you spend." Which of these three do you think was a neighbor to the man who fell into the hands of robbers?" He said, "The one who showed him mercy." Jesus said to him, "Go and do likewise" (Luke 10:30–37).

The philosopher Dallas Willard offers a helpful commentary on this parable: "In the story of the good Samaritan, Jesus not only teaches us to help people in need; more deeply, he teaches us that we cannot identify who . . . is 'in' with God, who is blessed, by looking at exteriors of any sort. That is a matter of the heart."[13]

So, in Christian ethics, as in Aristotle's ethics, virtue or character is fundamental. Rules or principles are derived from virtues and exist for the purpose of fostering virtue. On both theories, the moral life is about becoming a certain kind of person—someone possessing a virtuous character. The Christian ethicist Scott Rae writes:

At its heart Christian ethics is a blend of both virtues and principles. Morality is ultimately grounded in the character of God. . . . The virtues, or character traits, which are made clear by God's character and further clarified by Jesus's character, are the ultimate foundation for morality from a Christian worldview. God's commands are derived from his character. God issues the commands that he does because of the kind of [being] that he is. For example, God commands that we love our neighbors, ultimately not because "love makes the world go round," though that result is surely a good thing, but because he is [loving]. Likewise God mandates that we forgive not primarily because forgiveness restores relationships, though that is certainly true, but because God is fundamentally forgiving. The virtues, then, are primary, and the moral principles, or God's commands, are derived from them.[14]

And in Christian ethics as in the virtue theory of Aristotle, reason plays a strong role. For example, those with the virtue of peace—the peacemakers—respond to conflict in helpful ways. This requires the use of reason. Those with the virtue of compassion respond with love and concern to those in need and to those who are helpless and sick. This too requires the use of reason. And those with the virtue of humility are never prideful, or self-righteous. They give credit where it is due and are never heard saying, "I did it all by myself." This certainly requires the kind of critical thinking taught by Socrates, Plato, and Aristotle.

However, Christian ethics is not confined to the reading of scripture and the emulating of biblical models. Human reasoning plays an essential role. Christian philosophers draw a distinction between special and general revelation. Special revelation consists of God's Word received under inspiration and expressed in sacred scripture. General revelation is God's truth revealed outside of scripture—universal truth that can be discovered by anyone anywhere in the world using common human reason. Both the Old and New Testaments refer to a natural order that God inscribed on his creation, an order that can be known by anyone using just human reasoning. This is general revelation. Many Christian philosophers down through the ages have considered Aristotle's theory to be the general revelation complement to Christian virtue ethics. They believe that our common ability to reason is required as we plumb the depths of God's general revelation as well.

Augustine, one of the greatest philosophers of the Western tradition, was the first to give Christian ethics a deep and systematic philosophical expression and defense. Reasoning in harmony with scripture, Augustine argued that love is the highest expression of virtue. In each situation, we must ask, What would a loving person do? For obvious reasons Augustine's account of Christian virtue ethics is called *agapism* (Greek *agape*, "self-less, self-giving love").[15]

Virtue ethics, whether in the form worked out by Aristotle or the form taught by Christ and systematized by Augustine, is an incredibly hard ideal to live up to. However, it does not follow that the virtues are useless; they are guides. You fall down, you pick yourself up and try again. Do this every day.

Although this is not the place to enter this large topic, Christianity adds a doctrine of God's grace to ethical theory with the claim that we need God's help, or grace, as we strive to be as moral as we can be. No analogies are perfect, but Christian ethicists such as Augustine argue that (to use a personal example again) just as a loving grandpa might help his little grandson reach a higher shelf in the kitchen, God reaches down to help sinners reach higher than they otherwise might reach.

Questions for Reflection and Discussion 12.2

1. Has someone in your life served as a moral exemplar?
2. Can you name a public figure who is *not* a moral exemplar? Explain.
3. Is there someone in public life who is a moral exemplar for all of us?
4. What should we do when virtues conflict, as in the following case? During World War II, Dutch fishermen helped Jewish people escape the Nazi horror by hiding them in the holds of their boats. When Nazi

patrols stopped them and asked if they had any passengers, the captains faced a moral dilemma. Should they lie or tell the truth? Lying saved innocent lives and helped people in need. But it also violated the virtue of honesty. What would you do and why?

5. Here is another case where virtues seem to conflict. Suppose that at work you discover that one of your best friends on the job has been stealing from your employer. Reflection on the virtue of honesty suggests you should report him. However, thinking about the virtue of friendship suggests you should be loyal and not report him. What should you do?

6. Is there a middle path discernable by reason for every kind of activity?

7. Is moderation, or the middle path, always a good thing?

8. Compare and contrast Aristotle's theory with egoistic hedonism.

9. How are virtues acquired?

10. Does emotion play a role in the life of virtue?

AN INITIAL THEORY OF RIGHT AND WRONG — ETHICAL EGOISM

We've been examining the nature of moral goodness. The next topic is equally important. How do right and wrong relate to good and bad? As Socrates, Plato, Augustine, Aquinas, and many other philosophers since have argued, we seem to have a natural or built-in desire to pursue objective goodness. But is there a morally right way to pursue it? Questions about right and wrong arose as we examined the notion of irrational pleasure. It's time to take a closer look at this important moral category. What is the difference between moral right and wrong? How do right and wrong relate to good and bad? The focus will now be on moral *rightness* rather than moral goodness.

According to elementary ethical egoism, the first theory of moral rightness that we'll examine, we have only one fundamental moral obligation, and that is to always and only do that which is in our own self-interest as we understand it. For you, the morally right thing to do, on any occasion, is just that which you believe is in your own self-interest. For me, the morally right thing to do, on any occasion, is just that which I believe is in my own self-interest. So, no matter what you do, you are doing the right thing if you believe that your action is in your own self-interest.

As we proceed, keep in mind that this is not a hedonistic theory—there is no mention here of pleasure. Self-interest and pleasure are not always the same thing, for there are times when the pursuit of pleasure is not in your best interest. Egoistic hedonism was a theory of moral goodness; elementary ethical egoism is a theory of moral rightness.

If this initial theory of right and wrong is correct, you have no fundamental moral duties or obligations to other people; your *only* basic moral duty is to yourself. And that duty is to always further your own self-interest as you understand it. You may, on some occasions, help another person or do something that benefits someone else, but you are under no obligation to do so, and you should do so only if you think there is something in it for you that makes it worth the effort.

Compared to egoistic hedonism, which counsels each of us to exclusively pursue our own pleasure, elementary ethical egoism seems to be an improvement. For as we have noted, some pleasures are self-destructive and therefore clearly not in our best interest. Elementary egoism prohibits pleasures known to be self-destructive.

The theory may seem plausible at first, but there are severe problems. Imagine the following scenario. As you stroll leisurely along the shore of a beautiful lake on your day off, you see a toddler fall into the shallow water near the shore. The toddler goes under and obviously does not know how to swim. The mother has stepped away for a moment and doesn't realize that her child is drowning. You could wade into the two-foot-deep water and rescue the toddler in a couple of seconds, but you decide not to because you don't want to get your pants wet. According to ethical egoism in its elementary form, you have no moral obligation whatsoever to help the little child, and you *do nothing morally wrong if you continue your leisurely walk around the lake while the little person dies.* For according to this view, your only moral obligation is to do that which you believe benefits *you.* If you sincerely think it is in your self-interest to continue your leisurely stroll, then that is what you morally ought to do. You have no moral duty whatsoever to help another person, and in particular, there is no "duty of easy rescue" (as in this case). Indeed, if elementary ethical egoism is true, you have no fundamental duties to help others, period.

But does this sound right? Think about this situation as rationally and calmly as you can. Think about the enormous intrinsic value of an innocent human life. Surely you do something morally wrong if you stroll casually by and let the toddler drown, don't you? Given that the cost to you would be minimal, *don't you have a moral obligation to save his or her life?* Think about this as deeply and rationally as you can. Isn't it as certain as 1 + 1 = 2 that you ought to do *something* in this case? At least alert the mother. Isn't the obligation obvious to common sense and to critical reason? If you agree, then elementary ethical egoism is a false theory of right and wrong, for (again) according to elementary ethical egoism you do nothing at all morally wrong if you calmly walk by and let the toddler drown.

Perhaps another example is needed. Suppose that a stockbroker discovers he can steal money from some of his clients without getting caught. The amount he can siphon from their accounts will be enough to build a vacation home, and they will never know the difference. According to elementary ethical egoism, if he believes that stealing from his clients will promote his own self-interest, the stockbroker morally *ought to do so*. If elementary ethical egoism is true, it would be morally wrong *not* to steal the money.

But does this seem right? Think carefully about the effect his action has on the victims and their families. Aren't they intrinsically valuable beings? From a moral point of view, don't their interests count? Don't they deserve to be treated with more respect than that? Don't they have rights? Can the stockbroker's actions be defended rationally? Or is there a strong reason why the stockbroker's actions are morally wrong? What would society be like if everyone lived by this moral theory?[16]

Many similar hypothetical cases can be constructed. According to elementary ethical egoism, if you believe that it is in your own self-interest to lie, steal, or harm others in order to get ahead, and you believe you can get away with it, then you morally ought to do so. But think critically here. Suppose that you are in a situation where lying, stealing, and defrauding will get you ahead, and you know that you won't ever get caught. Would that make it right? Don't we have at least some duties to other people? Duties to treat them with respect? To treat them with civility? To aid them in a case of easy rescue? If so, then elementary ethical egoism, the view under consideration, is false.

I'm asking many questions, hoping that you will answer them for yourself on the basis of careful and realistic reasoning. Elementary ethical egoism clearly seems to call for antisocial and immoral behavior, doesn't it? Aren't these considerations good reasons to reject the theory? Notice again what we're doing: we're reasoning critically about morality. In philosophical ethics, as in philosophy in general, reason is our common currency.

UTILITARIANISM: THE FIRST "SCIENTIFIC" THEORY OF RIGHT AND WRONG

Introducing Jeremy Bentham

In the eighteenth century, a new theory of right and wrong that combined hedonism and a universal concern for all of humanity was first proposed and defended systematically by the English legal reformer and philosopher Jeremy Bentham (1748–1832). Bentham presented his theory as part of his campaign to make the harsh penal laws of his day more humane. And the laws were indeed harsh: in eighteenth-century England, people often received extremely cruel punishments for small offenses.[17]

Bentham began his major work, *An Introduction to the Principles of Morals and Legislation*, by stating that pleasure is the only thing that is intrinsically good and pain is the only thing that is intrinsically bad. His account of goodness is therefore hedonism. However, his account of right and wrong, named *utilitarianism*, is not egoistic. Rather, it is universalistic. The fundamental principle of morality, he argued, is not "Get for yourself as much pleasure as possible." Rather, it is the principle of utility, which can be stated this way: In any situation, the morally right thing to do, of all the available options, is that action which is expected to produce in its consequences the greatest net balance of pleasure over pain, measured and summed across everyone, with each person's pleasure counting equally.

The principle can be illustrated with a simple hypothetical example. Suppose that I have a choice of doing one of three things, action A, B, or C. Suppose further that I can reliably estimate the net balance of pleasure over pain that will result from each action, summed across everyone, with each person counting equally. Let the result of my calculation be this:

1. Action A would increase the net balance of pleasure over pain by ten units.

2. Action B would decrease the net balance of pleasure over pain by thirty units.

3. Action C would increase the net balance of pleasure over pain by sixty units.

Action C is the morally right choice, according to the principle of utility, for C adds more net pleasure to the world than any other available action.

Bentham had a lot to say about pleasure. Most importantly, he believed that all pleasures can be measured in common units. The pleasure gained by eating pie can be measured in the same units we use to measure the pleasure of reading a good novel or working for a good cause. He also believed that all kinds of pleasure are equal in moral value. That is, ten units of bodily pleasure derived from alcohol or drugs is as intrinsically valuable as ten units of intellectual pleasure produced by gazing at a beautiful work of art, enjoying a meaningful friendship, or reading an informative book.

Utilitarianism was a revolutionary idea when Bentham first proposed it. He hoped its adoption would make the penal code more humane, end slavery and oppression everywhere, and make the world a happier place.

John Stuart Mill Revises Bentham's Principle

John Stuart Mill (1806–73), one of the greatest thinkers of the nineteenth century, stepped forward to defend Bentham's theory but with one modification. Mill argued that Bentham was wrong to claim that all kinds of pleasure are equal in moral value and can be measured in common units. Rather, the pleasures gained from intellectual pursuits such as the attainment of knowledge, friendship, and the appreciation of beauty are qualitatively more valuable than the bodily pleasures such as those gained from sex, food, and drugs. This thought led Mill to modify Bentham's utilitarianism. An action is morally right, he argued, only if it is the one action, of all possible actions, that maximizes in its consequences both the quantity and the *quality* of pleasure summed across everyone. On Mill's "ideal" version of utilitarianism, the right action is the one that results in the largest net quantity *and quality* of pleasure in the world.

Some of Bentham's defenders countered that Mill's theory of value is elitist, for it places the pleasures of the egghead intellectual and the wealthy patron of fine art above the pleasures of working-class people with less money who enjoy simpler pleasures.

A second problem was raised by mathematicians who pointed out that it is not possible to maximize two variables at once. Yet Mill's formula requires that we maximize both the quantity and the quality of pleasure. His formula, they observed, cannot be mathematically satisfied, which means that it cannot be realistically applied.

Nevertheless, both Bentham and Mill believed that utilitarianism, suitably defined, would become the first "scientific" theory of morality. They hoped that one day, after science had progressed far enough, instruments would be invented to accurately measure quantities of pleasure and pain. Using a pleasure meter, or "hedometer," people would one day determine with scientific precision exactly the right thing to do.[18]

Application

Let's now see how utilitarianism might be used to make a realistic moral decision. Suppose that a city buys a large, forested tract of land, and the question is, Should the land be sold to private developers, or should a public park be developed instead? At the city council meeting, some citizens argue that the land ought to be made into a public park. They offer this utilitarian argument:

1. The right thing to do is always that which produces the greatest net balance of pleasure over pain for all affected.

2. If the land is sold to private developers, a few wealthy families will buy it and enjoy it exclusively.

3. If the land is turned into a public park, everyone in the city will have an opportunity to enjoy it.

4. If everyone has an opportunity to enjoy the land, the greatest net balance of pleasure over pain will result.

5. Therefore, the land (morally) ought to be turned into a public park.

Utilitarianism has many attractive features. It is impartial, for when we calculate the quantity of expected net pleasure, each person counts equally in the calculation. Ten units of pleasure experienced by a poor person counts the same as ten units of pleasure experienced by a rich person. And when you make a utilitarian moral decision, it is not all about you; rather, everyone matters (and counts equally). Universalistic hedonism—utilitarianism—is a very *un*selfish ethical theory. But there are problems.

Utilitarian Suggestion. When you throw a rock into a pond, waves spread out in every direction. Similarly, nearly every choice you make affects other people. When you are about to act, think about the effects your action will have on others. Avoid actions that benefit only yourself. Choose actions that benefit everyone affected.

DIFFICULTIES FOR UTILITARIANISM

Measurement Problems

Utilitarianism in either form requires that we measure, or at least estimate, quantities of pleasure and pain and then add them up. But can pleasure be measured, even roughly, and then added in an objective way? What is the unit of measurement? This is the measurement problem, which actually breaks down into two more specific problems, the intrapersonal comparison problem and the interpersonal comparison problem.

The intrapersonal problem is, How do we measure and then add up one person's own quantities of pleasure? Herman Snodgrass, for example, is hungry. Which would give him more pleasure at the moment, a burrito, a hot dog, or three hamburgers? Or would he derive more pleasure from a diet and a new book? What could possibly be the common unit of measurement?

Suppose that we have solved this problem and can measure the different pleasures of any given individual. How can we add the units of pleasure experienced by one person to the units of pleasure experienced by another? This is the interpersonal problem. Utilitarianism seems to require calculations such as this one:

If we enact policy X, then:

1. Person A will experience ten units of pleasure.

2. Person B will experience fifteen units of pleasure.

3. Person C will experience ten units of displeasure.

4. Therefore, the total net balance of pleasure over displeasure will be plus fifteen units.

A calculation like this would require a common unit of interpersonal pleasure, but no such unit has been found. Many theorists argue that the pleasures experienced by different individuals are incommensurable, that is, they cannot be compared on a common scale. If so, then the maximization of pleasure required by utilitarianism lacks a practical meaning.

Concerns about Justice

One of the most serious concerns is that in some realistic situations — including situations that have actually occurred — utilitarianism requires that we sacrifice the rights and well-being of the few (and thus decrease their pleasure) for the sake of the increased pleasures experienced by the majority, when doing so maximizes the total net pleasure experienced in society. This can happen if we adopt utilitarianism, for the goal of maximizing net pleasure overall takes priority over everything else, *including the way pleasure is distributed.* But sacrificing the interests of the few for the sake of the well-being of the many seems unjust when considered rationally, doesn't it?

Consider a realistic example. If maximizing the sum total of pleasure is all that matters, regardless of how it is distributed, then it seems to follow that the sheriff must violate the rights of one individual in order to bring about the greatest quantity of pleasure expected to be experienced by everyone in the community, as in a case such as the following:

> A riotous mob in a small town wants to hang a homeless man because they believe he committed a certain crime. However, the sheriff and judge know that the man is innocent. The problem is that if the man is not turned over to the mob, many people will be killed and much property will be damaged because the mob is about to go on a violent rampage. If the details of this hypothetical case are filled out in such a way that the total quantity of pleasure in society will be maximized by turning the innocent man over to the mob, then utilitarianism requires turning him over to the mob.

This example is hypothetical, but something similar has happened in the real world.[19] Consider this hypothetical possibility as calmly and rationally as possible. Would sacrificing the man's life in this way and for the reason given violate his fundamental right to a fair trial? Would it violate his basic human right to life? Aren't these individual rights that should not be overridden merely to increase the total quantity of pleasure in society? If so, then utilitarianism is a flawed moral theory. Thus:

1. In some cases, utilitarianism would justify sacrificing the rights of the few to increase the summed pleasures of the majority.

2. If a proposed moral theory would justify sacrificing the rights of the few to increase the pleasures of the majority, that theory is false.

3. Therefore, utilitarianism is false.

However, in defense of their theory, utilitarians ask questions such as these: How would sacrificing a man for the benefit of the majority affect the man's friends and family? Wouldn't they suffer? If so, shouldn't their suffering (displeasure) be subtracted from the total pleasure produced? Furthermore, what effect would sacrificing the rights of an innocent person have on the judicial system? Wouldn't the result be detrimental to the system overall? If so, shouldn't those long-term negative effects also be factored into the utilitarian calculation? It seems likely, defenders of utilitarianism argue, that when all the pleasures and pains are added up, sacrificing the man's life for the benefit of the majority might *not* produce the greatest net balance of pleasure over pain. Utilitarianism in this case might call for measures to protect innocent life.

But critics of utilitarianism still worry that utilitarian calculations could, in many realistic situations, require violating the rights of the few to promote the summed up pleasures of the many. For this reason, they argue, utilitarianism is not consistent with the idea of universal human rights or with the inherent dignity, inviolability, and absolute worth of the individual. Are these reasons to reject utilitarianism? The author of the next theory, Immanuel Kant, answered yes.

Questions for Reflection and Discussion 12.3

1. Explain utilitarianism in plain, down-to-earth terms, as if you are talking to your neighbor.
2. Compare and contrast Aristotle's theory of virtue ethics and utilitarianism.

3. Compare and contrast utilitarianism and elementary ethical egoism.
4. Is utilitarianism a scientific theory of ethics? Can the measurement problems be solved? Discuss.
5. Critically evaluate utilitarianism. Some questions you might consider: Does utilitarianism conflict with some of our most certain moral judgments about human rights? Are there things that should never be done to a human being, even if doing so would probably maximize net pleasure summed across everyone affected?
6. Select an issue you feel passionate about, and construct a moral argument on the issue from a utilitarian standpoint.

KANT'S THEORY OF UNIVERSAL RESPECT

The most influential moral theory today among philosophers is not utilitarianism, it is a theory first developed and defended in the eighteenth century by the German philosopher Immanuel Kant (1724–1804), one of the greatest philosophers of the Enlightenment period of European history. Using a priori reasoning that is hard to follow and even harder to summarize, Kant argued that (1) there is one foundational principle of morality; (2) this one principle is rationally self-evident, that is, it can be known to be true a priori; and (3) all other moral principles follow deductively from it the way theorems follow from self-evident axioms in geometry. As Kant saw it, then, all of morality can be articulated in the form of an axiom system that contains one axiom and many theorems.

The foundational moral principle proposed by Kant has nothing to do with utility or the production of hedonistic pleasure. It is also not about pure self-interest. The right thing to do, Kant argued, is not the rational mean between two extremes, as in the philosophy of Aristotle. The ultimate moral standard is also not love, as it is in *agapism*, the theory of Saint Augustine. Kant's theory departs radically from all previous ethical theories. As historians of ethics have noted and as we'll see, Kant's theory of morality introduced strong notions of impartiality, individual freedom, individual rights, and moral autonomy (moral self-rule) to the field of ethics in new and systematic ways.[20] Kant's theory is closely related to the modern doctrine of universal human rights. This will all make sense shortly. But as usual, some definitions are needed before we proceed.

Maxims, Universal Laws, and Imperatives

Every time you do something intentionally, you act for a reason that can be expressed as a rule. The rule, or principle, of an intentional action can be stated with a sentence of the following form: "In a circumstance of kind C, I'll perform an act of kind A for a reason R." For instance, suppose that you want to lose weight and decide that eating fewer carbs is the right strategy. The rule presupposed by your action is, "If I want to lose weight, I'll eat fewer carbs." Kant called a rule like this the "maxim" of the corresponding action. Maxims, then, are personal principles, or rules, that serve as rationales for intentional actions.

Next, suppose that you are about to act on the basis of a maxim M in a particular situation. Now imagine that all people have internalized your maxim and are committed to acting on it whenever they are in a similar situation. In this case, Kant would say that your maxim has become a "universal law."

Finally, an *imperative* is a command. There are two kinds of imperatives. A *hypothetical imperative* is a command that applies only conditionally, that is, only in certain circumstances. This kind of imperative is usually expressed in the form of a conditional sentence of the form "if X, then Y." For example, if I want to lose weight, then I'll eat fewer carbs. A hypothetical imperative, Kant noted, applies to a person only on the condition that the person has the particular desire or goal identified by the imperative. For example, the imperative just stated applies only to someone who wants to lose weight.

A *categorical imperative*, on the other hand, is a command that applies categorically, that is, unconditionally. Thus, it applies to all people, regardless of anyone's goals, desires, or situation. So, whereas the logical form of a hypothetical imperative is "If you want X, then do Y," the logical form of a categorical imperative is "Do Y!"

Next, Kant observed, it is part of our moral common sense that true moral principles apply categorically, or unconditionally. That is, if X is the morally right thing to do, then you ought to do X regardless of whether you want to at the moment, regardless of whether doing X will maximize profits, satisfy your desires, or bring you pleasure, wealth, or power. It follows that true moral principles must be expressible in the form of categorical, rather than hypothetical, imperatives.

We are almost ready to turn to the principle that Kant believed is the most fundamental moral principle of all, which he named the *categorical imperative*. Kant believed that this principle is a precise and philosophical version of the Golden Rule (Do unto others as you would have them do unto you).

One last complication. Kant probably did not intend to make things more complex than they need to be, but he did just that when he stated the categorical imperative in four different ways and then claimed that all four statements amount to the same underlying idea.[21] We'll now examine three of his four formulations.

THE FIRST FORMULATION OF
THE CATEGORICAL IMPERATIVE

The Formula of Universal Law

Kant's first statement of the categorical imperative goes like this:

> Act only according to that maxim whereby you can, at the same time, consistently will that it is a universal law.[22]

Many books have been written trying to explain exactly what Kant meant by this statement. The following, in my opinion, is the most reasonable interpretation of what scholars call Kant's "formula of universal law."

> Your action is morally permissible if, and only if, its underlying maxim is such that you could act on it and achieve your goal within a society in which everyone else has internalized the same maxim and likewise acts on it when in a similar situation.

A maxim of action that satisfies this standard is said to be "universalizable." Kant's first principle can therefore be shortened to the following: *An act is morally permissible if, and only if, its maxim is universalizable.*

What is the significance of this rule? If the maxim on which you are acting is universalizable, there is a sense in which you are acting in moral solidarity with everyone else in society. For you are acting on a principle that applies universally and that would be accepted and followed universally if everyone were to be fully rational. Most importantly, you are acting on a principle that makes no special exception for yourself or anyone else.

This suggests a four-step test to determine whether an action is morally permissible according to the first statement of the categorical imperative.

The Universalizability Test

Step 1. Formulate the maxim of your action as clearly as you can.

Step 2. Imagine that you live in a world in which everyone has internalized your maxim and acts on it when in a similar circumstance.

Step 3. Ask yourself, "Could I act on my maxim and accomplish my goal in such a world, in solidarity with everyone else internalizing the maxim and acting on it when in the same situation?"

Step 4. If the answer is yes, the maxim of your action is universalizable, and your action is morally permissible. If the answer is no, your maxim is not universalizable, and your action is not morally permissible.[23]

Application

Consider an individual named Joe who wants a certain book but doesn't want to pay for it. He decides he will steal it from the public library. His maxim is, "If I want a book and don't want to pay for it, then I'll steal it from the public library." Now, if everyone were to internalize Joe's maxim and act on it when in a similar situation, public libraries would probably go bankrupt and close, and it would no longer be possible to steal books from public libraries. Thus, if everyone were to internalize Joe's maxim, he would no longer be able to act on it in universal solidarity with everyone else and achieve his goal. His maxim, then, fails the categorical imperative test—his action is morally wrong.

In effect, the categorical imperative requires that when we make a moral decision, we step back from our own self-interested point of view and evaluate our actions from an *impartial* viewpoint that takes everyone into account. From an impartial point of view, we only follow principles that apply universally and thus make no special exceptions for ourselves.

The immoral person, on Kant's view, is someone who says, in effect, "Everyone else should follow the moral rules. I'm going to violate them because I'm special. I'm an exception."

A Kantian Suggestion: When you are about to perform a morally signifi-cant action, ask yourself, What maxim am I acting upon? Am I acting on a principle that I want others to follow? Can I act on this principle in moral solidarity with everyone else?

Problems

In *The Shape of the Good*, the philosopher Stephen Layman asks us to con-sider the case of an accountant in an extremely law-abiding society who figures out a way to secretly avoid paying his share of the taxes.[24] No one will ever find out. Furthermore, his method—let's call it "method X"—is one only a few specially situated insiders could ever get away with. Here is one way to put his maxim:

> If I can employ method X and secretly avoid paying my fair share of taxes, I'll do so.[25]

Now, since few would ever be in a position to employ method X, it would make no difference if everyone were to internalize this crooked maxim. This maxim therefore seems to pass Kant's universalizability test. And any maxim that passes the test counts as permissible on Kant's theory. Yet isn't it clear and distinct, from a moral point of view, that the accountant's plan is mor-ally wrong? There's no reasonable justification for such behavior, is there? It follows that Kant's first formulation of the categorical imperative—the for-mula of universal law—does not accurately state a sufficient condition for moral rightness. Some bad actions slip through.

Recall that Kant expressed his ultimate principle, the categorical im-perative, in four different ways and claimed that all four statements amount to the same underlying idea. Perhaps the problem we've been discussing can be resolved if we turn to his second formulation of the categorical imperative.

THE SECOND FORMULATION OF
THE CATEGORICAL IMPERATIVE

The Formula of Humanity as an End in Itself

Known as the "formula of humanity as an end in itself" but also called the "formula of universal respect," Kant's second statement of the categorical imperative can be summarized as follows:

> Always treat every human being, including yourself, as an *end* and never merely as a *means* to an end.

This will take on a deeper meaning after Kant's special terminology is clarified. First, recall that a good of some kind possesses intrinsic or absolute value if it is valuable in itself and not merely as a means to an end. Next, one of our basic moral insights is that each human being possesses absolute or intrinsic value. But what internal quality makes a human being so valuable? Kant argues that each person has absolute value by virtue of possessing two capacities, or abilities: (1) a capacity for moral autonomy, which includes the power of free will, and (2) a capacity for rationality.

Moral autonomy. The basic meaning of autonomy is self-rule. A morally autonomous being has the capacity to recognize, acknowledge, and freely choose to follow the moral law. Put another way, a morally autonomous being has the power to recognize the moral law and freely impose it on himself or herself by following it in good faith. This explains what Kant means when he calls morally autonomous beings "self-lawgivers." Notice that moral autonomy presupposes free will.

Rationality. Rational beings are capable of recognizing and following objective standards of critical thinking.

Now for Kant's definition of an "end." An *end* is a being possessing three characteristics: (1) absolute or intrinsic value, (2) a capacity for moral autonomy, (3) a capacity for rationality.

Putting this all together, the second formulation of the categorical imperative requires that we treat ourselves and all others as free, equal, morally autonomous, rational, intrinsically valuable beings and never merely as tools or means to an end. In condensed form, the principle is simply: Never merely *use* another person as if he or she is your tool.

This is not a merely other-regarding principle. Since I myself meet conditions 1 through 3, I am required to treat myself just as I would anyone else. This is crucial, for otherwise autonomy decays into a right to treat myself shabbily, or allow others to treat me poorly, as long I am willing to accept it.[26]

The following corollary is extremely important. Kant argues that the moral status of each human being as an end is rooted in the individual person's mere humanity alone. Thus, the moral status of being an end rather than a means is independent of a person's socioeconomic status, wealth, income, talents, race, gender, religion, ethnicity, health, and nationality. The claim is important: being an end is a property we all possess merely by virtue of being *human*.

So, on Kant's view, we treat our fellow human beings unethically when we treat them merely as tools put on earth for our use, as if they are *not* free, intrinsically valuable, autonomous rational beings with goals and projects of their own.

Slavery is an obvious example of using others immorally. We all agree that slavery is wrong. Kant's theory explains *why* it is wrong and why it is wrong categorically. Slavery is wrong because the master uses the slave as if the slave is nothing more than a tool put on earth for his use, when the slave is actually a human being, and as a human being is an end in himself or herself. As an end, the slave is a free, morally autonomous, rational, and valuable being *who is equal in intrinsic moral value to the master*. It follows that the slave is a being who cannot rightfully be the property of another person. Other obvious examples of immoral using include sex trafficking, armed robbery, kidnapping, stealing, riot, and assault.

Kant also specifies corresponding accounts of respect and dignity to accompany his principle. When we refuse to merely *use* another person as if he or she is nothing more than a tool, we respect that person's dignity as an end. The second formulation of the categorical imperative can therefore be reformulated without loss of meaning;

> Always treat yourself and your fellow human beings with the respect and dignity due a free, rational, intrinsically valuable, morally autonomous being.

A Kantian Suggestion: Kant's account of ethics sounds abstract and complicated at first, but it actually inspires realistic suggestions that can help anyone improve his or her life, including the following bit of advice. Make it a habit to always, in every interaction, treat others with the utmost respect, concern, and dignity. You can avoid many sins and a great deal of trouble in life if you vow to always follow this bit of Kantian advice.

Treating Others Merely as a Means to an End

One more aspect of Kant's principle requires clarification. What does Kant mean when he claims that it is morally wrong to treat another person "merely" as a means to an end? He has in mind the following distinction. When we treat another person as a tool—without any regard at all for that person's intrinsic value and status as a morally autonomous being—we use that person "merely" as a means to our end. This kind of using, Kant believes, is always wrong.

However, as we go about our daily lives, we often must rely on the services of others, for example, when we get our hair cut, take a bus, buy groceries, or hire someone to fix our car. Also, we often get help from others, enter into contractual relationships for our own benefit, hire people, take jobs, and so forth. Kant argues that there is nothing wrong with using the services of others, or receiving benefits from others, if we are at the same time respecting them as free, intrinsically valuable, morally autonomous ends.

And how do we respect someone as an end while we are also doing business with them or benefiting from a relationship with them? At the very least, we refrain from violating their rights. Generally, when two people engage in a mutually voluntary and transparent rights-respecting transaction, such as when A buys a car from B in an honest deal or when someone buys groceries or when someone gets his or her hair cut, neither party treats the other *merely* as a means.

Kantian Suggestions

- When people are behaving in an unnecessarily harsh, angry, and cruel manner, tell them so, but tell them calmly, and respectfully.

Do not return like for like. Modeling a calm and respectful response may require that you wait until you have composed yourself. Calmness is more effective than anger.

- The current statutes on sexual and racial harassment and discrimination make sense from a Kantian perspective. Such behavior is morally wrong because it fails to respect the other person as an intrinsically valuable end.
- Sexual and racial harassment and discrimination can also be criticized from a biblical point of view. Such actions are not a loving way to treat a fellow human being.

Kant's ethics of universal respect and the Christian ethic of love intersect on many points.

THE FINAL FORMULATION OF
THE CATEGORICAL IMPERATIVE

The Formula of the Kingdom of Ends

The last version of Kant's categorical imperative to be considered here is known as the "formula of the kingdom of ends." Imagine a kingdom in which everyone always treats everyone as an end and never as a mere means. Each person is treated as a free, intrinsically valuable, morally autonomous being deserving of equal respect and dignity. That would be a kingdom of ends. With that thought in mind, here is my summary of what I personally find to be Kant's most inspiring interpretation of the categorical imperative:

> Your action is morally permissible if, and only if, the maxim of your action is such that you could act on it and achieve your goal in solidarity with everyone else within a kingdom of ends.

Is Kant's categorical imperative, in one form or another, the most fundamental moral principle of all? You be the judge.

Recall that according to eyewitnesses, Socrates treated everyone he met as a moral equal and believed that everyone is capable of living a moral life.

This is why he was willing to engage anyone from any walk of life in philosophical discussion, even children. Although he lived centuries before Kant, was Socrates a Kantian at heart?

KANT AND MODERN HUMAN RIGHTS THEORY

Some contemporary theorists of universal human rights justify rights on a utilitarian basis, but most justify rights on a Kantian basis. The following is a simplified Kantian argument for the universal right to life, understood as the right that others not take your life, except in self-defense or to protect the life of an innocent person.

1. Each person must always be treated as an end, that is, as a free, rational, intrinsically valuable, morally autonomous being deserving of equal respect and dignity, and never merely as a means to an end.

2. Except in cases of self-defense or to protect innocent life, forcefully taking away someone's life treats that person as if he or she is not an end.

3. Therefore, it is morally wrong to forcefully take away a person's life, except in self-defense or to protect innocent life. This is a statement of the universal right to life.

Similar Kantian arguments have been given for the rights to liberty, to own property, to vote, to protest laws one believes are unjust, to petition the government, to form independent political parties, and to the freedoms of speech, association, and religion.

Rights, Duties, and Responsibilities

The familiar rights to "life, liberty, and the pursuit of happiness" that Jefferson placed in the Declaration of Independence are called "claim rights" by philosophers and legal theorists because they ground moral claims addressed to all others. Every claim right implies a corresponding duty. If everyone has a right to life, then it follows logically that everyone has a duty to not take the life of another person (except in self-defense or to protect an innocent life). Rights and duties thus fit together like two sides of the same coin. This is what human rights theorists mean when they say that rights and duties are "correlative." In a rights-respecting society, your rights are protected by the state. However, responsible, rights-respecting behavior is expected in return.

Another important distinction is the difference between negative and positive rights. A *negative* right is a right that others *not* do certain specified things to you. A *positive* right is a right to be given something or to have something done for you. Negative and positive claim rights imply different kinds of duties. Positive claim rights impose *duties of assistance*. If you have a positive claim right to something, then others have a duty to give you something or do something for you. Negative claim rights impose *duties of forbearance*. If you have a negative claim right of a certain kind, then others have a duty to not aggressively and forcefully interfere in your life in certain ways.

The familiar rights to life, liberty, and the pursuit of happiness have traditionally been understood as negative in character. For example, the right to life is the right that others *not* take your life (except in self-defense and so forth); it is not the (positive) right to be given everything you need to live. Kant argued that rights and duties are correlative; however, there is a debate (which we will not enter) as to whether he held that all basic rights are negative in character.

Rights as End-Constraints

As Kant understood them, human rights, like all moral principles, are categorical. As such, they supersede all other considerations, such as calculations of profit, pleasure, self-interest, and the utilitarian summed happiness of the majority. If Kant is correct, the rights of an individual cannot be overridden for any non-rights-based reason.

Thus, on the Kantian view, some things categorically cannot be done to any individual, no matter what, that is, no matter what alleged good may result someday. What sorts of things cannot ever be done to an individual? The actions blocked by negative rights. Human rights draw a moral boundary or fence around each person that categorically cannot be crossed *no matter what end goal one is pursuing*. Rights thus place categorical constraints on the ends one is pursuing.

For example, Peter can imagine lots of good things he could do with Paul's money. But no matter how good those things are, that fact does not justify violating Paul's property rights by stealing his money. During the twentieth century, many communist states violated the basic human rights of their people on massive scales to bring about what they claimed would be (in the distant future) a "worker's paradise."[27] On Kant's view, no matter how good the end result is thought to be, it is wrong to bring it about by violating human rights. In short: the end never justifies the means.

These thoughts are implied by the Kantian doctrine of the absolute value and moral inviolability of the individual person understood as an end. Kant's philosophy of human rights holds many implications for political philosophy, the subject we will briefly enter in chapter 13.

DIFFICULTIES FOR KANT'S THEORY

Kant argues that human beings are ends and that they are ends by virtue of possessing rationality, free will, and moral autonomy. But what about those who have lost these capacities, such as elderly people in nursing homes suffering from dementia or people born with severe impairments? Kant's theory seems to imply that they are not intrinsically valuable ends. But if they are not, then according to his theory, we have no moral obligations to them. Yet surely the elderly and the impaired are intrinsically valuable beings who *deserve* to be treated with the same respect we show to anyone else. Isn't it one of our deepest and most reasonable moral judgments that *every* person is worthy of the same respect and dignity, regardless of abilities and health?

Kant's theory could be modified to handle this objection by adding the following spiritual postulate. Suppose that each person is an immaterial soul temporarily animating a physical body. We examined this view in chapter 10—this is mind-body dualism. Suppose further that the absolute value of an individual is rooted *not* in that person's body or in his or her current abilities, but in that person's immaterial soul, understood as a creation of God and the basis of the human *potential* to reason, act freely, and exercise moral autonomy—whether those capacities are expressed, temporarily lost, or yet to be expressed. Supplemented in this way, Kant's theory implies that every person deserves categorical respect, even those who have lost their capacities through a disease such as dementia, even those born with disabilities, and even those who have not yet developed their capacities, such as babies and unborn persons.

Another objection concerns animals. Kant's theory, at least as he presented it, does not explain the moral respect we owe to our animal companions and other animals. Personally, one of my firmest moral convictions is that our beloved cats Orangie, Baby, and Worty, taken in as strays only to become members of the family, were intrinsically valuable beings who deserved to be treated with love and respect. Kant's theory leaves them out, for it only refers to autonomous beings who can be held morally responsible for their choices. Can his theory be modified to justify the respect we owe to nonhuman animals?

Each of the six major ethical theories we've examined has its strengths and weaknesses. Perhaps you will formulate your own theory by combining aspects of two, three, or of all six.

Questions for Reflection and Discussion 12.4

1. Explain one form of the categorical imperative. Describe a practical application.
2. What is the difference between treating someone merely as a means to an end and treating someone as an end.
3. Construct an argument against racial discrimination, on the basis of Kant's ethical theory.
4. Construct an argument against racial discrimination, on the basis of Christian virtue ethics.
5. Pick a recognized human right, and give a Kantian argument for that right.
6. Christians are called to love their neighbors as themselves. They are called to love every human being. What is the connection between respecting others in a Kantian sense and loving others in a Christian sense?
7. How does Kant's categorical imperative relate to the Golden Rule? Is his theory a philosophical version of that rule? What is the connection between respecting others in the Kantian sense and treating others as you would have them treat you?

Or Should We All Become
Moral Relativists?

BACK TO THE FUTURE

Different societies have different moral codes. Some things generally considered morally right in one society are generally considered morally wrong in others. The website antislavery.org estimates that 40.3 million people still live in legally condoned slavery in various parts of the world.[1] In some traditional cultures, wife-burning, arranged marriages (sometimes involving children), and honor killing are still accepted and practiced. According to Amnesty International, homosexuality carries the death penalty in many countries. At present, it is illegal to be transgender in seventy-seven nations around the world.

The ancient Greeks were the first to write about the diversity of morals across different cultures and to philosophize about the fact. Herodotus (ca. 484–ca. 425 BC), the founder of history as an academic subject, observed in his *Histories* that some actions thought to be morally right in one society are thought to be wrong in others. He also observed that people everywhere uncritically prefer the morals of their own culture.[2]

From the fact that moral beliefs differ from society to society, many people conclude that there are no objectively true and universally valid moral truths. Morality, they claim, is relative to society or culture. On this view, if a particular kind of action is deemed morally right in one society, then in that society that action *is* morally right. Furthermore, there is no objective or rational basis from which to criticize that society for its moral beliefs. So, if one society practices slavery and slavery is considered morally right in that society, then slavery is morally right in that society, and no one has any objective or rational basis for condemning or criticizing that society for practicing slavery. Likewise, if one society outlaws slavery and holds that it is morally wrong, then slavery is wrong in that society, and no one has any reasonable basis for objecting to that society's laws against slavery.

Others take the relativist idea further and argue that morality is relative to each person rather than to each culture or society. If an individual believes that some action is right, they say, then that action is right for that person and there is no objective basis from which to criticize that person for his moral views or actions. Each person is right on matters of morality; no person is ever wrong on any moral issue.

So, for example, if one person practices racial discrimination and believes it is morally right, then racial discrimination is right for that person, and there are no rational or objective grounds for objecting when that person discriminates.

Some people believe that moral relativism is a new, cutting-edge idea. They are wrong; it is as old as the hills. In Socrates's day, moral relativism was espoused by many of the Sophists, itinerant teachers who traveled around Greece offering private instruction in subjects such as rhetoric, athletics, writing, and poetry.

Socrates entered the *agora* to challenge the Sophistic relativists of his day and to argue that reasonable moral principles can be discovered using our critical-thinking skills and common sense. Before we go any further, we must clarify some basic terms, or things will get cloudy quickly.

SOME BASIC TERMINOLOGY

First, the meaning of *relative* needs clarification. Suppose that someone says or writes, "Los Angeles is near." Is this statement true or false? It depends. Before we can say, we need a definition of *near*, and we need to know where the person making the statement is located. Let *near* mean "within 50 miles." Now the question to ask is, "Near what?" Until the sentence is related to a location, it is incomplete and is neither true nor false.

If we complete the sentence as follows, it expresses the truth: "Los Angeles is near Long Beach." And if we complete the sentence this way it is false: "Los Angeles is near New York City." Thus, the sentence "Los Angeles is near" is "locationally relative" because it is neither true nor false until it is relativized to a specific location. Relative to Long Beach, the sentence is true; relative to New York City, the sentence is false. In general, relative statements are incomplete and only become complete when they are related to something.

Now, moral relativists believe that moral statements are relative. They claim that a moral statement such as "slavery is wrong" is like the statement "Los Angeles is near." Both statements, they say, are incomplete and only become complete (and thus true or false) when they are relativized to something. A statement such as "slavery is wrong" is thus true or false only relative to a particular society (says a societal relativist) or relative to an individual person (says an individual relativist), just as "Los Angeles is near" is true or false only relative to a physical reference point or location.

Moral objectivists disagree. They agree with Socrates and maintain that if we are willing to reason together, we will discover objectively true moral statements. What is an objectively true statement? In general, a statement is objectively true when its truth comports with the way the world is rather than to what we happen to believe about the world. Consider the proposition that the value of *pi* (the ratio of a circle's circumference to its diameter) is 3.14159. Anyone familiar with math knows that this statement is true, However, our belief that the statement is true is not what makes it true. The statement is true because it corresponds to the facts, specifically, the facts about the circle. And the facts about the circle are what they are regardless of what we believe about the circle. It would be true that *pi* equals 3.14159, even if we did not believe it to be true. *Pi* would be 3.14159, even if we had never discovered the fact. Indeed, even if a dictator were to conquer the world and convince everyone that *pi* is equal to 3, it would remain true that *pi* is 3.14159.

The point is that the value of *pi* is what it is whether or not we believe it. This is what makes the value of *pi* an objective truth—it is a truth about the way the world is rather than about what we believe about the world.

Another example is the claim that there are craters on the surface of the moon. Clearly also an objective truth.

Likewise, the moral objectivist claims that some moral statements are true *not* because we believe them but because they correspond to the facts or to reality. True moral statements are true because that is the way the world is. A closely related idea is that of an objective moral standard. Objective moral standards, if any exist, apply not because everyone accepts them but because they correspond to reality. They are true because they reflect the way the world really is. With the foregoing in mind, it is time to state the precise definitions that will help keep us on track.

- *Moral objectivism* is the view that at least some moral statements and standards are objectively true.
- *Moral universalism* is the related view that (1) objectively true moral principles exist, and (2) objectively true moral principles apply to every human being regardless of their culture, nationality, or beliefs.
- *Moral absolutism* is the view that true moral rules have no exceptions.

Not all moral objectivists accept moral absolutism. Many objectivists believe that true moral principles allow for principled exceptions. For instance, most objectivists would argue that it is wrong to kill another person, *except* in self-defense or to protect an innocent life. A moral objectivist could also believe that some objectively true moral principles have exceptions and others do not.

However, most moral objectivists are moral universalists, for most moral objectivists hold that objective moral principles apply to all human beings alike. Moral universalism, because it includes the claim that some objectively true moral principles exist, is a version of moral objectivism.

Moral relativism is the view that moral statements and standards are relative rather than objective or universal. There are two versions. According to societal relativism (also called cultural relativism), each society creates its own morality, and there is no universal or objective basis from which to judge the moral standards of any given society. Put another way, moral statements are only true relative to societies. So, if a society believes that slavery is morally right, then slavery is morally right *in that society* and there is no rational or objective basis for anyone to say that the slave-owning society is wrong to permit slavery.

According to individual relativism (also called moral subjectivism), moral standards are true only relative to individuals. If a person believes that beating up people at random just for fun is morally right, then beating up people for fun is morally right *for that person*, and there is no rational basis for anyone to say that the person is wrong when he assaults strangers on the street.

Moral nihilism (Latin *nihil*, "nothing") is a rejection of both moral objectivism and moral relativism. According to this view, moral properties and values (relative or objective) do not exist at all. Morality, whether objective or relative, is a total illusion. The world consists solely of morally neutral objects; it contains no moral values or properties in any sense. Both relativism and nihilism deny the existence of objective moral truths (and thus call for a skeptical attitude with respect to moral objectivity), but relativism at least admits the existence of relative moral truths. Nihilism goes further and claims that moral value, whether relative or objective, does not exist.

But moral nihilism has extremely counterintuitive consequences. If the world contains no moral properties and if all moral value is a complete illusion, then the Nazi Holocaust was not a morally bad thing, and the actions of one of the worst dictators in world history were not morally unjust. If moral nihilism is true, the Nazis violated no human rights (because human rights don't exist if moral nihilism is true); there is nothing morally wrong with racial discrimination, and genocide is not a morally bad thing at all. Nothing is morally wrong if moral nihilism is true because, according to moral nihilism, the world contains no moral properties or values at all.

Can anyone seriously believe that the world contains no moral qualities at all? Can anyone believe that there was nothing morally wrong with the Holocaust? Can anyone seriously say that there's nothing morally wrong with genocide? Moral nihilism is radically contrary to our shared moral common sense. And what kind of society would result if we all became moral nihilists? This is one view that will not be considered further in this book.

ARGUMENTS FOR SOCIETAL RELATIVISM

Some endorse societal relativism because they are convinced by the societal differences argument, sometimes called the "anthropologist's argument" because it has been given by prominent anthropologists.[3]

The Societal Differences Argument

1. Different societies have different moral codes.

2. No moral principle has won universal acceptance across all societies.

3. The best explanation of these facts is that objective moral truths do not exist; rather, morality is relative to each society.

4. Therefore, societal relativism is true.

Although this argument has seemed convincing to many, it has serious flaws. First, the second premise is false. As we saw in chapter 12, many moral principles are accepted universally. C. S. Lewis identifies numerous examples in *The Abolition of Man*.

Second, the argument is no better than the following parallel argument:

1. Different societies have different views on the causes of disease. In some societies people believe that diseases are caused by witches; in other societies people believe that diseases are caused by viruses and bacteria.

2. No theory of pathology has gained universal acceptance.

3. The best explanation of these facts is that there are no objective truths about the cause of disease; any theory of disease is true only relative to a given society's beliefs.

4. Therefore, pathological relativism is true.

Is this a strong argument? It is not. The third premise is false. Medical science has discovered many objective facts about disease, including that most disease is caused by bacteria and viruses. Those who believe that disease is caused by witches are simply ignorant. They need to learn more about the world. But if this argument does not work, then neither does the societal differences argument, which has the same logical structure.

In other words, just as we cannot reason from the fact that different societies have different beliefs about pathology to the claim that the truth about disease is relative to culture, we cannot reason from the fact that different societies have different beliefs about morality to the conclusion that societal relativism is true. Perhaps some societies are just mistaken on some moral matters. Perhaps people in these societies need to look in the mirror and engage in some serious critical thinking. The societal differences argument does not establish its conclusion.

Some have argued for societal relativism in this closely related way:

1. If moral objectivism is true, then we should expect everyone around the world to have the same moral beliefs.

2. But people around the world do not have the same moral beliefs.

3. Therefore, moral objectivism is false and societal relativism is true.

The problem with this argument is that there is no good reason to believe that its first premise is true. Furthermore, no moral objectivist claims that if moral objectivism is true, then everyone around the world agrees on all moral matters. The world contains a great deal of ignorance, including moral ignorance.

The Tolerance Argument

Others have endorsed societal relativism on the basis of the tolerance argument:

1. Tolerance is an extremely important moral value.

2. Everyone in every culture everywhere therefore ought to be tolerant of the moral codes of all other societies.

3. Moral universalism logically implies intolerance toward others, while societal relativism implies tolerance toward others.

4. So, societal relativism is the better theory.

This argument also has problems. Notice that premises 1 and 2 are *objective* and *universal* moral claims. Neither premise is a relative statement. A logically consistent societal relativist therefore cannot endorse the first two premises! Keep in mind that according to societal relativism, there are no true universal moral principles. Because the first two premises of this argument are presented as universally true, they actually contradict the tenets of societal relativism.

Furthermore, premise 3 of this argument is false. For contrary to popular belief, societal relativism does not logically imply tolerance, and moral universalism does not imply intolerance. Let's examine.

Societal relativism states that what's right in society A is determined only by society A's moral code. It follows, if societal relativism is true, that if you live in an *in*tolerant society, you should be intolerant of other societies, not tolerant. A consistent societal relativist therefore cannot consistently call for universal tolerance.

This point is so often missed in discussions on the topic that it deserves emphasis. According to societal relativism, if one society believes that intolerance is morally right, then intolerance is morally right in that society, period. When confronted with an intolerant society, a logically consistent relativist can only say, "There's nothing wrong with what they are doing." Only a moral universalist can consistently endorse universal tolerance.

The upshot surprises many people. If you believe in universal tolerance, you are a moral universalist, not a relativist, whether you realize it or not. The tolerance argument for societal relativism fails.

CHALLENGES FOR SOCIETAL RELATIVISM

If a theory has logical implications that are absurd or that contradict what seems extremely certain, that is a good reason to reject the theory. This is a principle of reasoning we employ in everyday life and in every academic subject. For instance, during the early part of the twentieth century, physicists in England and the United States discovered that atoms have an inner structure. However, when they applied the equations of Newtonian physics to the new data, the equations predicted events that did not subsequently occur. For example, the equations predicted that atoms are short-lived objects that collapse in a matter of minutes. Since an implication of the theory was obviously false, physicists began searching for a better theory.

Critics of societal relativism argue that the theory has logical implications that contradict propositions that are clearly and distinctly true. Five such implications of societal relativism will now occupy our attention.

Implication 1

If societal relativism is true, then critical thinking about our own society's moral values is impossible.

According to societal relativism, rational, cross-cultural moral judgments are impossible. That is, there is no rational or objective basis from which the moral code of another society can be judged. Therefore, we have no legitimate basis for criticizing the moral practices of another society, period.

This sounds right to many people today, but the claim has a surprising consequence. If there is no objective or rational basis from which to criticize the morals of another society, then there is no objective or rational basis from which to criticize the moral code of our *own* society. For any objective or rational basis suitable for criticizing our own society would also be a basis from which to criticize any other society. Societal relativism therefore implies that there is no rational or objective basis from which to criticize the moral code of our own society.

But is it true that critical thinking cannot be applied to the moral values of our society? As Socrates would say, let's examine. Isn't it just about as clear and distinct as anything can be that our society's moral code is not perfect and that it *can* be subjected to Socratic examination? Critical thinking means evaluating something on the basis of independent standards related to truth.

Isn't it just obvious that at least some aspects of our society's moral code can be judged on the basis of independent standards? For instance, on the basis of human rights? Or on the grounds of Kant's principle of universal respect? Not if societal relativism is true.

Our first argument against societal relativism therefore goes like this:

1. If societal relativism is true, then our society's moral code cannot be critically examined in a Socratic fashion,

2. But our society's moral code can be criticized and examined in a Socratic fashion.

3. Therefore, societal relativism is false.

Implication 2

If societal relativism is true, then social conformism follows.

This implication is related to the first. We've already seen that if societal relativism is true, there is no truth in morality higher than your own society's social mores. It follows that your own society's social mores cannot be criticized or critically examined. The only thing to do morally, then, is to accept and conform to your society's moral values. This position is known as *social conformism*: each of us ought to conform to our society's existing moral code and never question it. So, for example, if you live in a racist society, you should be a racist. If you live in a sexist society, you should be a sexist, and so forth. There is no need to think critically about morality—always simply do what your society's mores require. But surely social conformism is false. Thus:

1. If societal relativism is true, then social conformism is true.

2. But surely social conformism is false.

3. Therefore, societal relativism is false.

Implication 3

If societal relativism is true, then every society is infallible on matters of morality.

An authority is infallible if it cannot be mistaken. If societal relativism is true, it follows that each society is infallible on matters of morality. That is, no society anywhere on earth is, or even can be, mistaken on *any* moral matter. For if societal relativism is true, there are no objective standards by which the moral code of any society might be examined and found to be mistaken.

Is this implication of societal relativism believable? Don't we have strong reasons to believe that the Nazis were mistaken on at least *one* moral issue? For instance, on the matter of the Holocaust? Aren't there a few societies on earth today that need some correction? Not if societal relativism is true. Doesn't this implication of societal relativism—that every society is infallible on matters of morality—conflict with statements that are clearly and distinctly true? Thus:

1. If societal relativism is true, each society is infallible on matters of morality.

2. It is false that each society is infallible on matters of morality.

3. Thus, societal relativism is false.

Implication 4

If societal relativism is true, then moral reformers are always wrong.

A moral reformer is an individual who criticizes his or her society's moral code on the basis of independent moral standards. At the same time, the reformer urges positive change. The United States has a long history of efforts aimed at moral reform. Noteworthy reformers include the abolitionists of the nineteenth century, the great Frederick Douglass, advocates for workers' rights, Susan B. Anthony, the suffragettes, and Martin Luther King Jr.

However, as we've seen, if societal relativism is true, there is no rational or independent basis from which to criticize in a Socratic way *any* society on moral grounds. Furthermore, if societal relativism is true, every society is correct on all moral matters. Therefore, if societal relativism is true, it follows that no society needs correction, and every moral reformer is simply wrong to criticize.

Are these implications of societal relativism acceptable? Weren't the abolitionists clearly right to condemn slavery? Didn't they have the best reasons on their side? Wasn't Dr. King obviously right to criticize the system of legal segregation known as Jim Crow? Didn't he have the strongest reasons on his side? Not if societal relativism is true. Decide for yourself, on the basis of the best considerations. In short:

1. If societal relativism is true, social reformers have always been wrong.

2. But it is false that social reformers have always been wrong.

3. Therefore, societal relativism is false.

Implication 5

If societal relativism is true, then moral progress is impossible.

Progress implies improvement as measured by an independent standard of value. Suppose that Ed is one hundred pounds overweight, and a doctor tells him that his health will improve if he loses weight. Six months later, Ed has lost fifty pounds, and the doctor tells him that he has made great progress. The doctor is defining Ed's progress in terms of an independent standard of health, a standard above and beyond Ed's actual health. To say that Ed has made progress is to say that he has improved as measured by an objective medical standard.

As we've seen, societal relativism maintains that there is no objective moral standard above the moral code of any society by which it can be judged. It follows, if societal relativism is true, that there is no logical or objective basis from which to say that our society, or any society on earth, has improved morally over time. Indeed, if societal relativism is true, moral improvement is conceptually incoherent and logically impossible.

But isn't it obvious that the abolition of slavery in the United States (and in many other places around the world) in the nineteenth century constituted real moral progress? Wasn't the advent of universal adult suffrage a moral improvement? Aren't there good reasons to suppose so? Not if societal relativism is true.

In chapter 12, we examined reasons to believe that slavery was a grave moral injustice and that its abolition was moral progress. It was wrong because it violated universal human rights. It was wrong because freedom is a universal human value. It was also wrong because it is immoral to use another human being as if he or she is a mere tool, without regard to his or her humanity. The abolition of slavery was moral progress because it led to more just (if not yet perfectly just) societies around the world. The societal relativist, of course, disagrees. Which shows once again that societal relativism conflicts with things we have good reason to believe are true. Is this yet another reason to reject the theory? Or can the theory be defended? You decide.

1. If societal relativism is true, moral progress is impossible.

2. But moral progress has occurred.

3. Therefore, societal relativism is false.

IS INDIVIDUAL RELATIVISM TRUE?

According to individual relativism (also called "moral subjectivism"), if a person believes an action is right, then that makes the action right for that person, and there is no objective basis from which to say that the person's action is morally wrong. If individual relativism is true, there is no objective or rational basis from which to judge the actions of another person. It follows, if individual relativism is true, that there is no rational basis from which to criticize the actions of the infamous serial killer Gary Ridgway, a man who was convicted of killing forty-nine innocent women during the 1980s and 1990s.

An advocate of individual relativism must also say that there is no rational basis from which to criticize the actions of Adolf Hitler, Josef Stalin, Mao Tse-tung, and Pol Pot, including the decisions they made that sent millions of innocent men, women, children, and babies to their deaths. Critical thinking cannot be applied to their actions.

Are these implications of the view acceptable? Is there really no rational basis from which to criticize the morals of these mass killers? Or can the actions of these moral monsters be questioned and criticized on the basis of reasonable moral considerations?

Here is a start: the actions of these terrible human beings were objectively wrong because they violated the universal human rights of their victims. Isn't that a reasonable basis for criticism? Doesn't every human being have the right to life? Isn't it as reasonable and certain as anything can be that the actions of these moral monsters were wrong in an objective sense? Thus, we might argue:

1. If individual relativism is true, there is no objective basis from which to criticize the actions of mass killers such as Hitler, Stalin, Mao Tse-tung, and Pol Pot.

2. This implication of the theory is absurd—the actions of such moral monsters can be criticized on reasonable grounds.

3. Therefore, individual relativism is false.

Individual relativism has other problems. The individual relativist maintains that an action is morally right for a person if that person believes it is right, even if the person's belief is based on hatred, cognitive bias, prejudice, ignorance, faulty thinking, willful blindness, or unexamined cultural conditioning. Don't we all agree that these implications of individual relativism are also false?

Another logical implication of individual relativism is equally hard to accept: if the theory is true, each person is an infallible expert on matters of morality. For according to individual relativism, each person has his or her own moral code, and there is no basis from which to say that one person's code is mistaken—on anything. Therefore, if individual moral relativism is true, each person is right on every moral issue, no one has ever been mistaken on *any* moral matter. Is this consequence of the view believable? Is it reasonable to believe that Stalin and Hitler were never mistaken on even *one* moral issue? Stalin intentionally killed at least 5 million poor farmers in the Ukraine when they refused to turn over their pitiful supplies of grain to his army. Was Stalin really an infallible expert on morality? He was if individual relativism is true.[4]

REASON: OUR COMMON CURRENCY IN MATTERS OF MORALITY

The ethical objectivist claims that the moral codes of both societies and individuals can be questioned and subjected to Socratic examination on the basis of reasoned critical thinking. Perhaps there is something to the objectivist claim, given the problems we have found with both forms of moral relativism.

Socrates urged us to look in the mirror and examine our basic assumptions, beliefs, and values honestly on the basis of rational, reality-based criteria or standards. He firmly believed that if we will reason together calmly, accurately, and honestly, we will discover objectively true moral principles. Most moral philosophers agree. They believe that in matters of morality, we will make progress if we reason together using our own cognitive abilities. They believe, in short, that reason is our common currency.

Questions for Reflection and Discussion, Interlude 2

1. Compare and contrast moral absolutism, moral universalism, and moral objectivism.
2. In your own words, explain societal relativism. How does the view differ from individual relativism?
3. Evaluate one of the arguments for societal relativism.

4. Can a societal relativist advocate universal tolerance without inconsistency?

5. Are at least some moral values or principles accepted universally? Is the world moving toward agreement on some issues?

6. Can slavery be criticized on the basis of objective reasons? If so, what would those reasons be? Offer the most intelligent and strongest reasons you can for your position.

7. Can genocide be criticized on the basis of objective reasons? If so, what would those reasons be? Offer the most intelligent and strongest reasons you can for your position.

8. Can we make cross-cultural moral judgments on the basis of objective moral grounds? Offer the most intelligent and strongest reasons you can for your position.

9. Can the actions of a school shooter be criticized on rational moral grounds? If so, does this prove that individual relativism is false?

10. What would society be like if everyone believed that individual relativism is true?

THIRTEEN

Moral Reasoning
Applied to the State

THE BIRTH OF MODERN POLITICAL PHILOSOPHY

Political philosophy is the philosophical study of the nature and proper role of government, the rights and responsibilities of the individual, freedom, and related issues. In the *Republic*, Plato developed the first systematic political philosophy in written form in world history. Aristotle took the subject further in the *Politics*. During the thirteenth century, Thomas Aquinas produced an influential medieval theory in his "Treatise on Law," a part of his major work *Summa theologica*. Ancient and medieval political philosophy are required reading for anyone who wants to see in-depth how we arrived at our present understanding of government. But the modern framework within which most of us think today first took form in Europe during the sixteenth and seventeenth centuries as new ideas on freedom and the rights of the individual were circulated for debate in England and across the European continent in books, sermons, and public forums.[1]

The first distinctively modern political philosophy was originally called "liberalism" because it championed the freedom, or liberty, of the individual against the power of the state. As new variations on the original ideal of liberty emerged in Europe during the nineteenth and twentieth centuries, the first school of liberal thought became known as "classical liberalism," and the later theories that grew out of it were grouped under the heading "modern liberalism." In this chapter, we'll examine both classical and modern liberalism, and there will be plenty of food for thought.

THE IDEALS OF CLASSICAL LIBERALISM

The classical liberals certainly built on ideas going back to ancient Greece and Rome and to wisdom recorded in the Old and the New Testaments. But they added new elements of their own. The ideals they championed during the sixteenth and seventeenth centuries should sound familiar to all of us today.

1. Every human being—regardless of social status, wealth, income, nationality, religion, talents, looks, and so forth—possesses an absolute and equal value and dignity by virtue of his or her humanity alone that even the highest authorities must respect.
2. Each person by virtue of his or her humanity alone possesses inalienable rights that can be asserted against every other person and even against the highest authorities, including the state.
3. That among these rights are the (negative) rights to life, liberty, and property.
4. A legitimate government derives its authority not from God, heaven, or some higher realm above but from the rational and freely given consent of the people.
5. The primary purpose of any legitimate government is not to enrich the rulers, exploit the people, conquer territory, equalize income and wealth, build a perfect society, or force everyone to follow a particular religion or a prespecified form of life. Rather, it is to serve the people by protecting their inherent rights to life, liberty, and property—rights they possess by virtue of their God-given human nature alone.
6. The rights of the individual are most secure when they are protected by an elected government whose power is limited by a reasonable constitution or duly promulgated laws endorsed by the people on the basis of rational considerations.[2]

7. To prevent tyranny, the powers of the state should never be concentrated in the hands of one person or one governmental body; they should be separated and balanced.[3]

Keep in mind as we proceed that these are ideals. Ideals guide us as we seek to improve our present condition. They are aspirational rather than descriptive of reality as it currently is.

The classical liberal ideals sound commonplace today. It is easy to forget that they were revolutionary claims when the first liberals argued for them near the beginning of the modern period. Never before in the history of the world had such principles been championed by a political movement basing its claims on philosophical arguments. When the classical liberals began arguing for constitutionally limited, representative government, equality before the law, and universal human rights, most people around the world lived in societies where these philosophical concepts didn't even exist.[4]

Imago Dei

One fundamental doctrine motivating early classical liberal thought deserves special mention because of its historical and lasting significance. Most of the first classical liberals were inspired by a biblical idea that goes back to both the Jewish and Christian traditions, known as the doctrine of the *imago Dei*, "the image of God." This is the claim that the image of God is reflected in each human being, and by virtue of this reflection, each person possesses a sacredness, a dignity, an absolute value that must always be respected. The doctrine of the *imago Dei* appears in Genesis. It can also be found in the New Testament, in other world religions, and in the Greek and Roman philosophy of Stoicism. The seven classical liberal ideals listed above can all be supported on the basis of the doctrine using obvious arguments.[5]

IN SEARCH OF PHILOSOPHICAL FOUNDATIONS

We examined Kant's moral theory in chapter 12. Kant was a classical liberal, and his moral philosophy was a milestone in classical liberal thought. Many historians of philosophy believe that the classical liberal ideal received its fullest philosophical expression at the end of the eighteenth century in Kant's ethical theory. Intuitive considerations suggest that Kant's theory of universal respect provided a strong philosophical basis for the classical liberal ideals. However, a century before Kant, the English philosopher John Locke (1632–1704) offered a different but complementary basis in his *Two Treatises of Government* (1689). Locke's philosophy is as important as Kant's for an understanding of modern political thought.[6]

Locke's Argument for Classical Liberalism

When Locke began writing his two-volume defense of classical liberalism, the big question was, What is the logical basis of legitimate government? Locke approached the problem analytically. The method of analysis—to understand a complex whole, we must first break it down to its elementary parts—had already proved itself in physics, chemistry, and many other subjects. Applied to the state, the analytic approach requires that we uncover the elementary building blocks of legitimate government and then proceed from there.

The best way to do this, Locke argues, is to imagine that we have all been temporarily deposited in a *state of nature* (a state of affairs lacking all government) in which we are all free, equal, and reasoning at our best. Although government and human laws would not exist, the natural moral law would exist, and we would know it using our common human reason, for we would all know, using our rational faculties alone, the difference between right and wrong and good and bad.

Notice that Locke sides with Socrates on this matter—morality is an objective feature of the universe, and its laws can be discovered through critical reasoning. On matters of morality, reason is our common currency.

What specifically would we discover? If we reasoned at our best, Locke argues, we would know the first two axioms, or elementary principles, of the moral law, which political theorists of his day called the "natural law."

1. *The Axiom of Universal Moral Equality*: All human beings stand equal before the moral law.

2. *The Axiom of Individual Self-Ownership*: Each person is the morally rightful owner of his or her own self, "all being kings."

The meaning of the first axiom should be reasonably clear. Moral principles apply to all in the same way. No one is an exception; no one is above or below the moral law. The head of state, for example, must live by the same basic rules followed by everyone else. Does this principle seem reasonable to you?

The second axiom sounds puzzling at first glance. What does it mean to "own" yourself? Here is an imperfect analogy. If you own your car, then you are in charge of it. Others must ask your permission if they want to drive it or ride in it. On the other hand, it is your responsibility to change the oil, fill the gas tank, and take it in for service at regular intervals. And given that we are all morally equal, your control over your car has limits: you may not use it to impair the equal freedom of others to drive *their* cars.[7]

From these two axioms of the natural law, Locke claimed that the rights to life, liberty, and property follow logically. With a little fleshing out, his derivation in summary goes like this:

1. Axiom 1: Each person is equal before the moral law.

2. Axiom 2: Each person is the morally rightful owner of himself or herself.

3. If you own something, then you are in charge of it, you are responsible for it, and you can exclude others from using it.

4. Therefore, each person is in charge of his or her own life, is responsible for his or her life, and can exclude others from using his or her life.

5. Since all stand equal before the moral law, each person should have the liberty to do what he or she wishes with his or her life, provided that he or she allows everyone else the same liberty.

6. Therefore, no one may forcefully take the life or liberty of another person, except in cases of self-defense or to protect an innocent life. You may not take another person's life or liberty because those things belong to that person—they are not yours to take.

7. Given the rights to life and liberty thus established, it follows that a possession or item of property was legitimately acquired if it was received through a mutually voluntary, transparent exchange that respects the life and liberty of both parties, from someone who had in turn received it through a similar mutually voluntary, transparent exchange, and so forth back as far as records go. Examples of legitimate exchanges of property include receiving a gift on your birthday, bequeathing or

inheriting an heirloom, buying a good from a merchant, working for an agreed-upon wage, hiring someone for an agreed-upon wage, receiving agreed-upon interest on a loan, and receiving entrepreneurial profit after starting a business offering goods or services to willing customers.

8. Each person therefore has a natural right to own (legitimately acquired) property.[8]

9. In sum, each person, by virtue of his or her humanity alone, has natural universal rights to life, liberty, and property.

In approximately this way, Locke derived a set of basic human rights from the natural or moral law, using common human reasoning.[9]

Locke and other classical liberals called the rights to life, liberty, and property *natural rights* because they believed that we would possess them even in a state of nature. We would possess them even in the absence of government because they are part of our common human nature, which we would possess even in a state of nature. Life, liberty, and property are therefore *human* as well as natural rights.

The idea of natural or human rights had history-changing implications, including the following argument that eventually traveled around the world: Since fundamental rights are rooted in our common human nature, they are not dependent on social status, religion, nationality, wealth, or income. They are therefore *universal*. Each person in the world therefore has the same basic rights. Further logical implications include the following:

1. As inherent parts of human nature, rights preexist the state; they are therefore not conferred by the state.
2. Human beings are not born subject to a king or other earthly ruler. Rather, they are born free, possessing inherent rights that kings and all others ought to respect.
3. Human rights come from God since God created human nature.[10]
4. A state of nature is not a state of license. Even though government would be lacking, your liberty in a state of nature would not be the freedom to do anything you want to do, for your actions would be morally limited by the natural rights of others.

Locke next considers the nature of the state of nature. Once a state of nature reaches a certain level of development and population density, basic rights would be insecure, he argues, for violations would be wide-spread. Speaking in ideal terms, at this point it would be eminently reasonable for everyone to meet together, draw up a reasonable contract that specifies laws all should follow, and then form a government to enforce that contract. This agreement between the people and the state is called "the social contract."

And what provisions would a reasonable social contract (ideally) contain? Locke argues that free and equal individuals meeting in a state of nature and *reasoning at their best* would place strict limits on state power. The first and primary business of the state would be to protect the traditional rights of the individual to life, liberty, and property negatively conceived.[11]

The social contract described by Locke is only meant as an ideal, but even as an ideal, it is practical, for it gives us a rational basis for evaluating the basic structure or fundamental principles of any existing government: An existing state is just to the degree to which its basic principles match those we would choose in a state of nature if we were free, equal, educated, and reasoning at our best. Again, the ideal social contract is aspirational rather than factual.

This has been only a sketch of the deep theory of freedom, equality before the law, individual rights, and limited government developed by Locke in the 600-plus pages of his *Two Treatises of Government*, the most influential work of classical liberal political philosophy ever written.

Locke's writings were widely studied and admired in the American colonies. Jefferson, Madison, Franklin, and the other authors of the founding documents of the United States studied Locke's writings and were steeped in classical liberal political philosophy.[12] Although the U.S. Constitution did not fully implement the classical liberal ideal—it was, after all, a political compromise between parties with differing views on some matters—it contained a unique amendment procedure that made improvement possible. The philosopher William Talbott observes:

> What is remarkable about the U.S. Constitution is that it provides the framework for the system to become more just over time—indeed, it even provides the framework for the system to improve the processes by which it becomes more just. It is a constitution that regards no agent or branch of government as infallible and perfect. Nothing, not even the Constitution itself, is immune to revision. The procedures for amending the Constitution even apply to themselves.[13]

Thus, although American slavery was not ended when the Constitution was ratified, the seeds of its future demise were planted. In the history of the world, no document remotely like the U.S. Constitution had ever been written and agreed to by representatives of an existing polity.

The classical liberals were revolutionaries. When Locke was writing his *Two Treatises*, slavery was accepted as natural and was deeply embedded in the cultures of Africa, Asia, India, and the Middle East. Slavery was also widely practiced among the indigenous peoples of North, Central, and South America. The classical liberals launched the world's first antislavery crusade and took it around the globe against much opposition. During the nineteenth century, they also launched the first movements for the rights of women and the rights of workers.[14] In many places outside Europe, classical liberal writings inspired the first written constitutions, the first attempts at democratic government, and the first attempts to make rulers legally accountable to the people. The British philosopher A. C. Grayling observes in his fascinating history of freedom, *Toward the Light of Liberty: The Struggles for Freedom and Rights That Made the Modern Western World*, that the philosophical ideals championed by the classical liberals altered the course of history and changed the world. Modern history, Grayling argues, has been driven by philosophical ideas originating in Europe.[15]

Classical liberalism must be distinguished from classical conservatism, which emerged in Europe during the eighteenth century. Here are a few of the core conservative ideas as I understand them. We should respect and appreciate the good parts of our tradition, and we should be grateful toward those in the past who advanced the human condition. At the same time, we should recognize that no society is perfect. We should therefore work to improve our institutions and the human condition. But we can't tear everything down and start over on some new and untested basis without causing catastrophic suffering that could last for generations. Change should therefore not be radical and sudden. Rather, it should be piecemeal and thoughtful, guided every step of the way not by abstract, untested, a priori ideas of perfection sketched on paper by dreamy intellectuals but by the accumulated wisdom of the past tested by experience. By proceeding in this way, we conserve the best from the past as we advance to an even better future. The perfect is the enemy of the good.[16]

Questions for Reflection and Discussion 13.1

1. Give an argument for one of the classical liberal ideals based on the doctrine of the *imago Dei*.
2. What would life be like in a state of nature? If government did not exist, would we need to invent it?
3. What does Locke mean by *natural law*?
4. What did the classical liberals mean by natural rights? Why are they also called "human rights"?
5. In your own words, explain Locke's derivation of human rights from the natural law.
6. If you found yourself with many others in a state of nature, which principles would you propose for a reasonable social contract? Support your proposal with the best reasons you can think of.
7. Could a person lacking the right to own property nevertheless be free?

SHOULD THE STATE HELP THOSE IN NEED?

Locke writes the following in his *First Treatise of Government*:

> God has given no one of His children such a property in his peculiar portion of the things of this world, but that he has given his needy brother a right to the surplusage of his goods . . . when his pressing wants call for it. . . . Charity gives every man a title to so much out of another's plenty as will keep him from extreme want, where he has no means to subsist otherwise.[17]

Locke believed that human beings have a natural right to be helped when in serious need by those with a surplus. This is a positive right (a right to be given something) and the corresponding natural duty to aid (on the part of those with a surplus) is a positive duty (a duty to perform an action). For Locke, the positive duty to aid functions as a rider, or limit, on the right to private property.

Of course, this principle of charity requires a definition of *surplus* and of *need*. Locke leaves that to individuals, and to jurists and political officials who will apply the basic principles of justice to specific situations and institutions. Surely the application will be sensitive to time, place, and the general surplus already built up in a society through capital accumulation. It seems reasonable to suppose that the level of expected assistance will rise as an economy develops and the standard of living rises.

Locke's principle of charity reminds us of Jesus's parable of the Good Samaritan. Christians are called to be compassionate, generous, and kind to those in need of help. In addition, every major religion includes a duty of charity and a call for compassion toward those who are suffering. Locke generally supported his key political principles with citations from the Old and New Testaments and with reason-based derivations from the natural law. In this way, he tried to show that the basic principles of classical liberalism receive support from both reason and sacred scripture. This makes sense: Locke accepted the traditional view that reason and scripture must be in harmony because both stem from the same source. Since this is a philosophical discussion, Locke's strictly philosophical arguments will remain our focus.

So, to return to the issue, should the modern state be in the business of relieving human suffering? Should the (positive) rights and duties of assistance be enforced by the state and administered using tax revenue? The matter is not as simple as it may seem. Philosophers draw a distinction between enforceable and nonenforceable rights and duties. In our private lives, we have a natural moral duty to at least be polite to everyone we meet, but we also have the corresponding natural right to be treated in at least a polite way. But surely this duty and its corresponding right should not be written into law and enforced by the state. This is a nonenforceable right and correlative duty.

On the other hand, we also have a right to life and a corresponding duty not to take the life of another person (except in self-defense, etc.). Surely this right and its correlative duty should be written into law and enforced by the state.

So, should the moral duty to help those in extreme need be written into law and enforced by the state? Or should it be left a matter of individual conscience? There are two schools of Lockean thought on the matter: *libertarian Lockeanism* and *moderate Lockeanism*.

Libertarian Lockeans answer that assistance should be a matter of individual conscience and never a duty enforced by the state. The classical liberal French economist Frederic Bastiat (1801–50) argued for the libertarian Lockean position approximately as follows.[18] The only legitimate powers possessed by the state are those that the people — reasoning at their best — would rightly transfer to it in a state of nature. These are the moral powers individuals would already possess in a state of nature, namely, those they would rightly use to protect their natural rights to life, liberty, and property (negatively conceived). So, just as needy individuals in the state of nature would not have the moral right to force those with a surplus to come to their aid, and just as a group of individuals in a state of nature would not have the moral right to band together and forcibly take from those who have a surplus and give the proceeds to those in need, a morally ideal state would not have the right to use the tax system to forcefully redistribute the wealth from rich to poor. To do so, Bastiat claimed, would be nothing more than "legalized theft." Charity must therefore be a private matter, a voluntary act of love, an expression of brotherhood, sisterhood, solidarity, or community. Bastiat also believed that individuals, acting from conscience, in the private sector of a free society would step forward in sufficient numbers to provide all the assistance needed, without state enforcement. Bastiat had an optimistic view of human nature in this respect.

Libertarian Lockeans envision as their ideal a society in which social entrepreneurs, churches, and community groups of all kinds form private, voluntary organizations to help those in need and solve social problems, acting without state assistance. The ideal is feasible, they claim. For supportive evidence, they cite the enormous and unprecedented proliferation of nongovernmental organizations (NGOs) and charities that spontaneously sprang up in the United States during the nineteenth century — all inspired by the new freedom and all unprompted by state action. The 1800s saw the birth of thousands of benevolent societies, mutual-aid groups, self-help organizations, educational institutions, and other private philanthropic efforts that spread all over the nation.

Indeed, the American tradition of civic involvement, community service, and nonprofit group action already stood out in 1831 when one of Bastiat's countrymen, the French political scientist Alexis de Tocqueville, toured the United States. Tocqueville was amazed by the large number of voluntary civic and philanthropic organizations he found everywhere he went.[19]

Libertarian Lockeans also point to the existence today of large numbers of social entrepreneurs — smart, talented, and dynamic people everywhere who start NGOs to work on social problems. More than 1 million private humanitarian agencies currently operate in the United States alone. Libertarians applaud the myriad ways free people voluntarily give to the community and to people in need. They believe that this is (ideally) the way truly free people deal with social problems.

Moderate Lockeans disagree. First, they note that private individuals in a state of nature would not have the right to tax others to provide for the common good, but certainly the state has this right—government could not function otherwise, and government is a necessary institution. Therefore, Bastiat's second premise is false: some of the rights and moral powers possessed by the state would not be possessed by individuals in a state of nature.

Second, they argue, if there are no state assistance programs and all charity is voluntary, then many with a surplus are likely to reason this way: "Millions of other people will help those in need, whether or not I do. My contribution is therefore not necessary. I'll let others make the sacrifice and solve the problem, and I'll spend my surplus on myself." But if too many reason selfishly, which is likely, then not enough help will be provided to many who rightly ought to be helped. This is the free rider problem. History suggests that if the duty to aid others is left to individual conscience, many with a surplus will shirk their moral duty.

Third, argue the moderate Lockeans, if there is no state safety net, many others are likely to reason as follows: "Too few will contribute to help those in need. Therefore, if I contribute, my contribution will have a negligible effect on the problem. I won't contribute unless everyone does." But if too many reason this way, not enough will be done. This is the assurance problem.[20]

Fourth, there is the coordination problem. In *Capitalism with Morality*, D. W. Haslett argues for the following proposition: "Only government has the wherewithal to co-ordinate aid to the poor systematically so that large numbers do not get overlooked."[21] Moderate Lockeans conclude from these considerations that the libertarian solution would leave too many to suffer in isolation.

In light of these problems, moderate Lockeans conclude that the libertarian position on government aid does not adequately express the liberal belief in the absolute value and dignity of the individual and our commitment to regard each person as a being worthy of equal concern and respect. By building a state-supported safety net into the social contract, they argue, we guarantee that no one is overlooked by accident. At the same time, we express our belief in, and commitment to, the absolute value, autonomy, and dignity of each individual *regardless of social status*.

However, these Lockeans oppose a state monopoly on assistance. They argue that private charity has an important role to play in a free society. For without private charity, individuals would have no way to exercise their full moral powers, including the virtues of voluntary charity and compassion. The highest realistic stage of freedom, argue the moderate Lockeans, will be a society in which a galaxy of private organizations started by social entrepreneurs, churches, and civic groups help people in need develop their full potential, while the state, through modest taxation, provides complementary programs to ensure that no one in need of help is neglected by accident. The state, therefore, must not crowd out private efforts, for a vibrant private charitable sector is an important part of a free society.

The moderate Lockeans add one more caveat: aid should never be simply a dole. Given the liberal commitment to the moral autonomy and dignity of the individual, the purpose of aid should be to help individuals in need develop their full potential and advance on their own, which requires effort and responsibility on the part of those receiving help. As such, aid should never subsidize self-destructive or antisocial behavior.[22]

On the basis of this or similar reasoning, moderate Lockeans argue that a fully rational social contract drawn up by free and equal individuals reasoning at their best in a state of nature would include state programs aimed at relieving human suffering that complement private efforts. Nothing less would adequately express our commitment to the absolute worth, freedom, and dignity of *each* individual. This, they argue, is the reasonable ideal against which we should measure existing states.

Locke's political philosophy offered a moral justification for the system of *laissez-faire* (relatively unregulated) capitalism emerging in Europe during the seventeenth and eighteenth centuries. However, not all in the liberal tradition believed that the new economic system was being built on the right basis. It is time to turn to the arguments of the modern liberals.

Questions for Reflection and Discussion 13.2

1. What is the difference between libertarian and moderate Lockeanism?
2. Explain and evaluate an argument for libertarian Lockeanism.
3. Explain and evaluate an argument for moderate Lockeanism.

Capitalism is the economic system that came into existence in stages along with the spread of classical liberal ideas during the eighteenth and nineteenth centuries. The first capitalist societies — England, the Netherlands, France, Germany, and the United States — were those attempting to realize the newly articulated classical liberal ideals. How successful was the new economic system? Did capitalism advance the human condition? In his best-selling book, *Capital in the Twenty-First Century*, the French economist Thomas Picketty presents statistics showing that the average rate of economic growth around the world before the birth of capitalism was between one-tenth and one-twentieth of 1 percent per year. At that rate, the material standard of living of the average person around the world doubled every 500 to 1,000 years. After the birth of capitalism, the rate of economic growth in the emerging capitalist societies rose to between *ten and twenty times* that of all previous eras. The material standard of living of the average European began doubling every generation or two.[23] Real median income in England and the United States *tripled* during the nineteenth century — an advance unprecedented in world history. In the short span between 1860 and 1920, the real wages of workers in the United States doubled. At the same time, the average workweek was shortened from 66 to 50 hours.[24]

HOW MUCH INFLUENCE DOES LUCK HAVE IN LIFE?

Introducing John Rawls: Philosopher of Modern Liberalism

The Harvard philosopher John Rawls (1921–2001) was the most important political philosopher of the twentieth century. He is without a doubt the most influential modern liberal of our time. The argument Rawls stated against classical liberalism in his 600-page treatise, *A Theory of Justice*, is one of the most thought-provoking and debated arguments in modern political theory.[25] Rawls's book sold more than 300,000 copies — an amazing number for a purely academic work of philosophy. In just the ten years after its publication, its arguments were discussed in tens of thousands of scholarly articles and in hundreds of academic books.

His hugely influential argument challenging classical liberalism, known as the "moral arbitrariness argument," not only stimulated an avalanche of philosophical research, it is an argument anyone who cares about social justice ought to consider.[26]

New Terminology

Rawls's argument begins with some special terms. The talents, attributes, and natural abilities you are born with are your *natural assets*. These include your health, intelligence, looks, and any other natural "gifts" you possess from birth. Rawls also calls these your *natural endowment*. The process in nature that "distributes" natural assets to individuals before birth is the *natural lottery*. Thanks to the natural lottery, one person is born with amazing musical gifts, another can't sing a note on key; one person is gifted at math, another is not, and so forth.

Next, the family and social circumstances into which you were born constitute your *social endowment*, also called your *social assets*. The *social lottery* is the process that determines the circumstances of each person's birth. Thanks to the social lottery, one person is born into a poor family, another is born into a wealthy family, one was born into a loving family, and another is born into a dysfunctional family, and so on.

A consideration is *morally arbitrary* if it does not justify anything morally, and an attribute is morally arbitrary if the fact that a person possesses it justifies nothing morally. For example, the attribute of having brown eyes is morally arbitrary — the fact that your eyes are brown does not, by itself, morally justify paying you more, giving you extra vacation time, or granting you more rights. Or it may be true that you were born into the Smith family or in New England, but these facts alone don't justify giving you a promotion, a higher income, or special privileges.

The next idea is crucial: the talents and other natural assets you were born with and the family and social circumstances into which you were born, Rawls argues, are morally arbitrary attributes. Having been born with this or that talent or into this or that family or social situation does not by itself justify anything morally. For obviously, no one works for or earns or chooses or deserves the talents and other attributes he or she was born with or the family and social circumstances into which he or she was born.

So, the mere fact that you were born with a talent that is in high demand does not, by itself, morally justify your being paid more than someone else. It may be true that you were born into an affluent family, but that alone does not justify your having more wealth than the next person.

The gifts distributed by the natural and social lotteries, then, are morally arbitrary—their possession does not, by itself, justify anything.

If this still seems questionable, consider the fact that none of us worked for, earned, or deserved the talents, body, health, and other attributes we were born with. Nor did any of us work for, earn, or deserve the family and social circumstances into which we were born. Rawls writes:

> Perhaps some will think that the person with greater natural endow-
> ments deserves those assets. . . . Because he is more worthy in this
> sense, he deserves the greater advantages that he could achieve with
> them. This view, however, is surely incorrect. It seems to be one of the
> fixed points of our considered judgments that no one deserves his
> place in the distribution of native endowments, any more than one
> deserves one's initial starting place in society.[27]

Even the timing of a person's birth is a morally arbitrary natural asset. If Stevie Wonder had been born one hundred years earlier, he would not have become a rock star. But he didn't choose to be born at a certain time. He didn't work for the "gift" of being born just in time for the heyday of classic rock and roll.

The System of Natural Liberty

The next consideration concerns what Rawls calls "the system of natural liberty"—essentially a classical liberal society with a laissez-faire capitalist economy. In such a system, he argues, those lucky enough to have been born with talents in high demand in the marketplace will tend to profit greatly from their luck in the natural lottery, while others not as fortunate will have no such luck. This doesn't seem fair. Furthermore, those fortunate enough to have been born into favorable social or family circumstances will often benefit greatly from the lucky circumstances of their birth; others will not be so lucky. This too doesn't seem fair.

Now comes the most controversial step. Rawls claims that *most* differences in the income and wealth received on the relatively unregulated markets of a classical liberal system of laissez-faire capitalism are due to differing natural and social endowments rather than to effort, choice, or desert. In short, luck, rather than choice or effort, appears to be the decisive factor. This is offered as an empirical claim.

Given this, it follows that most differences in income and wealth received within a laissez-faire capitalist system governed by Lockean laws are neither worked for, nor earned, nor deserved. Rather, they are for the most part the result of luck in the natural and social lotteries. Therefore, most inequality within a classical liberal capitalist society is morally unjustified. Any society that allows luck to determine most of the outcomes in life seems unfair in a deeply moral sense. A classical liberal capitalist society is therefore a deeply immoral society.

It is important to include the modifier *most* in the preceding paragraph because, contrary to what some critics have insinuated, Rawls does not claim that *all* income and wealth received within a relatively free market system is due to morally arbitrary factors. He only claims that income and wealth received within capitalist markets are "for the most part" due to luck, that is, to morally arbitrary factors, rather than to choice, effort, or desert.

If Rawls is right, two things seem to follow. First, the rich and affluent in a system of classical liberal capitalism for the most part do *not* hold their wealth justly. Second, most poverty in such a system is not morally deserved or justified.

An Objection and a Reply

Some of Rawls's critics distinguish talents from skills. Talents are mere potentials at birth. Skills are developed talents. These critics argue that those born with exceptional talents who then receive high incomes as a result of developing their talents *chose* to develop their talents and put them to use. Many people have talents but never develop them into skills. In addition, most highly skilled people worked hard over long periods of time developing and honing their skills. But we normally give people moral credit for choosing to develop their skills and put them to use. We praise people for working hard. Doesn't this morally justify their success?

Critics also observed that those born into opportunity-rich environments must seize the opportunities available, or they will not go far. Many people are born into opportunity but choose not to take advantage of the possibilities staring them in the face—success is rarely automatic. But we normally congratulate people when they respond positively to opportunities. We suppose that their exemplary choices evidence good character. Doesn't this morally justify something?

Still other critics pointed to the strong work ethic, foresight, long years of preparation, and dedication usually displayed by successful people earning high incomes in the capitalist marketplace. Capitalist markets, they argue, don't reward people simply because they were born with talent. Rather, people are rewarded for their *developed* talents (i.e., skills) as well as for the way they chose to put their skills to use. In real life, choice—not birth—is usually decisive.

Similarly, these critics observe, capitalist markets don't simply reward people for being born into opportunity-rich environments; rather, they usually reward people for the way they responded to their environment. Again, many people are born into fortunate environments and ignore or reject the opportunities staring them in the face. Doesn't this justify success?

The suggestion here is that those receiving high incomes in a classical liberal capitalist system for the most part earned and therefore morally deserve their higher-than-average incomes because of (1) the way they developed their talents, (2) the way they responded to circumstances, (3) the choices they made, and (4) the extra effort, creativity, and foresight they displayed in offering their services or products to others.

Rawls was aware that this objection would be made; the rebuttal he included in his book has generated a great deal of discussion: "The assertion that a man deserves the superior character that enables him to make the effort to cultivate his abilities is equally problematic; for his character depends in large part upon fortunate family and social circumstances for which he can claim no credit. The notion of desert seems not to apply in these cases."[28]

In other words, the extra effort, strong work ethic, discipline, foresight, responsiveness to opportunity, choices, and other character traits generally associated with success in a capitalist marketplace are *themselves* to a large extent the product of undeserved and unearned family and social circumstances. Since these circumstances are undeserved and unearned, they are morally arbitrary factors for which the successful person can claim no credit. It would seem to follow that exceptional character traits are (for the most part) also morally arbitrary assets that justify nothing. Fleshed out, the argument would seem to go about like this:

Rawls's Moral Arbitrariness Argument

1. In a laissez-faire capitalist system based on classical liberal principles, most differences in income and wealth are due to luck, that is, to the distribution of natural talents at birth and the differing family, social, and economic circumstances into which people were born.

2. But no one works for, chooses, earns, or deserves the natural assets he or she was born with, nor does anyone work for, choose, earn, or deserve his or her initial starting place in life.

3. Even a person's present character, including his or her work ethic, choices in life, and developed skills and abilities, is to a large extent due to unchosen, undeserved, and unearned family and social circumstances.

4. Therefore, most differences in incomes and wealth received within a classical liberal free market capitalist system are due to unchosen, unearned, and undeserved factors.

5. Unchosen, unearned, and undeserved factors are morally arbitrary.

6. Therefore, most differences in incomes and wealth received within a classical liberal free market capitalist system are due to morally arbitrary factors.

7. Therefore, in a free market capitalist system based on classical liberal principles, differences in income and wealth, and differences in character, are (for the most part) morally unjustified.

8. Therefore, classical liberal capitalism is an unjust system.

Solution: Taming the Natural and Social Lotteries

According to Rawls's argument, the main problem with classical liberalism and its free market capitalist economy is that such a system gives the natural and social lotteries far too much sway, leaving too little to individual initiative. What should be done? Eliminate the natural lotteries? No, Rawls argues, they cannot be eliminated because they are an inescapable fact of human life. However, we do not have to allow them free rein. Just as we counteract the effects of the weather by constructing houses and making clothes and just as we mitigate the effects of disease by inventing medicines to curb their influence, we can use the power of the state to mitigate the morally arbitrary effects of the natural and social lotteries. Rawls proposes two fundamental principles of justice as the most reasonable way to tame the natural lotteries so as to socially affirm the equal value and dignity of each individual. Although these principles are usually referred to as "Rawls's two principles," the second has two independent clauses.

1. *The Greatest Equal Liberty Principle*: Each person is to have an equal right to the most extensive total system of equal basic liberties compatible with a similar system of liberty for all.

Clarification. Rawls believes that the traditional liberties (of speech, conscience, association, religion, etc.) form an interrelated system in which the character and value of one liberty depends on the way it and the others are defined. A single liberty cannot be defined on its own, apart from the others.[29] This makes sense. For instance, if freedom of speech is defined too broadly, then the rights to life and property will be restricted. (Defined too loosely, freedom of speech allows people to incite riots, to falsely shout "Fire!" in a crowded theater, and so forth.) Without rules of order in a convention, freedom of speech loses all value. (No meeting can function if freedom of speech is defined too loosely.) Ideally, the various liberties will be defined in a give-and-take process of argument and counterargument until a systemic maximum of total liberty is reached—subject to the moral constraint that all individuals have the *same* liberties.

2. *The Difference Principle and the Fair Equality of Opportunity Principle*: Social and economic inequalities are to be arranged so that they are both (1) to the greatest benefit of the least advantaged and (2) attached to offices and positions open to all under conditions of fair equality of opportunity. Clause (1) is known as the "difference principle," and clause (2) is called "the fair equality of opportunity principle."

Clarification. The *least advantaged* consists of those with the lowest levels of income, wealth, status, power, and opportunity. The difference principle allows a difference in income, wealth, status, power, or opportunity only if allowing that difference benefits the least advantaged by making them better off than they would be if the difference were *not* permitted.

Generally, a permitted inequality—for instance one person taking home a higher income than another—will satisfy the difference principle if it functions as a needed incentive for the extra effort and innovation that lead to higher levels of production, invention, and capital accumulation. For these, in turn, make possible a larger tax revenue supporting higher transfer payments to the least advantaged, better government programs that help the least advantaged, and greater economic opportunities and higher rates of economic growth that benefit the least advantaged.[30]

Put another way, the operation of the difference principle would reduce inequalities up to the point that any further reduction would diminish the incentives of the most productive, leaving less to be redistributed and thus less help for the least well off.

Turning to the principle of fair equality of opportunity, clause 2, Rawls distinguishes "formal" from "fair" equality of opportunity. Formal equality of opportunity exists when all laws apply to everyone impartially and equally in the abstract. If everyone is treated equally *before the law*, then formal equality exists. This is the ideal of equality endorsed by classical liberals.

However, Rawls observes, under a system of formal equality of opportunity, two equally motivated and equally talented individuals, starting from very unequal social backgrounds (for instance one is born into poverty and the other into wealth) will likely achieve very unequal levels of wealth, income, and powers of office. Imagine a child with mathematical talent born into a poor family in rural Mississippi and a kid with the same talent born into a rich and well-connected family in Boston. The latter has a much higher chance of developing and using his talents to the fullest. The problem, from the point of view of justice, is that this unequal outcome will be due largely (but not entirely) to the social conditions into which the two individuals were born, rather than to their respective effort, hard work, and choice.

Consequently, under formal equality of opportunity, although everyone is considered equal before the law, persons with similar talents and motivation will not always have equal life expectations. And the families and social conditions into which people are born, rather than effort and choice, are likely to play a big role in the distribution of wealth, income, and social status.

Fair equality of opportunity exists when government programs ensure that the social circumstances of a person's birth do not restrict what he or she can expect to accomplish in life. Under fair rather than formal equality of opportunity, an individual born into a poor family in a rural area who is good at science, for example, has the same chance of realizing his or her potential as someone born with the same talents and motivation into a rich and well-connected family in a large city.[31]

Rawls named his theory of justice, summed up by the two principles, "Justice as fairness."

CRITICISM FROM THE LEFT

Some of Rawls's critics on the left argue that his two principles are not sufficiently egalitarian. For one reason, they argue, the two principles call for and justify a capitalist welfare state. This is a capitalist system of private property in which wealth and income remain extremely unequal, a wealthy elite exercises disproportionate political power by virtue of the money it donates to large political parties, and many people live hopeless lives dependent on extensive state welfare programs that provide little incentive to advance.

Rawls disagreed. In his last book, *Justice as Fairness: A Restatement*, published in 2001 shortly before he died, Rawls argues that the system known in political theory as a "private-property-owning democracy"—not a capitalist welfare state—would best realize the two principles of his theory.[32]

In this kind of society, property is privately held, and markets are allowed to operate within limits. However, the state closely monitors the buildup and concentration of productive assets (capital), wealth, and income, and redistributes all three whenever inequalities become too large. Confiscation and redistribution of wealth and income are thus continuous processes.[33] As a result, private property is widely dispersed, socioeconomic inequality is minimized, and productive assets, including stocks and bonds, are owned as widely as possible.

For example, in a private-property-owning democracy, when a business becomes too large, as determined by law, the state buys it out at fair market value and redistributes the assets widely in the form of stocks and other financial instruments that pay dividends and interest. The owners of the business might receive a large payment; however, steeply graduated tax rates on income, wealth, gifts, and estates at death continuously redistribute wealth and income so that it is impossible for anyone to build up wealth, economic power, and the unfair political influence that comes with such power.

A good deal of redistributed wealth would take the form of stocks, bonds, and shares in mutual funds that would provide individuals with dividends and interest over their lifetimes. Of course, individuals would not be permitted to sell their financial assets and cash in on their endowments. And at death, assets would revert to the state, to be redistributed anew.

Rawls believed that a private-property-owning democracy, rather than a capitalist welfare state, is called for by his two principles.[34] This was his main response to his critics on the left. Most theorists consider a private-property-owning democracy to be a form of socialism called "market socialism."[35] Rawls apparently agreed.

> Our political terms *left* and *right* originated during the French Revolution (1789–94) when those members of the French National Assembly who wanted slow, gradual change sat on the right and those who wanted rapid and radical change sat on the left. Over the years, *right* and *left* have acquired new meanings.

CRITICISM FROM THE RIGHT

The first systematic critique of Rawls from the right came from an unexpected source. Three years after the publication (in 1971) of Rawls's *A Theory of Justice*, a book was published that caused a sensation in the world of academic philosophy. The book was *Anarchy, State, and Utopia*, by Robert Nozick (1938–2002), one of Rawls's colleagues in the Harvard Philosophy Department.[36] Nozick's book not only contained an extensive critique of Rawls's theory, it also presented a wide-ranging case for classical liberalism. Many still consider *Anarchy, State, and Utopia* to be the most significant philosophical defense to date of the claim associated with the classical liberals that, as Nozick puts it, "a minimal state limited to the narrow functions of protection against force, theft, fraud, enforcement of contract, and so on, is justified and that any more extensive state will violate persons' rights and is unjustified; and that the minimal state is inspiring as well."[37]

When it appeared in 1974, *Anarchy, State, and Utopia* drew widespread critical acclaim within the academic community and won the prestigious National Book Award for philosophy in 1975. It has sold more than 400,000 copies and has been translated into twenty languages. (Most original works of technical academic philosophy sell a few thousand copies.) The majority of the critics did not agree with the Lockean libertarian position Nozick defends — that moral considerations limit the power of the state to protecting the rights to life, liberty, and property, negatively conceived. The state therefore has no moral right to use tax money to assist those in need and solve major social problems. These tasks, Nozick argues, should be left to voluntary initiatives within the private sector. However, the critics applauded Nozick's book for its logical rigor and the creativity of its arguments.[38] Nozick's book is full of wide-ranging, complex, thought-provoking arguments employing the latest tools of decision theory and logic. His challenge to Rawls's moral arbitrariness argument will be our focus.

CHALLENGING RAWLS'S MORAL ARBITRARINESS ARGUMENT

Rawls's moral arbitrariness argument, Nozick argues, contains a logical gap. The gap appears between premises 6 and 7 in my summary of Rawls's argument.

6. Therefore, most differences in incomes and wealth received within a classical liberal free market capitalist system are due to morally arbitrary factors.

7. Therefore, in a free market capitalist system based on classical liberal principles, differences in income and wealth, and differences in character, are (for the most part) morally unjustified.

Nozick argues that even if we grant Rawls that a person's holdings (owned goods) are to a large extent due to luck or other morally arbitrary factors, it does not follow that the person's holdings are morally unjustified. For there is another way that holdings might be morally justified, which Rawls does not rule out.

In everyday life, we sometimes say that a person is morally entitled to a good regardless of whether he or she morally deserves it and apart from whether he or she earned it or even worked for it. Reflect on this example. For her sixteenth birthday, a young lady is given a modest, ten-year-old car with 100,000 miles on the odometer. The car was purchased legally by her parents, who chose to give it to her (and she chose to accept it). Her best friend received only a cheap book for her sixteenth birthday. It is part of our moral common sense that the first sixteen-year-old is morally *entitled* to (has a moral right to) her car, completely apart from whether she morally deserved it, worked for it, or otherwise earned it. And being morally entitled to her car means that she is morally justified in owning it. Her ownership is morally justified even though others received less for their sixteenth birthday. Why? She is morally entitled to her birthday present because she received it as the result of a voluntary and transparent transaction that violated no one's rights. Some might add, "Don't parents have a right to give birthday presents to their children?"

Consider this example. A young athlete trains hard and sacrifices for years before winning a spot on the U.S. Olympic team. When the big day arrives, the athlete wins a gold medal. Isn't it part of our moral common sense that the athlete has a right to the medal, and the recognition that comes with it? Isn't the athlete entitled to the award even though she did not deserve to be born with athletic talents and did not choose to be born into a supportive family or a society that values her talents? Isn't her ownership of the medal justified anyway, apart from the many morally arbitrary factors involved?

The first example suggests that we can be entitled to something (and justified in possessing it) even when we do not morally deserve it, even when we did not work for it or earn it, and even when we cannot claim credit for creating it. The second example suggests that we can be entitled to some reward, even though we did not create, or earn, or deserve all the many factors that went into our eventually receiving the reward.

If these judgments are correct, then premise 7 in Rawls's argument (as I presented it) does not follow from premise 6. Those with high incomes and wealth may not fully deserve their holdings, they may not have fully earned them, they may not have created all the factors that went into their eventual success, but they *may* be morally entitled to their rewards on the basis of commonsense considerations about rights, nonetheless.[39]

NOZICK'S ALTERNATIVE THEORY OF JUSTICE

Nozick looks for but does not find a Rawlsian argument that bridges the gap between premises 6 and 7. So, rejecting Rawls's arbitrariness argument against classical liberalism, he returns to the drawing board and presents a new argument for classical liberalism rooted in Locke's axioms. Here is my summary:

1. Each person stands equal before the moral law.

2. Each person is the morally rightful owner of himself or herself.

3. A person's natural and social assets are a part of that person's identity.

4. So, each person is the morally rightful owner of his or her own natural and social assets.

5. To rightfully own something is to be morally entitled to it.

6. As self-owners, then, people are morally entitled to their natural and social assets.

7. If people are morally entitled to an asset, they are entitled to whatever flows from that asset when they put it to use peacefully, that is, provided they violate no rights in the process, all exchanges are transparent and voluntary, and legitimate taxes are paid.

8. Therefore, people are morally entitled to what they receive from others through voluntary, transparent exchanges as they use their developed natural and social assets to produce goods or services which they offer to others (violating no rights in the process, etc.).

9. The holdings legally received by individuals on a free market governed by classical liberal principles generally flow from their developed natural and social assets used in this way.

10. Therefore, people are morally entitled to the after-tax wealth and income they receive on a free market governed by classical liberal principles.

11. If you are morally entitled to a good, then your possession of it is morally justified.

12. Therefore, capitalism governed by classical liberal principles is a morally just system.

The upshot of Nozick's argument is that individuals have a right or moral entitlement to their after-tax holdings, no matter how much wealth they accumulate, provided they received their holdings as a result of voluntary, transparent, non-rights-violating exchanges. Furthermore, they are entitled to their holdings whether or not they deserve the natural and social assets they were born with, whether or not they deserve their wealth, whether or not they created all the conditions and factors that led to their success, and whether or not they even made a productive contribution.

Nozick also argues that the state has no right to administer welfare programs of any kind, for (he argues) self-owners cannot rightly be forced to aid others, and a state welfare system does just that when it taxes their wealth and transfers it to others. Efforts on the part of those with a surplus to help those in need must be voluntary — they must stem from the private sector alone. Nozick thus sides with the libertarian Lockeans.[40]

Let's test Nozick's theory with the case of Michael Jordan, whose net worth exceeds $2 billion. The Nozickian questions to ask are these:

- Did he violate anyone's rights when he developed his natural talents and turned them into skills as he practiced basketball as a kid, in social circumstances that allowed him to develop his natural talents?
- Did the Chicago Bulls choose to offer him a contract? Did they violate anyone's rights when they did so? Did he choose to play for them?
- Did people choose to buy tickets to watch him play? Did fans violate anyone's rights when they bought tickets? Did he violate anyone's rights when he played in games all over the country, endorsed products, and so forth?

What are your answers to these questions? Nozick argues that if the individual transactions that led to Jordan becoming a billionaire were voluntary and violated no rights, then his holdings are just, even if he was born with more talent than others, even if he does not morally deserve his talents or the social situation into which he was born, *and even if he did not create all the factors that went into his success.* For on Nozick's account, the justice of a distribution of wealth and income is a matter of the justice of the individual transactions that led to it, not the income pattern it fits, the degree of equality, or considerations of moral desert.

Nozick named his account of justice "the entitlement theory." On his theory, then, desert, need, earning, and productive contribution are *not* what justify holdings or possessions. Holdings are justified if they were received through voluntary and transparent transactions that violated no rights, with transactions traced back as far as records allow. A true self-ownership society, Nozick believes, will allow people to develop and put their natural and social assets to use in any way they choose and to reap the fruits of their labor in the form of what others willingly offer them in return for their services or products—as long as they violate no one's natural rights in the process.

Two Views on the Nature of Liberal Capitalism

Rawls argues that a relatively unregulated classical liberal system of capitalism is unjust, for under such a system, income, wealth, and power are for the most part due to luck rather than choice, effort, or hard work. The system benefits a lucky few at the expense of the rest of society. Considerations of fairness and justice, he argues, suggest that the state should mitigate the effects of luck on income, wealth, and power, and the difference principle is the most reasonable way to do so.

Nozick argues that in a classical liberal capitalist system, when individuals are born with talents, how well they do in life generally depends crucially *not* on the talents with which they were born, nor on the social situation into which they were born, but on how they chose to develop their talents and on how they responded to their situation. For the capitalist marketplace generally rewards people for what they *do* with their talents, not for the raw, undeveloped talents they were born with. And it tends to reward people for the way they responded to their situation, not for the initial situation into which they were born.

Furthermore, Nozick argues, what people receive in a capitalist system generally reflects what others voluntarily offer them for the services and products they offer. In short, the market generally responds to choices, not to long past antecedents of choices.

What are we to make of this disagreement? Don't we normally give people credit for the choices they make in life? Don't we ordinarily say that they are entitled to the result (if no rights are violated in the process)? Isn't the fact that a system rewards non-rights-violating choices a morally desirable feature of that system? Aren't choices an essential aspect of freedom?

Rawls counters that in a relatively free market capitalist system, a small elite at the top reaps most of the rewards, for the most part thanks to luck. Nozick disagrees. People within a capitalist system who develop their talents and produce things of great economic value do not reap all the benefits. Rather, the benefits produced by their efforts spread out to many people and ultimately to society in general. We have all been made better off thanks to the many great musical geniuses, writers, entertainers, and artists who developed their native talents and offered the results on the marketplace. We are nearly all better off thanks to the many entrepreneurs who created new products, cheaper products, and new forms of economic organization that lowered prices for millions of consumers and created new opportunities for millions of workers.[41] We are nearly all better off thanks to the pioneers of digital computing who linked together and revolutionized the entire world.

Furthermore, Nozick argues, in a free market, those with talents in demand have a strong incentive to develop and use their talents to benefit others, for on a free market, income is generally earned by satisfying the needs and wants of others. The debate between Rawls and Nozick highlights many of the central political issues of our time.

BACK TO RAWLS

What can be said in defense of Rawls here? First, when Rawls claims that an individual's character and accomplishments are "for the most part" the product of morally arbitrary factors for which the individual cannot claim credit, he is not denying that people have free will. (Rawls does not mention free will in *A Theory of Justice*, but in other places, he indicates that he does believe that people possess it.) He is also not saying that people can never claim credit for their accomplishments. Rawls's view does not rule out taking pride in the skills you have developed or credit for the way you responded to the circumstances into which you were born. It only rules out the prideful attitude "I did it all by myself." President Obama was making a Rawlsian point in 2012 when he made his famous remark, "You didn't build this," referring to the state-provided infrastructure supporting profitable businesses in Massachusetts.

Second, Rawls's remarks on character and family upbringing urge humility. You can think of yourself in a Rawlsian way and still claim that you contributed to your success. But as a Rawlsian, you will also keep in mind that many other factors were also at work, including luck and contributions from others.

In response to Nozick, Rawls's defenders might also point to the deep pockets of misery, poverty, and despair that have been present in capitalist societies. And they might ask, "Does leaving some to languish in degrading conditions — that for the most part they did not cause — respect the equal dignity and absolute worth of each individual?" Does such a society embody the liberal ideal, that every person regardless of social status is equally worthy of dignity, respect, and concern?

A Rawlsian might add, "What good is Lockean self-ownership if you own few material goods and have little opportunity to develop your natural assets?" Rawls draws a distinction between liberty and the worth of liberty. On the basis of this distinction, his defenders ask, How valuable is your liberty if you are poor and lack the resources to use it?

Rawlsians argue that a society shaped by the difference principle, with comprehensive redistributive programs, minimal inequality, and a humane social safety net, best expresses our commitment to the absolute value of the individual and our shared belief that each person — by virtue of his or her humanity alone — is equally worthy of a humane level of concern, dignity, and respect.

A COMPROMISE?

There are two extreme views on state welfare programs. Libertarian Lockeans such as Nozick argue that a fully just society would have no state welfare programs at all. Social problems, including poverty, racism, and sexism, would be attacked by individuals in the private sector working through educational initiatives, churches, and all kinds of voluntary organizations formed by social entrepreneurs, concerned citizens, and so forth. Nozick believes that the private sector contains a sufficient number of smart and dedicated people who will constantly be finding new ways to respond constructively to social problems and help people in need improve their lives.

At the opposite extreme are those who argue that private charity is demeaning and that state aid alone is ennobling. The state, they argue, should be the sole provider of all programs designed to uplift the disadvantaged and solve social problems. A truly just society, they argue, would therefore have no private charitable organizations or aid groups at all. I will call this extreme the "communist solution" to the problem of poverty because the communist societies of the twentieth century—exemplified by the Soviet Union and Communist China—attempted to extinguish their independent civil sectors and in the process effectively outlawed nearly all organized private efforts aimed at solving social problems while giving the state a monopoly in this area.

We have already examined the problems associated with the libertarian position—the free rider, assurance, and coordination problems. The communist solution has problems as well. First, it does not let individuals exercise many of their moral powers, including their power to voluntarily and privately band together to help others in need out of the goodness of their hearts or out of a sense of solidarity, community, and so forth. Thus, it unduly restricts the moral autonomy of the individual.

Second, the communist solution gives the state far too much monopoly power. Totalitarianism is approaching when the state sector crowds out civil society, leaving nothing for community-minded individuals to do *as individuals*. And when the state controls every aspect of society, individuals are no longer free in any meaningful sense of the word.

What is the most reasonable solution? Since the issue is so important, I am going to offer my own argument, as food for thought. This will be a "both/and" position midway between Rawls and Nozick.

First, as Locke argues, each of us has a natural positive moral duty to help those in extreme need if we have a surplus. Locke, Nozick, and Rawls can agree on this.

Second, fully rational, equal, and free individuals in a state of nature, meeting to formulate an effective social contract and reasoning at their best, would choose an agreement that has the state protect the three classical liberal rights to life, liberty, and property negatively conceived. But a rational social contract, I maintain, would also have the state institute programs to help the least advantaged achieve their potential. These programs would be designed to complement, not crowd out, private-sector efforts launched by social entrepreneurs, churches, and community-minded individuals. However, state programs would not constitute a dole or mere handout, for a dole fails to respect the moral autonomy of its recipients. In addition, state programs would not subsidize irresponsible behavior. Rather, they would be designed to ensure that all in need receive enough resources and help to attain a decent, morally autonomous life with the opportunity to develop their talents and advance on their own initiative. Such programs would therefore expect effort and responsibility on the part of those helped.

In this way, rational social contractors would build into the fabric of their society the *imago Dei* and the associated liberal belief that each person possesses absolute value and, by virtue of this value, is equally deserving of respect and concern regardless of social status, wealth, income, color, or any other morally arbitrary factor.

Some might ask, What distinguishes the redistribution of wealth contained in this ideal proposal from that mandated by Rawls's difference principle? The answer is the cutoff point. As we've seen, Rawls's principle requires a private-property-owning democracy — a system mandating a massive, comprehensive, and continuous scheme of confiscation and redistribution that maximizes the condition of the least well off.[42] In contrast, the Lockean state programs that, I argue, express our commitment to help those in need would have an internal cutoff point far short of the level implicit in a private-property-owning democracy, for the Lockean limit on aid would not be related to the degree of inequality. Rather, help would be offered up to the point where individuals are morally autonomous and can advance on their own initiative. State assistance would not be an unending dole.

This stopping point reflects the claim — supported by plain observation — that help beyond a certain point creates dependency and lethargy, which in turn fails to respect the agency and moral autonomy of those in need.[43] Surely education is one of the most effective ways to prepare people to advance on their own. In political theory, the view I am defending is sometimes called *sufficientarianism*. I am suggesting a sufficientarian difference principle.[44]

A classical liberal society need not contain deep pockets of persistent poverty. A myriad of private-sector organizations, churches, and the efforts of innovative social entrepreneurs supplemented with effective government programs financed by moderate taxation could ensure that no citizen in need is accidentally neglected.[45]

CONCLUDING REFLECTIONS

Rawls drew our attention to the pervasive role that luck plays in our lives. Reflection on his moral arbitrariness argument ought to make any of us less judgmental and more compassionate toward those born into difficult circumstances and toward those born with disabilities of all kinds. Reflection on Rawls's theory—even if we do not agree with every aspect of it— should incline anyone to be more sensitive to and caring toward "those to whom life has been least kind."[46] Considering Rawls's argument also ought to make those who think they did it all by themselves think again.

On the other hand, Nozick draws our attention to the respect people are owed when they choose to develop their talents and put them to uses that others value and to the credit we give people when they respond in a positive way to the circumstances into which they were born.

In *Free to Choose*, Milton and Rose Friedman, two of the twentieth-century's leading defenders of free market capitalism, write:

> The amount of each kind of resource each of us owns is partly the result of chance, partly of choice by ourselves or others. Chance determines our genes and through them affects our physical and mental capacities. Chance determines the kind of family and cultural environment into which we are born and as a result our opportunities to develop our physical and mental capacity. . . . But choice also plays an important role. Our decisions about how to use our resources, whether to work hard or take it easy, to enter one occupation or another, to engage in one venture or another, to save or spend—these may determine whether we dissipate our resources or improve and add to them.[47]

Does this observation support Rawls or Nozick? Or both?

Questions for Reflection and Discussion 13.3

1. What is the difference between fair and formal equality of opportunity?
2. What laws and institutions would be required to realize fair equality of opportunity?

3. In your own words, explain Rawls's argument against classical liberal capitalism.
4. How does Rawls propose to mitigate the vagaries of the natural and social lotteries?
5. If someone's wealth is for the most part due to morally arbitrary factors, does it follow that his or her wealth is unjustly held?
6. Should there be a limit to the amount of wealth a person can accumulate?
7. What are the characteristics of a private-property-owning democracy?
8. Would a private-property-owning democracy be morally superior to a free market capitalist system?
9. In your own words, explain Nozick's argument for his version of classical liberalism.
10. Compare Rawls and Nozick on the role that luck plays in our lives.

FOURTEEN

God and Morality

OBSERVATIONS IN NEED OF EXPLANATION

In the previous two chapters, we've been discussing the moral law, also called the "natural law," that obligates us and that would obligate us even in a state of nature. As we've seen, modern political thought began with a recognition of a natural law that is higher than any man-made law.[1] In one of his most famous essays, "Letter from Birmingham City Jail," Dr. Martin Luther King Jr. attacked the segregation laws of the Jim Crow era based on this law, which he argues takes precedence over any human law:

> One may well ask "How can you advocate breaking some laws and obeying others?" The answer lies in the fact that there are two types of laws: just and unjust. I would be the first to advocate obeying just laws. One has not only a legal but a moral responsibility to obey just laws. Conversely, one has a moral responsibility to disobey unjust laws. Now, what is the difference between the two? How does one determine whether a law is just or unjust? A just law is a man-made

code that squares with the moral law or the law of God. An unjust law is a code that is out of harmony with the moral law. To put it in the terms of St. Thomas Aquinas: An unjust law is a human law that is not rooted in eternal law and natural law. Any law that uplifts human personality is just. Any law that degrades human personality is unjust. All segregation statutes are unjust because segregation distorts the soul and damages the personality. It gives the segregator a false sense of superiority and the segregated a false sense of inferiority. . . . Thus it is that I can urge men to obey the 1954 decision of the Supreme Court, for it is morally right; and I can urge them to disobey segregation ordinances, for they are morally wrong.[2]

We are all aware of something we call "moral obligation." When we are out in public and see someone fall and injure himself or herself, we naturally feel a strong obligation to help. Imagine that as you leisurely walk through a park, you see an old man lying on the ground calling for help. You could walk by without even calling 911. But could you walk by without feeling what the German philosopher Martin Heidegger named "the call of conscience"? Could you ignore the man without feeling shame at what you've just done? Without any sense that you had done something objectively wrong? The obligation to be moral presents itself to us as an objective aspect of reality, as something that calls us from above whether or not we want to respond. We can't get out of a moral obligation by simply ignoring it, can we?

C. S. LEWIS AND THE MORAL ARGUMENT FOR THEISTIC ETHICS

These are strong reasons to believe that there is an objective moral law and that this law imposes obligations on us. In other words, the moral law is normative rather than descriptive—it is a rule we ought to follow, not a description of how we do, in fact, always behave. But this is puzzling. Where does the moral law come from? What is its basis in reality? To answer this question, I am going to assemble several clues and then reason by inference to the best explanation to the conclusion that God is the source of the moral law. The inspiration for my presentation is the argument C. S.

Lewis developed in one of his most widely read books, *Mere Christianity*.[3] Many threads from the previous thirteen chapters of this book come together in this argument.

1. The moral law presents itself to us as an objective feature of the universe.

2. The moral law imposes obligations on us that take precedence over considerations of self-interest, ego, profit and loss, and the promptings of raw emotion and desire.

3. As Martin Luther King Jr. observed, not all human-made laws are just. Clearly, any human law can be critically evaluated on moral grounds.

4. The moral law therefore has authority over all human law.

5. As Lewis observed, any instinct, trait, or tendency said to be conferred by the process of natural selection can be evaluated based on moral considerations. If evolution gave us a tendency to behave in a certain way, that would not by itself *justify* behaving in that way, for behaving in that way might be immoral.

6. The moral law therefore has authority over traits conferred by natural selection.

7. Some social customs are moral, and others are not. Certainly, any social custom can be critically evaluated on moral grounds.

8. The moral law therefore has authority over social customs.

9. Any valid normative law comes from a lawgiver possessing the requisite authority.

10. It follows that the moral law stems from a moral lawgiver possessing moral authority over all human law, social customs, instincts, the human ego, and the other items cited.

11. The supreme moral authority cannot be mindless matter in motion, for atoms, subatomic particles, units of energy, and sheets of galaxies have no moral properties and certainly have no moral authority over us.

12. The supreme moral authority obviously cannot be a specific human being.

13. The supreme moral authority obviously cannot be a specific society or social group.

14. God, understood as a morally perfect supreme being, is the only reasonable candidate.

15. The best explanation of the data cited is therefore that God, understood as a morally perfect supreme being, is the source of the moral law.

16. Therefore, the most reasonable conclusion to draw is that God is the source of the moral law.

This is a best explanation argument for theistic ethics—the claim that morality originates in God or a supreme being. Since it is reasonable to assert the existence of that which is implied by our best explanations, this is also an argument for God's existence. In philosophy, this is called a "moral argument for God's existence."[4]

THE EUTHYPHRO DILEMMA:
A FAMOUS OBJECTION TO THEISTIC ETHICS

Many philosophers today reject the claim that morality originates in God. The most commonly given argument against theistic ethics was first stated by Socrates in a conversation with his friend Euthyphro, a priest, as recorded by Plato in the *Euthyphro*. Lewis confronted this argument, as we'll see.

As the dialogue begins, Socrates and Euthyphro are discussing morality. Euthyphro believes that morality consists of laws commanded by God. About halfway through the discussion, Socrates asks a question that has become one of the most famous in the history of philosophy. Here is one way to put his blockbuster question, known as the "Euthyphro dilemma."

Does God command (or will) that which is morally right *because* it is truly right, or is it right solely because *God commands (or wills) it*?

With this question, Socrates poses a logical dilemma for anyone who, like Euthyphro, maintains that morality consists of laws commanded by

God. The problem is that there appears to be only two ways to respond to the dilemma, but both answers seem to contradict traditional theism. The two possible answers, called the two "horns" of the dilemma, may be put this way:

> Answer 1. God commands what is right *because* it is truly right.
> According to this horn of the dilemma, God first recognizes that something is right and then, *on that basis*, commands it. Something is right entirely on its own, before God commands it, and then God sees that it is right and after seeing this, commands it.

> Answer 2. Things that are right are right *because* they are commanded by God.
> According to this horn of the dilemma, God's command *alone* makes something right. Something is neither right nor wrong on its own before God issues a command. Once the divine command is issued, it *becomes* right, and it becomes right solely by virtue of the divine command and not by virtue of anything more fundamental. Here is an analogy: a new ship has no name until someone in authority breaks a champagne bottle over it and formally christens it. The act of christening the ship gives it its name.

The Problem with Answer 1

God, according to Euthyphro and to traditional theists generally, is the ultimate authority in the universe: nothing stands above God; nothing outside of God obligates God or determines God's commands. (This is the doctrine of divine sovereignty.) It is natural to reason that if God is the supreme being, the ultimate source of all existence, then God is sovereign.

However, the first horn seems to contradict the doctrine of God's absolute sovereignty, for it says that God wills what is right *because it is truly right*. This seems to imply that God judges things in relation to an independent standard that exists above God—a standard God must follow. This would be a standard of moral rightness that has authority even over God. But if so, then morality is not actually based in God's commands at all. Instead, it comes from an authority above God, in which case (1) God is not universally sovereign, and (2) God is not really the ultimate source of the moral law.

The Problem with Answer 2

According to traditional theism, God, being the ultimate source of all things, is the source of reason. As the source of reason, God is rational to the highest degree possible. The problem with the second horn is that it implies that God is capricious rather than rational. For if what is right is right solely because it is commanded or willed by God, and nothing else, then it seems to follow that God decides what is right *on the basis of no objective reason whatsoever.* Before God issues his command, nothing is right or wrong. Something becomes right or wrong once God commands it, *and it is right for no underlying reason at all.* On the second horn, then, God's commands are arbitrary, irrational, like deciding an important issue by flipping a coin. God, in other words, is not a critical thinker! This horn of the dilemma avoids saying that God's commands are bound by an independent authority, but at the cost of making God's commands nonrational.

Answer 2 has other problems. If God's commands are arbitrary, then there are no limits to what God can command. It would seem to follow that *if God were to command that we all hate each other, then hatred would be morally right.* It would also seem to follow that *if* God were to command lying, then lying would be right, and so on. These consequences of answer 2 have seemed absurd to most who have thought hard about the matter. How could hate even possibly be morally right? The second horn has counterintuitive consequences.

The traditional theist thus appears to be caught in a dilemma, a double bind. It seems that only two answers are possible, and he must choose one. But either answer *contradicts his own view of God.* It seems to follow that the traditional theistic claim that the moral law is God's commands — understood as a component of traditional theism — is self-contradictory. If so, then it appears that the moral law cannot possibly be rooted in God.

THEISTIC RESPONSES

William Alston (1921–2009), a leading twentieth-century philosopher who taught for many years at Syracuse University, suggested one way the traditional theist can avoid the dilemma.[5] His argument begins with common ground agreed to by Socrates, Euthyphro, Plato, and many other moral philosophers since: When we correctly judge something to be morally right, our judgment (at least implicitly) refers to an objective, immaterial, standard known by reason.

Next, suppose that we agree with Socrates, Euthyphro, Plato, and most moral philosophers since that God exists. Now, if we hypothesize that the supreme, objective, immaterial standard of rightness *is identical to* the divine nature itself, then we have a solution to our dilemma.

For on the basis of this hypothesis, the traditional theist can grasp both horns of the Euthyphro dilemma without any self-contradiction. The theist can now agree that there is an objective, ultimate standard of moral rightness, independent of individual right things, and that God's commands always conform to this standard. This is to grasp the first horn of the dilemma: God commands what is right *because it is right*.

At the same time, the traditional theist can consistently maintain that God is sovereign—not bound by an external or higher standard. For according to this hypothesis, the supreme standard of rightness is internal to God, for it is identical to God's eternal nature. Thus, in commanding what is right, God is not succumbing to a standard above himself; God is merely commanding in conformity to his own nature.

Alston's hypothesis also allows the traditional theist to grasp the second horn of the dilemma and say that a right action is right because God commands it—God's command makes something right. This follows, for on Alston's hypothesis, God's commands directly reflect the supreme moral standard, namely, God's nature. As the philosopher Richard Purtill puts it, the laws of morality are the laws of God's very nature.[6] They proceed from God and therefore are not independent of God; yet they are not purely arbitrary or capricious, for God's nature is neither of the two. If Alston is right, the traditional theist has a logically consistent response to the Euthyphro dilemma. Lewis argues for a similar solution:[7]

> There were in the eighteenth century . . . theologians who held that "God did not command certain things because they are right, but certain things are right because God commanded them." To make the position perfectly clear, one of them even said that though God has, at it happens, commanded us to love him and one another, He might equally well have commanded us to hate Him and one another, and hatred would have been right. It was apparently a mere toss-up which He decided on. Such a view of course makes God a mere arbitrary tyrant.[8]

The more reasonable way to think of the matter, Lewis argues, is rather: "[God] is righteous and commands righteousness because He loves it. He enjoins what is good because it is good, because He is good. Hence His laws have truth, intrinsic validity, rock bottom reality, being rooted in His own nature."[9] On this view, the ultimate basis of objective moral truth is not God's commands, it is God's eternal and absolute goodness.

A SECOND OBJECTION TO THEISTIC ETHICS

The argument from the diversity and evolution of moral beliefs begins with this thought. If God imprinted in our hearts or on our rational faculty a knowledge of divine, objective moral values, as traditional theists often claim, then why is there so much moral disagreement both within and across cultures?[10] And why is our understanding of moral matters more advanced today than it was in the remote past? For example, in *The Better Angels of Our Nature: Why Violence Has Declined*, the Harvard psychologist Steven Pinker examines laws, institutions, and social practices of the past that appear terribly cruel and unjust when viewed from our present vantage point. In Europe as recently as the eighteenth century, horrible punishments were administered for small offenses.[11] Our moral knowledge and sensitivity have deepened over the centuries. But it seems that if God implanted moral knowledge in our hearts and minds at the start, then we would all have agreed on morality from the beginning. Therefore, it is not obvious that morality originates in God.

What can the advocate of theistic ethics say in response? Perhaps the following is a start. First, we should not overlook the fact that there is a great deal of universal agreement on most fundamental moral issues. As we saw in chapter 12, in *The Abolition of Man*, Lewis assembled a collection of moral principles and values accepted around the world. People everywhere, at least when at their best, value love, truth-telling, keeping one's word, friendship, loyalty, courage, respect for elders, and human life. The news tends to focus on our disagreements and failures; the good news and the many areas of universal agreement are usually not newsworthy.

Second, surely some moral disagreement can be explained with thoughts on the nature of free will. The possession of free will includes not only the power to grasp moral truth and follow it faithfully but also the power to willfully turn a blind eye to morality in order to rationalize bad or selfish behavior. The Christian ethicist Scott Rae observes that "many moral obligations conflict with self-interest, and this causes people to reject them, ignore them, and to rationalize immoral behavior."[12] Rationalizing bad behavior can distort anyone's conscience.

Socratic self-examination also reveals that each of us has moral blind spots due to selfishness and cognitive bias. Of course, the possession of free will also means that we also have the power to look in the mirror, realize our errors, and improve our lives.

Free will may explain some moral disagreements, but if God implanted knowledge of morality in the human heart or intellect, why has it taken humanity so long to figure out the basics on such matters as universal human rights and the nature of a free society? In other words, why has our knowledge of some moral matters grown over the years?

Irenaeus's soul-making theodicy, which we examined in chapter 7, offers one answer. His account suggests that God gave all of us the innate cognitive ability to discover for ourselves the moral truths of general revelation. But God also left us free to think for ourselves, discover, learn from others, and pass on our discoveries from generation to generation.

Metaethics vs. Normative Ethics

Philosophers divide philosophical ethics into two broad divisions. Normative ethics is the attempt to identify the correct principles or standards of ethical behavior. Metaethics is philosophical reflection on the logical status and nature of morality. Chapters 12 and 13 are introductions to normative ethics. This chapter falls within the subdivision of metaethics.

A THIRD OBJECTION TO THEISTIC ETHICS

Some argue that if we adopt the theistic view of morality and behave morally, then we will behave in the right way but for the wrong reason. We will be good out of fear of divine punishment and hope for a heavenly reward. But these are selfish, childish motives, not moral ones. Imagine seeing someone do a good deed and then finding out afterward that he or she only did it out of a crass hope of reward. The deed no longer looks morally good.

Furthermore, if we are good only because we desire reward or fear punishment, it follows that our commitment to morality is unreliable. For we would be bad if we were not going to be punished, or if we expected no reward for being good.

Theists offer this reply. Why can't believers, when at their best, be good out of love of God and out of love of their fellow creatures? Isn't love a moral motive? Furthermore, experience shows that our motives are usually mixed. Why can't self-interest and love both be parts of our motive when we perform a good act? We are, after all, imperfect creatures. Finally, a purely secular or nonreligious ethical view faces an analogous question: Are many secular people good only out of fear of punishment or desire for reward? If so, analogous problems arise.

POSSIBLE CONFUSIONS

Finally, some possible confusions must be cleared up. Theistic ethics does *not* include the claim that someone must believe in God to be a morally good person. Certainly, there are atheists who are morally good people. Nor does theistic ethics include the claim that believing in God makes one automatically a morally good person. Obviously, there are believers in God who have done morally abominable things. Theistic ethics also does *not* include the epistemological claim that one must know God to know the difference between right and wrong. Recall that theistic philosophers distinguish special from general revelation. The basic principles of morality, they claim, are present in general revelation, which can be known by anyone using reason, our common currency.

Moral Facts. As we saw in chapter 8, the correspondence theory of truth presupposes the existence of objective facts. The existence of objective moral truths implies the existence of objective *moral* facts. According to moral objectivism, just as it's a chemical fact that water boils at 212 degrees F (under standard conditions), it's an objective *moral* fact that (for example) armed robbery is wrong. The claim is that armed robbery—not our subjective feelings about armed robbery—has the property of moral wrongness. Likewise, since acts of kindness are morally right, acts of kindness have the objective property of moral rightness. They have this property whether or not someone believes they do. On the objective view of ethics, the world is dappled with moral facts or properties, that is, with *moral significance.* C. S. Lewis discusses in an especially clear way the difference between an objective and a subjective view of values in *The Abolition of Man.*[13]

JEAN-PAUL SARTRE AND THE MORAL ARGUMENT
AGAINST GOD'S EXISTENCE

Sometimes when considering an abstract issue, it helps to think about the matter from a different direction entirely. Another way to think about the relation between God and morality is exemplified by the writings of the French existentialist philosopher Jean-Paul Sartre (1905–80), an influential atheist who was especially popular among members of the 1960s youth counterculture. In *Existentialism and Human Emotions*, Sartre states that "existentialism is nothing else but the attempt to draw the full implications from a consistently atheist position."[14] However, he continues, giving up their belief in God leaves existentialists feeling forlorn, that is, sad and abandoned:

> When we speak of forlornness . . . we mean only that God does not exist and that we have to face all the consequences of this. The existentialist is opposed to a certain kind of secular ethics which would like to abolish God with the least possible expense. About 1880, some French teachers tried to set up a secular ethic which went something like this: God is a useless and costly hypothesis; we are discarding it; but, meanwhile, in order for there to be an ethics, a society, a civilization, it is essential that certain values be taken seriously and that they be considered as having an a priori existence. It must be obligatory, a priori, to be honest, not to lie . . . etc., etc. So we're going to try a little device which will make it possible to show that values exist all the same, inscribed in a heaven of ideas, though God does not exist.[15]

But existentialists reject any attempt to find an objective basis for morality apart from God.

> The existentialist, on the contrary, thinks it very distressing that God does not exist, because all possibility of finding values in [an objective] heaven of ideas disappears along with Him; there can no longer be an a priori Good, since there is no infinite and perfect consciousness to think it. Nowhere is it written that the Good exists, that we must be honest, that we must not lie, because the fact is we are on a plane where there are only men. Dostoevsky said, "If God didn't exist, everything would be permitted." That is the very starting point of existentialism. Indeed, everything is permissible if God does not exist, and as a result

man is forlorn, because neither within him nor without does he find anything to cling to. . . . If God does not exist, we find no values or commands to turn to. . . . That is the idea I shall try to convey when I say that man is condemned to be free.[16]

So, according to Sartre, if there *are* objective moral truths, then God exists. And if God does not exist, then objective moral truths do not exist. But God does not exist, Sartre declares; therefore, there are no objective moral truths, and each of us is radically free to create his or her own system of good and bad, right and wrong. Indeed, each of us *must*.[17]

The Australian philosopher J. L. Mackie (1917–81) was another influential atheist who argued from the same premises. In *The Miracle of Theism*, Mackie argues that the traditionally conceived moral properties such as right and wrong and good and bad cannot be explained naturalistically, that is, in terms of the fundamental categories of physics, or matter, or in terms of anything that is part of the natural world around us. Therefore, "Moral properties constitute so odd a cluster of properties and relations that they are most unlikely to have arisen in the ordinary course of events without an all-powerful God to create them."[18]

Mackie argues in his book that (1) God does not exist, (2) objective moral values exist only if God exists, (3) therefore there is no objective basis for morality, and (4) this leaves each individual radically free to "invent" his or her own morality.

Notice that in this discussion, the theist and the atheist start from the same premise, namely, if God does not exist, then objective moral truths do not exist. From here, they reach opposite conclusions via differing second premises. The theist argues this way:

1. If God does not exist, then objective moral truths do not exist.

2. But objective moral truths *do* exist.

3. Therefore, God exists.

The atheist argues this way:

1. If God does not exist, then objective moral truths do not exist.

2. God does not exist.

3. Therefore, objective moral truths do not exist.

Both arguments are valid (if the premises are true, then the conclusion must be true). Do objective moral truths exist? If the answer is yes, it follows validly that God exists, given the shared premise that if God does not exist, then objective moral standards do not exist.

The radical implications of the atheist view proposed by Sartre and Mackie are not always noted. If there are no objective moral truths and each person is absolutely free to create his or her own morality, then there is no objective standard by which a person's freely chosen moral beliefs can be judged or evaluated. It follows that there is no objective basis from which to say that one person's moral beliefs are true and another's are false, or that one person's moral beliefs are better than another's. So, if one person advocates hatred and another advocates love, there is no objective basis from which to say that the first person is wrong and the second is right.

Let's put this in even more personal and realistic terms. Was Dr. King right when he argued in his "Letter from Birmingham City Jail" that there is a transcendent justice above any human code of justice? That there is a natural moral law on which human laws can be judged?[19] Recalling Kant and Rawls, do we have an objective moral obligation to treat each other with concern and respect? If so, then, given the key premise noted above, the premise shared by many atheists and theists, God does exist. You decide.

Questions for Reflection and Discussion 14

1. In your own words, summarize the best explanation argument for theistic ethics.
2. According to the Euthyphro argument, what is the problem with supposing that God commands what is right because it is right? What is the problem with supposing that something is right because God commands it?
3. How does Alston claim to resolve the Euthyphro dilemma?
4. Explain an objection to theistic ethics, and offer a theistic response.
5. Choose any idea in Sartre's argument, and discuss it philosophically.
6. Choose any idea in King's famous letter, and discuss it philosophically.
7. Is God the ultimate source of the moral law? Offer the most intelligent and strongest reasons you can for your position.

NOTES

To the Instructor

1. James Beilby, ed., *Naturalism Defeated? Essays on Plantinga's Evolutionary Argument against Naturalism* (Ithaca, NY: Cornell University Press, 2002), 1.

ONE. *How Philosophy Began*

1. "Khnemu (Khnum)," Ancient Egypt: The Mythology, http://www.egyptian myths.net/khnemu.htm.

2. See http://zhang.digitalscholar.rochester.edu/china/tag/pangu/#:~:text =Pangu.

3. See https://en.wikipedia.org/wiki/Mdombo.

4. See https://www.ancient-literature.com/greece_hesiod_theogony.html.

5. The ancient Hebrews are a second exception to this generalization: they too preserved in detail the names, dates, and biographical information of their major figures. The Hebrews also reflected deeply on the big questions of life. The book of Job is only one of many fine examples. Their writings, however, are not considered philosophy in the strict sense of the word because they do not contain philosophical *arguments*. We'll examine the idea of an argument in more depth in chapter 2, but for now, as philosophers use the term, an "argument" is one or more premises offered as evidence for a conclusion. A strictly philosophical argument reaches its conclusion using unaided reasoning and observation alone. The Hebrew scriptures, also called the Old Testament, are a collection of religious rather than strictly philosophical writings.

6. Some have claimed that the ancient Egyptians invented philosophy and taught the Greeks to philosophize. The Greeks, they claim, stole all their ideas

from the Egyptians. Greek philosophy is therefore a stolen intellectual legacy, a "cultural appropriation." However, this claim has been thoroughly examined and debunked by mainstream historians. Not a single document in the historical records of ancient Egypt contains even one philosophical argument. Myth, pronouncements of priestly authority, magic, rituals, and unexamined tradition do not constitute philosophy. Others have claimed that philosophy began in India and was copied by the Greeks. The charge, again, is that Greek philosophy is nothing but stolen goods. This also requires a reply. On the Indian subcontinent, the first reflections on the big questions appear in the *Vedas* (Sanskrit for "sacred knowledge")—four collections of religious writings transmitted by priests and considered divinely inspired. Each of the four (*Rigveda, Samaveda, Yajurveda,* and *Atharvaveda*) has four parts: hymns to the gods; directions on how to voice these hymns; commentary on these directions; and the *Upanishads,* or speculative commentary on the preceding three parts. In each of the Vedas, the Upanishads appear last, as appendices, and some do contain the beginnings of philosophical thought. However, none of the Upanishads can be reliably dated to the early sixth century BC. Furthermore, there is no evidence of any contact between the scholars of India and Greece as early as the days of Thales. Something similar can be said regarding the earliest dated writings of ancient China. The *Analects* of Confucius (551–479 BC) do not contain a single argument, let alone a philosophical argument. This may be because his followers selected only the key points of his teaching. A century or more after his death, however, as his thoughts became influential, Chinese thinkers began to debate his ideas on the basis of reason, and a golden age of Chinese philosophy began. The fact remains that a tradition of back-and-forth, reasoned philosophical debate on the big questions, preserved in written form with dates, makes its first appearance in the historical record in only one place—the land of the Greeks during the sixth century BC. The issue of historical priority would not matter were it not for the current attacks on Western civilization within the academy, harsh attacks which falsely present Western thought as stolen goods and Western civilization as nothing but a parasite from the start. I owe thanks to my colleague Mark Storey (Bellevue College) for many helpful discussions that clarified my understanding of the early history of philosophical thought in India, China, and other ancient civilizations. See Mary R. Lefkowitz and Guy MacLean Rogers, eds., *Black Athena Revisited* (Chapel Hill: University of North Carolina Press, 1996), and Mary Lefkowitz, *Not Out of Africa: How Afrocentrism Became an Excuse to Teach Myth As History* (New York: New Republic Books, 1997).

7. See Patricia F. O'Grady, *Thales of Miletus: The Beginnings of Western Science and Philosophy* (Burlington, VT: Ashgate, 2002). Unfortunately, none of his writings survived; we know of his arguments through commentaries written by later philosophers, including Aristotle.

8. James Fieser and Norman Lillegard, *A Historical Introduction to Philosophy* (New York: Oxford University Press, 2002), 5.

9. David Stewart, *Exploring the Philosophy of Religion* (Englewood Cliffs, NJ: Prentice-Hall, 1980), 77.

10. L. P. Gerson, *God and Greek Philosophy: Studies in the Early History of Natural Theology* (New York: Routledge, 1990), 14.

11. Thomas Nagel, *Mind and Cosmos: Why the Materialist Neo-Darwinian Conception of Nature Is Almost Certainly False* (New York: Oxford University Press, 2012), 16. Nagel also argues that the amazing things we have learned about the deep structure of the universe are strong evidence that the universe *is* intelligible down to the most fundamental level.

12. *Albert Einstein, Ideas and Opinions* (New York: Crown, 1954), 261–62.

13. Merrill Ring, *Beginning with the Pre-Socratics* (Mountain View, CA: Mayfield Publishing, 1987), 22.

14. See https://novoscriptorium.com/2019/11/04/theological-views-of -thales-from-miletos/.

15. The Hebrews, of course, were monotheists long before this, but not for strictly philosophical reasons. They preserved their religious experiences and thoughts in the Old Testament.

16. Wallace Matson, *A New History of Philosophy* (New York: Harcourt Brace Jovanovich, 1987), 1:4. I am using the terms *theory* and *hypothesis* interchangeably here to mean "a proposed explanation offered as the starting point for further investigation." We often use these two words in this way in everyday life. Some prefer the more technical definitions: A *hypothesis* is "a proposed explanation based on limited data and offered as a basis for further study"; a *theory* is "a proposed explanation that is already well-confirmed."

17. J. V. Luce, *An Introduction to Greek Philosophy* (Dublin: Thames and Hudson, 1992), 22.

18. Quoted in Laurence BonJour, *Epistemology: Classic Problems and Contemporary Responses* (New York: Rowman and Littlefield, 2010), 1. Originally from Wilfrid Sellars, *Science, Perception, and Reality* (London: Routledge & Kegan Paul, 1963), 1.

19. Laurence BonJour, *Epistemology: Classic Problems and Contemporary Responses* (New York: Rowman and Littlefield, 2010),viii.

20. Francis Collins, *The Language of God: A Scientist Presents Evidence for Belief* (New York: Free Press, 2007).

21. Edward Feser, *Five Proofs of the Existence of God* (San Francisco: Ignatius, 2017), 281.

22. Karl Popper, *The World of Parmenides: Essays on the Pre-Socratic Enlightenment* (London: Routledge, 1998), 36.

23. Matson, *New History of Philosophy*, 15–16.

24. Luce, *Introduction to Greek Philosophy*, 9.

25. For those who want to delve into the pre-Socratics, a good place to begin is Frederick Copleston, *A History of Philosophy*, Vol. 1, *Greece and Rome: From the Pre-Socratics to Plotinus*, rpt. ed. (New York: Image Books, 1993). I also recommend Ring, *Beginning with the Pre-Socratics*.

26. See Thomas Heath, *A History of Greek Mathematics* (New York: Dover, 1981), 1:122.

27. W. W. Rouse Ball, *A Short Account of the History of Mathematics* (New York: Dover, 1960), 14.

28. Heath, *History of Greek Mathematics*, 128. Heath's book runs to more than 1,000 pages and only provides a summary of the Greek accomplishment. As Heath notes, the word *geometry* is of Greek origin.

29. Burton, *History of Mathematics*, 85.

30. Dirk J. Struik, *A Concise History of Mathematics* (New York: Dover, 1967), 38.

31. Burton, *History of Mathematics*, 85.

32. Struik, *A Concise History of Mathematics*, 38.

33. J. M. Roberts, *A Short History of the World* (New York: Oxford University Press, 1993), 117. For more on the place of the Greeks in world history, see the short but excellent M. I. Finley *The Ancient Greeks* (New York: Viking Press, 1965), and H. D. F. Kitto, *The Greeks* (New York: Pelican, 1958). Two popular books are Thomas Cahill, *Sailing the Wine Dark Sea: Why the Greeks Matter* (New York: Doubleday, 2003), and Edith Hamilton, *The Greek Way* (New York: W. W. Norton & Co., 1930).

34. In private correspondence with Andrew Jeffery, August 2017.

35. Hamilton, *Greek Way*, 14. Hamilton's classic book is required reading for anyone seeking a deeper understanding of the ancient Greeks. For history buffs, on the topic of what we owe the Greeks, I recommend two books to complement Hamilton's classic study: Bruce Thornton, *Greek Ways: How the Greeks Created Western Civilization*, rev. ed. (New York: Encounter Books, 2002), and Victor Davis Hanson, *Carnage and Culture: Landmark Battles in the Rise to Western Power* (New York: Anchor, 2001).

TWO. *The Socratic Method*

1. Quoted in W. K. C. Guthrie, *Socrates* (Cambridge: Cambridge University Press, 1972), 53.

2. Some question whether his military service is relevant to his life as a philosopher. Surely it helped shape his character. Perhaps his distaste for violence and force in personal life stemmed in part from his experience in battle.

3. See Nicholas Sekunda, *Greek Hoplite 480–323 BC: Weapons, Armour, Tactics* (Elms Court, UK: Osprey, 2000).

4. Socrates's student Plato re-created this argument in the dialogue *Crito*.

5. On voluntary simplicity today, see the blogs *Choosing Voluntary Simplicity*, http://www.choosingvoluntarysimplicity.com/, and *Enjoy Simple Living*, http://www.enjoysimpleliving.blogspot.com/.

6. See "A Brief History of the Idea of Critical Thinking," The Foundation for Critical Thinking, http://www.criticalthinking.org/pages/a-brief-history-of-the-idea-of-critical-thinking/408. Parts of my account of the Socratic method and critical thinking are adapted from a textbook that I wrote, Paul Herrick, *Think with Socrates: An Introduction to Critical Thinking* (New York: Oxford University Press, 2014).

7. Ronald Gross, *Socrates' Way: Seven Master Keys to Using Your Mind to Its Utmost* (New York: Jeremy P. Tarcher/Putnam, 2002), 9.

8. See C. C. W. Taylor, *Socrates: A Very Short Introduction* (New York: Oxford University Press, 1998), 26.

9. Alfred North Whitehead, *Process and Reality* (New York: Free Press, 1979), 39.

10. Plato's dialogues are available in many inexpensive editions, for example, C. D. C. Reeve, ed., *A Plato Reader: Eight Essential Dialogues* (New York: Hackett, 2012). For the complete works, see Edith Hamilton, Huntington Cairns, and Lane Cooper, eds., *The Collected Dialogues of Plato: Including the Letters* (Princeton, NJ: Princeton University Press, 1981).

11. Alcoholics Anonymous adds that a full program of recovery includes the recognition of a higher power and the act of calling upon that power for help. If he were alive today, Socrates would be in full agreement with this wonderful organization that has helped many thousands of individuals deal effectively with addiction.

12. Plato, *Apology* 29d.

13. The vote was 280 to convict, 220 to acquit.

14. At the Prytaneum, a state-sponsored mess hall reserved for Olympic champions. He also offered a nominal fine as an alternative punishment, again knowing it would not be accepted.

15. For an account of his argument, see Plato's *Crito*.

16. Plato, *Phaedo* 116c.

17. Ibid., 116d.

18. Ibid., 117d. Plato is sparing his readers the gruesome details. A death by hemlock would usually involve vomiting, feelings of suffocation, and violent seizures.

19. Read this online at http://www.nlnrac.org/classical/cicero.

20. Gregory Vlastos, "The Paradox of Socrates," in *The Philosophy of Socrates: A Collection of Critical Essays*, ed. Gregory Vlastos (New York: Anchor Books, 1971), 20.

21. An ideal that humanity is still struggling to achieve, 2,400 years after Socrates. The same ideal was advanced about the same time by the Chinese philosopher Mozi (ca. 470–ca. 391 BC), who rejected the Confucian aristocratic morality of his day and argued for a morality of universal concern, love, and impartiality toward all human beings. Like Socrates, Mozi also argued for the existence of God and taught that reason can discover truth when it follows objective criteria. He is the founder of the first school of formal logic in the Chinese tradition. Unfortunately, we know very little about Mozi's thought or the work of the Mohist logicians because a powerful Chinese emperor executed the Mohists and burned their books. One of the lessons of history is that unelected authoritarian rulers do not want the people to reason critically, independently of their overlords.

22. Gross, *Socrates' Way*, 2. For further research on Socrates, in addition to the sources already cited I recommend Gregory Vlastos, *Socrates: Ironist and Moral Philosopher* (Ithaca, NY: Cornell University Press, 1991).

THREE. *And a Few Principles of Logic*

1. The information presented in this chapter is adapted from Paul Herrick, *Introduction to Logic* (New York: Oxford University Press, 2012).

2. Benson Mates, *Elementary Logic*, 2nd ed. (New York: Oxford University Press, 1972), 206. *Ex nihilo* is Latin for "out of nothing" and means "from scratch" in this context. We'll examine this idea applied to the universe as a whole in chapter 6.

3. J. V. Luce, *Introduction to Greek Philosophy* (Dublin: Thames and Hudson, 1992), 95.

4. See Jonathan Barnes, *Aristotle: A Very Short Introduction* (New York: Oxford University Press, 2009, 4. Also recommended is J. L Ackrill, *Aristotle the Philosopher*. (New York: Oxford University Press. 1981). For the reader interested in delving into Aristotle's thought, I recommend Richard McKeon, ed., *The Basic Works of Aristotle*, ed. (New York: Random House, 1941), and W. D. Ross, *Aristotle* (New York: Meridian Books, 1959).

5. Logicians like technical definitions. In logic, a proposition, claim, or state of affairs counts as "possible" if it is not self-contradictory. A statement is self-contradictory if it is a self-contradiction or implies one. A self-contradiction is any statement of the form "P and it is not the case that P," where P is a variable standing in for any declarative sentence. If we consistently give the words their usual meanings, the following statement is a self-contradiction: The car is ten years old and it is not the case that the car is ten years old. Now, although it is highly improbable that a person wins the New York State lottery one million times in a row, it is (logically) possible, for the supposition is not self-contradictory. Thus, it is logically possible (though not likely) someone wins the New York State lottery one million times in a row. On the other hand, it is not logically possible that there is a man who is older than all men, for the statement (that there is a man who is older than all men) is self-contradictory.

FOUR. *The Design Argument*

1. This story is my imaginative account of the thoughts that probably led Socrates to give his design argument for the existence of God or a supreme being. In Socrates's time, many philosophers in Athens thought along these lines.

2. In his memoirs, Socrates's student Xenophon reports hearing his teacher give this argument. See Xenophon, *Conversations with Socrates* (New York: Barnes and Noble, 2005), "Socrates Proveth the Existence of a Deity," chap. 4.

3. According to ancient historians, Pythagoras discovered that the harmonic intervals on the musical scale reflect whole number mathematical ratios between vibrating physical objects rather than the material properties of the physical objects themselves. For instance, an octave results when the ratio between the lengths of vibrating strings is 2:1, the fourth note is produced by a 3:2 ratio, and the fifth by a 4:3 ratio. The beauty within musical harmony is thus a function of abstract mathematical structure rather than of anything purely physical. During the seventeenth century, Pythagoras was honored by many of those who founded modern science for his early insights into the mathematical structure of the world, including his pioneering work that launched the science of acoustics by connecting math, physics, sound, and beauty.

4. Douglas Hofstadter and Emmanuel Sander, *Surfaces and Essences: Analogy as the Fuel and Fire of Thinking* (New York: Basic Books, 2013).

5. Steven Weinberg, *Dreams of a Final Theory* (New York: Vintage Books, 1994), 6. Most leading physicists today believe that the universe displays one overall, comprehensive order. See James Trefil, *Reading the Mind of God: In Search*

414   Notes to Pages 66–72

of the Principle of Universality (New York: Doubleday, 1989); Paul Davies, *The Mind of God: The Scientific Basis for a Rational World* (New York: Simon and Schuster, 1992).

6. Epicurus hypothesized that this happened an infinite number of times in the past producing in time every possible combination of atoms. As we'll see, a chance process like this requires an intelligently designed background order.

7. My argument here was inspired by a similar argument Alvin Plantinga gives in Plantinga, *Where the Conflict Really Lies: Science, Religion, & Naturalism* (New York: Oxford University Press, 2011), 214.

8. Complexity actually increases as we go from observable entities to the theoretical levels that explain them.

9. For further reading on the design argument I recommend Richard Swinburne, *The Existence of God*, 2nd ed. (Oxford: Clarendon 2004), chap. 8, "Teleological Arguments," 153–91, and Elliott Sober, *The Design Argument* (Cambridge: Cambridge University Press, 2018).

10. Thomas Nagel, *The Last Word* (New York: Oxford University Press, 1997), 150.

11. Thomas Nagel, *Mind and Cosmos: Why the Materialist Neo-Darwinian Conception of Nature Is Almost Certainly False* (New York: Oxford University Press, 2012), 16–17.

12. See Stephen C. Meyer, *Return of the God Hypothesis: Three Scientific Discoveries That Reveal the Mind behind the Universe* (New York: HarperOne, 2021); Meyer, *Darwin's Doubt: The Explosive Origin of Animal Life and the Case for Intelligent Design* (New York: HarperOne, 2013); Meyer, *Signature in the Cell: DNA and the Evidence for Intelligent Design* (New York: HarperOne, 2010); Michael J. Behe, *Darwin's Black Box: The Biochemical Challenge to Evolution* (New York: Free Press, 2001); and Behe, *The Edge of Evolution: The Search for the Limits of Darwinism* (New York: Free Press, 2007); and William Dembski, *The Design Inference: Eliminating Chance through Small Probabilities* (Cambridge: Cambridge University Press, 2006).

13. Thomas Nagel, *Mind and Cosmos*, 18.

14. Ibid., 18. On the disgraceful, anti-intellectual way intelligent design theorists have been treated and indeed smeared by some scientific elites, see Ben Stein's movie *Expelled*.

15. See Edward Grant, *The Foundations of Modern Science in the Middle Ages: Their Religious, Institutional, and Intellectual Contexts* (Cambridge: Cambridge University Press, 1996), and Rodney Stark, *How the West Won: The Neglected Story of the Triumph of Modernity* (Wilmington, DE: Intercollegiate Studies Institute Press, 2015). Another important source is the classic Alfred North Whitehead, *Science and the Modern World* (New York: Mentor Books, 1925). White-

head argues that medieval Christianity provided "the soil, the climate, the seeds" for the birth of modern science" (ibid., 22).

16. Incidentally, the universities of Europe that gave birth to modern science had all been founded by the Catholic Church and were administered by churchmen. The pioneers in many branches of modern science were monks and priests who combined scientific research with duties in their religious orders. See James Hannam, *The Genesis of Modern Science: How the Christian Middle Ages Launched the Scientific Revolution* (Washington, DC: Regnery, 2011), and Thomas Woods Jr., *How the Catholic Church Built Western Civilization.*(Washington DC: Regnery, 2005). Woods writes: "The Catholic contribution to science went well beyond ideas—including theological ideas—to accomplished practicing scientists, many of whom were priests. For example, Father Nicolaus Steno . . . is often identified as the father of geology. The father of Egyptology was Father Athanasius Kircher. The first person to measure the rate of acceleration of a freely falling body was yet another priest, Father Giambattista Riccioli. Father Roger Boscovich is often credited as the father of modern atomic theory. Jesuits so dominated the study of earthquakes that seismology became known as 'the Jesuit science.' Even though some thirty-five craters on the moon are named for Jesuit scientists and mathematicians, the Church's contributions to astronomy are all but unknown to the average educated American" (ibid., 5). Modern mathematics was born in Europe in the same historical context. See any standard history of mathematics, for instance: Florian Cajori, *A History of Mathematics*, 5th ed. (New York: Chelsea, 1991), and Victor Katz, *A History of Mathematics: An Introduction* (New York: Harper Collins, 1993).

17. Quoted in Ernan M. McMullin, ed., *Evolution and Creation* (Notre Dame, IN: University of Notre Dame Press, 1985), 28. For Ray's argument, see Alan Olding, *Modern Biology and Natural Theology* (New York: Routledge, 1991), x–xi. According to the biologist Ernst Mayr, Ray's *Historia Plantarum* catalogued 18,665 plant species.

18. Quoted in McMullin, ed., *Evolution and Creation*, 126.

19. Quoted in John Marks Templeton, ed., *Evidence of Purpose* (New York: Continuum, 1994), 50.

20. I. Bernard Cohen, *The Birth of a New Physics* (Garden City, NY: Doubleday, 1960), 152–53.

21. David Hume, *Dialogues concerning Natural Religion* (Indianapolis, IN: Hackett, 1980), 48.

22. Ibid., 36.

23. Weinberg, *Dreams of a Final Theory*, 6. Most leading physicists today believe that the universe displays one overall, comprehensive order. See Trefil, *Reading the Mind of God*; Davies, *The Mind of God*; and Davies, *Accidental Universe*, chap. 2.

24. Craig J. Hogan, *The Little Book of the Big Bang: A Cosmic Primer* (New York: Springer-Verlag, 1998).

25. David Hume, *Dialogues concerning Natural Religion*, 49–51.

26. I am using David Hume, *Enquiries concerning the Human Understanding and concerning the Principles of Morals*, 2nd ed., ed. L. A. Selby-Bigge, reprinted from the Posthumous Edition of 1777 (Oxford: Oxford University Press, 1902), 136.

27. For a longer and more in-depth response to the question, Who designed the designer?, see William Lane Craig, "Richard Dawkins on Arguments for God," in *God Is Good, God Is Great*, ed. William Lane Craig and Chad Meister (Downers Grove, IL: InterVarsity Press, 2009), loc. 361–91, Kindle ed. For the reader interested in exploring modal logic, simplicity, necessary existence, and the way philosophers have employed these concepts to reach an ultimate explanation, I recommend Kenneth Konyndyk, *Introductory Modal Logic* (South Bend, IN: University of Notre Dame Press, 1986); Jeffrey E. Brower, "Simplicity and Aseity," in *The Oxford Handbook of Philosophical Theology*, ed. Thomas P. Flint and Michael C. Rea (Oxford: Oxford University Press, 2009), 105–29; and Timothy O'Conner, *Theism and Ultimate Explanation: The Necessary Shape of Contingency* (Oxford: Wiley-Blackwell, 2012).

28. David Hume, *Dialogues concerning Natural Religion*, 89.

29. Ibid., 11.

FIVE. *Design and Evolution*

1. Of Paley, Darwin writes, "I was charmed and convinced by the long line of argumentation [in *Natural Theology*]"; see George Gaylord Simpson, ed., *The Book of Darwin* (New York: Washington Square, 1982), 42.

2. On the intellectual debate that preceded the introduction of Darwin's theory, see Michael Ruse, *The Darwinian Revolution* (Chicago: University of Chicago Press, 1979).

3. Charles Darwin, *On the Origin of Species by Means of Natural Selection, or the Preservation of Favoured Races in the Struggle for Life* (New York: Mentor, 1959), 443.

4. Ibid., 450.

5. Quoted in Robert Augros and George Stanciu, *The New Biology: Discovering the Wisdom in Nature* (Boston: New Science Library, 1987), 228–29.

6. Quoted in William Dembski, *Mere Creation: Science, Faith, and Intelligent Design* (Downers Grove, IL: InterVarsity, 1998), 73.

7. Quoted in Augros and Stanciu, *New Biology*, 188.

8. Richard Dawkins, *The Blind Watchmaker: Why the Evidence of Evolution Reveals a World without Design* (New York: W. W. Norton, 1987).

9. Ibid., 45.

10. I am paraphrasing Dawkins here (ibid., 46–49).

11. See Paul C. W. Davies, *The Accidental Universe* (Cambridge: Cambridge University Press, 1982), chap. 2. See also John Barrow and Frank Tippler, *The Anthropic Cosmological Principle* (New York: Oxford University Press, 1986); and Joseph Silk, *The Big Bang*, rev. ed. (New York: W. H. Freeman, 1989).

12. See John Gribbin and Martin Rees, *Cosmic Coincidences: Dark Matter, Mankind, and Anthropic Cosmology* (New York: Bantam, 1989), 4.

13. See Davies, *Accidental Universe*; Tippler and Barrow, *Anthropic Cosmological Principle*; John Gribbin and Martin Rees, *Cosmic Coincidences*; George Greenstein, *Symbiotic Universe* (New York: William Morrow, 1987); and Paul Davies, *God and the New Physics* (New York: Simon and Schuster, 1983).

14. Quoted by Alvin Plantinga, *Where the Conflict Really Lies: Science, Religion, and Naturalism* (New York: Oxford University Press, 2011), 195.

15. Paul C. W. Davies, "The Unreasonable Effectiveness of Science," in *Evidence of Purpose*, ed. John Templeton (New York: Templeton Press, 1997), 49.

16. Barrow and Tippler, *Anthropic Cosmological Principle*, 360.

17. See Heinz Pagels, "A Cozy Cosmology," reprinted in John Leslie, ed., *Physical Cosmology and Philosophy* (New York: Macmillan, 1990), 174.

18. Gribbin and Rees, *Cosmic Coincidences*, 269.

19. Ibid., 10.

20. John Barrow, *The Artful Universe* (Oxford: Clarendon, 1995), 34–35.

21. Ibid.

22. In addition, each proton is composed of two "up" quarks bound to one "down" quark by the exchange of mysterious particles called "gluons." Electrons are not composed of smaller particles.

23. Greenstein, *Symbiotic Universe*, 64–65.

24. Ibid., 64.

25. Ibid.

26. Ibid., chap. 3; Gribbin and Rees, *Cosmic Coincidences*, chap. 1.

27. Paul Edwards, *Physical Cosmology and Philosophy* (New York: Macmillan, 1990), 16.

28. See Gribbin and Rees, *Cosmic Coincidences*, 18.

29. Ibid.

30. Ibid., 26.

31. George Seielstad, *Cosmic Ecology: The View from the Outside In* (Los Angeles: University of California Press, 1983), 65.

32. This website lists 140: https://www.cltruth.com/ /2019/factors-fine-tuning
-life-universe/.

33. See Freeman Dyson, "The Argument from Design," an essay reprinted in
Dyson, *Disturbing the Universe* (New York: Basic Books, 1981), 250. Dyson argues that the improbable arrangement of the fundamental constants is evidence
of design.

34. Ibid.

35. Ibid., 95.

36. Stephen Hawking, *A Brief History of Time*, 10th anniversary ed. (New
York: Bantam, 1998), 129.

37. By "discontinuous" I mean that no signals or information or entities can
pass from one mini-universe to another.

38. Victor Stenger, *God and the Multiverse: Humanity's Expanding View of the
Cosmos* (Amherst, NY: Prometheus, 2014), 351.

39. Davies, *Accidental Universe*, 128.

40. See C. Stephen Layman, *Letters to a Doubting Thomas: A Case for the
Existence of God* (New York: Oxford University Press, 2007), 130.

41. The many universes theory originated within physics as an interpretation
of quantum mechanics, apart from any debates about the existence of God. The
original article was Hugh Everett III, "'Relative State' Formulation of Quantum
Mechanics," *Review of Modern Physics* 29, no. 454 (1957). For those who want to
probe Everett's theory, I recommend Simon Saunders, Jonathan Barrett, Adrian
Kent, and David Wallace, eds., *Many Worlds? Everett, Quantum Theory, and Reality*
(New York: Oxford University Press, 2010). For the reader who wants to explore
the multiverse idea further, I recommend: Klaas Kraay, ed., *God and the Multiverse:
Scientific, Philosophical, and Theological Perspectives* (New York: Routledge, 2014).

42. Plantinga, *Where the Conflict Really Lies*, 213–14.

43. For further problems with the many worlds hypothesis, see Robert
Spitzer, *New Proofs for the Existence of God: Contributions of Contemporary Physics
and Philosophy* (Grand Rapids, MI: William B. Eerdmans, 2010), 67–73.

44. Darwin's son reported a conversation between his father and the Duke of
Argyll, a biologist. According to Darwin's son, the duke referenced some of his
own books and observations he had made of the wonderful contrivances for
certain purposes in nature, and then said that "it was impossible to look at these
without seeing that they were the effect and the expression of mind." Darwin
replied, "Well, that often comes over me with overwhelming force; but at other
times," and he shook his head vaguely, adding, "it seems to go away" (originally
from Charles Darwin, *Life and Letters*, 316n); George Douglas Campbell, "What
Is Science?," in *Good Words for 1885*, ed. Donald MacLeod (London: Isbester &

Co., 1885), 26:244. I owe this reference to my colleague Jim Slagle. It appears in Slagle, *The Evolutionary Argument against Naturalism* (New York: Bloomsbury, 2021), 62–63.

45. Van Inwagen, *Metaphysics*, 146. For an in-depth study of the fine-tuning argument, I recommend Robin Collins, "The Teleological Argument: An Exploration of the Fine-Tuning of the Universe," in *The Blackwell Companion to Natural Theology*, ed. William Lane Craig and J. P. Moreland (Oxford: Wiley-Blackwell, 2012), 202–81.

SIX. *The Cosmological Argument*

1. Jim Holt, *Why Does the World Exist? An Existential Detective Story* (New York: W. W. Norton, 2012), 3–4.

2. Heinz Pagels, *Perfect Symmetry* (New York: Bantam, 1985), 137.

3. See Norman Malcolm, *Ludwig Wittgenstein: A Memoir* (London: Oxford University Press, 1958), 70.

4. See Plato, *Theaetetus* 155c-d, in *Plato: The Collected Dialogues*, trans. Jowett et al., ed. Edith Hamilton and Huntington Cairns (Princeton, NJ: Princeton University Press, 1961; Aristotle, *Metaphysics* 982b, in *Basic Works of Aristotle*, trans. Richard McKeon (New York: Random House, 1941).

5. Stephen Hawking and Leonard Mlodinow, *The Grand Design* (New York: Bantam, 2010).

6. No empirical evidence of any kind could ever prove that something popped into existence out of nothing.

7. David Albert, "On the Origin of Everything," *New York Times*, March 23, 2012, 20.

8. Ibid., 135.

9. Hawking and Mlodinow, *Grand Design*, 180.

10. See Steven Weinberg, "A Designer Universe?," in *Science and Religion: Are They Compatible?*, ed. Paul Kurtz (Amherst, NY: Prometheus Books, 2003), 33.

11. Letting s = solid, l = liquid, g = gas, and aq = aqueous (in water).

12. Stephen Hawking, *A Brief History of Time: From the Big Bang to Black Holes* (New York: Bantam Books, 1988), 174.

13. Aquinas divides his work into questions rather than chapters.

14. Thomas Aquinas, *Summa theologica* I, q. 2, a. 3, trans. Fathers of the English Dominican Province (Westminster, MD: Christian Classics), 1981.

15. Aquinas and other medieval philosophers drew a distinction between an *essentially* ordered (or *per se*) series of causes and an *accidentally* ordered (or *per*

accidens) series. In an accidentally ordered cause-and-effect regress, each cause in the series occurs before its effect in time. In such a series, some causes that operated long ago may no longer be operating now. Imagine, for example, a series of parents producing children, who in turn become parents producing children, and so forth over hundreds of years. The ancestors of long ago are no longer alive today. In contrast, in an essentially ordered regress of causes, the causes are all operating at the same time. In another context, Aquinas offers this example: a hand moves a staff, which moves a stone. Hand, staff, and stone are all in motion simultaneously. I am leaving out Aquinas's distinction between accidentally ordered and essentially ordered causes because the argument I develop works with both kinds of causal regress and is easier to understand.

16. Craig J. Hogan, *The Little Book of the Big Bang: A Cosmic Primer* (New York: Springer-Verlag, 1998).

17. Steven Weinberg, *Dreams of a Final Theory* (New York: Vintage, 1994), 6. Most leading physicists today believe that the universe displays one overall, comprehensive order. See James Trefil, *Reading the Mind of God: In Search of the Principle of Universality* (New York: Doubleday, 1989); Paul Davies, *The Mind of God: The Scientific Basis for a Rational World* (New York: Simon and Schuster, 1992); Davies, *Accidental Universe*, chap. 2; and J. H. Mulvey, *The Nature of Matter* (Oxford: Oxford University Press, 1981).

18. Aquinas, *Summa theologica* I, q. 2, a. 3.

19. William L. Rowe, *Philosophy of Religion: An Introduction* (New York: Cengage), 32.

20. Ibid., 32.

21. Richard L. Purtill, *Reason to Believe* (Grand Rapids, MI: Eerdmans, 1974), 81–83. For a rigorous, book-length defense of the PSR, see Alexander Pruss, *The Principle of Sufficient Reason: A Reassessment* (Cambridge: Cambridge University Press, 2010).

22. See James S. Trefil, *The Moment of Creation* (New York: Charles Scribner's Sons, 1983), 5.

23. See David Hume, *Dialogues concerning Natural Religion* (Indianapolis, IN: Hackett, 1980), pt. 9.

24. Richard Purtill, *Philosophically Speaking* (Englewood Cliffs, NJ: Prentice Hall, 1975), 12.

25. Robert Martin, *Epistemology: A Beginner's Guide* (London: Oneworld, 2014), 65.

26. See Keith M. Parsons, "No Creator Need Apply: A Reply to Roy Abraham Varghese," Internet Infidels, 2006, http://infidels.org/library/modern/keith_parsons/varghese.html.

27. Richard Taylor, *Metaphysics* (New York: Prentice Hall, 1963), 106.

28. Hawking, *Brief History of Time*, 174.

29. Roger Penrose is quoted in Alan Lightman and Roberta Brawer, eds., *Origins: The Lives and Worlds of Modern Cosmologists* (Cambridge, MA: Harvard University Press, 1990), 433.

30. For those who would like to delve into philosophical theology, I recommend Thomas V. Morris, *Our Idea of God: An Introduction to Philosophical Theology* (Notre Dame, IN: University of Notre Dame Press, 1991), and Thomas P. Flint and Michael Rea, eds., *The Oxford Handbook of Philosophical Theology* (New York: Oxford University Press, 2011).

31. Hogan, *Little Book of the Big Bang*.

32. Bertrand Russell, *Why I Am Not a Christian: And Other Essays on Religion and Related Subjects* (New York: Touchstone, 1967), 6.

33. See Moreland's website at http://www.jpmoreland.com/articles/who-or -what-caused-god/. For the reader interested in the notion of a first cause understood as a final explanation, I recommend Timothy O'Connor, *Theism and Ultimate Explanation: The Necessary Shape of Contingency* (Oxford: Wiley-Blackwell, 2012).

34. Richard Purtill presents this argument in Purtill, *Reason to Believe*, chap. 3. Incidentally, quantum events and virtual particles are not an exception. On *one* interpretation of quantum mechanics, quantum events have no causes. However, quantum events occur only within, and because of, preexisting quantum fields. Thus, even if they lack causes, they do not pop into existence out of nothing.

35. William Lane Craig and Quentin Smith, *Theism, Atheism, and Big Bang Cosmology* (Oxford: Oxford University Press, 1993), 63–64. For more on the cosmological argument, I recommend William Lane Craig, *The Cosmological Argument from Plato to Leibniz* (New York: Harper & Row, 1980), and Richard Swinburne, *The Existence of God*, 2nd ed. (Oxford: Clarendon, 2004), 133–52.

36. Lewis's intriguing book is available from several publishers. Here is one: C. S. Lewis, *The Pilgrim's Regress* (New York: HarperOne, 2014).

37. The respected historian of medieval science Edward Grant notes that "between 1902 and 1916, Pierre Duhem, a famous French physicist turned historian, wrote fifteen volumes on medieval science. Duhem was the first to blow away the dust of centuries from manuscript codices that had lain untouched since the Middle Ages. What he discovered led him to make the startling claim that the Scientific Revolution, associated with the glorious names of Nicholaus Copernicus, Galileo Galilei, Johannes Kepler, Rene Descartes, and Isaac Newton, was but an extension and elaboration of physical and cosmological ideas formulated . . . primarily . . . at the University of Paris"; see Grant, *The Foundations of*

Modern Science in the Middle Ages: Their Religious, Institutional and Intellectual Contexts (New York: Cambridge University Press, 1996), xi. See also Jean Gimpel, *The Medieval Machine: The Industrial Revolution of the Middle Ages* (New York: Barnes & Noble Books, 1976), chap. 8, "Reason, Mathematics, and Experimental Science," 171–98.

38. Many academics today denigrate the medieval scholars (known as the "scholastics") and present them as pointy-headed intellectuals interested only in arguing about abstruse questions such as "How many angels can dance on the head of a pin?" On the contrary, Albert did work in natural science and was one of the pioneers of the empirical investigation of nature. The man even had himself lowered over a cliff in a basket so he could observe eagle eggs hatching. Every aspect of God's creation is worthy of study, argued Albert, and no question is unworthy of the Christian scholar. Albert's writings helped pave the way for the birth of modern science, which occurred in Europe three centuries later.

39. "Ransom of my soul" is a reference to Christ and reflects the Christian doctrine of the atonement, the claim that Christ as the Son of God took on human flesh and died to atone for the sins of humanity to bring about a new oneness between human beings and their creator.

40. Robert Pasnau and Christopher Shields, *The Philosophy of Aquinas* (New York: Westview Press, 2004), vii.

INTERLUDE ONE. *A Survey of Modern Cosmology*

1. The refracting telescope was invented by Dutch lens makers in about 1608, but Italian mathematician, physicist, and astronomer Galileo was the first to build a model and observe the heavens with it in 1609. The reflecting telescope was invented by English mathematician, physicist, and astronomer Isaac Newton. A refracting telescope uses lenses to magnify images; the reflecting telescope uses a mirror and a lens.

2. An excellent account of the rise of modern science is I. Bernard Cohen, *The Birth of a New Physics*, rev. ed. (New York: W. W. Norton, 1985).

3. This law states that the entropy (disorder) of a closed system must increase over time.

4. John Farrell, *The Day without Yesterday: Lemaître, Einstein, and the Birth of Modern Cosmology* (New York: Thunder's Mouth Press, 2005), 80.

5. Ibid., 90.

6. It is true that before Lemaître published his theory, some astronomers had raised the possibility that the nebulae might be receding from each other.

However, the data had been inconclusive and everyone had been reluctant to drop the assumption of a static universe.

7. The Hooker telescope at Mount Wilson remained the largest telescope in the world until 1949.

8. See John Farrell, *The Day without Yesterday*, 104.

9. Ibid., 106.

10. Ibid.

11. Ibid., 100.

12. Ibid., 115.

13. Ibid., 80.

14. See Fred Hoyle, *Frontiers of Astronomy* (New York: Mentor Books, 1957), 42.

15. The steady state model incorporates what's called the "perfect cosmological "principle": no point in space or time is special. The cosmologist Herbert Dingle quipped that calling this principle "perfect" is "like calling a spade a perfect agricultural instrument." Dingle's statement is quoted in John D. Barrow, *Theories of Everything: The Quest for the Ultimate Explanation* (Oxford: Clarendon, 1991), 46.

16. Joseph Silk, *The Big Bang*, rev. and updated ed. (New York: W. H. Freeman, 1989), 108.

17. Farrell, *Day without Yesterday*, from the book's dust jacket.

18. If you want to follow the latest cosmological research, two good popular sources are *Sky and Telescope* magazine and *Astronomy* magazine.

19. See Steven Weinberg, *The First Three Minutes: A Modern View of the Origin of the Universe* (New York: Basic Books, 1993), 154, and James Trefil, *The Moment of Creation* (New York: Charles Scribner's Sons, 1983), 215.

20. William Lane Craig and Quentin Smith, *Theism, Atheism, and Big Bang Cosmology* (Oxford: Clarendon, 1995), 135.

21. For further reasons why the oscillating universe model fails, see Robert Spitzer, *New Proofs for the Existence of God: Contributions of Contemporary Physics and Philosophy* (Grand Rapids, MI: William B. Eerdmans, 2010), "Why a Bouncing Universe Cannot Have Been Bouncing Forever," chap. 1, 27–30.

22. Steven Duncan, *Analytic Philosophy of Religion: Its History since 1955* (Penrith, CA: Humanities-Ebooks, 2010), 165.

23. See his full presentation, in William Lane Craig, "The Kalam Cosmological Argument," in *The Blackwell Companion to Natural Theology*, ed. William Lane Craig and J. P. Moreland (Oxford: Wiley-Blackwell, 2012), 101–201. A more compact version can be found here in Craig, "The Kalam Cosmological Argument," in *Two Dozen (or so) Arguments for God*, ed. Jerry Walls and Trent Dougherty (New York: Oxford University Press, 2018), 389–405.

24. For the reader who wants to probe the scientific cosmological issues discussed in this interlude, I recommend Weinberg, *The First Three Minutes*, and Trefil, *The Moment of Creation*. An advanced work is Jeffrey Koperski, *The Physics of Theism: God, Physics, and the Philosophy of Science* (Oxford: Wiley-Blackwell, 2014).

SEVEN. *The Problem of Evil*

1. Timothy Snyder, *Bloodlands: Europe between Hitler and Stalin* (New York: Basic Books, 2012), viii. Snyder notes that if we include civilian deaths that resulted from other policies enacted by Hitler and Stalin, the number rises to between 17 million and 21 million. For the reader who wants to research another of the great tragedies of the twentieth century, I recommend Stéphane Courtois, Nicolas Werth, Jean-Louis Panné, Andrzej Paczkowski, Karel Bartosek, and Jean-Louis Margolin, *The Black Book of Communism: Crimes, Terror, Repression* (Cambridge, MA: Harvard University Press, 1999). The authors, all scholars (and former communists), provide archival documentation and eyewitness testimony that communist governments, in their drives for power during the twentieth century, killed without trial between 80 million and 100 million unarmed civilians. From the cover: "Already famous throughout Europe, this international bestseller plumbs recently opened archives in the former Soviet bloc to reveal the actual, practical accomplishments of Communism around the world: terror, torture, famine, mass deportations, and massacres. Astonishing in the sheer detail it amasses, the book is the first comprehensive attempt to catalogue and analyze the crimes of Communism over seventy years."

2. Snyder, *Bloodlands*, vii.

3. Ibid., vii.

4. Ibid., viii.

5. The name "logical argument from evil" derives from the fact that the main premise of this argument is claimed to be "a priori" or "logically" true. In philosophy, a proposition is said to be logically, or a priori, true if its truth can be grasped by an internal process of pure logical reasoning alone, without reliance on sense experience or empirical data. We'll examine the notion of a priori truth in chapter 8 when we enter the field of philosophy known as *epistemology* (theory of knowledge).

6. The name "evidential argument" derives from the fact that the main premise of this argument is an empirical claim, that is, a claim based on evidence gained from our sense experience of the world. We'll also examine the notion of empirical data in the following chapter.

7. J. L. Mackie, "Evil and Omnipotence," in *The Problem of Evil: Selected Readings*, ed. Michael Peterson (Notre Dame, IN: University of Notre Dame Press, 1992), 89.

8. See Alvin Plantinga, *God, Freedom, and Evil* (Grand Rapids, MI: Eerdmans, 1974), 7–57. For an even deeper argument, see Plantinga, *The Nature of Necessity* (New York: Oxford University Press, 1974), chap. 9. *The Nature of Necessity* is Plantinga's masterpiece contribution to modern modal logic. This book revolutionized the field and ended with a fascinating modal logic response to the problem of evil and a deep modal argument for God's existence, with God understood in the traditional way as omnipotent, omnibenevolent, and so forth. Pike's seminal contribution can be found in Nelson Pike, "Hume on Evil," in *The Problem of Evil*, ed. Marilyn McCord Adams and Robert Merrihew Adams (New York: Oxford University Press, 1990), 38–52.

9. Plantinga was able to show that the assumption Mackie needed is false without stating a theodicy. He called his rebuttal to Mackie a "defense" of theism rather than a theodicy. In my opinion, because of its technical nature, Plantinga's full argument is best reserved for an advanced course in philosophy of religion.

10. Philosophers distinguish *intrinsic* and *extrinsic* values, or goods. Something is extrinsically valuable if it is valuable only as a means to something else that is valuable. It is valuable only as a means to an end. Something is intrinsically valuable if it is valuable in itself, apart from anything it leads to or produces.

11. For his full theodicy, see Augustine, *City of God* (New York: Random House, 1950), bks. 11–12. For excerpts, see Peterson, ed., *Problem of Evil*, 191–97. For further treatment, see Christopher Kirwan, *Augustine* (New York: Routledge, 1989), and John Hick, *Evil and the God of Love* (New York: Palgrave Macmillan, 2010), pt. 2.

12. C. Stephen Layman, *Letters to a Doubting Thomas: A Case for the Existence of God* (New York: Oxford University Press, 2007), 189. In his first work of Christian apologetics, *The Pilgrim's Regress*, and in his spiritual autobiography, *Surprised By Joy*, C. S. Lewis develops a profound argument for immortality that I summarize like this: (1) Throughout the ages poets, romantics, artists, and other sensitive souls have testified to the existence within human nature of an innate desire for complete transcendence. (2) The transcendence longed for is a life after death in a heavenly realm united in eternity with our loved ones and our Creator. (3) An object exists corresponding to each of the other innate, natural desires (for instance, we have a natural desire for food and food exists, we have a natural longing for love and love exists, etc.). (4) Therefore, by the standard rules of analogical reasoning, it is likely that an object exists corresponding to our desire or longing for complete transcendence. Lewis's famous "argument from desire" is an

argument for God's existence, heaven, and life after death all in one. His reasoning is worthy of careful reflection, but it is outside the scope of this introduction to philosophy. For further reflection, in addition to Lewis's writings, see Todd Buras and Michael Cantrell, "C. S. Lewis's Argument from Nostalgia: A New Argument from Desire," in *Two Dozen (or so) Arguments for God*, ed. Jerry Walls and Trent Dougherty (New York: Oxford University Press, 2018), 356–71.

13. J. R. Lucas, *Freedom and Grace* (Grand Rapids, MI: Eerdmans, 1976), 39.

14. Augustine, *City of God* (Cambridge, MA: Harvard University Press, 1957), 1:22. I was drawn to this passage when reading Anthony Meredith, S.J., *Christian Philosophy in the Early Church* (New York: T&T Clark, 2012).

15. The story of Joseph and his brothers, told in Genesis 37–50, is a biblical illustration of sinful people committing an evil act, which God uses to further his plan of salvation. Joseph said to his guilty brothers, "But now, do not therefore be grieved or angry with yourselves because you sold me here, for God sent me before you to preserve life. . . . And God sent me before you to preserve a posterity for you in the earth, and to save your lives by a great deliverance. So now it was not you who sent me here, but God" (Gen. 45:5, 7–8a, NKJV). Thanks to Karen Olson for bringing these verses to my attention.

16. Augustine actually did offer an explanation of natural evil, but his explanation was religious rather than philosophical. On the basis of scripture, he argued that God created higher orders of beings (angels) and gave them the power of free will. Unfortunately, some used their free will to rebel against God, and they were cast out of heaven. Natural evils such as earthquakes and disease are caused by the fallen angels (devils) who are always attempting to ruin God's experiment in human freedom. Since this was a religious rather than a philosophical theory, it will not be discussed here.

17. Thus, whereas Augustine interprets the garden of Eden story as a "fall downward" from perfection and grace to imperfection and sin, Irenaeus interprets it as a "fall upward," from imperfection to moral growth and ultimately redemption. I owe this insight to my colleague Steven Duncan.

18. Hick, *Evil and the God of Love*, 324–25.

19. For those who still put Lenin, the founder of the Soviet Union, on a pedestal, I recommend a scholarly book by Richard Pipes, *The Unknown Lenin: From the Secret Archive* (New Haven, CT: Yale University Press, 1996). Pipes was a renowned historian of communism and for many years professor of history at Harvard University. During Lenin's first six months in power, his secret police shot without trial more than 50,000 political opponents. When peasants in the province of Penza protested the Soviet confiscations of their grain, Lenin ordered the Red Army to seize one hundred farmers at random and hang them publicly with-

out trial in the village squares—in front of their wives and children—to produce total submission. Lenin launched a campaign against the Orthodox Church. According to his personal orders, priests who resisted seizures of church property were to be shot on the spot and "the more the better." In some of the archival documents, Lenin calls for the burning of entire cities that were resisting his orders and for the extermination of entire regions of people. During the 1930s, Stalin, Lenin's successor, starved to death at least 5 million peasants in the Ukraine when they resisted his orders; see Anne Applebaum, *Red Famine: Stalin's War on Ukraine* (New York: Doubleday, 2017), and Robert Conquest, *The Great Terror: A Reassessment*, 40th anniversary ed. (New York: Oxford University Press, 2007). Mao Tse-tung, the founder of communist China, executed 750,000 political opponents without trial during his first year in power alone, but the total number of deaths attributable to his despotic rule likely exceeds 30 million; see *Black Book of Communism*, chap. 21: "China: A Long March into Night." On Mao, I also recommend Jasper Becker, *Hungry Ghosts: Mao's Secret Famine* (New York: Henry Holt, 1996), and Frank Dikotter, *Mao's Great Famine* (New York: Bloomsbury, 2010). On Ho Chi Minh and Pol Pot, see chaps. 23 and 24 of the *Black Book of Communism* for similar crimes against humanity, but on smaller scales.

20. Satguru Sivaya Subramuniyaswami, *Dancing with Siva: Hinduism's Contemporary Catechism* (Honolulu: Himalayan Academy: 1993), 93.

21. Ibid.

22. Ibid.

23. Read Rowe's argument in William Rowe, "The Problem of Evil and Some Varieties of Atheism," and "The Evidential Argument from Evil: A Second Look," in *The Evidential Argument from Evil*, ed. Daniel Howard-Snyder (Indianapolis: Indiana University Press, 1996), 1–11, 262–86. See also William L. Rowe, "Ruminations about Evil," in *Philosophical Perspectives*, Vol. 5, *Philosophy of Religion*, ed. James E. Tomberlin (Atascadero, CA: Ridgeview, 1991), 69–88. My summary of the argument has been influenced by Chris Tweedt, "Defusing the Common Sense Problem of Evil," *Faith and Philosophy* 32, no. 4 (2015): 391–403.

24. Rowe, "Problem of Evil and Some Varieties of Atheism," 4.

25. Ibid.

26. Read Alston's argument here in William Alston, "The Inductive Argument from Evil and the Human Cognitive Condition," in *The Evidential Argument from Evil*, ed. Daniel Howard-Snyder (Indianapolis: Indiana University Press, 1996), 97–126.

27. For a number of excellent articles dealing with the issues raised by Rowe's argument, see Howard-Snyder, ed., *Evidential Argument from Evil*.

28. In my view, skeptical theism supplements, but does not make unnecessary, the accounts of evil provided by the free will and moral qualities theodicies.

29. Alston, "Inductive Argument from Evil," 31.

30. Read Wykstra's argument here: Stephen Wykstra, "Rowe's No-see-um Arguments from Evil," in Howard-Snyder, ed., *Evidential Argument from Evil*, 126–51.

31. Wykstra puts the underlying principle this way: "On the basis of cognized situation S, human H is entitled to claim 'it appears that p' only if it is reasonable for H to believe that, given her cognitive faculties and the use she has made of them, if p were not the case, S would likely be different than it is in some way discernable to her." See Wykstra, "Rowe's No-see-um Arguments from Evil," in Howard-Snyder, ed., *Evidential Argument from Evil*, 128. For example, a doctor looks at a mask and does not see any bacteria on it. Is she justified in concluding that the mask contains no bacteria? Clearly not, for the mask would not look any different if it did contain bacteria.

32. C. Stephen Evans and R. Zachary Manis, *Philosophy of Religion: Thinking about Faith*, 2nd ed. (Downers Grove, IL: IVP Academic, 2009).

33. Plantinga, *God, Freedom, and Evil*, 10.

34. Plantinga lists two dozen or so here: https//meta-religion.com/philosophy/articles/metaphysics/theistic_arguments.htm. See also Jerry Walls and Trent Dougherty, eds., *Two Dozen (or so) Arguments for God: The Plantinga Project* (New York: Oxford University Press, 2018).

35. Richard Swinburne, *The Existence of God*, 2nd ed. (New York: Oxford University Press, 2004). To get a sense of the wide variety of arguments for God's existence that have been rigorously defended by philosophers, see Walls and Dougherty, eds., *Two Dozen (or so) Arguments for God*. Theistic philosophers argue that in the final analysis, every aspect of the universe points, in one way or another, toward God. For an opposing view, see J. L. Mackie, *The Miracle of Theism* (New York: Oxford University Press, 1983).

EIGHT. *What Can We Know?*

1. Scholars have identified around 30 Sophists, but there were as many as 150 at the height of the sophistic movement in ancient Greece. This was an extraordinary number of professional teachers for such a small country at the time. See W. K. C. Guthrie, *The Sophists* (Cambridge: Cambridge University Press, 1971).

2. Socrates also believed that democracy is a breeding ground for demagoguery.

3. Guthrie sums up Gorgias's teaching as the claim that "nothing exists (or is real), that if it did we could not know it, and if we could know it, we could not communicate our knowledge to one another" (Guthrie, *The Sophists*, 180).

4. My argument is based on a similar argument Thomas Nagel gives in his critique of postmodernism; see Nagle, *The Last Word* (New York: Oxford University Press, 2001), 15. My statement is stronger thanks to suggestions from an anonymous reviewer from the University of Notre Dame Press.

5. Stated most clearly in Plato's *Meno* and *Theaetetus*.

6. Recall that a proposition is not the same thing as a sentence. Two different sentences can express one and the same proposition. Technically, a proposition is the claim expressed by a declarative sentence. You won't go wrong if you think of a proposition as the meaning of a declarative sentence. When two different sentences mean the same thing, they express the same proposition.

7. For instance, *Gorgias*, *Cratylus*, and *Charmides*.

8. *Theaetetus* 187a–201d.

9. Laurence BonJour, *Epistemology: Classic Problems and Contemporary Responses* (New York: Rowman and Littlefield, 2010), 15.

10. Laurence BonJour and Ernest Sosa, *Epistemic Justification: Internalism vs. Externalism, Foundations vs. Virtues* (Oxford: Blackwell, 2003), 1.

11. BonJour, *Epistemology*, 35.

12. See Plato's *Apology*.

13. Laurence BonJour, *In Defense of Pure Reason* (Cambridge: Cambridge University Press, 1998), 2.

14. "Sense data" is the term epistemologists use for the states of mind produced directly by our physical senses that we experience immediately.

15. Some reply as follows: "But we must use our senses to read the sentences and to hear the arguments. Thus, our knowledge in these cases is partly based on the senses and empirical data." This objection is mistaken. We use our senses to understand the *meanings* of the propositions involved, not their *truth*. We use pure reason alone to see that the propositions in question, once understood, are true (and must be true).

16. Dan O'Brien, *An Introduction to the Theory of Knowledge* (Cambridge: Polity, 2006), 25–26.

17. The material in this section is adapted from Paul Herrick, *Think with Socrates: An Introduction to Critical Thinking* (New York: Oxford University Press, 2014), chap. 7.

18. Ibid., 56.

19. See James Gleick, *Genius: The Life and Science of Richard Feynman* (New York: Vintage, 1993).

20. I owe thanks to Steve Duncan for suggesting this caveat in private correspondence.

21. See Edmund Gettier, "Is Justified True Belief Knowledge?," in *Epistemology: Contemporary Readings*, ed. Michael Huemer (London: Routledge, 2002), 444–46. https://fitelson.org/proseminar/gettier.pdf.

22. I will be closely paraphrasing Gettier's argument.

23. Edmund L. Gettier, "Is Justified True Belief Knowledge?," *Analysis* 23, no. 6. (1963): 123.

24. My discussion has benefited from and follows the clear analysis in Robert Martin, *Epistemology: A Beginner's Guide* (London: Oneworld Publications, 2014).

25. Jim Slagle, *The Epistemological Skyhook: Determinism, Naturalism, and Self-Defeat*, Routledge Studies in Contemporary Philosophy (New York: Routledge, 2016), 35.

26. Ibid., 34.

27. A good place to begin is BonJour, *Epistemology*.

NINE. *C. S. Lewis and the Argument from Reason*

1. Although Lewis became famous as a tutor of English literature and a leading scholar in that subject, he also trained in the philosophical classics and began his career at Oxford teaching philosophy (during the 1924 to 1925 terms). After teaching at Oxford for nearly thirty years, Lewis was appointed chair of Medieval and Renaissance Literature at Cambridge University, where he taught until shortly before his death on November 22, 1963 — the same day John F. Kennedy died.

2. C. S. Lewis, *Miracles: A Preliminary Study* (New York: Macmillan, 1947), 11.

3. Ibid., 10.

4. Ibid., 19.

5. Ibid., 20.

6. Ibid., 21

7. Ibid., 21. In the first edition of *Miracles*, Lewis used the term "irrational cause." After debating the Catholic philosopher Elizabeth Anscombe (1919–2001) at a famous meeting of the Oxford Socratic Club in 1948, he revised his argument and changed this premise to refer to a "nonrational cause." Upon reading the revised version, Anscombe complimented Lewis, saying that

the revised argument was much better and "corresponds more to the depth and difficulty of the problem." See Victor Reppert, *C. S. Lewis's Dangerous Idea: In Defense of the Argument from Reason* (Downers Grove, Il: Intervarsity Press, 2003), 70.

8. Ibid., 21.

9. Ibid., 22.

10. Ibid., 20.

11. Ibid., 22.

12. I owe this point to my colleague Jim Slagle, assistant professor of philosophy at the University of Portland, in private correspondence. He is the author of a powerful defense of Lewis's argument which I heartily recommend: see Slagle, *The Epistemological Skyhook: Determinism, Naturalism, and Self-Defeat* (New York: Routledge, 2016).

13. Peter van Inwagen, "Genesis and Evolution," in *Reasoned Faith: Essays in Philosophical Theology in Honor of Norman Kretzmann*, ed. Eleonore Stump (Ithaca, NY: Cornell University Press, 1993), 93.

14. Ibid.

15. Ibid.

16. From my colleague Steve Duncan in private correspondence.

17. Slagle, *Epistemological Skyhook*, 152.

18. See William J. Talbott, "A New Reliability Defeater for Evolutionary Naturalism," *Philosophy and Phenomenological Research* 113, no. 3 (2016): 538–64. Although Talbott has criticized naturalistic theories of the origin of our cognitive abilities, he is also a critic of the argument from reason.

19. For the reader who wants to delve into Lewis's argument I recommend Slagle, *Epistemological Skyhook*, chaps. 7–10, and Reppert, *C. S. Lewis's Dangerous Idea*.

20. Alvin Plantinga, *Where the Conflict Really Lies: Science, Religion, and Naturalism* (New York: Oxford University Press, 2011). A useful collection of critical essays on an early version of Plantinga's argument (accompanied by Plantinga's replies and defense) is James Beilby, ed., *Naturalism Defeated? Essays on Plantinga's Evolutionary Argument against Naturalism* (Ithaca, NY: Cornell University Press, 2002).

21. Plantinga, *Where the Conflict Really Lies*, 350.

22. For another rigorous and in-depth defense of Plantinga's evolutionary argument against naturalism, I recommend Jim Slagle's new book (as of this writing): Slagle, *The Evolutionary Argument against Naturalism: Context, Exposition, and Repercussions* (New York: Bloomsbury Academic, 2021).

23. See Slagle, *Epistemological Skyhook*, 226.

TEN. *The Mind-Body Problem*

1. Kathleen Weldon, "Paradise Polled: Americans and the Afterlife," *Huffington Post*, https://www.huffingtonpost.com/kathleen-weldon/paradise-polled-americans_b_7587538.html.

2. For a defense of property dualism, see David Chalmers, *The Conscious Mind: In Search of a Fundamental Theory* (New York: Oxford University Press, 1996), chap. 4.

3. Historians consider Descartes's writings to be the founding documents of modern philosophy because of the radical break he made with the philosophy of the Middle Ages. During the medieval period metaphysical issues took center stage in philosophy. Beginning with Descartes, epistemological concerns moved to the front. The mainstream view is that Descartes shifted philosophy in an epistemological direction. In addition, his pioneering work in mathematics and physics contributed to the birth of modern math and physics. On Descartes's contributions, I recommend A. C. Grayling. *Descartes: The Life and Times of a Genius* (New York: Walker & Company, 2005).

4. René Descartes, *Meditations on First Philosophy*, trans. Laurence J. Lafleur (Indianapolis: Bobbs-Merrill), 81. Read the *Meditations* here: https://www.earlymoderntexts.com/assets/pdfs/descartes1641.pdf

5. For the purposes of this introductory level argument, I am assuming that a "part" of the body contains at least two atomic particles.

6. For logic purists, technically, premise 2 is the contrapositive of Leibniz's law. (The contrapositive of "If P, then Q" is "If not Q, then not P.") Every conditional, or "if, then," proposition is logically equivalent to its contrapositive and therefore implies (and is implied by) its contrapositive.

7. Edward Feser, *Philosophy of Mind* (London: Oneworld Publications), loc. 45, Kindle.

8. Robert C. Koons and George Bealer, eds., *The Waning of Materialism* (New York: Oxford University Press, 2010), 18.

9. Ibid., 18.

10. For those who would like to explore recent philosophical arguments for dualism, including the four we have just examined, I recommend Andrea Lavazza and Howard Robinson, eds., *Contemporary Dualism: A Defense* (New York: Routledge, 2016); Jonathan J. Loose, Angus J. L. Menuge and J. P. Moreland, eds., *The Blackwell Companion to Substance Dualism*. Blackwell Companions to Philosophy (Oxford: Wiley-Blackwell, 2018), and John Foster, *The Immaterial Self: A Defense of the Cartesian Dualist Conception of the Mind* (New York: Routledge, 1991).

11. See Patrick Lee and Robert P. George, *Body-Self Dualism in Contemporary Ethics and Politics* (Cambridge: Cambridge University Press, 2009), Kindle ed.

12. Edward Feser, *Philosophy of Mind: A Beginner's Guide* (Oxford: Oneworld, 2005), 16.

13. For further exploration of the identity theory, see Cynthia Macdonald, *Mind-Body Identity Theories* (London: Routledge, 1989). See also Keith Campbell, *Body and Mind* (Garden City, NY: Doubleday, 1970); and Paul Churchland, *Matter and Consciousness* (Cambridge: The MIT Press, 2013), 26–36. An important early defense of the theory is David Armstrong, *A Materialist Theory of the Mind* (London: Routledge & Kegan Paul, 1968).

14. The case of Phineas Gage is often mentioned in this connection. In the 1840s, Gage was working on a railroad construction crew, setting dynamite charges, when a horrible accident occurred. A stick of dynamite exploded prematurely, sending a three-foot-long iron tamping rod through his left cheek and out the top of his skull. Amazingly, Gage survived, but the rod destroyed part of the front of his brain (his prefrontal cortex). After he recovered, his friends and associates noticed a drastic change in his personality. My colleague Steve Duncan in correspondence suggested one way to interpret this case: perhaps Gage's personality change was his real self coming out after damage to his frontal cortex made it impossible for him to suppress his true nature.

15. See J. J. C. Smart, "Sensations and Brain Processes," in *Materialism and the Mind-Body Problem*, ed. David Rosenthal (Indianapolis: Hackett, 1987), 54.

16. The philosophers David Lewis and David Armstrong were the first to propose functionalist theories of the mind, in 1966 and 1968, respectively.

17. Discussed in Owen J. Flanagan Jr., *The Science of the Mind* (Cambridge, MA: MIT Press, 1984), chap. 1.

18. In framing my explanation, I am indebted to Anthony Appiah, *Necessary Questions* (Englewood Cliffs, NJ: Prentice-Hall, 1989), 22.

19. For further development of this line of reasoning, see John Searle, *Minds, Brains, and Science* (Cambridge, MA: Harvard University Press, 1984).

20. See Ned Block, "Psychologism and Behaviorism," *The Philosophical Review* 90, no. 1 (1981): 5–43. And Block, "Troubles with Functionalism," in *Readings in the Philosophy of Psychology*, ed. Ned Block (Cambridge, MA: Harvard University Press, 1980), 1:276.

21. See David Chalmers, *The Conscious Mind: In Search of a Fundamental Theory* (New York: Oxford University Press, 1996), xii.

22. The hard problem also includes this related question: How can there be *something it is like* to be a bundle of nerve fibers? See David Chalmers, *The Character of Consciousness* (Oxford University Press, 2010), and Chalmers, *Conscious Mind*.

434 Notes to Pages 260–276

23. Chalmers, *Conscious Mind*, xii. As Chalmers notes, brain scientists work up elegant theories, but their theories explain only the neural functioning, not the subjective experiences: "After explaining the physical mechanism, there remains the experience. Something further needs explaining" (ibid., xii).

24. For further exploration of this interesting point, see Thomas Nagel, "What Is It Like to Be a Bat?," in *Mortal Questions* (Cambridge: Cambridge University Press, 1979), 165–80.

25. The neuroscientist John C. Eccles, who was awarded the Nobel Prize in Physiology or Medicine, defends a dualist account of the mind-brain relationship in Karl Popper and John C. Eccles, *The Self and Its Brain: An Argument for Interactionism* (New York: Routledge, 1984) and John C. Eccles, *How the Self Controls Its Brain* (New York: Springer-Verlag, 1994).

26. For further research on this argument, I recommend J. P. Moreland, *Consciousness and the Existence of God: A Theistic Argument* (New York: Routledge, 2010).

ELEVEN. *Do We Have Free Will?*

1. Robert Coburn, *The Strangeness of the Ordinary: Problems and Issues in Contemporary Metaphysics* (Savage, MD: Rowman & Littlefield, 1990), chap. 2. Coburn was a beloved professor of philosophy who taught at the University of Chicago and then for four decades at the University of Washington. He was a prolific writer. He was also my teacher, my mentor, and my dissertation supervisor.

2. Actually, this has already been done. Two people were hooked together via the Internet, and an intention formed by one person involuntarily moved the arm of the other.

3. The examples are mine. I am elaborating a little on the basic premise of Coburn's thought experiment.

4. Coburn, *Strangeness of the Ordinary*, 24.

5. A valuable collection of readings on the topic of moral responsibility is John Martin Fischer, ed., *Moral Responsibility* (Ithaca, NY: Cornell University Press, 1986). See also Jennifer Trusted, *Free Will and Responsibility* (Oxford: Oxford University Press, 1984).

6. My explanation of causation is influenced by the way Coburn explains it in *Strangeness of the Ordinary*.

7. Quoted in Louis Pojman, *Philosophy: The Pursuit of Wisdom* (Belmont, CA: Wadsworth, 1994), 231.

8. Quoted in Daniel C. Dennett, *Elbow Room: The Varieties of Free Will Worth Wanting* (Cambridge, MA: MIT Press, 1984), 50.

9. See Peter van Inwagen, *An Essay on Free Will* (New York: Oxford University Press, 1983), 154–57.

10. Ibid., 156–61.

11. I am patterning this argument on an argument van Inwagen constructs in *Essay on Free Will*.

12. The contradiction, in this case, is pragmatic rather than logical: one cannot successfully live as one's principles dictate.

13. Is *judging* which argument is the better argument a *choice*? If so, then rational thought presupposes free will.

14. Van Inwagen, *Essay on Free Will*, 209.

15. Ibid., 209.

16. Ibid., 207.

17. In the 1980s, the neuroscientist Benjamin Libet conducted brain experiments that, he claimed, show that free will does not exist. Others repeated his experiments. I am not discussing the "Libet-style" experiments here because philosophers have shown that the experimental results can be interpreted in more than one way and that at least one interpretation of the data implies the existence of free will. The issue is outside the scope of this discussion.

18. For my argument, I owe much to the analysis developed by van Inwagen in *Essay on Free Will*, chap. 4.

19. Van Inwagen, *Essay on Free Will*, 131.

20. For an in-depth study of Epicurus's view, see Timothy O'Keefe, *Epicurus on Freedom* (Cambridge: Cambridge University Press, 2005).

21. Technically, agent causation is a specific theory within the broader category of free will theories called "libertarianism." Libertarianism with respect to free will has nothing to do with the political/economic theory of the same name. We'll discuss political libertarianism in chapter 13. Agent causation is the most fully developed and most commonly discussed libertarian theory of free will. It is also representative of the larger category. The broader term "libertarian" is problematic because it is easily confused with the political theory of the same name. For these reasons, agent causation will be our focus.

22. Roderick Chisholm, "Freedom and Action," in *Freedom and Determinism*, ed. Keith Lehrer (New York: Random House, 1966), 11–44.

23. Richard Taylor, *Metaphysics*, 2nd ed. (Englewood Cliffs, NJ: Prentice Hall, 1974), 54.

24. Ibid.

25. A related account of free will worth careful study is Steven M. Duncan, *How Free Will Works: A Dualist Theory of Human Action* (Eugene, OR: Wipf & Stock, 2011). This book is best read in tandem with Steven M. Duncan, *Determinism and Causality* (Seattle: Amazon CreateSpace, 2017).

26. For the reader who wants to explore the idea of agent causation, I recommend Timothy O'Connor, *Persons and Causes: The Metaphysics of Free Will* (New York: Oxford University Press, 2000); Thomas M. Crisp, Steven L. Porter, Gregg A. Ten Elshof, eds., *Neuroscience and the Soul: The Human Person in Philosophy, Science, and Theology* (Grand Rapids, MI: William B. Eerdmans, 2016); and Roderick Chisholm, *Person and Object: A Metaphysical Study* (New York: Routledge, 2014).

27. Richard Purtill, "From Street Corner to Classroom," in *Falling in Love with Wisdom*, ed. David D. Karnos and Robert G. Shoemaker (New York: Oxford University Press, 1993), 117.

28. Joseph M. Boyle Jr., Germain Grisez, and Olaf Tollefsen, *Free Choice: A Self-Referential Argument* (Notre Dame, IN: University of Notre Dame Press, 1976), 5.

29. Chisholm, "Freedom and Action," in Lehrer, ed., *Freedom and Determinism*, 23.

30. I am indebted here to Ted Honderich, *How Free Are You? The Determinism Problem* (New York: Oxford University Press, 1993).

31. For further research on this issue I recommend Richard Swinburne, *Mind, Brain, and Free Will* (New York: Oxford University Press, 2013).

TWELVE. *Can We Reason about Morality?*

1. Martin Luther King Jr., "Letter from Birmingham City Jail," in *A Testament of Hope: Essential Writings and Speeches of Martin Luther King Jr.*, ed. James M. Washington (New York: Harper One, 1986), 289–302.

2. C. S. Lewis, *The Abolition of Man* (New York: Macmillan, 1947), 56.

3. Ibid., 59.

4. See Aristotle, *Nicomachean Ethics* (London: Oxford University Press, 1954). *Nicomachean Ethics* is also contained in *The Basic Works of Aristotle*, ed. Richard McKeon (New York: Random House, 1941). For additional discussion, see James T. Walsh and Henry Shapiro, eds., *Aristotle's Ethics: Issues and Interpretations* (Belmont, CA: Wadsworth, 1967); and Amelie Oksenberg Rorty, ed., *Essays on Aristotle's Ethics* (Berkeley: University of California Press, 1980). See also W. D. Ross, *Aristotle* (New York: Meridian Books, 1959); and Henry B. Veatch, *Aristotle: A Contemporary Appreciation* (Bloomington: Indiana University Press, 1974). A helpful introduction to Aristotle's thought may also be found in Donald M. Borchert and David Stewart, *Exploring Ethics* (New York: Macmillan, 1986).

5. *Nicomachean Ethics*, bk. 1, 1098, in McKeon, ed., *Basic Works of Aristotle*, 942.

6. Of course, many overcome an abusive or unloving environment and grow up to become moral and productive adults.

7. Aristotle, *Ethics* 2.4, 1105b7–18. I am indebted to the analysis in Gerard J. Hughes, *Aristotle on Ethics* (London: Routledge, 2001). This passage is quoted in Hughes, ibid.,13.

8. Aristotle, *Ethics* 2.2, 1103b26–31.

9. My interpretation of Aristotle here is indebted to John E. Hare, *God and Moral Obligation: A Philosophical Inquiry* (Oxford: Blackwell, 2007).

10. Ibid., 14–15.

11. Ibid., 18.

12. All biblical references are to NRSV unless otherwise specified. See W. H. Bellinger Jr. and Todd. D. Still, eds., *Baylor Annotated Study Bible* (Waco, TX: Baylor University Press, 2019).

13. Dallas Willard, *The Divine Conspiracy: Rediscovering Our Hidden Life in God* (New York: HarperColliins, 1998), 112.

14. Scott B. Rae, *Moral Choices: An Introduction to Ethics*, 4th ed. (Grand Rapids, MI: Zondervan Academic, 2018), 68–69.

15. On ways to apply *agapism*, or "the law of love," to everyday life, I recommend Murray Bodo, OFM, *Surrounded by Love: Seven Teachings from Saint Francis* (Cincinnati: Franciscan Media, 2018). Of course, books on the lives of the saints are always helpful.

16. The novelist Ayn Rand (1906–82) is sometimes thought to have advocated elementary ethical egoism. She did not. In *The Virtue of Selfishness: A New Concept of Egoism* and in *Capitalism: The Unknown Ideal*, she argues that our sole moral duty is to pursue our *rational* self-interest. Her view, rational ethical egoism, differs in many ways from the version of egoism we are examining. For instance, on Rand's view, it is always in our rational self-interest to respect the rights of others to life, liberty, and property. Rand gave her ethical theory a literary expression in novels such as *The Fountainhead*, *Atlas Shrugged*, and *Anthem*.

17. See Steven Pinker, *The Better Angels of Our Nature: Why Violence Has Declined* (New York: Penguin, 2011), chap. 1.

18. For the reader who wants to delve into utilitarianism, I recommend John Stuart Mill, *Utilitarianism*, ed. George Sher (Indianapolis: Hackett, 2002), and Ben Eggleston and Dale E. Miller, *The Cambridge Companion to Utilitarianism* (Cambridge: Cambridge University Press, 2014).

19. Watch the movie *Rosewood*, directed by John Singleton.

20. See J. B. Schneewind, *The Invention of Autonomy: A History of Modern Moral Philosophy* (Cambridge: Cambridge University Press, 1997).

21. Kant offered no argument in support of his claim that the four formulations of the categorical imperative are logically equivalent. Most philosophers argue that the four statements of the categorical imperative are not equivalent.

22. See Immanuel Kant, *Groundwork of the Metaphysics of Morals*, trans. H. J. Paton (New York: Harper & Row, 1964), 70. For a detailed study, see H. J. Paton, *The Categorical Imperative: A Study in Kant's Moral Philosophy* (Philadelphia: University of Pennsylvania Press, 1948). An excellent study of Kant's ethical theory is Allen W. Wood, *Kantian Ethics* (Cambridge: Cambridge University Press, 2008). Kant's writings on ethics are collected in *Practical Philosophy: The Cambridge Edition of the Works of Immanuel Kant*, ed. Mary J. Gregor; intro. Allen W. Wood (Cambridge: Cambridge University Press, 1999).

23. In settling upon my explanation of Kant's categorical imperative, I have been influenced by Russ Shafer-Landau, *Fundamentals of Ethics* (New York: Oxford University Press, 2012), 159, and Lewis Vaughn, *Philosophy Here and Now*, 2nd ed. (New York: Oxford University Press, 2014), chap. 3.

24. C. Stephen Layman, *The Shape of the Good: Christian Reflections on the Foundations of Ethics* (Notre Dame, IN: University of Notre Dame Press, 1991), 90.

25. Ibid., 91.

26. I owe thanks to my colleague Steven Duncan for brining this issue to my attention, in conversation.

27. I recommend Stéphane Courtois, Nicolas Werth, Jean-Louis Panné, Andrzej Paczkowski, Karel Bartosek, and Jean Louis Margolin, *The Black Book of Communism: Crimes, Terror, Repression* (Cambridge, MA: Harvard University Press, 1999), and Richard Pipes, *Communism: A History* (New York: Modern Library, 2001).

INTERLUDE TWO.   *Or Should We All Become Moral Relativists?*

1. See "What Is Modern Slavery?," Anti-Slavery, https://www.antislavery .org/slavery-today/modern-slavery/. This group is a reliable source.

2. Herodotus, *Histories* 3.38. I have excerpted this passage from the Internet Classics Archive, http://classics.mit.edu/Herodotus/history.html.

3. For example, the English anthropologist E. E. Evans-Pritchard (1902–73) and the American anthropologist Ruth Benedict (1887–1948).

4. See Anne Applebaum, *Red Famine: Stalin's War on Ukraine* (New York: Doubleday, 2017), and Robert Conquest, *The Great Terror: A Reassessment*, 40th anniversary ed. (New York: Oxford University Press, 2007). See also the first

massive scholarly study on Stalin's mass murders in the Ukraine: Robert Conquest, *The Harvest of Sorrow: Soviet Collectivization and the Terror Famine* (New York: Oxford University Press, 1987); originally published in 1968. For a survivor's view, see Miron Dolot, *Execution by Hunger: The Hidden Holocaust* (New York: W. W. Norton, 1987). For broader research, I recommend Jasper Becker, *Hungry Ghosts: Mao's Secret Famine* (New York: Henry Holt, 1996), and Frank Dikotter, *Mao's Great Famine* (New York: Bloomsbury, 2010). As we mentioned in chapter 7, experts estimate that during the twentieth century, communist dictators were directly responsible for the deaths of between 80 and 100 million innocent victims. See Stéphane Courtois, Nicolas Werth, Jean-Louis Panné, Andrzej Paczkowski, Karel Bartosek, and Jean-Louis Margolin, *The Black Book of Communism: Crimes, Terror, Repression* (Cambridge, MA: Harvard University Press, 1999).

THIRTEEN. *Moral Reasoning Applied to the State*

1. On the history of freedom and the development of our modern understanding, I recommend the magisterial Donald Treadgold, *Freedom: A History* (New York: New York University Press, 1990). Treadgold was a beloved history professor and highly respected scholar who taught at the University of Washington for four decades. I was privileged to take several of his classes. I also recommend John Rawls, *Lectures on the History of Political Philosophy* (Cambridge, MA: Harvard University Press, 2007); David Schmidtz and Jason Brennan, *A Brief History of Liberty* (Oxford: Wiley Blackwell, 2010); and Orlando Patterson, *Freedom in the Making of Western Culture* (New York: Basic Books, 1991).

2. Nearly all the ideas championed by the classical liberal philosophers can be found in Reformation political thought, especially in Puritan and Calvinist writings. However, classical liberal philosophers such as Hobbes, Locke, and Kant gave these ideas a philosophical rather than a purely religious or biblical foundation.

3. The English philosopher and classical liberal theorist Thomas Hobbes (1588–1679) famously disagreed with this principle. The classical liberals did not agree on everything, but Hobbes was in the minority when he argued for an absolute monarch in his masterpiece *Leviathan* (1651).

4. No records exist of any public philosophical debates on the modern political ideals in any non-Western society during the sixteenth, seventeenth, and eighteenth centuries. The classical liberals were the intellectual pioneers of these ideas in the modern world. To paraphrase Edith Hamilton (chapter 1), all societies around the world have been schooled in political theory by the West.

5. The Oxford historian J. M. Roberts is one of many scholars who includes the influence of biblical images such as the *imago Dei* in their histories of the development of freedom. See J. M. Roberts, *The Triumph of the West: The Origin, Rise, and Legacy of Western Civilization* (London: British Broadcasting Corporation, 1985). Roberts's classic work is now available in many editions.

6. Many editions are available. I am using *John Locke: Two Treatises of Government* (New York: New American Library, 1965), with an introduction and notes by Peter Laslett. A generation before Locke, Hobbes also offered an original foundation for the classical liberal ideals in *Leviathan*. Locke's theory was more widely accepted, perhaps because Hobbes argued for absolute monarchy whereas Locke argued for republican government, strong individual rights as counters to state power, and the right of revolution, among the other liberal ideals. In political theory, a government is "republican" (lowercase *r*) if the citizens take an active part in their own governance.

7. The theological interpretation of self-ownership would presumably be that God created each person and put each in charge of his or her own soul, each to be judged individually in the end.

8. The right to own property can thus be derived from the rights to life and liberty. Classical liberals generally believed that if a person has no *right* to own property, which includes food, clothing, and personal possessions, then that person lives at the beck and call of others, and that person is not truly free. And as the classical liberals saw it, rightful ownership of some item entails the right to exclude others from using or taking that item.

9. Recall the distinction between special revelation and general revelation. *Special* revelation consists of God's Word received under inspiration and expressed in scripture. *General* revelation is God's truth revealed outside of scripture — universal truths that can be discovered using our unaided human cognitive abilities. Both the Old and New Testaments refer to a natural order that God inscribed on his creation, a fixed structure that can be studied and understood using our common human reasoning apart from special revelation. Locke considered the natural moral law to be part of God's general revelation. In his day, it was common for philosophers to call the axioms of natural law "the laws of nature and of nature's God." A beautifully written study of modern natural law ideas, including Locke's place in the tradition, is the classic Carl Becker, *The Declaration of Independence: A Study in the History of Political Ideas* (New York: Vintage, 1942).

10. It was almost universally accepted in Locke's day that God exists and that God created human nature. Locke gave a profound philosophical argument for God's existence in chapter 10 of his treatise on epistemology, *An Essay Concerning Human Understanding* (1689), the first work of philosophy to propose a systematic epistemological basis for modern science.

11. The right to life, then, is the right that others not take your life; it is not the right to be given what you need to live. The right to property is the right that others not take your (legitimately acquired) property; it is not the right to be given property, and so forth.

12. See Morton White, *The Philosophy of the American Revolution* (Oxford: Oxford University Press, 1978), and White, *Philosophy, the Federalist, and the Constitution* (Oxford: Oxford University Press, 1987). For another excellent study of Locke's influence on the Founding Fathers, see Becker, *Declaration of Independence*. Also of value is Alfred H. Kelly and Winfred A. Harbison, *The American Constitution: Its Origin and Development*, 5th ed. (New York: W. W. Norton, 1976), and Alexander Hamilton, James Madison, and John Jay, *The Federalist Papers* (New York: The New American Library, 1961).

13. William Talbott, *Which Rights Should Be Universal?* (New York: Oxford University Press, 2005), 37. On how unlikely it was at the time that the document we know as the Constitution would pass, see Carol Berkin, *A Brilliant Solution: Inventing the American Constitution* (New York: Mariner Books, Houghton Mifflin Harcourt, 2003), and Catherine Drinker Bowen, *Miracle at Philadelphia: The Story of the Constitutional Convention May–September 1787*, foreword by Warren E. Burger (New York: Back Bay Books, 1986).

14. In 1787, as the U.S. Constitution was being drafted, slavery was a world-wide institution, practiced and accepted as natural across Africa, Asia, the Middle East, and India.

15. A. C. Grayling, *Toward the Light of Liberty: The Struggles for Freedom and Rights That Made the Modern Western World* (New York: Walker Publishing, 2007).

16. The founding document of classical conservatism is Edmund Burke's *Reflections on the Revolution in France* (1790). Many editions are available. Also important is Burke's *A Philosophical Enquiry into the Origin of our Ideas of the Sublime and Beautiful* (1757). Burke (1729–97) was an Irish philosopher, statesman, and member of Parliament. The American philosopher Russell Kirk (1918–94) is the most prolific contemporary scholar and interpreter of Burke's political philosophy. Kirk's *The Conservative Mind* (1953) is widely considered to be the founding document of modern conservatism.

17. *John Locke: Two Treatises of Government*, 42.

18. Frederic Bastiat, *Selected Essays on Political Economy*, trans. Seymour Cain; ed. George B. de Huszar (Irvington-on-Hudson, NY: The Foundation for Economic Education, 1964), chap. 2.

19. Alexis de Tocqueville, *Democracy in America* (New York: Dover, 2017).

20. This is not the same problem as the famous assurance problem developed in Hobbes's philosophy. To put it roughly, Hobbes argued that we have

no obligation to be moral unless we can be assured that others will be moral in return. In a state of nature we have no assurance that others will be moral if we are moral. Hence, in a state of nature we have no obligation to be moral. We are only obliged to be moral once the state exists and enforces written laws with punishments that give everyone a strong incentive to treat each other in accord with the moral or natural law. In contrast, Locke (and Kant) held that moral obligation would exist even in a state of nature.

21. D. W. Haslett, *Capitalism with Morality* (Oxford: Clarendon, 1994), 69.

22. For a wise and bipartisan study of state welfare programs that suggests tested ways to improve the existing system and help individuals achieve their potential while respecting and promoting individual initiative and autonomy, see Ron Haskins and Isabel Sawhill, *Creating an Opportunity Society* (New York: Brookings Institution Press, 2009). The authors are two leading poverty researchers at the Brookings Institution.

23. See Thomas Piketty, *Capital in the Twenty-First Century* (Cambridge, MA: Harvard University Press, 2014), 73–74.

24. See Edwin J. Perkins and Gary M. Walton, *A Prosperous People: The Growth of the American Economy* (Englewood Cliffs, NJ: Prentice-Hall, 1985), 141. For deep research on the exponential increase in productivity unleashed by the birth of liberal capitalism, I recommend: Joel Mokyr. *The Lever of Riches: Technological Creativity and Economic Progress* (New York: Oxford University Press, 1992); Eric Jones, *The European Miracle: Environments, Economies, and Geopolitics in the History of Europe and Asia*, 3rd ed. (Cambridge: Cambridge University Press, 2003); David S. Landes, *The Wealth and Poverty of Nations: Why Some Are so Rich and Some so Poor* (New York: W. W. Norton, 1999); and Nathan Rosenberg and L. E. Birdzell Jr., *How the West Grew Rich: The Economic Transformation of the Industrial World* (New York: Basic Books, 1986).

25. John Rawls, *A Theory of Justice* (Cambridge, MA: Harvard University Press, 1971). A good collection of articles on Rawls is Norman Daniels, ed., *Reading Rawls: Critical Studies on Rawls' "A Theory of Justice"* (Stanford, CA: Stanford University Press, 1989). I also recommend Thomas Pogge, *John Rawls: His Life and Theory of Justice* (New York: Oxford University Press, 2007). For a shorter version of his complex argument, see John Rawls and Erin Kelly, ed., *Justice as Fairness: A Restatement* (Cambridge, MA: Harvard University Press, 2001). I also recommend Paul Graham, *Rawls* (Oxford: Oneworld, 2007), and Jon Mandle, *Rawls's A Theory of Justice: An Introduction* (Cambridge: Cambridge University Press, 2009).

26. Rawls presents this argument within a larger argument for a rational social contract.

27. Rawls, *A Theory of Justice*, 104.

28. Ibid., 101.

29. Ibid., 203.

30. The difference principle thus allows incentives to economic activity but taxes away economic rents — payments not needed to draw forth extra effort and action.

31. However, Rawls cautions that likely no social system will ever achieve perfection. Although we hope that poverty won't exist in a well-ordered, fully just society, it is possible there will remain some kinds of poverty we simply do not know how to cure, for example the poverty of those who drop out of the system and refuse to better themselves, refuse aid, refuse to work, and so forth. In *Justice as Fairness: A Restatement*, he writes that even within a fully just society, "we hope that an underclass will not exist; or, if there is such a small class, that is the result of social conditions we do not know how to change, or perhaps cannot even identify or understand. When society faces this impasse, it has at least taken seriously the idea of itself as a fair system of cooperation between its citizens" (Rawls and Kelly, eds., *Justice as Fairness: A Restatement*, 140).

32. See Rawls and Kelly, eds., *Justice as Fairness: A Restatement*, pt. IV.

33. Rawls explicitly stated that the difference principle requires the periodic redistribution of income, wealth, status, and power, even if everyone acts justly and even if society is perfectly just and well ordered. See John Rawls, *Political Liberalism* (New York: Columbia University Press, 2005), 283–84.

34. Ibid.

35. For more on property-owning democracy, see Martin O'Neill and Thad Williamson, eds., *Property-Owning Democracy: Rawls and Beyond* (Malden, MA: Wiley-Blackwell, 2012). It is interesting that Thomas Paine (1736–1809), the colonial author of the most influential case for revolution of the time, *Common Sense* (1776), argues in his later writings for an early version of private-property-owning democracy. Paine was one of the first to propose a universal basic income guaranteed by the state. He also argues that each person should receive from the state a property endowment upon reaching adulthood.

36. Robert Nozick, *Anarchy, State, and Utopia* (New York: Basic Books, 1974).

37. Ibid., 1.

38. A valuable collection of critical articles treating Nozick's work is Jeffrey Paul, ed., *Reading Nozick* (Totowa, NJ: Rowman & Littlefield, 1981). For a book-length critical study of Nozick's theory, see Jonathan Wolff, *Robert Nozick: Property, Justice, and the Minimal State* (Stanford, CA: Stanford University Press, 1991). Also recommended is David Schmidtz, *Robert Nozick: Contemporary*

Philosophy in Focus (New York: Cambridge University Press, 2002); Edward Feser, *On Nozick* (New York: Cengage Learning, 2003); Alan Lacey, *Robert Nozick* (New York: Routledge, 2014); Ralf M. Bader and John Meadowcroft, eds., *The Cambridge Companion to Nozick's "Anarchy, State, and Utopia"* (Cambridge: Cambridge University Press, 2011); and Lester Hunt, *"Anarchy, State, and Utopia": An Advanced Guide* (Oxford: Wiley-Blackwell, 2015).

39.   Nozick suggests another problem for Rawls. Even if we grant that individuals do not deserve their natural and social assets, it does not logically follow that others deserve a share of the goods produced when high-income individuals put their natural assets to work.

40.   Here is a standard libertarian argument for Nozick's position. Just as you cannot rightly be forced to let others drive your car if you are its rightful owner, a self-owner cannot rightly be forced to aid others. A self-owner might, however, help others voluntarily, just as the owner of a car might voluntarily allow someone to borrow it.

41.   I recommend Larry Schweikart, *The Entrepreneurial Adventure: A History of Business in the United States* (Belmont, CA: Wadsworth, 1999).

42.   The difference principle maximizes the condition of the least well off in the sense that it transfers to them an amount such that if any more were to be transferred, they would actually receive less due to the disincentive effects of heavy taxation and redistribution.

43.   One problem, of course, is that some become so comfortable with their aid that they don't want to advance to the point of independence.

44.   The philosopher George Sher has argued for sufficientarianism in a number of books. I recommend Sher, *Equality for Inegalitarians* (Cambridge: Cambridge University Press, 2014).

45.   The economist Ludwig von Mises pointed out that under capitalism, as the economy develops, average real income rises, mass poverty declines, and charitable giving rises. See Ludwig von Mises, *Human Action: A Treatise on Economics*, 3rd rev. ed. (New Haven CT: Yale University Press, 1963), 837. On the potentials of the American private charity sector, see Karl Zinsmeister, *The Almanac of American Philanthropy* (Washington, DC: The Philanthropy Roundtable, 2016). Some of the statistics presented in this scholarly study are eye-opening. In the United States, per capita individual charitable giving adjusted for inflation rose 350 percent between 1954 and 2012 (ibid., 1114). Individuals are responsible for 81 percent of U.S. charitable giving, corporations and foundations make up the remaining 19 percent (ibid., 1118). In terms of annual private giving as a percent of GDP, the United States ranks as the most charitable country in the world, with giving at levels three to fifteen times the levels of the other developed

countries (ibid., 1166). The United States also ranks at the top of the chart for private donations for overseas aid, with giving at eight times the level of its closest rival, Japan (ibid., 1162). The output of the U.S. nonprofit sector as a percent of GDP has risen from 1.8 in 1930 to 5.6 in 2014 (ibid., 1124). In 2010, 10.6 percent of the U.S. workforce was employed in the nonprofit sector, up from 8.8 percent in 1998 (ibid., 1122). See these charts online at http://www.philanthropy roundtable.org/almanac/statistics/u.s.-generosity.

46. David Schmidtz, *The Elements of Justice* (Cambridge: Cambridge University Press, 2006), 188.

47. Milton Friedman and Rose Friedman, *Free to Choose: A Personal Statement* (New York: Avon, 1980), 13. I owe thanks to my colleague Art DiQuattro for drawing my attention to this passage.

FOURTEEN. *God and Morality*

1. Of course, a recognition of a natural law that is higher than any human law goes back to the ancient Greeks and Romans. A recognition of natural law can also be found in the Old and New Testaments.

2. Martin Luther King Jr., "Letter from Birmingham Jail," in *Testament of Hope: The Essential Writings and Speeches of Martin Luther King, Jr.*, ed. James M. Washington (New York: HarperOne, 2003), 289–302.

3. C. S. Lewis, *Mere Christianity* (New York: Macmillan, 1943), 45, 52, bk. 1.

4. For the reader who wants to research the moral argument, I recommend Mark Murphy, *God and Moral Law: On the Theistic Explanation of Morality* (New York: Oxford University Press, 2011), Angus Ritchie, *From Morality to Metaphysics: The Theistic Implications of Our Ethical Commitments* (New York: Oxford University Press, 2013), David Baggett and Jerry Walls, *The Moral Argument: A History* (New York: Oxford University Press, 2019), and Philip L. Quinn, *Divine Commands and Moral Requirements* (Oxford: Clarendon Press, 1978).

5. William P. Alston, "What Euthyphro Should Have Said," in *Philosophy of Religion: A Reader and Guide*, ed. William Lane Craig (Edinburgh: Edinburgh University Press, 2002), 283–98.

6. Richard L. Purtill, *Reason to Believe* (Grand Rapids, MI: Eerdmans, 1974), 96.

7. See C. S. Lewis, *Reflections on the Psalms*, rpt. ed. (New York: HarperOne, 2017), 119: "God is righteous and commands righteousness because He loves it. He enjoins what is good because it is good, because He is good. Hence His laws have 'truth,' intrinsic validity, rock bottom reality, being rooted in His own nature." Lewis is commenting on Psalm 70.

8. Harold Lindsell, ed., *The Best of C. S. Lewis* (Grand Rapids, MI: Baker Book House, 1961), 61.

9. Lewis, *Reflections on the Psalms*, 119.

10. I owe thanks to an anonymous reviewer for the University of Notre Dame Press for suggesting that I take up this objection.

11. Steven Pinker, *The Better Angels of Our Nature: Why Violence Has Declined* (New York: Penguin, 2011).

12. Scott B. Rae, *Moral Choices: An Introduction to Ethics*, 4th ed. (Grand Rapids MI: Zondervan Academic, 2018), 44.

13. C. S. Lewis, *The Abolition of Man* (New York: Macmillan, 1947), chap. 1.

14. Jean-Paul Sartre, *Existentialism and Human Emotions* (Secaucus, NJ: Carol Publishing, 1998), 21.

15. Ibid., 21.

16. Ibid., 23.

17. But if each of us *must* create his or her own morality, where does *this* objective moral obligation come from?

18. J. L. Mackie, *The Miracle of Theism: Arguments for and against the Existence of God* (New York: Oxford University Press, 1983), 115.

19. King, "Letter from Birmingham Jail," in Washington, ed., *Testament of Hope*, 289–302. For the reader interested in the philosophical ideas that shaped King's mature worldview, I recommend Rufus Burrow Jr., *God and Human Dignity: The Personalism, Theology, and Ethics of Martin Luther King, Jr.* (South Bend, IN: University of Notre Dame Press, 1992). King's primary philosophical influence was "Boston Personalism"—a school of philosophy founded by Borden Parker Bowne (1847–1910), a professor of philosophy at Boston University who was also a Methodist clergyman. King was introduced to personalism in his philosophy classes at Boston University. The Boston personalists argued for these interrelated ideas: (1) Reality is ultimately personal in nature, being grounded in God, a supreme person; personhood is therefore the ultimate category of explanation; (2) there is an objective moral order in the universe, a "natural" law expressing God's nature; (3) this natural law or objective morality calls us to recognize "the infinite, inviolable worth of the person as such and a personal God to whom persons are of supreme value"; (4) our creation by God as beings of inviolable worth is the ground of human dignity; (5) human nature has a communitarian, relational dimension—we were meant to be related to each other in holy ways rooted in mutual love and respect; and (6) human beings have a natural desire for a beloved community anchored in God. Although these core ideas can be found in Western philosophy going back to ancient times, Bowne and others at Boston, including Edgar S. Brightman (1884–1953), developed the personalist theme in unique ways. Many threads of this book come together in the theistic personalism of Dr. Martin Luther King Jr.

INDEX

Abolition of Man (Lewis), 304, 400, 402

Academy, Plato's, 40

agapism, 321

agent causation theory, 288
  account of free will, 288–89
  arguments against, 292–95
  arguments for, 290–92
  dualism and, 295–97
  theism and, 295–97

Albert the Great, 422n.38

Alcoholics Anonymous
  Socratic method and, 32, 411n.11

Alston, William
  Euthyphro dilemma and, 398–99
  moral argument and, 398–99
  skeptical theism and, 178–79

Analects of Confucius, 407–8n.6

analogy, 59, 61

Anarchy, State, and Utopia (Nozick), 381–82

Anaximander, 5, 9

Anaximenes, 5, 9

Anthony, Susan B., 354

Aquinas, Thomas, 62, 359
  free will and, 295
  life of, 137–39
  Second Way, 114–21

arche, 7, 106

argument
  deductive, 42–45
  —defined, 33, 41
  —sound, 44
  —valid vs. invalid, 43–46
  inductive
  —analogical, 59
  —best explanation, 64, 65–66
  —cogent, 48
  —defined, 42
  —strong vs. weak, 47

argument from evil
  evidential version, 176–78
  initial statement of, 159
  logical version, 161

argument from neuroscience, 248

argument from reason
  C. S. Lewis's statement of, 211–14
  cognitive abilities and, 214
  evolutionary objection to, 214
  intelligibility of the universe and, 220
  Plantinga and, 223

Aristotle
  and the founding of logic, 39–40
  life, 40–41
  on mind-body problem, 245–46
  moral responsibility and, 280

Aristotle (*cont.*)
  Politics, 359
  on Thales, 5
  theory of the good life, 312–18
  on wonder, 108
assets
  natural, 373
  social, 373
atomism
  design argument and, 66–67
  founded, 66
Augustine, Saint, 62
  ethics and, 321
  problem of evil and, 164–67
autonomy (moral), 336
axiom of individual self-ownership, 362
axiom of universal moral equality, 362
axiom system, 16

Barrow, John, 94–95
Bastiat, Frederic, 368–69
Behe, Michael, 71
Bentham, Jeremy, 325–27
best explanation argument
  for agent causation, 290–91
  for the big bang, 152
  defined, 64
  from dualism to theism, 295–97
  fine-tuning argument, 98–100
  from free will to theism, 295–97
  for intelligent design, 64–66
  from objective moral truth to theism,
    395–96
big bang, theory of
  argument for, 152
  God and, 150
  Lemaître and development of,
    144–50
blind chance (hypothesis), 66–67,
    77–78
Block, Ned, 258
BonJour, Laurence, 10, 192, 193, 197,
    198, 241, 242

Boyle, Joseph, Jr., 292
Boyle, Robert, 73
Brahmins, 75
Burke, Edmund, 441n.16

capitalism
  charity and, 367–71, 444n.45
  the human condition and, 372,
    442n.24
  laissez faire, 371
  —Rawls's critique of, 374–77
  liberal, 386–87
  two views of, 386–87
capitalist welfare state, 380–81
categorical imperative (Kant), 332
  four forms of, 333–40
Catholic Church, birth of modern
  science and, 415n.16
causation, event vs. agent, 290
cause (and effect)
  accidentally vs. essentially ordered,
    419n.15
  cosmological argument and, 116–22
  defined, 271
  free will and, 271
Chalmers, David
  hard problem of consciousness, 260
  zombie argument of, 259–60
charity
  capitalism and, 444n.45
  classical liberalism and, 367–71
  communism and, 389
  contemporary, 444n.45
  Locke and, 367–71
  Locke's principle of, 367
Chinese room argument. *See*
  functionalism
Chisholm, Roderick, 288–89, 295
Christ, Jesus, 318–21
Cicero, 37
Coburn, Robert, 267–68, 434n.1
communism, 424n.1, 438n.4
compatibilism. *See* determinism

computer, development of, 49–50
  Aristotle and, 49
  logical theory and, 49
Confucius, 305, 407–8n.6
conservatism
  classical, 366
  modern, 441n.16
Constitution, U.S., 365
constitutionalism, birth of, 18
Copleston, Frederick, cosmological
  argument and, 134
cosmic coincidences
  defined, 95
  examples of, 93, 95–97
  physicists' comments on, 97–98
cosmic microwave radiation, 150,
  151–53
cosmological constant (Einstein),
  143, 149
cosmology
  cosmological argument and, 107
  defined, 28
cosmos
  defined, 59
  design argument and, 59
Craig, William Lane
  cosmological argument and, 136
  kalam argument and, 154
creationism, 85
  vs. evolutionism, 86
critical thinking
  criteria of, 26
  logic and, 26
  Socrates as founder of, 26

Darwin, Charles, 85
  critique of Paley, 87
  theory of evolution, 86–87, 105
  universe as expression of a mind,
  418n.44
Davies, Paul, 94, 97, 103
Dawkins, Richard, critique of
  intelligent design, 89–90

defeater, 208–9
definition
  defined, 33
  essential and nominal distinguished,
  33
deliberation argument. *See* van
  Inwagen, Peter
Dembski, William, 71
democracy
  ancient Greek philosophy and, 18
  birth of, 18
  defined, 18
  private-property-owning, 380–81
Descartes, René, 232–35
  divisibility argument, 232
  mind-body problem and, 232–39
determinism
  defined, 272
  hard, 273–76
  —argument against, 277–80
  —argument for, 273
  soft (compatibilism), 281–83
  —account of free will, 281
  —argument against, 283–85
  —argument for, 282
dialectic
  defined, 14
  pre-Socratics and, 14–15
Dialogues concerning Natural Religion
  (Hume), 74–81, 123
difference principle, 378, 443n.33,
  444n.42
dilemma of determinism argument, 287
dissociative identity disorder, 236–37
divisibility argument. *See* Descartes,
  René
Doppler, Christian, 147
Doppler effect, 147
Douglass, Frederick, 354
dualism (mind-body), 229–31
  epiphenomenalism and, 246
  hylomorphism and, 230–31, 245–46
  property, 231, 246–47

dualism (mind-body) (*cont.*)
  substance, 230, 246
  theism and, 263–65
Duncan, Steve, 219
duty, 340–41, 367–71
  positive vs. negative, 341
Dylan, Bob, mind-body problem and,
  234
Dyson, Freeman, 97

Eddington, Arthur, 143–44, 148
egoism. *See* ethics
Einstein, Albert
  big bang and, 146, 148–49
  general theory of relativity, 142–44
  on intelligibility of universe, 8
Elisabeth, Princess, 237
  challenge to Descartes, 237–39
emotion
  moral life and, 316
  the soul and, 30–31
ends, vs. means to an end, 336
*Enquiry concerning Human
  Understanding* (Hume), 79–80
entitlement, 383–86
entitlement theory (Nozick), 386
  argument for, 384–85
Epicurus
  design argument and, 414n.6
  free will and, 285–87
  swerve, 286
epiphenomenalism. *See* dualism
epistemic justification, 193
epistemology
  birth of, 190
  defined, 190
  Socrates and, 190–92
equal liberty principle, 378
equal opportunity, 378–79
  fair vs. formal, 379
equal opportunity principle (Rawls),
  379

ethics (moral philosophy), 304
  Aristotelian, 312–18
  Christian, 318–21
  defined, 304
  elementary egoism and, 322–24
  — Rand, Ayn, and, 437n.16
  emotions and, 316
  hedonism and, 306–12
  Kant's theory of, 331–43
  metaethics vs. normative ethics, 401
  Socratic theory of, 307–10
  utilitarian, 325–31
  virtue, 314–16
eudaimonia, 309, 310, 318
Euthyphro dilemma, 396–98
evil
  argument from, 159
  — evidential argument, 176–78
  — logical argument, 161–63
  defined, 159
  human vs. natural, 168
  problem of, 159
evolution, theory of, 86–89
  naturalistic vs. theistic, 100
evolutionism. *See* creationism
ex nihilo nihil fit principle, 133, 412n.2
examination of conscience, 28
existentialism, 403

fair opportunity principle, 378
faith, 136
Feser, Ed
  argument against scientism, 13
  dualism and, 239, 247
fine-tuning argument, 91–100
  birth of, 91–93
  cosmic coincidences and, 93–98
  multiverse objection to, 100–102
Five Ways, Aquinas's, 114
freedom, civic
  first philosophical expressions of, 18
  history of, 439n.1

free rider problem, 370
Free to Choose (Friedman), 391
free will
    account of, 270
    agent causation account of,
        288–91
    Augustine's theodicy and, 165
    compatibilist account of, 281–83
    dualism and, 295–97
    self-referential argument for, 292
    simple indeterminist account of,
        285–87
    Socratic critical thinking and, 298
    theism and, 295–97
French National Assembly, 381
    and origin of left vs. right, 381
Friedman, Milton, and Rose Friedman,
    391
Friedmann, Alexander, 144
functionalism
    arguments against
    — Chinese room, 256–57
    — gigantic mind, 258–59
    — zombie, 259–60
    arguments for, 254–55
    defined, 253–54
fundamental forces of nature, 92
fundamental particles of matter, 92

Galileo, 72
Gamow, George, 150
general theory of relativity, 141–44
geometry, 16–17, 141–42
Gettier, Edmund, 206
Gettier paradoxes, 206–10
goodness, extrinsic vs. intrinsic, 306
Gorgias of Leontini, 188
Grayling, A. C. 366
Greek miracle, 19–20
Gribbin, John, 93, 94
Grisez, Germain, 292
Gross, Ronald, 38

Hamilton, Edith, 20, 410n.35
hard problem of consciousness.
    See Chalmers, David
Harrison, George, and the search for
    God, 136
Hawking, Stephen
    cosmological argument and, 110,
        128
    fine-tuning argument and, 98
Hebrews (ancient), 407n.5
hedonism
    egoistic, 306–7, 311
    universalistic, 325
Heidegger, Martin, 265, 394
Herodotus, 19
    cultural relativism and, 344
    founding of history and, 19
Hick, John, 171
Hippocrates, 19
    birth of scientific medicine and,
        19
history, birth of, 19
Hitler, 157–58
Hobbes, Thomas, 439n.3, 440n.6
Hofstadter, Douglas, 61
Hogan, Craig, 77, 116
Holbach, Baron Paul-Henri d', 275
Hoyle, Fred, 149–52
Hubble, Edwin, 147–80
Hubble constant, 146
human rights
    Kantian moral theory and,
        340–42
    positive vs. negative, 341
Hume, David, 62, 74
    criticism of the cosmological
        argument, 123–27
    on design argument, 62–81
    — agreement with, 81
    — objections to, 74–81
Huxley, Julian, 88
hylomorphism, 230–31, 245

identity
  qualitative, 234, 248
  quantitative (numerical), 234, 248
identity theory (of mind), 247–53
imago Dei, doctrine of, 361, 390
immortality
  argument for, 425n.12
  problem of evil and, 166–67
  Socrates and, 309
imperatives, categorical vs.
    hypothetical, 332
incompatibilism
  argument for, 274
  hard determinism and, 275
indeterminism, 285–91
  defined, 285
  Epicurus and, 285–86
  free will and, 285–86
  simple, 285–87
infinite regression
  Aquinas's Second Way and, 116,
    118–19
  argument against, 118–19, 124–28
  circular vs. linear, 126
  defined, 80
  design argument and, 80–81
  Hume and, 123–27
  intelligibility thesis and, 118–19
intelligence, artificial, strong vs. weak,
    258
intelligent design theorists, 71
intelligible universe thesis, 7–8
  argument from reason and, 220
  cosmological argument and, 118–21
  design argument and, 81
  Einstein and, 8
  Nagle, Thomas, and, 8
  as requirement of science, 8
  Thales and, 7–8
intentionality
  argument against identity theory, 251
  argument for dualism, 241–42
  defined, 240

interaction problem, 238
Irenaeus, Bishop, 164, 169–72

James, William, 287
Jeffery, Andrew, 20
Job, book of, 182
Jordan, Michael, 385
Justice as Fairness (Rawls), 380
justification, epistemic, 193
  a posteriori, 197–99
  a priori, 198–201

kalam cosmological argument, 154
Kant, Immanuel
  classical liberalism and, 361
  cosmology and, 140–41
  human rights and, 340–42
  theory of ethics, 331–43
karma, theory of, 173
  as solution to problem of evil, 173–75
King, Martin Luther, Jr.
  moral argument for theism and,
    393–95, 405
  moral reform and, 354
  personalism and, 446n.19
  philosophical ethics and, 303
  theism and, 446n.19
kingdom of ends, 339
Kirk, Russell, 441n.16
knowledge
  a posteriori (or empirical), 197–99
  a priori (or ratiocinative), 197–201
  classical theory of, 190–94
  —justification and, 193, 197–98
  cultural relativism and, 196
  objective truth and, 187–88
  Socrates and, 191–93
Krauss, Lawrence, cosmological
    argument and, 109–10

Laertius, Diogenes, 9
lambda, 143, 149
Laplace, Pierre-Simon, 275–76

laws of chemistry, 112
Layman, C. Stephen, 103
  multiverse hypothesis and, 103
  problem of evil and, 166–67
least advantaged, 378
left-right distinction (politics), 381
Leibniz, Gottfried, 62
Leibniz's Law, 235
Lemaître, Georges
  big bang theory and, 144–53
  discovery of cosmic background
    radiation, 153
  Einstein and, 146, 148–49
Lenin, 426n.19
"Letter from Birmingham City Jail"
    (King), 393, 405, 446n.19
Leucippus of Miletus, 66
  design argument and, 66
Lewis, C. S., 136, 211, 349
  argument from reason, 211–14
  Euthyphro dilemma and, 399
  moral argument for theism,
    394–96
  moral law and (*Tao*), 304–5
  search for God and, 136
liberalism
  classical
  —ideals of, 360–361
  —introduced, 359
  —Locke's argument for, 362–64
  —Nozick and, 381–82, 385
  modern, 360
  —John Rawls and, 372–80
libertarianism (free will), 435n.21
libertarianism (political), 368–79, 385
Libet experiments, 435n.17
life after death, 35, 166–67, 230,
    425–26n.12
Locke, John, 367
  charity and, 367–71
Lockeans
  libertarian, 368–70
  moderate, 370–71

logic
  Aristotle and, 39–41
  in computing, 49–50
  critical thinking and, 26
  deductive arguments, 42
  —sound, 44
  —valid vs. invalid, 43–48
  defined, 26, 39
  founding of, 39–40
  inductive arguments, 42–43
  —cogent, 48
  —strong vs. weak, 46–49
lottery
  natural, 373
  social, 373
Lucas, J. R., 167
luck, 374–75
Lull, Raymond, 49
  and invention of the computer, 49
Lyceum, 40, 41

Mackie, J. L.
  argument from evil and, 161
  moral argument and, 404–5
Mao Tse-tung, 172, 356, 426n.19
materialism
  defined, 231
  mind-body, 231, 247–53
mathematics
  Babylonian and Egyptian, 15–16
  birth of, 15–18
  distinguished from mensuration, 16
  Thales and, 16–17
maxim, 332
medicine, scientific, birth of. *See*
    Hippocrates
mensuration. *See* mathematics
mere theism. *See* theism
metaphysics, defined, 187
Meyer, Stephen, 71
microwave radiation, 151–53
Mill, John Stuart, 326–27
Miracles (Lewis), 211, 225

Mises, Ludwig von, 444n.45
modern science
  birth of, 414n.15, 414n.16
  first steps toward, 8, 19
monotheism
  defined, 9
  Ockham's razor and, 13
  Thales and, 9
Monte Cassino, 138
moral absolutism, 347–48
moral arbitrariness, 373–74
moral arbitrariness argument, 377
  Nozick's challenge, 382–83
moral argument, Lewis, C. S. and,
  394–95, 399
moral nihilism, 348
moral objectivism, 347
moral relativism, individual vs. societal,
  347–48
moral responsibility
  argument, van Inwagen's, 279
  defined, 269
moral universalism, 347
Moreland, J. P., cosmological argument
  and, 132
Mozi, 412n.21
multiverse hypothesis, 100–105
  Layman's objection to, 103
  Ockham's razor challenge, 103
  Plantinga on, 104
  this universe objection to, 104
myth, 3
  distinguished from philosophy, 4
  examples of, 4

Nagel, Thomas
  argument from reason and, 224
  design argument and, 67–69
  functionalism and, 261
  intelligibility thesis and, 8
  mind-body problem and, 242–43
natural endowment (assets), 373
natural law, 362–63, 394

natural liberty, system of, 374
natural lottery, 373
natural selection, defined, 86–87
  argument from reason and, 215–21
  Darwin and, 86–87
  design argument and, 87
  required background order, 91
  Richard Dawkins's model of, 89–90
naturalism
  defined, 100, 211–12
  Lewis's argument against, 211–14,
  221–23
  vs. supernaturalism, 211–12, 222–24
  vs. theism, 222–24
naturalistic Darwinism, 100
naturalistic evolutionary theory, 221
nebulae, 140
necessary condition, 192
  vs. sufficient condition, 192
necessary truth, 133
neuroscience, argument from, 248–49
New Atheists, 75, 109
Newton, Isaac, 73–74
new watchmaker argument. *See* fine-
  tuning argument
nihilism (moral), 348
no-see-um inference, 180
Nozick, Robert, 381
  argument for libertarian Lockeanism,
  384
  critique of Rawls, 382–83
  entitlement theory of, 384–86
  liberal capitalism and, 386

Ockham, William of, 76
Ockham's razor
  argument for identity theory, 250
  cosmological argument and, 130–31
  defined, 76
  design argument and, 76–77
  monotheism and, 135
one over the many, 6–7, 9
oscillating universe theory, 153–54

Pagels, Heinz, 94, 108
Paley, William, 83
    watchmaker argument, 83–84
    —Darwin's rejection of, 85–88
Parfit, Derek, 128
Parsons, Keith, cosmological argument
    and, 128–29
Pascal, Blaise, 48, 50
Penrose, Roger, 128
Penzias, Arnold, 151–52
personalism, 446n.19
Phaedo, 36
    on death of Socrates, 36–37
philosophy
    birth of, 4
    defined, 5, 10–11
    distinguished from myth, 4
physicalism, 231
Picketty, Thomas, 372
Pinker, Steven, 400
Plantinga, Alvin
    argument from reason and, 223–24
    evolutionary argument against
        naturalism, 223
    multiverse hypothesis and, 104
    problem of evil and, 163, 181
Plato, 29, 35–36, 40, 190–91, 231
praise and blame principle, 269
pre-Socratics, 14–21
    retrospective on, 20–21
principle of alternate possibilities, 269
principle of sufficient reason
    Aquinas's Second Way and, 119–21
    defined, 120
principle of testimony. *See* testimony
principle of utility, 325
privacy
    argument against identity theory, 252
    argument for dualism, 244
    defined, 244
problem of evil
    evidential problem, 176
    logical problem, 159

problem of the one and the many.
    See Thales of Miletus
property-owning democracy, 380–81,
    443n.35
psychology experiment, the, 267–68
Purtill, Richard
    defense of ex nihilo principle, 133–34
    free will and, 291
    moral argument for theism and, 399
    principle of sufficient reason and, 121
Pythagoras, 60
    and musical scale, 413n.3

qualia
    argument against identity theory, 251
    defined, 239
    argument for dualism, 240
quantum mechanics, 418n.41, 421n.34

Rae, Scott, 320
Ramaglia, Vincenzo, 98
Rand, Ayn, and rational ethical egoism,
    437n.16
Rawls, John, 372
    moral arbitrariness argument, 377,
        382
    two principles of justice, 378–79
Ray, John, 73
Rees, Martin, 93, 97
Reformation political theorists, 439n.2
Reid, Thomas, 203
relativism
    alethic, 185–87
    meaning of, 345–46
    Socrates and, 187
    Sophists and, 187
relativism, moral
    cultural (societal)
    —arguments for, 348–51
    —challenges for, 351–55
    individual (subjectivism), 345, 348
    —challenges for, 355–57
Republic (Plato), 359

revelation, special vs. general, 320–21,
440n.9
rights
as claims, 340
duties and, 341
as end-constraints, 341–42
first philosophical expressions of, 18
human (universal), 340, 364
Kant's theory and, 340–42
life, liberty, and property, 340, 360,
363–64
modern human rights theory, 340
natural, 364
positive vs. negative, 341
utilitarianism and, 329–30
Rowe, William R., 176
and evidential argument from evil,
176–79
rule of law, first philosophical
expressions of, 18
Russell, Bertrand, 131
cosmological argument and, 131–32,
134–35

Sartre, Jean Paul
atheism and, 403
existentialism and, 403
moral argument and, 403–5
science, birth of, 19
design argument and, 72–74
modern science, birth of, 72
scientism, 11–13
Searle, John, 256–57
Second Way, Aquinas's, 114–21
self (mind-body problem), 230–31
self-contradiction, 413n.5 (chap. 3)
self-defeat (self-refutation), 214, 221–24
self-ownership. *See* axiom of individual
self-ownership
self-referential argument for free will,
292
Sim Universe, 98–99
Sitter, Willem de, 143

skeptical theism
defined, 181
Plantinga and, 181
as response to problem of evil,
178–81
skepticism
absolute, 187–88
defined, 187
Socrates and, 188
Sophists and, 188
skills, 375
vs. talents, 375
Slagle, Jim, 208, 219, 224, 431n.12,
431n.22
slavery, 344–45, 366
Smart, J. J. C., 250
Smith, Quentin, 153
social contract, 365
social endowment, 373
socialism, market, 381
societal differences argument, 349–50
Socrates, 21, 23–38, 57–59, 231, 357
account of the soul, 30–33, 307–10
birth of critical thinking and, 26
design argument and, 57–63
Euthyphro objection and, 396
freedom and, 38
on hedonism, 307–10
method of thought, 25–28
as midwife, 28
military service, 24
modern psychology and, 32
moral equality and, 25, 38
self-reform and, 32
vs. the Sophists, 307–9
theism and, 31, 309
theory of ethics, 305, 307–10
trial of, 34–35
two favorite questions, 32–33
on wonder, 108
youth, 24
Sophists, 307
egoistic hedonism and, 307

soul, the
  modern psychology and, 32
  Socrates's account, 30–32, 308–10
split-brain syndrome, 236–37
Stalin, 157–58, 426–27n.19
state of nature, 362, 365
steady-state theory, 150–53
Stenger, Victor, 100
  multiverse hypothesis, 101
subjectivity
  argument against identity theory,
    252
  argument for dualism, 243
  defined, 242–43
Subramuniyaswami, Sivaya, 174
substance, 230
sufficient condition. *See* necessary
    condition
sufficientarianism, 390
Summa theologica, 114, 129, 359
supernaturalism. *See* naturalism
Swinburne, Richard, 182
system of natural liberty, 374

Talbott, William, 220
talents, 373
  moral arbitrariness and, 373–74
  vs. skills, 375
Taylor, Richard, 128, 224, 289–90
testimony
  defined, 202
  expert, 204–5
  justification and, 203–4
  principle of, 203
  Reid, Thomas, and, 203
Thales of Miletus, 5–10
  cosmological argument and, 135
  and problem of the one and the
    many, 6
  in retrospect, 9–10
theism
  Aquinas and, 130
  defined, 9

first philosophers and, 9
  mere, 130
  — problem of evil and, 160
  skeptical, 178–81
  Thales and, 8–9
theodicy
  defined, 164
  free will, 164–67
  moral qualities, 169–73
  rug maker, 167–69
theology
  defined, 85
  natural vs. revealed, 85
  philosophical, 129, 421n.30
theory (vs. hypothesis), 409n.16
Theory of Justice (Rawls), 372, 387
theos, 9
Tollefsen, Olaf, 292
tolerance, and moral relativism, 350
tolerance argument, 350–51
trial of Socrates, 34–35
  speech to the jury, 35
truth
  coherence theory of, 189
  correspondence theory of, 189
  — moral facts and, 402
  objective, 187–90, 346
  pragmatic theory of, 189–90
  relativism and, 185–87
  Socrates and, 188
  subjective, 190
Turing, Alan, 50
Two Treatises of Government (Locke),
    362, 364

United States Constitution, 365–66
universal constants
  defined, 93
  examples of, 95–97
universal human rights, 364
  Socrates and, 38
universal tolerance, 350–51
universalizability test, 334

utilitarianism
  Bentham's version, 325–26
  difficulties for
  —concerns about justice, 329–30
  —measurement problems, 328–29
  Mill's version, 326–27

value (absolute or intrinsic), 336
van Inwagen, Peter
  on the Arche, 106
  deliberation argument, 277–78
  on Lewis's *Miracles* argument, 218–
    19, 224
  moral responsibility argument, 279–80
Vedas, 407–8n.6
virtue
  Aristotle's theory (*see* Aristotle)
  defined, 314
  ethics (*see* Aristotle)
  intellectual vs. moral, 316–17
Vlastos, Gregory, 37–38
voluntary simplicity, 24

watchmaker argument. *See* Paley,
    William
ways of knowing, 196
Weinberg, Steven, 63
  cosmological argument and,
    116–17
  design argument and, 63
  quantum theory and, 111
welfare state, capitalist, 380
Whitehead, Alfred North, 29
Wilson, Robert, 151–52
Wittgenstein, Ludwig, 108
Wykstra, Stephen
  no-see-um inference, 180
  skeptical theism and,179–81

Xanthippe, 25
Xenophon, 23, 24, 413n.2

zombies, 259
  argument (*see* functionalism)
  See also Chalmers, David

PAUL HERRICK

is professor of philosophy at Shoreline Community College.
He is the author of six previous textbooks in philosophy and logic,
including *The Many Worlds of Logic*, *Introduction to Logic*,
and *Think with Socrates: An Introduction to Critical Thinking*.

CPSIA information can be obtained
at www.ICGtesting.com
Printed in the USA
LVHW010812170522
718971LV00008B/223